James Anthony Froude

History of England from the fall of Wolsey to the death of Elizabeth

Volume III

James Anthony Froude

History of England from the fall of Wolsey to the death of Elizabeth
Volume III

ISBN/EAN: 9783742822277

Manufactured in Europe, USA, Canada, Australia, Japa

Cover: Foto ©ninafisch / pixelio.de

Manufactured and distributed by brebook publishing software (www.brebook.com)

James Anthony Froude

History of England from the fall of Wolsey to the death of Elizabeth

HISTORY OF ENGLAND

FROM

THE FALL OF WOLSEY

TO

THE DEATH OF ELIZABETH.

BY

JAMES ANTHONY FROUDE, M.A.
LATE FELLOW OF EXETER COLLEGE, OXFORD.

AUTHORIZED EDITION.

VOLUME III.

LEIPZIG:
F. A. BROCKHAUS.

1861.

CHAPTER XII.

FOREIGN AND DOMESTIC ASPECTS OF THE REFORMATION IN ENGLAND.

In the sensitive condition of Europe the effect of events was felt beyond their natural consequence. The death of Catherine of Arragon led to the renewal of the war between France and the Empire. Paul III., in real or pretended reluctance to proceed to the last extremity, had for a time suspended the Bull of Deposition which he had drawn against the King of England.[1] It was idle to menace while he was unable to strike; and the two great Catholic powers had declined, when his intention was first made known to them, to furnish him with the necessary support. Francis I., who trifled, as it suited his convenience, with the court of London, the see of Rome, the Smalcaldic League, and the Divan at Constantinople, had protested against a step which would have compelled him to a definite course of action. The Emperor, so long as Solyman was unchecked upon the Danube, and Moorish corsairs swept the Mediterranean and ravaged the coasts of Italy, had shrunk from the cost and peril of a new contest.

A declaration of war, in revenge for the injuries of the divorced queen, would indeed have been welcomed with enthusiasm by the gentlemen of Spain. A London merchant, residing at Cadiz, furnished his government with unwelcome evidence of the spirit which was abroad in the Peninsula: 'I have perceived,' he wrote to Cromwell, 'the views and manners of these countries, and favour

[1] He told Sir Gregory Cassalis that he had been compelled by external pressure to issue threats, 'quæ tamen nunquam in animo habuit ad exitum perducere.'—Sir Gregory Cassalis to Henry VIII.: *MS. Cotton. Vitellius,* B 14, fol. 215.

that these Spaniards do bear towards the King's Grace and his subjects, which is very tedious in their hearts both in word and deed, with their great Popish naughty slanderous words in all parts. And truly the King's Grace hath little or no favour now. We be all taken in derision and hated as Turks, and called heretics, and Luterians, and other spiteful words; and they say here plainly they trust shortly to have war with England, and to set in the Bishop of Rome with all his disciples again in England.'[1] The affront to a Castilian princess had wounded the national honour; the bigotry of a people to whom alone in Europe their creed remained a passion, was shocked by the religious revolution with which that affront had been attended; and the English and Irish refugees, who flocked to their harbours, found willing listeners when they presented themselves as the missionaries of a crusade.[2] Charles himself was withheld only by prudence from indulging the inclination of his subjects. He shared to the full their haughty sensitiveness; again and again in his private consultations with the Pope he had spoken of the revenge which he would one day exact against his uncle; and one of the best informed statesmen of the age, whose memoirs have descended to us, declares that every person who understood anything of the condition of Europe, believed assuredly that he would at last execute his threat.[3]

But as yet no favourable opportunity had offered itself. His arms were occupied with other enemies; the Irish rebellion had collapsed; the disaffection in England seemed unable to coalesce with sufficient firmness to encourage an invasion in its support. It was not till the close of the year 1535, when Charles returned to Naples covered with glory from his first expedition into Africa, that means and leisure for his larger object at length offered themselves. His power and his fame were now at their zenith. He had destroyed the Moslem fleet; he had wrested Tunis from the dreaded Barbarossa; he had earned the

[1] Richard Ebbes to Cromwell: *MS. Cotton. Vespasian*, B 7, fol. 87.
[2] 'There he here both Englishmen and Irishmen many that doth daily invent slander to the realm of England, with as many naughty Popish practices as they can and may do, and specially Irishmen.'—Ibid.
[3] 'L'Empéreur a deux fois qu'il avoit parlè audit Evesque luy avoit faict un discours long et plein de grande passion de la cruelle guerre qu'il entendoit faire contre le dit Roy d'Angleterre, au cas qu'il ne reprinst et restituast en ses honneurs la Reyne Catherine sa tante, et luy avoit declarè les moyens qu'il avoit exeouter vivement icelle guerre, et principalement au moyen de la bonne intelligence ce qu'il disoit avoir avec le Roy d'Ecosse.'—MARTIN DU BELLAY: *Memoirs*, p. 110.

gratitude of the Catholic world by the delivery of twenty thousand Christian slaves. The last ornament might now be added to his wreath of glory, if he would hush down the tumults of heresy as he had restored peace to the waters of the Mediterranean.

With this intention Charles remained in Italy for the winter. The Pope again meditated the publication of the Bull of Deposition;[1] a circular was issued from the Vatican, copies of which were sent even to the Lutheran princes, inviting a crusade against England,[2] and Cardinal Granvelle was instructed to sound the disposition of Francis, and persuade his co-operation. The Emperor would be moderate in his demands; an active participation would not be required of him;[3] it would be sufficient if he would forget his engagement with an excommunicated sovereign to whom promises were no longer binding, and would remain passive.

There was reason to believe that Granvelle's mission would be successful. The year preceding Charles had played off a hope of Milan as a bribe to disunite the French from England; he was ready now to make a definite promise. With the first slight inducement Francis had wavered; while again, in point of religion his conduct was more satisfactory than had been expected. He adhered in appearance to the English alliance, but he had deceived Henry's hopes that he would unite in a rupture with Rome; he had resisted all entreaties to declare the independence of the Gallican church; he had laboured to win back the Germans out of schism, partly to consolidate the French influence in Europe as opposed to the Imperial, but partly also, as he had taken pains to prove, that no doubt might be entertained of the position of France in the great question of the Reformation. He had allowed himself, indeed, as a convenience, to open negotiations for a treaty with Solyman; but the Turks, in the eyes of devout Catholics, were less obnoxious than heretics;[4] and the scandal was obscured by an open repen-

[1] Reginald Pole states that the issue was only prevented by the news of Queen Catherine's death.—Pole to Prioli: *Epistles*, vol. i. p. 442.
[2] SLEIDAN. [3] DU BELLAY'S *Memoirs*, p. 135.
[4] 'The Turks do not compel others to adopt their belief. He who does not attack their religion may profess among them what religion he will; he is safe. But where this pestilent seed is sown, those who do not accept, and those who openly oppose, are in equal peril.'— REGINALD POLE: *De Unitate Ecclesiæ*. For the arch-enemy of England even the name of heretic was too good. 'They err,' says the same writer elsewhere, 'who call the King of England heretic or schismatic. He has no claims to name so honourable. The heretic and schismatic acknowledge the power and providence of God. He takes God utterly away.'—*Apology to Charles the Fifth*.

tance for past shortcomings, and a declaration that for the future he would eschew the crime of toleration, and show no mercy to any Protestant who might fall within his grasp. An English stranger saw Francis of France march through the streets of Paris with the princes of the blood, the queen, the princesses, the bishops, cardinals, dukes, lords, counts, the 'blue blood' of the nobility. They had torches, and banners, and relics of the saints, the whole machinery of the faith: and in the presence of the august assemblage six heretics were burnt at a single fire; the king gave thanks to God that he had learnt his obligations as a Christian sovereign; and, imploring the Divine forgiveness because in past years he had spared the lives of some few of these wretches whom it was his duty to have destroyed, he swore that thenceforward they should go all, as many as he could discover, to the flames.[1]

Thus, therefore, good hopes were entertained of Francis; but inasmuch it was known with what a passion he had set his heart on Milan, Charles resolved not to trust too entirely to his zeal for orthodoxy; and, either through Granvelle or through his ambassadors, he signified his consent to an arrangement which would have consigned Italy conclusively to a Gallican supremacy. Sforza, the last reigning duke, whose claims had hitherto been supported by the Imperialists, had died childless in the previous October. The settlement which had been made in the treaty of Cambray had thus been rendered nugatory; and Francis desired the duchy for his second son, the Duke of Orleans, who, in right of his wife, Catherine de' Medici, would inherit also the dukedoms of Florence and Urbino. If the Emperor was acting in good faith, if he had no intention of escaping from his agreement when the observance of it should no longer be necessary, he was making no common sacrifice in acquiescing in a disposition the consequence of which to the House of

---

[1] 'Sire, je pense que vous avez entendu du supplication que le Roy fit, estant la present luy mème allant en ordre apres les reliques me teste portant ung torche en son mayn avecques ses fils, ses evesques, et cardinaulz devant luy, et les ducs, contes, seigneurs, seneschals, esquieres, et aultres nobles gens apres luy; et la Reyne portée par deux hommes avecques la fille du Roy et ses propres. Apres toutes les grosses dames et demoiselles suivants a pié. Quant tout ceci fit fayt on brûlait vi. a ung feu. Et le Roy pour sa part remercioit Dieu qu'il avoit donne cognoissance de si grand mal le priant de pardon qu'il avoit pardonne a ung ou deux le en passé; et qu'il ne pas este plus diligente en faysant execution; et fit apres serment que dicy en avant il les brulerait tous tous tant qu'il en trouveroit.'—Andrew Baynton to Henry VIII.: *MS. State Paper Office,* temp. Henry VIII. second series, vol. iv.

Austria he so clearly foresaw.[1] He, however, seemed for the present to have surrendered himself to the interests of the Church;[2] and, in return for the concession, Francis, who had himself advised Henry VIII. to marry Anne Boleyn,—Francis, who had declared that Henry's resistance to the Papacy was in the common interest of all Christian princes,—Francis, who had promised to make Henry's cause his own, and, three years previously, had signed a treaty, offensive and defensive, for the protection of France and England against Imperial and Papal usurpations,—sank before the temptation. He professed his willingness to join hand and heart with the Emperor in restoring unity to Christendom and crushing the Reformation. Anticipating and exceeding the requests which had been proposed to him, he volunteered his services to urge in his own person on Henry the necessity of submitting to the universal opinion of Christendom; and, to excuse or soften the effrontery of the demand, he suggested, that, in addition to the censures, a formal notice should be served upon all Christian princes and potentates, summoning them to the assistance of the Papacy to compel the King of England with the strong hand to obey the sentence of the See of Rome.[3] A Catholic league was now on the point of completion. The good understanding so much dreaded by English ministers, between France, the Empire, and the Papacy, seemed to be achieved. A council, the decision of which could not be doubtful, would be immediately convoked by Paul, under the protectorate of the two powers; and the Reformation would become a question no longer of argument, but of strength.

Happily, the triple cord was not yet too secure to be broken by an accident. The confederacy promised favourably till the new year. At the end of January it be-

[1] 'The Duke of Orleans is married to the niece of Clement the Seventh. If I give him Milan, and he be dependent only on his father he will be altogether French.... he will be detached wholly from the confederacy of the Empire.'—Speech of Charles the Fifth in the Consistory at Rome: *State Papers*, vol. vii. p. 641.

[2] Charles certainly did give a promise, and the date of it is fixed for the middle of the winter of 1535-6 by the protest of the French court, when it was subsequently withdrawn. 'Your Majesty,' Count de Vigny said, on the 18th of April, 1536, 'promised a few months ago that you would give Milan to the Duke of Orleans, and not to his brother the Duke of Angouleame.'—Ibid.: *State Papers*, vol. vii.

[3] 'Bien estoit d'advis quant au faict d'Angleterre, afin qu'il eust plus de couleur de presser le Roy dudit pays a se condescendre a l'opinion universelle des Chrétiens, que l'Empereur fist que notre Sainct Pere sommast de ce faire tous les princes et potentats Chrétiens; et a luy assister, et donner main forte pour faire obeir le dit Roy à la sentence et determination de l'Eglise.'—DU BELLAY: *Memoirs*, p. 136.

came known in Italy that the original cause of the English quarrel existed no longer—that Queen Catherine was no more. On the first arrival of the news there was an outburst of indignation. Stories of the circumstances of her death were spread abroad with strange and frightful details. Even Charles himself hinted his suspicions to the Pope that she had been unfairly dealt with, and fears were openly expressed for the safety of the Princess Mary.[1] But, in a short time, calmer counsels began to prevail. Authentic accounts of the queen's last hours must have been received early in February from the Spanish ambassador, who was with her to the end; and as her decease gave no fresh cause for legitimate complaint, so it was possible that an embarrassing difficulty was peacefully removed. On both sides there might now, it was thought, be some relaxation without compromise of principle; an attempt at a reconciliation might at least be made before venturing on the extremity of war. Once more the Pope allowed the censures to sleep.[2] The Emperor, no longer compelled by honour to treat Henry as an enemy, no longer felt himself under the necessity of making sacrifices to Francis. He allowed his offer of Milan to the Duke of Orleans to melt into a proposal which would have left uninjured the Imperial influence in Italy; and Francis, who had regarded the duchy at last as his own, was furious at his disappointment, and prepared for immediate war. So slight a cause produced effects so weighty. Henry, but a few weeks before menaced with destruction, found himself at once an object of courteous solicitation from each of the late confederates. The Pope found a means of communicating to him the change in his sentiments.[3] Francis, careless of all considerations beyond revenge, laboured to piece together the fragments of a friendship which his own treachery had dissolved; and Charles, through his resident at the court of London, and even with his own hand in a letter to Cromwell, condescended to request that his good brother would forget and forgive what was past. The occasion of their disagreement being removed, he desired

---

[1] DU BELLAY: *Memoirs*. 'Hic palam obloquuntur de morte illius ac verentur de Puellâ regiâ ne brevi sequatur.' 'I assure you men speak here tragice of these matters which is not to be touched by letters.'—Harvel to Starkey, from Venice, Feb. 5, 1535-6: ELLIS, second series, vol. ii.
[2] Pole to Prioli: *Epist*. vol. i. p. 442.
[3] 'There hath been means made unto us by the Bishop of Rome himself for a reconciliation.'—Henry VIII. to Pace: BURNET'S *Collectanea*, p. 476.

to return to the old terms of amity. The Princess Mary might be declared legitimate, having been at least born *in bonâ fide parentum;* and as soon as this difficulty should have been overcome, he promised to use his good offices with the Pope, that, at the impending council, his good brother's present marriage should be declared valid, and the succession arranged as he desired.[1] Finally, that he might lose no time in reaping the benefit of his advances, he reminded Henry that the old treaties remained in force by which they had bound themselves to assist each other in the event of invasion; that he looked to his good offices and his assistance in the now imminent irruption of the French into Italy.

The English government lavished large sums as secret service money in the European courts. Though occasionally misled in reports from other quarters, they were always admirably informed by their agents at Rome.[2] Henry knew precisely the history of the late coalition against him, and the value which he might attach to these new professions. He had no intention of retracing any step which he had taken. For his separation from the rest of Christendom, Rome and the other powers were alone responsible.

Events would now work for him. He had only to stand still. To the Pope he sent no answer; but he allowed Sir Gregory Cassalis to hold an indirect commission as his representative at the Papal court. To Francis he remained indifferent. The application on the part of the Emperor had been the most elaborate, and to him his answer was the most explicit. He received the Spanish ambassador in an audience at Greenwich, and, after a formal declaration had been made of Charles's message, he replied with the terms on which he would consent to forget the events of the preceding years. The interruption of friendly relations between England and Spain was the fault wholly and entirely, he said, of the Emperor. When the crown of the Cæsars was last vacant, it had been at the disposal of himself; and he it was who had permitted the choice to fall on its present wearer. In Charles's difficulties he had lent him money: to him Charles was indebted for his power, his influence, and his fame; and, in return, he had met only with ingratitude. To remember injuries, however, was not in his nature. 'We can continue our displeasure to no man,' he said, 'if

---

[1] Henry VIII. to Pace: BURNET's *Collectanea,* p. 476. LORD HERBERT, p. 196. DU BELLAY'S *Memoirs.*

[2] DU BELLAY.

he do once remove the cause thereof; so if he which is a prince of honour, and a personage whom we once chose and thought worthy for his virtue and qualities to be advanced, will by his express writings, either desire us to put his doings towards us in oblivion, or by the same purge himself and declare that such things wherein we have noted unkindness at his hands have been unjustly imputed to him, we shall gladly embrace his offer touching the reconciliation.' Being the injured party, he could receive no advance and treat of no conditions unless with this necessary preliminary. Let the Emperor deal with him frankly, and he should receive a reasonable answer to all his reasonable requests.

'For the Bishop of Rome, he had not,' he continued, 'proceeded on so slight grounds as he would alter any one piece of his doings. In all his causes he had laid his foundation upon the laws of God, nature, and honesty, and established his works made upon the same with consent of the states of the realm in open and high court of parliament.' The Bishop, however, had himself made known his desire for a return to a better understanding with him, and he did not think it expedient that a third party should interfere.[1]

The haughty answer concealed a less indifferent feeling. Henry was seriously conscious of the danger of the isolation of the country; and though he chose in words to defend his self-respect, though he saw, perhaps, in a high bearing the surest means to command the respect of others, he was anxious from his heart to resume his old relations with Spain and Flanders, so important for English commerce, and still more important for the tacit sanction of his past conduct, which would be implied in a renewed treaty with the nephew of Catherine. He directed the English resident at the Imperial court to report the manner in which his reply had been received: he desired him at the same time to lose no opportunity of impressing, both on Charles and on his ministers, the benefits which would accrue to all Christendom, as well as to themselves, if they were again on good terms.[2]

So matters hung uncertain through the spring. The court of Rome continued hopeful,[3] although at that very time the English parliaments were debating the contents of the Black Book, and decreeing the dissolution of the smaller monasteries. Rumour was still favourable to a

[1] Henry VIII. to Pace: BURNET's *Collectanea*, p. 476.
[2] Ibid.
[3] Pole to Prioli, March, 1536; *Epis. Reg. Poli*, vol. 1.

reconciliation, when, for the moment, all other considerations were absorbed in the breaking out of the French war.

Francis had not waited for the declaration of a change of policy on the part of Charles to collect an army. On the first hint of a difficulty he saw what was intended. Milan, after all, was not to be surrendered. His chief military successes had been gained by a suddenness of movement which approached to treachery. Instantly that he knew Charles to be hesitating, he took advantage of some trifling Border differences to open a quarrel; and he declared war and struck his first blow at the same moment. His troops entered Savoy, and the brilliant D'Annebault, who commanded in chief, sweeping all before him, had overrun Piedmont and had secured and fortified Turin, before a man had been raised to oppose him.

This unwelcome news found the Emperor at Naples in the middle of March. Report slightly, but only slightly, anticipating the reality, brought information at the same time of a Franco-Turkish alliance, and of the approach of a fresh Ottoman fleet; and in the first burst of anger and mortification Charles swore that this time he would not lay down his arms till either he or his rival had ceased to wear a crown.[1] Antonio de Leyva was left to collect and equip an army; Charles himself went in the first week in April to Rome, to make a public protest against the French aggression. On the seventeenth of that month, Pope, prelates, cardinals, and foreign ambassadors being all assembled in the consistory, he rose, and with his bonnet in his hand poured out in Spanish a long and passionate invective, denouncing the King of France as the enemy of God and man — the wanton and wicked disturber of the world. When peace was necessary before all things to compose schism, and to repel the Turks, Francis was breaking that peace — was bringing in the Turks — was confounding heaven and earth only for his own ambition. In the interests of Europe, even now he would give Milan to the Duke of Angoulesme; the union of the duchies was too formidable a danger to allow him to bestow it on the Duke of Orleans. This was his last concession: if it was refused, he challenged Francis to decide their differences in single combat, laying Burgundy in gage against Lombardy, the victor to have both in undisputed possession.

Explosions of passion were not unfrequent with Charles, and formed the most genuine feature in his character.

[1] Sir Gregory Cassalis to Cromwell: *State Papers*, vol. vii. p. 641.

His audience, however, were fluttered by his violence. His own prudence taught him the necessity of some explanation. On the following day the consistory reassembled, when, in calmer tones, he reaffirmed his accusations, and renewed his proposals.

'I am not against peace,' he said; 'those who so accuse me slander me. The Pope is the common friend of myself and the King of France. Without his Holiness's permission I should not have spoken as I spoke yesterday. I bear no personal malice. I received the sacrament before I entered your assembly, and many as are my errors and infirmities, I am not so bad a Christian as to communicate while in mortal sin. But a confederate of the Empire is attacked—it is my duty to defend him. The Duke of Savoy is my near relative; but were he a stranger, so long as he is one of my lieges, I must expose my life for him, as he would expose his life for me. I have challenged the King of France to mortal combat; but not in malice, not in vain bravado or appetite for glory. Wise men do not thrust themselves into desperate duels, least of all with an antagonist so strong and skilful. I offered him the alternative of this combat only if peace was impossible, that the terrible evils which menace Christendom might be thus avoided. For here I say it, and while I say it I do but claim my proper privilege as an honest sovereign, not only would I expose my person to peril, but gladly would I sacrifice my life for the welfare of the Christian world.'[1]

The challenge might naturally have touched Francis, whose one sound quality was personal courage; but on this occasion the competitors had exchanged their characters. Francis had the start in the field: he had twelve thousand picked troops in Turin; the remainder of the invading force was distributed in impregnable positions over Piedmont and Savoy.[2] For once he determined to win a reputation for prudence as well as daring, and he left Charles to seek his remedy where he could find it. The Pope entreated, but in vain; and the campaign followed which was so disastrous to the Empire, which for a time reversed so signally the relative position of the two princes, and defeated the expectations of the keenest statesmen.

Finding himself too late, without delay and difficulty,

---

[1] An interesting account of these speeches and of the proceedings in the consistory is printed in the *State Papers*, vol. vii. p. 646. It was probably furnished by Sir Gregory Cassalis.
[2] Sir Gregory Cassalis to Cromwell: *State Papers*, vol. vii.

to expel the French out of their Italian conquests, Charles, in spite of the remonstrance of his generals, and relying, as was thought, on a repetition of the treason of the Duke of Bourbon, by one or more of the Gallican nobility,[1] led his army into Provence. He trusted either that he would find the country undefended, or that the French chivalry, when attacked in their homes, would, with their usual recklessness, risk a decisive battle; or, at least, that in a fertile district he would find no difficulty in procuring provisions. In each of his calculations he found himself fatally mistaken. The inhabitants of Provence had themselves destroyed their crops, and driven away their cattle. In his front, Montmorency lay intrenched at Avignon, and Francis between Lyons and Valence, in fortified camps. Time and necessity had on this occasion been enlisted as the allies of France; and with the garrison of Marseilles in his rear intercepting his supplies, unable to advance, and shut up in a country which had been left barren as an Arabian desert, the Emperor sate still in the sultry summer heats, while his army melted away from him with famine and disease. De Leyva, his ablest commander, and thirty thousand veterans, miserably perished. He escaped only from being driven into the sea by a retreat; and crept back into Italy with the broken remnant of his forces, baffled and humiliated in the only European war into which no fault of his own had plunged him.

Of the feelings with which these events were regarded by Henry, we have little evidence. No positive results followed from the first interchange of messages; but Charles so far endured the tone in which his advances had been received, that fresh communications of moderate friendliness were interchanged through Sir Gregory Cassalis at the beginning of the summer.[2] In July Henry offered his services as a mediator with the court of France both to the Emperor and to the Queen Regent of the Netherlands.[3] At the same time English engineers were in the French camp in Provence, perhaps as professional students of the art of war, perhaps as volunteers indirectly countenanced by the government.[4] The quarrel, in reality,

---

[1] 'Omnes qui sollerti judicio ista pensitare solent, ita statuunt aliquid proditionis in Galliâ esse paratum non dissimile Ducis Borboniæ proditioni. Non enim aliud vident quod Cæsarem illuc trahere posset.' —Sir Gregory Cassalis to Cromwell: *State Papers*, vol. vii.

[2] See Cassalis's Correspondence with Cromwell in May, 1536: Ibid.

[3] The clearest account which I have seen of the point in dispute between Charles V. and Francis I. is contained in a paper drawn by some English statesman apparently for Henry's use.—*Rolls House MSS.* first series, No. 757.

[4] When the English army was in the Netherlands, in 1543, the

admitted of no solution except by the sword; and if the English felt no absolute satisfaction in seeing two powers crippling each other's strength, who, a few months previously, were in league for their own ruin, the government at least saw no reason to co-operate with either side, in a cause which did not concern them, or assist in bringing a dispute to a close which had broken out so opportunely for themselves.

Meanwhile the probabilities of a reunion with Rome had for a moment brightened. It was stated at the close of the last volume that, on the discovery of the adulteries of the queen, a panic arose among the Reformers, lest the king should regard her crime as a judgment upon the divorce, and in the sudden revulsion retrace his steps. It was seen, too, that after her punishment their fears were allayed by an act of parliament against the Papal usurpations, the most emphatic which had yet been passed, and that the country settled back into an equilibrium of permanent hostility. There are circumstances remaining to be explained, both with respect to the first alarm and to the statute by which it was dispelled.

The partial advances which had been made by the Pope had been neither accepted nor rejected, when, on the 20th of May, a courier from England brought the news of Anne's misdemeanours to Rome. The consistory would have been more than mortal if they had not been delighted. From the first they had ascribed the king's conduct to the infatuating beauty of Catherine's rival. It was she who, tigress-like, had thirsted for the blood of their martyrs, and at her shrine they had been sacrificed.[1] Her character appeared at last in its true colours; the enchantment was broken, and the abhorrence with which Henry's name had so lately been regarded was changed throughout Italy to a general feeling of pity.[2] The pre-

Emperor especially admired the disposition of their entrenchments. Sir John Wallop, the commander-in-chief, told him he had learnt that art some years before in a campaign, of which the Emperor himself must remember something, in the south of France.

[1] Pole, in writing to Charles V., says that Henry's cruelties to the Romanists had been attributed wholly to the 'Lerna' at his side; and 'when he had shed the blood of her whom he had fed with the blood of others,' every one expected that he would have recovered his senses.—POLI *Apologia ad Carolum Quintum*.

[2] 'The news, which some days passed were divulged of the queen's case, made a great tragedy, which was celebrated by all men's voices with admiration and great infamy to that woman to have betrayed that noble prince after such a manner, who had exalted her so high, and put himself to peril not without perturbation of all the world for her cause. But God showed Himself a rightful judge to discover such treason and iniquity. All is for the best. And I reckon this to the king's great fortune, that God would give him grace to see and touch

cious sheep who had been lost to the Church would now return to the fold, and the Holy Father would welcome back his erring child with paternal affection.¹ This seems to have been the general expectation; unquestionably it was the expectation of the Pope himself. Paul sent again for Sir Gregory Cassalis, and after expressing his delight that God had delivered the king from his unhappy connexion, he told him that he waited only for the most trifling intimation of a desire for reunion to send a nuntio to England to compose all differences and to grant everything which the king could reasonably demand.² Limiting, like a man of business, the advantages which he had to offer to the present world, the Pope suggested that Henry, in connexion with himself, might now become the arbiter of Europe, and prescribe terms to the Empire as well as to France. For himself and for his office he said he had no ambition. The honour and the profit should alike be for England. An accession of either to the pontificate might prove its ruin.³ He lauded the king's early character, his magnanimity, his generous assistance in times past to the Holy See, his devotion to the Catholic faith. Forgetting the Holy League, glossing over the Bull of Deposition as an official form which there had been no thought of enforcing, he ventured to say that for himself he had been Henry's friend from the beginning. He had urged his predecessor to permit the divorce; at Bologna he had laboured to persuade the Emperor to consent to it.⁴ He had sent a red hat to the Bishop of Rochester only that he might have the benefit of his assistance at the approaching council; and when he heard of his death, being surrounded by solicitations and clamours for vengeance, he had but seemed for a time to consent to measures which would never have been executed.

A warmer overture could scarcely have been conceived,

with his hand what great enemies and traitors he lived withal.'—Harvel to Starkey, from Venice, May 26: ELLIS, second series, vol. ii. p. 77.

¹ Pole to Contarini: *Epist.* vol. i. p. 437.

² 'Dicerem in ipso me adeo bonum animum reperisse ut procul dubio vestra Majestas omnia de ipso sibi polliceri possit.'—Sir Gregory Cassalis to Henry VIII.: *MS. Cotton. Vitellius*, B 14, fol. 215.

³ Neque ea cupiditate laborare ut suas fortunae in immensum augeat aut Pontificales fines propaget unde accidere posset ut ab hâc . . . . institutâ ratione recederet.—Ibid. The MS. has been injured by fire —words and paragraphs are in places wanting. In the present passage it is not clear whether Paul was speaking of the Papal authority generally, or of the Pontifical states in France and Italy.

⁴ Causâ vero matrimonii et in consistoriis et publice et privatim apud Clementem VII. se omnia quæ [potuerit pro] vestrâ Majestate egisse; et Bononiæ Imperatori per [horas] quatuor accurate persuadere conatum fuisse.—Ibid.

and Cassalis ventured to undertake that it was made in good faith.[1] It was true that, as Cardinal of Ravenna, Paul III. had been an advocate for Henry; and his abrupt change on his election to the see proves remarkably how the genius of the Papacy could control the inclination of the individual. Now, however, the Pope availed himself gladly of his earlier conduct, and for a month at least nothing transpired at Rome to damp his expectation. On the 5th of June Cardinal Campeggio wrote to the Duke of Suffolk to feel his way towards the recovery of his lost bishopric of Salisbury.[2] As late as St. John's day (June 24th) the Papal council were rejoicing in the happy prospect which seemed to be re-opening. Strange it was, that so many times in this long struggle some accident or some mistake occurred at a critical contingency to ruin hopes which promised fairly, and which, if realized, would have changed the fortunes of England. Neither the king nor the country would have surrendered their conquered liberties; the Act of Appeals would have been maintained, and, in substance if not in name, the Act of Supremacy. It is possible, however, that if at this juncture the Pope would have relinquished the high pretensions which touched the allegiance of subjects, Henry, for the sake of peace, would have acknowledged in the Bishop of Rome a titular primacy.

Many times a good cause has been ruined by the overzeal of its friends. If there really existed such a danger, England may thank a young nobleman for its escape, who was permitted to do his country a service far different from his intentions. Once already we have seen Reginald Pole in reluctant employment in Paris, receiving opinions on the divorce. Henceforth for some years he will fill a prominent place in this history, and he must be introduced with a brief account of his life.

Reginald, second son of Margaret Plantagenet, Countess of Salisbury, was born in the year 1500. His mother, so long as the first of the Tudor princes was on the throne, remained in obscurity. The titles and estates of the Nevilles being afterwards restored to her and to her eldest son, Reginald shared the benefits of the revival of his family, and was selected by Henry VIII. for particular favour.

He was educated under the king's eye, and at the king's expense; he was pensioned and endowed, according to

[1] Sir Gregory Cassalis to Henry VIII.: *MS. Cotton. Vitellius*, B 14, fol. 215.
[2] *State Papers*, vol. vii. June 5, 1536.

the fashion of the time, while still a boy, with an ecclesiastical benefice; and he was designed, should his inclination permit him, for the highest office in the English church. These general kindnesses he himself gratefully acknowledges; and he professes to have repaid Henry's care with a child's affection. He says that he loved the king for his generosity to himself and his family; that he loved him for his own high and noble qualities, his liberality, his gentleness, his piety, his princely illustrious nature.[1] Nor did he fail to profit by the advantages which were heaped upon him. He studied industriously at Paris and at Padua, acquiring, as he believed, all knowledge which living teachers could impart to him; and he was himself so well satisfied with the result, that at the mature age of thirty-six he could describe himself to Henry as one who, although a young man, 'had long been conversant with old men; had long judged the eldest man

[1] Since Pole, when it suited his convenience, could represent the king's early career in very different colours, it is well to quote some specimens of his more favourable testimony. Addressing Henry himself, he says: 'Quid non promittebant præclaræ illæ virtutes quæ primis annis principatûs tui in te maxime elucebant. In quibus primum pietas quæ una omnium aliarum, et totius humanæ felicitatis quasi fundamentum est se proferebat. Cui adjunctæ erant quæ maxime in oculis hominum elucere solent justitia clementia liberalitas, prudentia denique tanta quanta in illâ tenerâ ætate esse potuit. Ut dixit Ezechiel de Rege Assyriorum, in paradiso Dei cedrus te pulcrior non inveniebatur.'—*De Unitate Ecclesiæ*, lib. 3.

Again, writing to Charles V., after speaking of the golden splendour of Henry's early reign, his wealth, his moderation, the happiness of the people, and the circle of illustrious men who surrounded his throne, he goes on—

'Hi vero illam indolem sequebantur quam Regi Deus ipsi prius dederat cujus exemplar in Rege suo viderunt. Fuit enim indoles ejus aliquando prorsus regia. Summum in eo pietatis studium apparebat et religionis cultus; magnus amor justitiæ; non abhorrens tamen natura ut tum quidem videbatur a clementiâ.'

And the time at which the supposed change took place is also marked distinctly:—

'Satanas in carne adhuc manentem naturâ hominis jam videtur spoliasse . . . enâ induisse . . . in quâ nihil præter formam videtur reliquisse quod sit hominis; . . . . ne vitia quidem . . . sed cum omni virtute et donis illis Dei cœlestibus quibus cum optimis Regum comparari poterat, antequam in vicariatum Filii ejus se ingereret [præditus est] postquam illum honorem impie ambivit et arripuit, non solum virtutibus omnibus privatus est sed etiam,' etc.—POLI *Apologia ad Carolum Quintum*.

It was 'necessary to the position' of Romanist writers to find the promise of evil in Henry's early life, after his separation from the Papacy; and stories like those which we read in SANDERS grew like mushrooms in the compost of hatred. But it is certain that so long as he was orthodox he was regarded as a model of a Catholic prince. Cardinal Contarini laments his fall, as a fall like Lucifer's: 'Qui fieri potuit per Deum immortalem,' he wrote to Pole, 'ut animus ille tam mitis tam mansuetus ut ad bene merendum de hominum genere a naturâ factus esse videatur sit adeo immutatus.'—*Epist. Reg. Poli*, vol. ii. p. 31.

that lived too young for him to learn wisdom from.'[1] Many ambitious youths have experienced the same opinion of themselves; few have ventured on so confident an expression of it. But for his family's sake as much as for his own, the king continued to regard him with favour; and could he have prevailed upon himself to acquiesce in the divorce of Queen Catherine, it is possible that he would have succeeded Warham in the English primacy.

From conviction, however, or from the tendency to contradiction characteristic of a peculiar kind of talent, Pole was unable to adopt an opinion so desirable for his interests. First doubtfully, and afterwards emphatically and positively, he declared his dissent from the resolutions of parliament and convocation. He had witnessed with his own eyes the means by which the sentences had been obtained of the universities abroad. He was satisfied of the injustice of the cause. He assured himself that to proceed in it would be perilous to the realm.

His birth and the king's regard for him gave an importance to his judgment which it would not otherwise have obtained. Repeated efforts were made to gain him. His brother, Lord Montague, the Duke of Norfolk, even Henry himself, exerted all their powers of persuasion. On the death of Wolsey the archbishopric of York was held out to him as the reward of compliance.[2] Once only he wavered. He had discovered, as he imagined, a means of making a compromise with his conscience, and he went down to Whitehall to communicate his change. But, as he rather theatrically relates, when he found himself in the presence-chamber he could not utter the words which he had intended to use; either he was restrained by a Higher Power, or the sight of that Henry whom he loved so tenderly paralysed his tongue; he burst into tears, and the king left him in displeasure.[3] On retiring from the palace he wrote a letter of apology; accompanying it, perhaps, with the formal statement of the grounds of his opposition, which about this time he submitted to the government.[4] His defence was received kindly; but, though clever, it was little to the purpose. The arguments were chiefly political; and Henry, who listened patiently to any objection on the ground of principle, paid no very high respect to the opinion of a university student in matters

[1] Pole to Henry VIII.: STRYPE's *Memorials*, vol. ii. p. 305.
[2] Pole to the English Council: *Epist*. vol. i.
[3] Ibid.
[4] Said by Cranmer to have been an able paper: 'He suadeth with such goodly eloquence, both of words and sentences, that he is like to persuade many.'—CRANMER's *Works*, edit. JENKYNS, vol. i. p. 2.

of state. Pole, finding his position increasingly uneasy, in 1532 applied for and obtained permission to reside for a time at Avignon. In his absence the divorce was completed; and England becoming more than ever distasteful to him, he removed to the monastery of Carpentras, and thence to his old quarters at Padua. Meantime Henry's personal kindness towards him remained undiminished. His leave of absence was indefinitely extended. His pension was continued to him; the revenues of the deanery of Exeter were regularly paid to his account; and he was exempted specially from the general condition required of all holders of ecclesiastical benefices, the swearing allegiance to the children of Queen Anne. He could himself neither have desired nor expected a larger measure of forbearance.[1]

This was his position in the year 1535, when, in common with all other English noblemen and gentlemen, he was requested to send in his opinion on the authority in foreign countries claimed by the see of Rome, and at the same time to state whether his sentiments on the previous question remained unchanged. The application was not formally made through the council. A civilian, a Mr. Starkey, a personal acquaintance, was entrusted with the commission of sending it; and Starkey took the opportunity of advising his friend to avoid the errors into which he had previously fallen. Pole's opinion on political perils, foreign invasions, internal commotions, was not wanted. 'As touching the *policy* of the separation from Rome, and the divorce, and of the bringing them to effect, whether it were done well or ill,' Starkey ironically wrote, 'his Grace requireth no judgment of you, as of one that of such things hath no great experience as yet. Whether it should be *convenient* that there should be one head in the Church, and that the Bishop of Rome .... set this aside .... and in the matrimony, whether the policy he hath used therein be profitable to the realm or no .... leave that aside .... only shew you whether the supremacy which the Bishop of Rome has for many ages claimed be of Divine right or no .... and if the first matrimony were to make, you would approve it then or no .... and the cause why you would not.'

Finally, as Pole once before had been tempted to give an opinion against his conscience, Starkey warned him to reply sincerely and honestly; to think first of God and the truth; and only when his conscience would permit

[1] PHILLIPS' *Life of Cardinal Pole.*

him, to consider how he could satisfy the king. 'His Grace said to me,' the letter concluded, 'that he would rather you were buried there than you should, for any worldly promotion or profit to yourself, dissemble with him in these great and weighty causes.'[1]

The tone of this concluding passage teaches us not to rely too absolutely on Pole's own version of the attempts which had before been made upon his constancy. Perhaps the admonition, perhaps the irony, of his correspondent galled him. At any rate, the king desired the truth, and the truth he should have. Other things had been in rapid development since Pole left England. He, too, had chosen his course, and his mind had not stood still. It was now the winter of 1535, when the scheme of the crusade was first taking shape. At this juncture he sat down to comply with the king's demands. Instead of brief answers to brief questions, he composed a considerable volume; and as the several parts were completed, they were submitted to the inspection of Cardinal Contarini. Had the project of war gone forward, and had other matters remained unchanged, it is possible that Contarini would have found no fault with a composition which afterwards was regarded in the Catholic world with so much complacency. Under the actual circumstances, his language alarmed by its violence. The cardinal protested against an invective which could only irritate, and entreated Pole to reconsider what he had written.

If Pole had been honest—if he had desired only the interests of the Catholic church—he would have listened to advice; but he replied that he well knew the king's character, and that the evil had risen to its present height because no one had ventured to speak the truth to him. Henry was not a man who could be moved by gentleness. Long ago the heaviest censures of the Church ought to have been launched upon him, and by that time he would have returned to his obedience. He said also (and this is especially to be noticed), that he was not so much addressing the king as addressing the English nation, who were impassive and hard to move. He was determined to open their eyes to the delusion into which they were betrayed, and he must go beyond the matter and beside it, and insinuate when he was unable to assert.[2]

---

[1] STRYPE's *Memorials*, vol. Ii. p. 281.
[2] 'Quibus si rem persuadere velis multa præter rem sunt dicenda multa insinuanda.'—*Epist. Reg. Pol.* vol. i. p. 434. And again: 'Illum librum scribo non tam Regis causâ quam gregis Christi qui est universus Regni populus, quem sic deludi vix ferendum est.'—Ibid. p. 437. I draw attention to these words, because in a subsequent defence of

In this mood, and while the book was still unsent, he learnt with utter mortification of the relinquishment of the Emperor's intended enterprise, and the possible peaceful close of the quarrel. He had proposed to himself a far different solution. It may be that he was convinced that no such peaceful close could lead to good. It may have been, that the white rose was twining pure before his imagination, with no red blossoms intermixed, round the pillars of a regenerated church. Or, perhaps, many motives, distinct and indistinct, were working upon him. Only the fact is certain, that he might have mediated, but that he was determined rather to make mediation impossible; the broken limb should not be set in its existing posture.

In March he heard that the Pope was softening. He wrote, urgently entreating that his Holiness would commit himself in nothing till in possession of secrets which he could communicate.[1] Contarini having desired that he might show the book to Paul, he refused, under the plea that others might see it, and that he was bound to give Henry the first perusal; an honourable answer, if his other insincerity allowed us to accept his word. We may believe, with no want of charity, that his real fear was, lest Paul should share the feelings of Contarini, and for the present discourage its despatch.[2] His letters at this time display an unveiled anxiety for immediate open hostility. His advice to the Pope was to send out his bull without more delay. He passionately deplored the change which the death of Catherine had worked upon Charles. 'Alas!' he said, 'that the interests of the Church should be affected by the life or death of a single woman! Oh that his Holiness could but convince the Emperor of his blessed privileges as the champion of the Catholic faith!'[3] 'The Emperor preferred to fight against the Turks. What were the Turks compared with the antichrist of England? What advantages would be gained if the Crescent were driven

---

himself to the English Privy Council, Pole assured them that his book was a private letter privately sent to the king; that he had written as a confessor to a penitent, under the same obligations of secrecy: 'Hoc genere dicendi Regem omnibus dedecorosum et probrosum reddo? Quibus tandem illustrissimi Domini? Hisne qui libellum nunquam viderunt? an his ad quos legendum dedi? Quod si hic solus sit Rex ipse, utinam ipse sibi probrosus videretur. Ad eum certe solum misi; quocum ita egi ut nemo unquam a confessionibus illi secretior esse potuisset hoc tantum spectans quod confessores ut illi tantum sua peccata ostenderem.'—Apologia ad Ang. Parl.: *Epist.* vol. i. p. 181. So considerable an inconsistency might tempt a hasty person to use hard words of Pole.

[1] Pole to Priuli: *Epist.* vol. i. p. 441.
[2] Ibid. p. 442.   [3] Ibid. p. 443.

out of Europe, and England were lost? Let him strike at once while the wound was green: it would soon gangrene and mortify, and then it would be too late.'

This language, under some aspects, may appear pardonable—may, perhaps, be admired as the expression of a fine enthusiasm. Those whose sympathy with sentimental emotions is restrained within the prosaic limits of ordinary law, would call it by a harder name. High treason, if it be not a virtue, is the worst of crimes; and for a subject to invite a foreign power to invade his country is the darkest form of treason. An unjust exile might be pleaded as a faint palliation—a distinct religious obligation might convert the traitor into a patriot. Neither of these pretexts could be urged at the existing crisis in defence of Reginald Pole.

The book was completed in the middle of the winter; the correspondence connected with it extended through February, March, and April. In May came the news of Anne Boleyn's crimes, and the fresh impulse which I have described to the hopes of the Pope and his more moderate advisers. The expectation of a reconciliation was approaching to a certainty, and if he waited longer it might be too late. That particular time he selected to despatch his composition, and rouse again (it is idle to suppose that he was blind to the inevitable consequence) the full storm of indignation and suspicion.[1]

A production, the effect of which was so considerable, requires some analysis. It shall be as brief as is consistent with the due understanding of the feeling which the book created.[2]

'Whether to write or not to write,' commenced the youthful champion of the faith, 'I cannot tell; when to write has cost the lives of so many and so noble men,

[1] Tunc statim misi cum ille e medio jam sustulisset illam quæ illi et regno totius hujus calamitatis causa existimabatur.—*Apolog. ad Carol. Quint.*

[2] A MS. copy of this book, apparently the original which was sent by Pole, is preserved among the *Records* in the Rolls House, scored and underlined in various places, perhaps by members of the Privy Council. A comparison of the MS. with the printed version, shows that the whole work was carefully re-written for publication, and that various calumnies in detail, which have derived their weight from being addressed directly to the king, in what appeared to be a private communication by a credible accuser—which have, therefore, been related without hesitation by late writers as ascertained facts—are not in the first copy. So long as Pole was speaking only to the king, he prudently avoided statements which might be immediately contradicted, and confined himself to general invective. When he gave his book to the world he poured into it the indiscriminate slanders which were floating in popular rumour. See *Appendix* to the Fourth Volume.

and the service of God is counted for the worst of crimes. Duty urges me to write; yet what shall I write? The most faithful servant may hesitate in what language to address his sick master, when those who so far have approached his bed have forfeited their lives. Yet speak I will—I will cry in your ears as in the ears of a dead man—dead in your sins. I love you—wicked as you are, I love you. I hope for you, and may God hear my prayer. You desire the truth; I should be a traitor, then, did I conceal from you the truth. I owe my learning to your care. I will use against yourself the weapons with which yourself have armed me.

'You have done no wrong, you say. Come, then, I will show you your wrong. You have changed the constitution of your country, and that is wrong. When the Church had but one head, you have made her a monster with a separate head in every realm, and that is wrong. You, of all princes (bad and impious as many of them have been), are the first who has ventured so enormous an impiety. Your flatterers have filled your heart with folly; you have made yourself abhorred among the rulers of Christendom. Do you suppose that in all these centuries the Church has failed to learn how best she should be governed? What insolence to the bride of Christ! What insolence to Christ Himself! You pretend to follow Scripture! So say all heretics, and with equal justice. No word in Scripture makes for you, except it be the single sentence, 'Honour the king.' How frail a foundation for so huge a superstructure!'

Having thus opened the indictment, he proceeded to dissect a book which had been written on the Supremacy by Dr. Sampson. Here he for some time expatiated, and having disposed of his theological antagonist, opened his parallels upon the king by a discussion of the principles of a commonwealth.

'What is a king?' he asked. 'A king exists for the sake of his people; he is an outcome from Nature in labour;[1] an institution for the defence of material and temporal interests. But inasmuch there are interests beyond the temporal, so there is a jurisdiction beyond the king's. The glory of a king is the welfare of his people; and if he knew himself, and knew his office, he would lay his crown and kingdom at the feet of the priesthood, as in a haven and quiet resting-place. To priests it was said, 'Ye are gods, and ye are the children of the Most High.'

---

[1] Partus Naturæ laborantis.

Who, then, can doubt that priests are higher in dignity than kings. In human society are three grades—the people—the priesthood, the head and husband of the people—the king, who is the child, the creature, and minister of the other two.'[1]

From these premises it followed that Henry was a traitor, a rebel against his true superior; and the first section closed with a fine rhetorical peroration.

'Oh, Henry!' he exclaimed, 'more wicked than Ozias, who was smitten with leprosy when he despised the warnings of Azariah—more wicked than Saul, who slew the priests of the Lord—more wicked than Dathan and Abiram, who rose in rebellion against Aaron—what hast thou done? What! but that which is written in the Scripture of the prince of pride—'I will climb up into heaven; I will set my throne above the stars; I will sit me down on the mount of the covenant; I will make myself even with the Most High.' .... He shall send his vengeance upon thee—vengeance sudden, swift, and terrible. It shall come; nor can I pray that it may longer tarry. Rather may it come and come quickly, to the glory of his name. I will say, like Elijah, 'Oh, Lord! they have slain thy prophets with the edge of the sword; they have thrown down thine altars; and I only am left, and they seek my life to take it away. Up, Lord, and avenge the blood of thy holy ones.''

He now paused for a moment in his denunciation of Henry, and took up his parable against the English bishops, who had betrayed the flock of Christ, and driven them into the den of the villain king. 'You thought,' he said to these learned prelates, 'that the Roman pontiff slept—that you might spoil him with impunity, as the robber Cacus spoiled the sleeping Hercules. Ah! but the Lord of the sheep sees you. He sees you from his throne in heaven. Not we only who are left yet alive tell, with our bleating voices, whither you have driven us; but, in louder tones than ours, the blood of those whom ye have slain, because they would not hear your hireling voices, cries out of the dust to Christ. Oh, horrible!—most horrible! No penalty which human justice could devise can reach your crimes. Men look to see when some unwonted vengeance shall light upon you, like that which fell on Korah and his company, in whose footsteps ye now are following. If the earth open her mouth and swallow you up

---

[1] Populus enim regem procreat.

quick, every Christian man will applaud the righteous judgment of the Almighty.'

Again he passed back to the king, assailing him in pages of alternate argument and reprobation. In most modern language he asserted the responsibility of sovereigns, calling English history to witness for him in the just rebellions provoked by tyranny; and Henry, he said, had broken his coronation oath and forfeited his crown. This and similar matter occupied the second part. It had been tolerably immoderate even so far, but the main torrent had yet to flow.

The third and most important section divides itself into an address, first to the king and then to England; finally to the foreign powers—the Emperor particularly, and the Spanish army.

'I have spoken,' he commenced, 'but, after all, I have spoken in vain. Wine turns to vinegar in a foul vessel; and to little purpose have I poured my truth into a mind defiled with falsehood and impurity. How shall I purify you? How, indeed! when you imagine that yourself, and not I, are in possession of the truth; when you undertake to be a teacher of others; when, forsooth, you are head of a church. But, come, listen to me. I will be your physician. I will thrust a probe into those envenomed wounds. If I cause you pain, believe that it is for your good. You do not know that you have a wound to probe. You pretend that you have only sought to do the will of God. You will say so. I know it. But, I beseech you, listen to me. Was it indeed your conscience which moved you? Not so. You lusted after a woman who was not your wife. You would make the Word of God bear false witness for you; and God's providence has permitted you to overwhelm yourself in infamy. I say, you desired to fulfil your lusts. And how, you ask, do I know this? How can I see your heart? Who but God can read those secrets? Yes, oh prince; he also knows—to whom God will reveal the heart. And I tell you that I am he to whom God has revealed yours. You will cry out against my arrogance. How should God open your heart to me? But contain yourself a little. I do not say that God has shewn more to me than he has shewn to any man who will use his understanding.[1] You think that the offspring of your harlot will be allowed to sit on the throne, that the pure blood of England will endure to be her subjects.

---

[1] In the printed copy the king is here accused of having intrigued with Mary Boleyn before his marriage with Anne. See *Appendix*.

No, truly. If you dream thus, you have little of your father's wisdom. There is not a peer in all the land who will not hold his title better than the title of a harlot's bastard. Like Cadmus, you have flung a spear among your people, and armed them for mutual slaughter. And you—you, the vilest of plunderers—a thief—a robber—you call yourself supreme head of the Church! I acquit the nation of the infamy of their consent. They have not consented. The few suffrages which you can claim have been extorted by terrour. Again, how do I know this? I, who was absent from my country? Yes, I was absent. Nor have I heard one word of it from any creature. And yet so it is. I have a more sure testimony than the testimony of eyes and ears, which forbids me to be mistaken.'

The witness was the death of Sir Thomas More, Bishop Fisher, and the Charterhouse monks; and the story of their martyrdom was told with some power and passion.

The remedy for all its evils rested with England. England must rebel. He called on it, with solemn earnestness, to consider its position: its church infected with heresy, its saints slaughtered, its laws uprooted, its succession shattered; sedition within, and foreign war imminent from without; and the single cause of these accumulated miseries a licentious tyrant. 'And oh! my country,' he exclaimed, 'if any memory remains to you of your antient liberties, remember—remember the time when kings who ruled over you unjustly were called to account by the authority of your laws. They tell you that all is the king's. I tell you that all is the commonwealth's. You, oh! my country, are all. The king is but your servant and minister. Wipe away your tears, and turn to the Lord your God.'

Of his own conduct he would give Henry fair warning. 'I myself,' he said, once more addressing him, 'I myself shall approach the throne of your last ally, the King of France. I shall demand that he assist you no longer; that, remembering the honour of his father, with his own past fidelity to the Church of Christ, he will turn against you and strike you down. And think you that he will refuse my petition? How long dream you that God will bear with you? Your company shall be broken up. The scourge shall come down upon you like a wave. The pirates who waste the shores of the Mediterranean are less the servants of Satan than you. The pirates murder but the bodies of men. You murder their souls.

Satan alone, of all created beings, may fitly be compared with you.'

So far I have endeavoured to condense the voluminous language into a paraphrase, which but languidly approaches the blaze and fury of the original. Vituperation, notwithstanding, would have been of trifling consequence; and the safe exhortations of refugees, inciting domestic rebellions, the dangers of which they have no intention of sharing, are a form of treason which may usually be despised. But it is otherwise when the refugee becomes a foreign agent of his faction, and not only threatens to invite invasion, but converts his menace into act. When the pages which follow were printed, they seemed of such grave moment that they were extracted and circulated as a pamphlet in the German States. The translation, therefore, will now adhere closely to the text.

'I call to witness,' he went on, 'that love of my country which is engrafted in me by nature—that love of the Church which is given to me by the Son of God —did I hear that the Emperor was on the seas, on his way against Constantinople, I would know no rest till I was at his feet—I would call to him were he in the very narrows of the Bosphorus—I would force myself into his presence—I would address him thus: 'Cæsar,' I would say, 'what is this which you are doing? Whither are you leading this mighty army? Would you subdue the enemies of Christendom? Oh! then, turn, turn your sails. Go where a worse peril is threatening—where the wound is fresh, and where a foe presses more fearful far than the Turk. You count it a noble thing to break the chains of Christian captives: and noble, indeed, it is. But more glorious is it, to rescue from eternal damnation the many thousand souls who are torn from the Church's bosom, and to bring them back to the faith of Christ. What will you have gained when you have driven back the Turks, if other Turks be sprung up meanwhile amidst ourselves? What are Turks save a sect of Christians revolted from the Church? The beginning of the Turks is the beginning of all heretics. They rejected the Head which was set over them by Christ, and thus by degrees they fell away from the doctrine of Christ. What then? See you not the seed of these self-same Turks scattered at home before your doors? Would, indeed, it were so scanty that there was any difficulty in discerning its presence! Yes; you see it, sad to say, in your own Germany. The disease is there, though not as yet in its worst form. It is not yet set forth by authority. The German church may even now cast forth the seed of the adulterers, and bear again the true fruit of Catholic truth. But for England! Alas! in England that seed is sown thick and broad; and by the sovereign's hand. It is sown, and it is quickening, and the growing blade is defended by the sword. The sword is the answer to all opponents. Nay, even silence is an equal crime. Thomas More, the wisest, the most virtuous of living men, was slain for silence. Among the monks, the more holy, the more devout they be, the greater is the peril. All lips are closed by fear of death. If these fine beginnings do not prove to you what it is to forsake the head of the Church, what other evidence do you desire? The Turks might teach you: they, too, forsook him—they, too, brought in the power of the sword; by the sword these many ages they have maintained themselves, and now the memory of their mother has perished, and too late the Church cries to her lost children to return to her.[1] Or, again, Germany may teach you. How calm, how tranquil, how full of piety was Germany! How did Germany flourish while it held steadfast by the faith! How has it been torn with wars, distracted with mutinies, since it has revolted from its allegiance! There is no hope for Germany, unless, which God grant, it return to the Church—our Supreme Head. This is the Church's surest bulwark; this is the first mark for the assaults of heretics; this is the first rallying point of true Catholics; this, Cæsar, those heroic children of the Church in England have lately died to defend, choosing rather to give their naked bodies to the swords of their enemies than desert a post which was the key to the sanctuary.

"That post was stormed—those valiant soldiers were slain. What wonder, when the champion of the foemen's host was a king! Oh, misery! worse than the worst which ever yet has befallen the spouse of Christ! The poison of heresy has reached a king, and, like the Turk, he shakes his drawn sword in the face of all who resist him. If he

---

[1] Elsewhere in his letters Pole touches on this string. If England is to be recovered, he is never weary of saying, it must be recovered at once, while the generation survives which has been educated in the Catholic faith. The poison of heresy is instilled with so deadly skill into schools and churches, into every lesson which the English youth are taught, that in a few years the evil will be past cure. He was altogether right. The few years in fact were made to pass before Pole and his friends were able to interfere; and then it was too late; the prophecy was entirely verified. But, indeed, the most successful preachers of the Reformation were neither Cranmer nor Parker, Cromwell nor Burleigh, Henry nor Elizabeth, but Pole himself and the race of traitors who followed him.

affect now some show of moderation, it is but to gain time and strength, that he may strike the deadlier blows; and strike he will, doubt it not, if he obtain his desire. Will you then, Cæsar—you who profess that you love the faith—will you grant him that time? When the servants of Christ cry to you, in their agony, for help,—when you must aid them now, or your aid will be for ever useless, —will you turn your arms on other foes? will you be found wanting to the passionate hope of your friends, when that hope alone, that simple hope, has held them back from using their own strength and striking for themselves? Dream not, Cæsar, that all generous hearts are quenched in England—that faith and piety are dead. Judge rather those who are alive by the deaths of those who have gone to the scaffold for religion's sake. If God reserved for Himself seven thousand in Israel who had not bowed the knee to Baal, when Ahab and his cursed Jezebel slew his prophets, think not that, in these days of greater light, our Jezebel, with all her scent for blood, has destroyed the whole defenders of the truth. There are legions in England yet unbroken who have never yet bent their knees. Go thither, and God, who has been their Saviour, will bid them rally to your banners. They are the same English, Cæsar, who, unaided, and in slighter causes, have brought their princes to their judgment bar —have bidden them give account for moneys wasted to the prejudice of the commonwealth, and when they could not pass their audit, have stripped them of crown and sceptre. They are the same; and long ago, in like manner, would they have punished this king also, but that they looked to you. In you is their trust—in your noble nature, and in your zeal for God. Their cause is yours, peculiarly yours; by you they think the evil can be remedied with less hurt to England than by themselves. Wisely, therefore, they hold their hand till you shall come.

"And you—you will leave them desolate; you turn your back upon this glorious cause; you waste yourself in a distant enterprise. Is it that your soldiers demand this unhappy preference? are your soldiers so eager to face their old eastern enemies? But what soldiers, Cæsar! Your Spaniards?—your own Spaniards? Ah! if they could hear the noble daughter of Isabella, wasted with misery, appealing in her most righteous cause to their faithful hearts! The memory of that illustrious lady, well I know, is not yet so blotted from their recollection that a daughter worthy of so great a mother could pray to them in vain. Were they told that a princess of Spain, child of the proudest sovereign of that proud empire, after twenty years of marriage, had been driven out as if she had been the bastard of some clown or huckster that had crept from her filth into the royal bed, and to make room for a vile harlot—think you they would tamely bear an injury which the basest of mankind would wash out in blood? Think you that, when there scarce breathes a man so poor of soul who would not risk his life to requite so deep an indignity, the gentlemen of Spain will hesitate to revenge the daughter of their sovereign? Shall it go ont among the nations to your shame and everlasting ignominy, that Spain sits down under the insult because she is faint-hearted—because she is feeble, and dares not move? It cannot be. Gather them together, Cæsar. Call your musters; I will speak to them—I will tell them that the child and grandchild of Isabella of Castile are dishonoured and robbed of their inheritance, and at the mention of that name you shall see them reverse their sails, and turn back of themselves their vessels' prows.

"But not for Catherine's sake do I now stand a suitor either to you or them. For herself she desires nothing; she utters no complaint over her most unrighteous fate. You are now in the meridian of your glory, and some portion of its lustre should be hers; yet she is miserable, and she endures her misery. Each fresh triumph of your arms entails on her some fresh oppression; but hers is no selfish sorrow for herself or for her cause. She implores you, Cæsar, for the sake of England, of that England into which from her own noble stem she was once engrafted, which she loves and must love as her second country. Her private interests are nothing to her; but if it so happen that the cause of this illustrious and most dear land is so bound up in hers—that if she be neglected, England must forfeit her place among the nations—must be torn with civil distractions, and be plunged in ruin and disaster irretrievable—if the cause of religion be so joined to her cause that her desertion is the desertion of the Holy Church, that the ancient faith will be destroyed, new sects will spring up, not in that island only, which at her coming she found so true to its creed, but spreading like contagion, and bringing to confusion the entire communion of the faithful (and this is no conjectural danger: it is even now come—it is among us; already, in England, to be a friend to the old customs of the Church is fraught with deadly peril)—finally, if in this matter there be every motive which ought to affect a prince who loves the name of Christ—then—then she does entreat you not to delay longer in hastening to deliverance of the Christian commonwealth, because it happens that the common cause is her cause—because Ferdinand of Spain was her father—because Isabella was her mother—because she is your own aunt—because her most ruthless enemies have never dared to hint that in word or deed she has been unworthy of her ancestors, or of the noble realm from which she sprang.

"She implores you, if God has given you strength to defy so powerful an enemy as the Turk, in that case, not to shrink from marching against a foe more malignant than the Turk, where the peril is nothing, and victory is sure. By the ties of blood, which are so close between you and her—by the honour of Spain which is compromised—by the welfare of Christendom, which ought to be so dear to us all—she beseeches you, on her knees, that you will permit no mean object to divert you from so holy, so grand, so brilliant an enterprise, when you can vindicate at once the honour of your family and the glory of that realm which has made you famous by so many victories, and simultaneously you can shield the Christian commonwealth from the worst disasters which have menaced it for centuries."

Here terminated this grand apostrophe, too exquisite a composition to be lost—too useful when hereafter it was to be thrown out as a firebrand into Europe, although Catherine, happily for herself, had passed away before her chivalrous knight flung down his cartel for her. A few more words were, however, in reserve for Henry.

'I have spoken of Cæsar,' he turned and said to him; 'I might have spoken of all Christian princes. Do you seriously think that the King of France will refuse obedience when the Pope bids him make peace with the Emperor, and undertake your chastisement? He will obey, doubt it not; and when you are trampled down under their feet there will be more joy in Christendom than if the Turks were driven from Constantinople. What will you do? What will become of your subjects when the ports of the Continent are closed, as closed they will be, against them and their commerce? How will they loathe you then? How will you be cast out among the curses of mankind?[1] When you die you shall have no lawful burial, and what will happen to your soul I forbear to say. Man is against you; God is against you; the universe is against you. What can you look for but destruction?'

These paragraphs are a condensation of five pages of invective.

The hurricane had reached its height; it spent its fury in its last gusts. The note changed, the threats ceased, and the beauty of humiliation and the promises of forgiveness to the penitent closed the volume.

Thus wrote an English subject to his sovereign, and professed afterwards to be overwhelmed with astonishment when he learnt that his behaviour was considered unbecoming. As Samuel to Saul, as Nathan to David, as Elijah to Ahab, so was Reginald Pole to Henry the Eighth, the immediate messenger of Heaven, making, however, one central and serious error; that, when between Henry the Eighth and the Papacy there lay to be contended for, on the one side, liberty, light, and justice—on the other, tyranny, darkness, and iniquity, in this great duel the Pope was God's champion, and Henry was the devil's. No pit opened its mouth to swallow the English bishops; no civil wars wrecked the prosperity of the country; no foreign power overwhelmed it; no dishonour touched its arms, except in the short interval when Catherine's daughter restored the authority of the Papacy, and Pole was Archbishop of Canterbury, and the last relic of the empire of the Plantagenets in France was lost for ever. He was pleased with his composition, however. He determined, in spite of Contarini, to send it. He expected the English council to believe him when he declared that he had no sinister intention, that he seriously imagined that a monarch who had taken the Pope by the beard and hurled him out of the kingdom, would be frightened by the lectures and threats of a petulant youth.

On the 27th of May the book was despatched to England by a messenger from Venice, and with it Pole sent two letters, one to the king, the other to his friend Cuthbert Tunstall, the Bishop of Durham. The first contained little more than the credentials of the bearer. The letter to Tunstall, as well as a verbal message by which it was accompanied, was to the effect, that the book was long, too long for the king himself to read; he desired his friend to undertake, and the king to permit him to undertake, the first perusal. The contents were to be looked upon as a secret communication between himself and his Majesty; no eye had seen more than a small portion of what he had written, and that against his own will. The addresses and apostrophes inserted here and there, which might seem at first sight questionable, were dramatically introduced only to give effect to his argument.[1]

---

[1] Reginald Pole to the King, Venice, May 27. *MS. penes me.* In-

These statements seem somewhat adventurous when we think of the correspondence with Cardinal Contarini, and of Pole's assertion that he was writing less for the king than to undeceive the English people; nor do we readily acquiesce in the belief that the invocation to Charles was not intended for Charles's eyes, when the writer very soon after submitted it to those eyes, and devoted the energies of years to bring the Spaniards into England.

The messenger arrived early in June. Parliament had just met to receive the report of the queen's crimes and execution, and the king, occupied with other business, gladly complied with Pole's request, and left to others the examination of so bulky a volume. It was placed in the hands of Tunstall and Starkey. Whether Henry ever read it is not certain. If he saw it at all, it was at a later period.[1] At once, if any hope or thought had existed of a return to communion with the Papacy, that hope was at an end. Written from Italy, the book was accepted as representing the feeling if not dictated by the instructions of the Ultra-Catholics; and in such a mood they could only be treated as enemies. So much of its character as was necessary was laid before Henry, and, on the 14th of June, within a day or two therefore of its receipt, a courier was despatched with replies both from Henry himself, from the Bishop of Durham, Starkey, and Cromwell. If Pole expected to be regarded as a formidable person his vanity was seriously mortified. The substance of what he had written was seen to be sufficiently venomous, but the writer himself was treated rather as foolish than as wicked, and by the king was regarded with some kind of pity. Henry wrote (it would seem briefly) commanding him on his allegiance, all excuses set apart, to return to England and explain himself.[2]

---

structions to one whom he sent to King Henry by Reginald Pole.—BURNET'S *Collectanea*, p. 478.

[1] Starkey to Pole: STRYPE'S *Memorials*, vol. ii. p. 282.

[2] In his *Apology to Charles the Fifth* Pole says that Henry in his answer to the book said that he was not displeased with him for what he had written, but that the subject was a grave one, and that he wished to see and speak with him. He, however, remembered the fable of the fox and the sick lion, and would not show himself less sagacious than a brute. Upon this LINGARD and other writers have built a charge of treachery against Henry, and urged it, as might be expected, with much eloquent force. It did not occur to them that if Henry had really said anything so incredible, and had intended treachery, the letters of Tunstall and Starkey would have been in keeping with the king's; they would not have been allowed to betray the secret and show Pole their true opinions. Henry's letter was sent on the 14th of June; the other letters bore the same date, and went by the same post. But, indeed, the king made no mystery of his displeasure. He may have written generally, as knowing only so much

The summons was more fully explained by Starkey and Tunstall. The former declared that at the first reading of the book he was so much amazed and astonished that he knew not what to think except that he was in a dream.[1] The Bishop of Durham, on whose support Pole seems to have calculated, condescended to his arguments, and replied in formal Anglican language, that to separate from the Pope was not to separate from the unity of the Church: the Head of the Church was Christ, and unity was unity of doctrine, to which England adhered as truly as Rome: Pole had made a preposterous mistake, and it had led him into conduct which at present, if properly atoned for, might be passed over as folly, and covered and forgotten: if persevered in it would become a crime; but it was a secret so far, and if promptly repented of, should remain a secret from all eyes for ever.[2] He was commanded by the government, he was implored by his friends to return to England, to make his peace in person, and entreat the king's forgiveness.

But neither his friends nor the king understood Pole's character or comprehended his purpose. He was less foolish, he was more malicious than they supposed. When the letters reached him he professed to be utterly surprised at the reception which his book had met with. He regretted that the Supremacy Act made it impossible for him to comply with a command to present himself in England; but he protested so loudly that he had meant neither injury nor disrespect, he declared so emphatically that his book was a *bonâ fide* letter addressed to the king only, and written for his own eyes and no other's, that at last Henry believed him, accepted his assurance, and consented to pass over his impertinence. In July or August he was informed by Starkey 'that the king took the intolerable sharpness of his writings even as they that most friendly could interpret them. He thought, as few would think, that the exaggerations, the oft-returning to the same faults, the vehement exclamations, the hot sentences, the uncomely bitings, the despiteful comparisons, and likenings, all came of error and not of evil intent. His Grace supposed his benefits not forgotten, and Pole's love towards his Highness not utterly quenched.

of the book as others had communicated to him. That he affected not to be displeased is as absurd in itself as it is contradicted by the terms of the refusal to return, which Pole himself sent in reply.—STRYPE's *Memorials*, vol. ii. p. 295.

[1] Starkey to Pole: Ibid. p. 282.
[2] Tunstall to Pole: *Rolls House MS.* BURNET's *Collectanea*, p. 479.

His Majesty was one that forgave and forgot displeasure, both at once.' For his own part, however, Starkey implored his friend, as he valued his country, his honour, his good name, to repent himself, as he had desired the king to repent; the king would not press him or force his conscience; if he could be brought to reconsider his conduct, he might be assured that it would not be remembered against him.' Simultaneously with, or soon after this letter, the Bishop of Durham wrote also by the king's order, saying that, as he objected to return, it should not be insisted on; inasmuch, however, as he had affirmed so positively that his book was a private communication, there could be no further reason for preserving any other copies of it, and if he had such copies in his possession he was called upon to prove his sincerity by burning them. On his compliance, his property, which would be forfeited under the Supremacy Act, should remain in his hands, and he was free to reside in any country which he might choose.[2]

Pole did not burn his book, nor was it long before he gave the government reason to regret their forbearance towards him. For the time he continued in receipt of his income, and the stir which he had created died away.

There are many scenes in human life which, as a great poet teaches us, are either sad or beautiful, cheerless or refreshing, according to the direction from which we approach them.[3] If, on a morning in spring, we behold the ridges of a fresh-turned ploughed field from their northern side, our eyes, catching only the shadowed slopes of the successive furrows, see an expanse of white, the unmelted remains of the night's hailstorm, or the hoarfrost of the dawn. We make a circuit, or we cross over and look behind us, and on the very same ground there is nothing to be seen but the rich brown soil swelling in the sunshine, warm with promise, and chequered perhaps here and there with a green blade bursting through the surface. Both images are true to the facts of nature. Both pictures are created by real objects really existing. The pleasant certainty, however, remains with us, that the winter is passing away and summer is coming; the promise of the future is not with the ice and the sleet, but with the sunshine, with gladness, and hope.

[1] Starkey to Pole: *Rolls House MS.*
[2] Phillips' *Life of Cardinal Pole*, vol. i. p. 148. Reginald Pole to Edward VI.: *Epist. Reg. Pol.*
[3] Wordsworth's *Excursion*, book v.

Reginald Pole has shown us the form in which England appeared to him, and to the Catholic world beyond its shores, bound under an iron yoke, and sinking down in despair and desolation. To us who have seen the golden harvests waving over her fields, his loud raving has a sound of delirium: we perceive only the happy symptoms of lengthening daylight, bringing with it once more the season of life, and health, and fertility. But there is a third aspect—and it is this which we must now endeavour to present to ourselves—of England as it appeared to its own toiling children in the hour of their trial, with its lights and shadows, its frozen prejudices and sunny gleams of faith; when day followed day, and brought no certain change, and men knew not whether night would prevail or day, or which of the two was most divine—night, with its starry firmament of saints and ceremonies, or day, with the single lustre of the Gospel sun. It is idle to try to reproduce such a time in any single shape or uniform colour. The reader must call his imagination to his aid, and endeavour, if he can, to see the same object in many shapes and many colours, to sympathize successively with those to whom the Reformation was a terror, with those to whom it was the dearest hope, and those others—the multitude—whose minds could give them no certain answer, who shifted from day to day, as the impulse of the moment swayed them.

When parliament met in June, 1536, convocation as usual assembled with it. On Sunday, the ninth of the month, the two houses of the clergy were gathered for the opening of their session in the aisles of St. Paul's— high and low, hot and cold, brave and cowardly. The great question of the day, the Reformation of the Church, was one in which they, the spirituality of England, might be expected to bear some useful part. They had as yet borne no part but a part of obstruction. They had been compelled to sit impatiently, with tied hands, while the lay legislature prescribed their duties and shaped their laws for them. Whether they would assume a more becoming posture, was the problem which they were now met to solve. Gardiner was there, and Bonner, Tunstall, and Hilsey, Lee, Latimer, and Cranmer; mitred abbots, meditating the treason for which, before many months were passed, their quartered trunks would be rotting by the highways; earnest sacramentaries, making ready for the stake: the spirits of the two ages—the past and the future—were meeting there in fierce collision; and above them all, in his vicar-general's chair, sate Cromwell, proud and powerful, lording over the scowling crowd. The present hour was his. His enemies' turn in due time would come also.

The mass had been sung, the roll of the organ had died away. It was the time for the sermon, and Hugh Latimer, Bishop of Worcester, rose into the pulpit. Nine-tenths of all those eyes which were then fixed on him would have glistened with delight, could they have looked instead upon his burning. The whole multitude of passionate men were compelled, by a changed world, to listen quietly while he shot his bitter arrows among them.

We have heard Pole; we will now hear the heretic leader. His object on the present occasion was to tell the clergy what especially he thought of themselves; and Latimer was a plain speaker. They had no good opinion of him. His opinion of them was very bad indeed. His text was from the sixteenth chapter of St. Luke's Gospel: 'The children of this world are wiser in their generation than the children of light.'

The race and parentage of all living things, he said, were known by their fruits. He desired by this test to try the parentage of the present convocation. They had sat—the men that he saw before him—for seven years, more or less, session after session. What measures had come from them? They were the spiritualty—the teachers of the people, divinely commissioned; said to be and believed to be, children of light; what had they done? . . . . Mighty evils in those years had been swept away in England . . . . but whose hands had been at the work?—was it theirs? For his part, he knew that they had burned a dead man's bones; he knew that they had done their best to burn the living man who was then speaking to them. . . . . What else they had done he knew not.

The end of your convocation shall show what ye are, he said, turning direct upon them; the fruit of your consultations shall show what generation ye be of. What now have ye engendered? what have ye brought forth? What fruit has come of your long and great assembly? What one thing that the people have been the better of a hair? That the people be better learned and taught now than they were in time past, should we attribute it to your industry, or to the providence of God and the foreseeing of the King's Grace? Ought we to thank you or the King's Highness? Whether stirred the other first?—you the king, that ye might preach, or be you, by his letters, that ye should preach more often? Is it unknown, think you, how both ye and your curates were in manner by violence enforced to let books be made, not by you, but by profane and lay persons? I am bold with you; but I speak to the clergy, not to the laity. I speak to your faces, not behind your backs.

If, then, they had produced no good thing, what had they produced? There was false money instead of true. There were dead images instead of a living Saviour. There was redemption purchased by money, not redemption purchased by Christ. Abundance of these things were to be found among them .... and all those pleasant fictions which had been bred at Rome, the canonizations and expectations, the totquots and dispensations, the pardons of marvellous variety, stationaries and jubilaries, manuaries and oscularies, pedaries, and such other vanities —these had gracious reception; these were welcomed gladly in all their multiplicity. There was the ancient purgatory pickpurse—that which was suaged and cooled with a Franciscan's cowl laid upon a dead man's back, to the fourth part of his sins; that which was utterly to be spoiled, but of none other but the most prudent father the Pope, and of him as oft as he listed—a pleasant invention, and one so profitable to the feigners, that no emperor had taken more by taxes of his living subjects than those truly begotten children of the world obtained by dead men's tributes.

This was the modern Gospel—the present Catholic faith,—which the English clergy loved and taught as faithfully as their brothers in Italy. 'Ye know the proverb,' the preacher continued, "An evil crow an evil egg.' The children of this world that are known to have so evil a father the world, so evil a grandfather the devil, cannot choose but be evil—the devil being such an one as never can be unlike himself. So of Envy, his well-beloved leman, he begot the World, and left it with Discord at nurse; which World, after it came to man's estate, had of many concubines many sons. These are our holy, holy men, that say they are dead to the world; and none are more lively to the world. God is taking account of his stewards, as though he should say, 'All good men in all places accuse your avarice, your exactions, your tyranny. I commanded you that ye should feed my sheep, and ye earnestly feed yourselves from day to day, wallowing in delights and idleness. I commanded you to teach my law; you teach your own traditions, and seek your own glory. I taught openly, that he that should hear you should hear Me; he that should despise you should despise

Me. I gave you also keys—not earthly keys, but heavenly. I left my goods, that I have evermore esteemed, my Word and sacraments, to be dispensed by you. Ye have not deceived Me, but yourselves: my gifts and my benefits shall be to your greater damnation. Because ye have despised the clemency of the Master of the house, ye have deserved the severity of the Judge. Come forth; let us see an account of your stewardship.'

'And He will visit you; in his good time God will visit you. He will come; He will not tarry long. In the day in which we look not for Him, and in the hour which we do not know, He will come and will cut us in pieces, and will give us our portion with the hypocrites. He will set us, my brethren, where shall be wailing and gnashing of teeth; and here, if ye will, shall be the end of our tragedy.'[1]

Our glimpses into these scenes fall but fitfully. The sermon has reached us; but the audience—the five hundred fierce vindictive men who suffered under the preacher's irony—what they thought of it; with what feelings on that summer day the heated crowd scattered out of the cathedral, dispersing to their dinners among the taverns in Fleet-street and Cheapside—all this is gone, gone without a sound. Here no friendly informer comes to help us; no penitent malcontent breaks confidence or lifts the curtain. All is silent.

Yet, although the special acts of this body were of no mighty moment, although rarely have so many men been gathered together whose actual importance has borne so small a proportion to their estimate of themselves, yet not often, perhaps, has an assembly collected where there was such heat of passion, such malignity of hatred. For the last three years the clergy had remained torpid and half stunned, doggedly obeying the proclamations for the alterations of the service, and keeping beyond the grasp of the law. But, although too demoralized by their defeat to attempt resistance, the great body of them still detested the changes which had been forced upon their acceptance, and longed for a change which as yet they had not dared to attempt actively to compass.[2] The keener among the leaders had, however, by this time, in some degree collected themselves. They had been already watching their enemies, to strike, if they could see a

[1] *Sermons of Bishop Latimer*, Parker Society's edition, p. 33.
[2] In the State Paper Office and the Rolls House there are numerous 'depositions' as to language used by the clergy, showing their general temper.

vulnerable point, and had masked batteries prepared to unveil. Latimer taunted them with their inefficiency: he should find, perhaps to his cost, that their arms had not wholly lost their ancient sinew. To keep clear of suspicion of favouring heresy, in their duel with the Pope and Papal idolatries, they knew to be essential to the position of the government. When taunted with breaking the unity of the Church, the Privy Council were proud of being able to point to the purity of their doctrines; and although fighting against a stream too strong for them—contending, in fact, against Providence itself—the king, Cromwell, and Cranmer struggled resolutely to maintain this phantom stronghold, which they imagined to be the key of their defences. The moving party, on the other hand, inevitably transgressed an unreal and arbitrary boundary; and through the known sensitiveness of the king on the real presence, with the defence of which he regarded himself as especially entrusted by the supremacy, the clergy hoped to recover their advantage, and in striking heresy to reach the hated vicar-general.

The sermon was preached on the 9th of June; on the 23rd the lower house of convocation indirectly replied to it, by presenting a list of complaints on the doctrines which were spreading among the people, the open blasphemy of holy things, and the tacit or avowed sanction extended by certain members of the council to the circulation of heretical books. As an evidence of the progress in the change of opinion, this document is one of the most remarkable which has come down to us.[1]

After a preface, in which the clergy professed their sincere allegiance to the crown, the renunciation, utter and complete, of the Bishop of Rome and all his usurpations and injustices, the abuses which they were going to describe had, nevertheless, they said, created great disquiet in the realm, and required immediate attention.

To the slander of this noble realm, the disquietness of the people, and damage of Christian souls, it was commonly preached, thought, and spoke, that the sacrament of the altar was lightly to be esteemed.

Lewd persons were not afraid to say, 'Why should I see the sacring of the high mass? Is it anything but a piece of bread or a little pretty piece Round Robin?'

Of baptism it was said that 'It was as lawful to baptize in a tub of water at home or in a ditch by the way-

---

[1] Printed in Strype's *Memorials*, vol. ii. p. 260. The complaints are not exaggerated. There is not one which could not be illustrated or strengthened from depositions among the *Records*.

side as in a font of stone in the church. The water in the font was but a thing conjured.'

Priests, again, were thought to have no more authority to minister sacraments than laymen. Extreme unction was not a sacrament at all, and the hallowed oil, 'no better than the Bishop of Rome's grease and butter.' Confession, absolution, penance, were considered neither necessary nor useful. Confession 'had been invented' (here a stroke was aimed at Latimer) 'to have the secret knowledge of men's hearts and to pull money out of their purses.' 'It were enough for men each to confess his own sins to God in public.' The sinner should allow himself to be a sinner and sin no more. The priest had no concern with him. Purgatory was a delusion. The soul went straight from the body to heaven or to hell. Dirige, commendations, masses, suffrages, prayers, almsdeeds, oblations done for the souls departed out of the world, were vain and profitless. All sins were put away through Christ. If there were a place of purgatory Christ was not yet born.

The Church was the congregation of good men, and prayer was of the same efficacy in the air as in a church or chapel. The building called the church was made to keep the people from the rain and wind, a place where they might assemble to hear the Word of God. Mass and matins were but a fraud. The saints had no power to help departed souls. To pray to them, or to burn candles before their images, was mere idolatry. The saints could not be mediators. There was one Mediator, Christ. Our Lady was but a woman, 'like a bag of saffron or pepper when the spice was out.'[1] It was as much available to pray to saints 'as to whirl a stone against the wind.' Hallowed water, hallowed bread, hallowed candles, hallowed ashes, were but vanities. Priests were like other men, and might marry and have wives like other men.'[2]

---

[1] This, again, was intended for Latimer. The illustration was said to be his; but he denied it.

[2] Many of the clergy and even of the monks had already taken the permission of their own authority. Cranmer himself was said to be secretly married; and in some cases women, whom we find reported in this letter of Cromwell's visitors as concubines of priests, were really and literally their wives, and had been formally married to them. I have discovered one singular instance of this kind.

Ap Rice, writing to Cromwell in the year 1535 or 6, says:

'As we were of late at Walden, the abbot, then being a man of good learning and right sincere judgment, as I examined him alone, shewed me secretly, upon stipulation of silence, but only unto you, as our judge, that he had contracted matrimony with a certain woman secretly, having present thereat but one trusty witness; because he, not being able, as he said, to contain, though he could not be suffered

'The saying and singing of mass, matins, and evensong, was but roaring, howling, whistling, mumming, conjuring, and juggling,' and 'the playing of the organs a foolish vanity.' It was enough for a man to believe what was written in the Gospel—Christ's blood was shed for man's redemption, let every man believe in Christ and repent of his sins. Finally, as a special charge against Cromwell, the convocation declared that these heresies were not only taught by word of mouth, but were set out in books which were printed and published *cum privilegio*, under the apparent sanction of the crown.

Thus were the two parties face to face, and the king had either to make his choice between them, or with Cromwell's help to coerce them both into moderation. The modern reader may imagine that he should have left both alone, have allowed opinion to correct opinion, and truth to win its own victory. But this 'remedy for controversy,' so easy now, was then impossible — it would have been rejected equally by the governors and the governed. Deep in the hearts of all Englishmen in that century lay the conviction, that it was the duty of the magistrate to maintain truth, as well as to execute justice. Toleration was neither understood nor desired. The protestants clamoured against persecution, not because it was persecution, but because truth was persecuted by falsehood; and, however furiously the hostile factions exclaimed each that the truth was with them and the falsehood with their enemies, neither the one nor the other disputed the obligation of the ruling powers to support the truth in itself. So close the religious convictions of men lay to their hearts and passions, that if opinion had been left alone in their own hands, they would themselves have fought the battle of their beliefs with sharper weapons than argument. Religion to them was a thing to die for, or it was nothing. It was therefore fortunate, most fortunate, for the peace of England, that it possessed in the

---

by the laws of man, saw he might do it lawfully by the laws of God; and for the avoiding of more inconvenience, which before he was provoked unto, he did thus, having confidence in you that this act should not be anything prejudicial unto him.'—*MS. State Paper Office*, temp. Henry VIII., second series, vol. xxxv.

Cromwell acquiesced in the reasonableness of the abbot's proceeding; he wrote to tell him 'to use his remedy,' but to avoid, as far as possible, creating a scandal.—*MS. Ibid.* vol. xlvi.

The government, however, found generally a difficulty in knowing what to resolve in such cases. The king's first declaration was a reasonable one, that all clergy who had taken wives should forfeit their orders, 'and be had and reputed as lay persons to all purposes and intents.'—Royal Proclamation: WILKINS's *Concilia*, vol. iii. p. 776.

king a person whose mind, to a certain extent, sympathized with both parties; to whom both, so long as they were moderate, appeared to be right; to whom the extravagances of both were wrong and to be repressed. Protestant and Anglican alike might look to him with confidence — alike were obliged to fear him; neither could take him for their enemy, neither for their partisan. He possessed the peculiarity which has always distinguished practically effective men, of being advanced, as it is called, only slightly beyond his contemporaries. The giddy or imaginative genius soars on its own wings, it may be to cleave its course into the sunlight, and be the wonder of after times, but more often to fall like Icarus. The man of working ability tempers his judgment by the opinion of others. He leads his age—he bears the brunt of the battle—he wins the victory; but the motive force which bears him forward is not in himself, but in the great tidal wave of human progress. He is the guide of a great movement, not the creator of it; and he represents in his own person the highest average wisdom, combined necessarily in some measure with the mistakes and prejudices of the period to which he belongs.[1]

On receiving the list of grievances, the king, then three weeks married to Jane Seymour, in the first enjoyment, as some historians require us to believe, of a guilty pleasure purchased by an infamous murder, drew up with his own hand,[2] and submitted to the two houses of convocation, a body of articles, interesting as throwing light upon his state of mind, and of deeper moment as the first authoritative statement of doctrine in the Anglican church.

By the duties of his princely office, he said, he held himself obliged, not only to see God's Word and commandment sincerely believed and reverently kept and observed, but to prevent also, as far as possible, contentions and differences of opinion. To his regret he was informed that there was no such concord in the realm as he desired, but violent disagreement, not only in matters of usage and ceremony, but in the essentials of the Christian faith. To avoid the dangerous unquietness, therefore, which might, perhaps, ensue, and also the great peril to the souls of his subjects, he had arrived at the

---

[1] Luther, by far the greatest man of the sixteenth century, was as rigid a believer in the real presence as Aquinas or St. Bernard.

[2] We were constrained to put our own pen to the book, and to conceive certain articles which were by you, the bishops, and the whole of the clergy of this our realm agreed on as Catholic.— Henry VIII. to the Bishops and Clergy: WILKINS's *Concilia*, vol. iii. p. 825.

following resolutions, to which he required and commanded obedience.

I. As concerning the faith, all things were to be held and defended as true which were comprehended in the whole body and canon of the Bible, and in the three creeds or symbols. The creeds, as well as the Scripture, were to be received as the most holy, most sure and infallible words of God, and as such, 'neither to be altered nor couvelled' by any contrary opinion. Whoever refused to accept their authority 'was no member of Christ, or of his spouse the Church,' 'but a very infidel, or heretic, or member of the devil, with whom he should be eternally damned.'

II. Of sacraments generally necessary to all men there were three—baptism, penance, and the sacrament of the altar.[1]

[a] Of baptism the people were to be taught that it was ordained in the New Testament as a thing necessary for everlasting salvation, according to the saying of Christ, 'No man can enter into the kingdom of heaven except he be born again of water and the Holy Ghost.' The promises of grace attached to the sacrament of baptism appertained not only to such as had the use of reason, but also to infants, innocents, and children, who, therefore, ought to be baptized, and by baptism obtain remission of sin, and be made thereby sons and children of God.

[b] Penance was instituted in the New Testament, and no man who, after baptism, had fallen into deadly sin, could, without the same, be saved. As a sacrament it consisted of three parts—contrition, confession, and amendment. Contrition was the acknowledgment of the filthiness and abomination of sin, a sorrow and inward shame for having offended God, and a certain faith, trust, and confidence in the mercy and goodness of God, whereby the penitent man must conceive certain hope that God would forgive him his sins, and repute him justified, of the number of his elect children, not for any worthiness of any merit or work done by the penitent, but for the only merits of the blood and passion of Jesus Christ. This faith was strengthened by the special application of Christ's words and promises, and therefore, to attain such certain faith, the second part of penance was necessary; that is to say, confession to a priest (if it might be had), for the abso-

---

[1] Whether marriage and ordination were sacraments was thus left an open question. The sacramental character of confirmation and extreme unction is *implicitly* denied.

lution given by a priest was instituted of Christ, to apply the promises of God's grace to the penitent. Although Christ's death was a full, sufficient sacrifice, oblation, and satisfaction for which God forgave sinners their sin, and the punishment of it; yet all men ought to bring forth the fruits of penance, prayer, fasting, and almsdeeds, and make restitution in will and deed to their neighbour if they had done him any wrong, and to do all other good works of mercy and charity.

[c] In the sacrament of the altar, under the form and figure of bread and wine, was verily, substantially, and really contained and comprehended the very self-same body and blood of our Saviour Christ, which was born of the Virgin Mary, and suffered upon the cross for man's redemption; and under the same form and figure of bread and wine was corporeally, really, and in very substance exhibited, distributed, and received of all them which receive the said sacrament.

III. By justification was signified remission of sin and acceptance into the favour of God; that is to say, man's perfect renovation in Christ. Sinners obtained justification by contrition and faith, joined with charity; not as though contrition, or faith, or works proceeding therefrom, could worthily merit the said justification, for the only mercy and grace of the Father promised freely unto us for the Son's sake, and the merits of his blood and passion, were the only sufficient and worthy causes thereof; notwithstanding God required us to show good works in fulfilling his commands, and those who lived after the flesh would be undoubtedly damned.

In these articles, which exhausted the essential doctrines of the faith, the principles of the two religions are seen linked together in connexion, yet without combination, a first effort at the compromise between the old and the new which was only successfully completed in the English Prayerbook. The king next went on to those matters of custom and ritual, which, under the late system, had constituted the whole of religion, and which the Reformers were now trampling upon and insulting. Under mediæval Catholicism the cycle of life had been enveloped in symbolism; each epoch from birth to death was attended with its sacrament, each act of every hour with its special consecration: the days were all anniversaries; the weeks, the months, the seasons, as they revolved, brought with them their sacred associations and holy memories; and out of imagery and legend, simply taught and simply believed, innocent and beautiful practices had expanded as never-fading flowers by the road-side of existence.

Concerning these Henry wrote: 'As to having vestments in doing God's service, such as be and have been most part used—the sprinkling of holy water to put us in remembrance of our baptism, and the blood of Christ sprinkled for our redemption on the cross—the giving of holy bread, to put us in remembrance of the sacrament of the altar, that all Christians be one body mystical in Christ, as the bread is made of many grains, and yet but one loaf—the bearing of candles on Candlemas-day, in memory of Christ the spiritual light—the giving of ashes on Ash-Wednesday, to put in remembrance every Christian man in the beginning of Lent and penance that he is but ashes and earth, and thereto shall return—the bearing of palms on Palm Sunday, in memory of the receiving of Christ into Jerusalem a little before his death, that we may have the same desire to receive Him into our hearts —creeping to the cross, and humbling ourselves on Good Friday before the cross, and there offering unto Christ before the same, and kissing of it in memory of our redemption by Christ made upon the cross—setting up the sepulture of Christ, whose body, after his death, was buried—the hallowing of the font, and other like exorcisms and benedictions by the ministers of Christ's Church, and all other like laudable customs, rites, and ceremonies, —they be not to be contemned and cast away, but to be used and continued as good and laudable, to put us in remembrance of those spiritual things that they do signify, not suffering them to be forgot, or to be put in oblivion, but renewing them in our memories. But none of these ceremonies have power to remit sin, but only to stir and lift up our minds unto God, by whom only our sins be forgiven.'

So, too, of the saints. 'The saints may be honoured because they are with Christ in glory; and though Christ be the only Mediator, yet we may pray to the saints to pray for us and with us unto Almighty God; we may say to them, 'All holy angels and saints in heaven, pray for us and with us unto the Father, that for his dear Son Jesus Christ's sake we may have grace of Him and remission of our sins, with an earnest purpose to keep his holy commandments, and never to decline from the same again unto our lives' end.''

Finally, on the great vexed question of purgatory. 'Forasmuch as the due order of charity requireth, and the books of Maccabees and divers antient doctors plainly shew, that it is a very good, charitable deed to pray for souls departed; and forasmuch as such usage hath continued in the Church for many years, no man ought to be grieved with the continuance of the same. But forasmuch as the place where they be, the name thereof, and kind of pains there, be to us uncertain by Scripture, therefore this with all other things we remit unto Almighty God, unto whose mercy it is meet and convenient for us to commend them, trusting that God accepteth our prayers for them. Wherefore it is much necessary that such abuses be clearly put away, which, under the name of purgatory, hath been advanced; as to make men believe that through the Bishop of Rome's pardons men might be delivered out of purgatory and all the pains of it, or that masses said at any place or before any image might deliver them from their pain and send them straight to heaven.'[1]

We have now before us the stormy eloquence of Pole, the iconoclasm of Latimer, the superstitions of the complaining clergy—representing three principles struggling one against the other, and the voice of the pilot heard above the tempest. Each of these contained some element which the other needed; they were to fret and chafe till the dust was beaten off, and the grains of gold could meet and fuse.

The articles were debated in convocation, and passed because it was the king's will. No party were pleased. The Protestants exclaimed against the countenance to superstition; the Anglo-Catholics lamented the visible taint of heresy, the reduced number of the sacraments, the doubtful language upon purgatory, and the silence—dangerously significant—on the nature of the priesthood. They were signed, however, by all sides; and by Cromwell, now Lord Cromwell, lord privy seal, and not vicar-general only, but appointed vicegerent of the king in all matters ecclesiastical, they were sent round through the English counties, to be obeyed by every man at his peril.[2]

The great matters being thus disposed of, the business of the session concluded with a resolution passed on the 20th of July, respecting general councils. The Pope, at the beginning of June, had issued notice of a council to

---

[1] *Formularies of Faith*, temp. Henry VIII., Oxford edition, 1825. Articles devised by the King's Majesty to stablish Christian quietness and unity, and to avoid contentious opinions.

[2] Cromwell's patent as lord privy seal is dated the 2nd of July, 1536. On the 9th he was created Baron Cromwell, and in the same month vicegerent *in rebus ecclesiasticis.*

be assembled, if possible, at Mantua, in the following year. The English government were contented to recognise a council called *ad locum indifferentem*, with the consent of the great powers of Europe. They would send no delegates to a petty Italian principality, where the decrees would be dictated by the Pope and the Emperor. The convocation pronounced that the Pope had gone beyond his authority: a general council could not legally be called without the consent of all Christian princes; to princes the right belonged of determining the time and place of such an assembly, of appointing the judges, of fixing the order of proceeding, and of deciding even upon the doctrines which might lawfully be allowed and defended.[1]

This was the last act of the year; immediately after, the convocation was prorogued. From the temper which had been displayed, it was easy to see that trouble was impending. The form which it would assume was soon to show itself.

Meanwhile, an event occurred of deeper importance than decrees of councils, convocation quarrels, and moves and counter-moves on the political chessboard; an event not to be passed by in silence, though I can only glance at it.

The agitation caused by the queen's trial had suspended hitherto the fate of the monasteries. On the dispersion of the clergy a commission was appointed by Cromwell, to put in force the act of dissolution;[2] and a series of injunctions were simultaneously issued, one of which related to the articles of faith, another to the observance of the order diminishing the number of holydays; a third forbade the extolling the special virtue of images and relics, as things which had caused much folly and superstition; the people should learn that God would be better pleased to see them providing for their families by honest labour, than by idling upon pilgrimages; if they had money to spare, they might give it in charity to the poor.

The paternoster, the apostles' creed, and the ten commandments had been lately published in English. Fathers of families, schoolmasters, and heads of households were to take care that these fundamental elements of the Christian faith should be learnt by the children and servants under their care; and the law of the land was to be better observed, which directed that every child

[1] The judgment of the convocation concerning general councils, July 20, 28 Henry VIII.: BURNET'S *Collectanea*, p. 88.
[2] BURNET'S *Collectanea*, p. 89.

should be brought up either to learning or to some honest occupation, 'lest they should fall to sloth and idleness, and being brought after to calamity and misery, impute their ruin to those who suffered them to be brought up idly in their youth.'

An order follows, of more significance: 'Every parson or proprietary of every parish church within this realm shall, on this side of the feast of St. Peter ad Vincula next coming,[1] provide a book of the whole Bible, both in Latin and also in English, and lay the same in the quire, for every man that will to read and look therein; and shall discourage no man from reading any part of the Bible, but rather comfort, exhort, and admonish every man to read the same, as the very word of God and the spiritual food of man's soul; ever gently and charitably exhorting them, that using a sober and modest behaviour in the reading and inquisition of the true sense of the same, they do in nowise stiffly or eagerly contend or strive one with another about the same, but refer the declaration of those places that be in controversy to the judgment of the learned.'

The publication of the English translation of the Bible, with the permission for its free use among the people — the greatest, because the purest victory so far gained by the Reformers — was at length accomplished; a few words will explain how, and by whom. Before the Reformation, two versions existed of the Bible in English — two certainly, perhaps three. One was Wicliffe's; another, based on Wicliffe's, but tinted more strongly with the peculiar opinions of the Lollards, followed at the beginning of the fifteenth century; and there is said to have been a third, but no copy of *this* is known to survive, and the history of it is vague.[2] The possession or the use of these translations was prohibited by the Church, under pain of death. They were extremely rare, and little read; and it was not till Luther's great movement began in Germany, and his tracts and commentaries found their way into England, that a practical determination was awakened among the people, to have before them, in their own tongue, the book on which their faith was built.

I have already described how William Tyndal felt his heart burn in him to accomplish this great work for his

---

[1] The Feast of St. Peter ad Vincula was on the 1st of August. These injunctions could hardly have been issued before August, 1536; nor could they have been later than September. The clergy were, therefore, allowed nearly a year to provide themselves.

[2] LEWIS's *History of the English Bible*.

country; how he applied for assistance to a learned bishop; how he discovered rapidly that the assistance which he would receive from the Church authorities would be a speedy elevation to martyrdom; how he went across the Channel to Luther, and thence to Antwerp; and how he there, in the year 1526, achieved and printed the first edition of the New Testament. It was seen how copies were carried over secretly to London, and circulated in thousands by the Christian Brothers. The council threatened; the bishops anathematized. They opened subscriptions to buy up the hated and dreaded volumes. They burnt them publicly in St. Paul's. The whip, the gaol, the stake, did their worst; and their worst was nothing. The high dignitaries of the earth were fighting against Heaven, and met the success which ever attends such contests. Three editions were sold before 1530; and in that year a fresh instalment was completed. The Pentateuch was added to the New Testament; and afterwards, by Tyndal himself, or under Tyndal's eyes, the historical books, the Psalms and Prophets. At length the whole canon was translated, and published in separate portions.

All these were condemned with equal emphasis—all continued to spread. The progress of the work of propagation had, in 1531, become so considerable as to be the subject of an anxious protest to the crown from the episcopal bench. They complained of the translations as inaccurate—of unbecoming reflections on themselves in the prefaces and side notes. They required stronger powers of repression, more frequent holocausts, a more efficient inquisitorial police. In Henry's reply they found that the waters of their life were poisoned at the spring. The king, too, was infected with the madness. The king would have the Bible in English; he directed them, if the translation was unsound, to prepare a better translation without delay. If they had been wise in their generation they would have secured the ground when it was offered to them, and gladly complied. But the work of Reformation in England was not to be accomplished, in any one of its purer details, by the official clergy; it was to be done by volunteers from the ranks, and forced upon the Church by the secular arm. The bishops remained for two years inactive. In 1533, the king becoming more peremptory, Cranmer carried a resolution for a translation through convocation. The resolution, however, would not advance into act. The next year he brought the subject forward again; and finding his brother prelates fixed in their neglect, he divided Tyndal's work into ten parts, sending one part to each bishop to correct. The Bishop of London alone ventured an open refusal; the remainder complied in words, and did nothing.[1]

Finally, the king's patience was exhausted. The legitimate methods having been tried in vain, he acted on his own responsibility. Miles Coverdale, a member of the same Cambridge circle which had given birth to Cranmer, to Latimer, to Barnes, to the Scotch Wishart, silently went abroad with a licence from Cromwell; with Tyndal's help he collected and edited the scattered portions; and in 1536[2] there appeared in London, published *cum privilegio* and dedicated to Henry VIII., the first complete copy of the English Bible. The separate translations, still anomalously prohibited in detail, were exposed freely to sale in a single volume, under the royal sanction. The canon and text book of the new opinions—so long dreaded, so long execrated--was thenceforth to lie open in every church in England; and the clergy were ordered not to permit only, but to exhort and encourage, all men to resort to it and read.[3]

In this act was laid the foundation-stone on which the whole later history of England, civil as well as ecclesiastical, has been reared; the most minute incidents become interesting, connected with an event of so mighty moment.

'Caiphas,' said Coverdale in the dedicatory preface, 'being bishop of his year, prophesied that it was better to put Christ to death than that all the people should perish: he meaning that Christ was a heretic and a deceiver of the people, when in truth he was the Saviour of the world, sent by his Father to suffer death for man's redemption.

'After the same manner the Bishop of Rome conferred on King Henry VIII. the title of Defender of the Faith, because his Highness suffered the bishops to burn God's Word, the root of faith, and to persecute the lovers and ministers of the same; where in very deed the Bishop, though he knew not what he did, prophesied that, by the righteous administration of his Grace, the faith should be so defended that God's Word, the mother of faith, should have free course through all Christendom, but especially in his own realm.

'The Bishop of Rome has studied long to keep the Bible from the people, and specially from princes, lest

[1] Lewis's *History of the English Bible*.
[2] The printing was completed in October, 1535.
[3] There is an excellent copy of this edition in the Bodleian Library at Oxford.

they should find out his tricks and his falsehoods, lest they should turn from his false obedience to the true obedience commanded by God; knowing well enough that, if the clear sun of God's Word came over the heat of the day, it would drive away the foul mist of his devilish doctrines. The Scripture was lost before the time of that noble king Josiah, as it hath also been among us unto the time of his Grace. Through the merciful goodness of God it is now found again as it was in the days of that virtuous king; and praised be the Father, the Son, and the Holy Ghost, world without end, which so excellently hath endowed the princely heart of his Highness with such ferventness to his honour and the wealth of his subjects, that he may be compared worthily unto that noble king, that lantern among princes, who commanded straitly, as his Grace doth, that the law of God should be read and taught unto all the people.

'May it be found a general comfort to all Christian hearts—a continual subject of thankfulness, both of old and young, unto God and to his Grace, who, being our Moses, has brought us out of the old Ægypt, and from the cruel hands of our spiritual Pharaoh. Not by the thousandth part were the Jews so much bound unto King David for subduing of great Goliah as we are to his Grace for delivering us out of our old Babylonish captivity. For the which deliverance and victory I beseech our only Mediator, Jesus Christ, to make such mean with us unto his heavenly Father, that we may never be unthankful unto Him nor unto his Grace, but increase in fear of God, in obedience to the King's Highness, in love unfeigned to our neighbours, and in all virtue that cometh of God, to whom, for the defending of his blessed Word, be honour and thanks, glory and dominion, world without end.'[1]

Equally remarkable, and even more emphatic in the recognition of the share in the work borne by the king, was the frontispiece.

This was divided into four compartments.

In the first, the Almighty was seen in the clouds with outstretched arms. Two scrolls proceeded out of his mouth, to the right and the left. On the former was the verse, 'the word which goeth forth from me shall not return to me empty, but shall accomplish whatsoever I will have done.' The other was addressed to Henry, who was kneeling at a distance bareheaded, with his crown

---

[1] Preface to COVERDALE's *Bible*.

lying at his feet. The scroll said, 'I have found me a man after my own heart, who shall fulfil all my will.' Henry answered, 'Thy word is a lantern unto my feet.'

Immediately below the king was seated on his throne, holding in each hand a book, on which was written 'the Word of God.' One of these he was giving to Cranmer and another bishop, who with a group of priests were on the right of the picture, saying, 'Take this and teach;' the other on the opposite side he held to Cromwell and the lay peers, and the words were, 'I make a decree that, in all my kingdom, men shall tremble and fear before the living God.' A third scroll, falling downwards over his feet, said alike to peer and prelate, 'Judge righteous judgment. Turn not away your ear from the prayer of the poor man.' The king's face was directed sternly towards the bishops, with a look which said, 'Obey at last, or worse will befal you.'

In the third compartment, Cranmer and Cromwell were distributing the Bible to kneeling priests and laymen; and, at the bottom, a preacher with a benevolent beautiful face was addressing a crowd from a pulpit in the open air. He was apparently commencing a sermon with the text, 'I exhort therefore that, first of all, supplications, prayers, intercessions, and giving of thanks be made for all men—for kings'—and at the word 'kings' the people were shouting 'Vivat Rex!—Vivat Rex!' children who knew no Latin lisping 'God save the King!' and, at the extreme left, at a gaol window, a prisoner was joining in the cry of delight, as if he, too, were delivered from a worse bondage.

This was the introduction of the English Bible—this the seeming acknowledgment of Henry's services. Of the translation itself, though since that time it has been many times revised and altered, we may say that it is substantially the Bible with which we are all familiar. The peculiar genius—if such a word may be permitted—which breathes through it—the mingled tenderness and majesty —the Saxon simplicity—the preternatural grandeur—unequalled, unapproached, in the attempted improvements of modern scholars—all are here, and bear the impress of the mind of one man—William Tyndal. Lying, while engaged in that great office, under the shadow of death, the sword above his head and ready at any moment to fall, he worked, under circumstances alone perhaps truly worthy of the task which was laid upon him—his spirit, as it were divorced from the world, moved in a purer element than common air.

His work was done. He lived to see the Bible no longer carried by stealth into his country, where the possession of it was a crime, but borne in by the solemn will of the king—solemnly recognised as the word of the Most High God. And then his occupation in this earth was gone. His eyes saw the salvation for which he had longed, and he might depart to his place. He was denounced to the regent of Flanders; he was enticed by the suborned treachery of a miserable English fanatic beyond the town under whose liberties he had been secure; and with the reward which, at other times as well as those, has been held fitting by human justice for the earth's great ones, he passed away in smoke and flame to his rest.

CHAPTER XIII.

THE PILGRIMAGE OF GRACE.

The Nun of Kent's conspiracy, the recent humour of convocation, the menaces of Reginald Pole, alike revealed a dangerous feeling in the country. A religious revolution in the midst of an armed population intensely interested in the event, could not be accomplished without an appeal being made at some period of its course to arms; and religion was at this time but one out of many elements of confusion. Society, within and without, from the heart of its creed to its outward organization, was passing through a transition, and the records of the Pilgrimage of Grace cast their light far down into the structure and inmost constitution of English life.

The organic changes introduced by the parliament of 1529 had been the work of the king and the second house in the legislature; and the peers had not only seen measures pass into law which they would gladly have rejected had they dared, but their supremacy was slipping away from them; the Commons, who in times past had confined themselves to voting supplies and passing without inquiry such measures as were sent down to them, had started suddenly into new proportions, and had taken upon themselves to discuss questions sacred hitherto to convocation. The upper house had been treated in disputes which had arisen with significant disrespect; ancient and honoured customs had been discontinued among them against their desire;[1] and, constitutionally averse to change,

---

[1] 'The Lord Darcy declared unto me that the custom among the Lords before that time had been that matters touching spiritual authority should always be referred unto the convocation house, and not for the parliament house: and that before this last parliament it was accustomed among the Lords, the first matter they always com-

they were hurried powerless along by a force which was bearing them they knew not where. Hating heretics with true English conservatism, they found men who but a few years before would have been in the dungeons of Lollards' Tower, now high in court favour, high in office, and with seats in their own body. They had learnt to endure the presence of self-raised men when as ecclesiastics such men represented the respectable dignity of the Church; but the proud English nobles had now for the first time to tolerate the society and submit to the dictation of a lay peer who had been a tradesman's orphan and a homeless vagabond. The Reformation in their minds was associated with the exaltation of base blood, the levelling of ranks, the breaking down the old rule and order of the land. Eager to check so dangerous a movement, they had listened, some of them, to the revelations of the Nun. Fifteen great men and lords, Lord Darcy stated, had confederated secretly to force the government to change their policy;[1] and Darcy himself had been in communication for the same purpose with the Spanish ambassador, and was of course made aware of the intended invasion in the preceding winter.[2] The discontent extended to the county families, who shared or imitated the prejudices of their feudal leaders; and these families had again their peculiar grievances. On the suppression of the abbeys the peers obtained grants, or expected to obtain them, from the forfeited estates. The country gentlemen saw only the desecration of the familiar scenes of their daily life, the violation of the tombs of their ancestors, and the buildings themselves, the beauty of which was the admiration of foreigners who visited England, reduced to ruins.[3] The abbots had been their personal friends, 'the

muned of, after the mass of the Holy Ghost, was to affirm and allow the first chapter of Magna Charta touching the rights and liberties of the church; and it was not so now. Also the Lord Darcy did say that in any matter which toucheth the prerogative of the king's crown, or any matter that touched the prejudice of the same, the custom of the Lords' house was that they should have, upon their requests, a copy of the bill of the same, to the intent that they might have their council learned to scan the same; or if it were betwixt party and party, if the bill were not prejudicial to the commonwealth. And now they could have no such copy upon their suit, or at the least so readily as they were wont to have in parliament before.'—Examination of Robert Aske in the Tower: *Rolls House MS.* A 2, 29, p. 197.

[1] 'The said Aske saith he well remembereth that the Lord Darcy told him that there were divers great men and lords which before the time of the insurrection had promised to do their best to suppress heresies and the authors and maintainers of them. and he saith they were in number fifteen persons.'—*Rolls House Miscellaneous MSS.* first series, 414.

[2] Richard Coren to Cromwell: *State Papers*, vol. i. p. 558.

[3] 'The abbeys were one of the beauties of the realm to all

trustees for their children and the executors of their wills;'[1] the monks had been the teachers of their children; the free tables and free lodgings in these houses had made them attractive and convenient places of resort in distant journeys; and in remote districts the trade of the neighbourhood, from the wholesale purchases of the corndealer to the huckstering of the wandering pedlar, had been mainly carried on within their walls.[2]

'The Statute of Uses,' again, an important but insufficient measure of reform, passed in the last session of parliament but one,[3] had created not unreasonable irritation. Previous to the modification of the feudal law in the year 1540, land was not subject to testamentary disposition; and it had been usual to evade the prohibition of direct bequest, in making provision for younger children, by leaving estates in 'use,' charged with payments so considerable as to amount virtually to a transfer of the property. The injustice of the common law was in this way remedied, but remedied so awkwardly as to embarrass and complicate the titles of estates beyond extrication. A 'use' might be erected on a 'use;' it might be extended to the descendants of those in whose behalf it first was made; it might be mortgaged, or transferred as a security to raise money. The apparent owner of a property might effect a sale, and the buyer find his purchase so encumbered as to be useless to him. The intricacies of tenure thus often passed the skill of judges to unravel;[4] while, again, the lords of the fiefs were unable to claim their fines or fees or liveries, and the crown, in cases of treason, could not enforce its forfeitures. The Statute of Uses terminated the immediate difficulty by creating, like the recent Irish Encumbered Estates Act, parliamentary titles. All persons entitled to the use of lands were declared to be to all intents and purposes the lawful possessors, as much as if such lands had been made over to

strangers passing through.'—Examination of Aske: *Rolls House MS.* A 2, 29.

[1] Examination of Aske: MS. ibid. I am glad to have discovered this most considerable evidence in favour of some at least of the superiors of the religious houses.

[2] 'Strangers and buyers of corn were also greatly refreshed, horse and man, at the abbeys; and merchandize was well carried on through their help.'—Examination of Aske: ibid.

[3] 27 Henry VIII. cap. 10.

[4] Among the unarranged MSS. in the State Paper Office is a long and most elaborate explanation of the evils which had been created by the system of uses. It is a paper which ought to find its place in the history of English landed tenure; and when the arrangement of these MSS. now in progress is completed, it will be accessible to any inquirer.

them by formal grant or conveyance. They became actual owners, with all the rights and all the liabilities of their special tenures. The embarrassed titles were in this way simplified; but now, the common law remaining as yet unchanged, the original evil returned in full force. Since a trust was equivalent to a conveyance, and land could not be bequeathed by will, the system of trusts was virtually terminated. Charges could not be created upon estates, and the landowners complained that they could no longer raise money if they wanted it; their estates must go wholly to the eldest sons; and, unless they were allowed to divide their properties by will, their younger children would be left portionless.[1]

Small grievances are readily magnified in seasons of general disruption. A wicked spirit in the person of Cromwell was said to rule the king, and everything which he did was evil, and every evil of the commonwealth was due to his malignant influence.

The discontent of the noblemen and gentlemen would in itself have been formidable. Their armed retinues were considerable. The constitutional power of the counties was in their hands. But the commons, again, had their own grounds of complaint, for the most part just, though arising from causes over which the government had no control, from social changes deeper than the Reformation itself. In early times each petty district in England had been self-supporting, raising its own corn, feeding its own cattle, producing by women's hands in the cottages and farmhouses its own manufactures. There were few or no large roads, no canals, small means of transport of any kind, and from this condition of things had arisen the laws which we call shortsighted, against engrossers of grain. Wealthy speculators, watching their opportunity, might buy up the produce not immediately needed, of an abundant harvest, and when the stock which was left was exhausted, they could make their own market, unchecked by a danger of competition. In time no doubt

---

[1] 'Masters, there is a statute made whereby all persons be restrained to make their will upon their lands; for now the eldest son must have all his father's lands; and no person, to the payment of his debts, neither to the advancement of his daughters' marriages, can do nothing with their lands, nor cannot give to his youngest son any lands.'—Speech of Mr. Sheriff Dymock, at Horncastle: *Rolls House MS.* A 2, 29.

'They want the Statute of Uses qualified, that a man be allowed to bequeath part of his lands by will. It will invade the old accustomed law in many things.'—Examination of Aske: MS. ibid. 'Divers things should be reformed, and especially the Act of Uses. Younger brothers would none of that in no wise.'—Earl of Oxford to Cromwell: *Miscellaneous MSS.* State Paper Office, second series, vol. i.

the mischief would have righted itself, but only with the assistance of a coercive police which had no existence, who would have held down the people while they learnt their lesson by starvation. The habits of a great nation could only change slowly. Each estate or each township for the most part grew its own food, and (the average of seasons compensating each other) food adequate for the mouths dependent upon it.

The development of trade at the close of the fifteenth century gave the first shock to the system. The demand for English wool in Flanders had increased largely, and holders of property found they could make their own advantage by turning their corn-land into pasture, breaking up the farms, enclosing the commons, and becoming graziers on a gigantic scale.

I have described in the first chapter of this work the manner in which the Tudor sovereigns had attempted to check this tendency, but interest had so far proved too strong for legislation. The statutes prohibiting enclosures had remained, especially in the northern counties, unenforced; and the small farmers and petty copyholders, hitherto thriving and independent, found themselves at once turned out of their farms and deprived of the resource of the commons. They had suffered frightfully, and they saw no reason for their sufferings. From the Trent northward a deep and angry spirit of discontent had arisen which could be stirred easily into mutiny.[1]

---

[1] The depositions of prisoners taken after the rebellion are full of evidence on this point. George Gisborne says: 'We were in mind and will to meet for certain causes, the which concerned the living of the poor people and commons, the which they say be sore oppressed by gentlemen, because their livings is taken away.'—*Rolls House MS. miscellaneous, first series, 132.*

Wm. Stapleton says: 'Among the causes of the insurrection were pulling down of villages and farms, raising of rents, enclosures, intakes of the commons, worshipful men taking yeomen's offices, that is, becoming dealers in farm produce.'—*Rolls House MS.*

I am tempted to add a petition sent from one of the discontented districts to the crown, which betrays great ignorance of political economy, although it exhibits also a clear understanding both of the petitioners' sufferings and of the immediate causes of those sufferings.

'Please it your noble Grace to consider the great indigence and scarcity of all manner of victual necessary to your subjects within this realm of England, which doth grow daily more and more, by reason of the great and covetous misusages of the farms within this your realm; which misusages and the inconveniences thereof hath not only been begun and risen by divers gentlemen of the same your realm, but also by divers and many merchant adventurers, clothmakers, goldsmiths, butchers, tanners, and other artificers and unreasonable covetous persons, which doth encroach daily many farms more than they can occupy in tilth of corn; ten, twelve, fourteen, or sixteen farms in one man's hands at once; when in time past there hath been in every farm of them a good house kept, and in some of them three,

Nor were these the only grievances of the northern populace. The Yorkshire knights, squires, sheriffs, and justices of the peace, intent, as we see, on their own interests, had been overbearing and tyrannical in their offices. The Abbot of York, interceding with Cromwell in behalf of some poor man who had been needlessly arrested and troubled, declared that 'there was such a company of wilful gentlemen within Yorkshire as he thought there were not in all England besides,'[1] and Cromwell in consequence had 'roughly handled the grand jury.' Courts of arbitration had sate from immemorial time in the northern baronies where disputes between landlords and tenants had been equitably and cheaply adjusted. The growing inequality of fortunes had broken through this useful custom. Small farmers and petty leaseholders now found themselves sued or compelled to sue in the courts at Westminster, and the expenses of a journey to London, or of the employment of London advocates, placed them virtually at the mercy of their landlords. Thus the law itself had been made an instrument of oppression, and the better order of gentlemen, who would have seen justice enforced, had they been able, found themselves assailed daily with 'piteous complaints' which they had no power to satisfy.[2] The occupation of the council with the larger questions of the Church, had left them too little leisure to attend to these disorders. Cromwell's occasional and abrupt interference had created irritation, but no improvement; and mischiefs of all kinds had grown unheeded till the

four, five, or six ploughs kept and daily occupied, to the great comfort and relief of your subjects of your realm, poor and rich. For when every man was contented with one farm, and occupied that well, there was plenty and reasonable price of everything that belonged to man's sustenance by reason of tillage; forasmuch as every acre of land tilled and ploughed hore the straw and the chaff besides the corn, able and sufficient with the help of the shakke in the stubbe to succour and feed as many great beasts (as horses, oxen, and kine) as the land would keep: and further, by reason of the hinderflight of the crops and seeds tried out in cleansing, winnowing, and sifting the corn, there was brought up at every barn-door hens, capons, geese, ducks, swine, and other poultry, to the great comfort of your people. And now, by reason of so many farms engrossed in one man's hands, which cannot till them, the ploughs be decayed, and the farmhouses and other dwelling-houses; so that when there was in a town twenty or thirty dwelling-houses they be now decayed, ploughs and all the people clean gone, and the churches down, and no more parishioners in many parishes, but a neatherd and a shepherd instead of three score or four score persons.'—*Rolls House MS.* miscellaneous, second series, 854.

[1] Abbot of York to Cromwell.—*Miscellaneous MS.* State Paper Office, second series, vol. lii.

[2] See a very remarkable letter of Sir William Parr to Cromwell, dated April 8, 1536, a few months only before the outbreak of the rebellion: Ibid. vol. xxxi.

summer of 1536, when a fresh list of grievances, some real, some imaginary, brought the crisis to a head.

The convocation of York, composed of rougher materials than the representatives of the southern counties, had acquiesced but tardily in the measures of the late years. Abuses of all kinds instinctively sympathize, and the clergy of the north, who were the most ignorant in England, and the laity whose social irregularities were the greatest, united resolutely in their attachment to the Pope, were most alarmed at the progress of heresy, and most anxious for a reaction. The deciding act against Rome and the king's articles of religion struck down the hopes which had been excited there and elsewhere by the disgrace of Queen Anne. Men saw the Papacy finally abandoned, they saw heresy encouraged, and they were proportionately disappointed and enraged.

At this moment three commissions were issued by the crown, each of which would have tried the patience of the people, if conducted with the greatest prudence, and at the happiest opportunity.

The second portion of the subsidy (an income-tax of two and a half per cent. on all incomes above twenty pounds a year), which had been voted in the autumn of 1534, had fallen due. The money had been required for the Irish war, and the disaffected party in England had wished well to the insurgents, so that the collectors found the greatest difficulty either in enforcing the tax, or obtaining correct accounts of the properties on which it was to be paid.

Simultaneously Legh and Layton, the two most active and most unpopular of the monastic visitors, were sent to Yorkshire to carry out the Act of Suppression. Others went into Lincolnshire, others to Cheshire and Lancashire, while a third set carried round the injunctions of Cromwell to the clergy, with directions further to summon before them every individual parish priest, to examine into his character, his habits and qualifications, and eject summarily all inefficient persons from their offices and emoluments.

The dissolution of the religious houses commenced in the midst of an ominous and sullen silence. The act extended only to houses whose incomes were under two hundred pounds a year, and among these the commissioners were to use their discretion. They were to visit every abbey and priory, to examine the books, examine the monks—when the income fell short, or when the character of the house was vicious, to eject the occupants, and place the lands and farm-buildings in the hands of lay tenants for the crown. The discharge of an unpopular office, however conducted, would have exposed those who undertook it to great odium. It is likely that those who did undertake it were men who felt bitterly on the monastic vices, and did their work with little scruple or sympathy. Legh and Layton were accused subsequently of having borne themselves with overbearing insolence; they were said also to have taken bribes, and where bribes were not offered, to have extorted them from the houses which they spared. That they went through their business roughly is exceedingly probable; whether needlessly so must not be concluded from the report of persons to whom their entire occupation was sacrilege. That they received money is evident from their own reports to the government; but it is evident also that they did not attempt to conceal that they received it. When the revenues of the crown were irregular and small, the salaries even of ministers of state were derived in great measure from fees and presents; the visitors of the monasteries, travelling with large retinues, were expected to make their duties self-supporting, to inflict themselves as guests on the houses to which they went, and to pay their own and their servants' 'wages' from the funds of the establishments. Sums of money would be frequently offered them in lieu of a painful hospitality; and whether they took unfair advantage of their opportunities for extortion, or whether they exercised a proper moderation, cannot be concluded from the mere fact that there was a clamour against them. But beyond doubt their other proceedings were both rash and blameable. Their servants with the hot puritan blood already in their veins, trained in the exposure of the impostures and profligacies of which they had seen so many, scorning and hating the whole monastic race, had paraded their contempt before the world; they had ridden along the highways, decked in the spoils of the desecrated chapels, with copes for doublets, tunics for saddle-cloths,[1] and the silver relic-cases hammered into sheaths for their daggers.[2] They had been directed to enforce an abrogation of the superfluous holydays; they had shown such excessive zeal that in some places common markets had been held under their direction on Sundays.[3]

[1] It was said that the visitors' servants had made apparel, doublets, yea, even saddlecloths, of the churches' vestments.—Examination of John Dakyn: Rolls House MS. miscellaneous, first series, 402.
[2] Rolls House MS.
[3] Ibid. miscellaneous, first series, 402.

Scenes like these working upon tempers already inflamed, gave point to discontent. Heresy, that word of dread and horror to English ears, rang from lip to lip. Their hated enemy was at the people's doors, and their other sufferings were the just vengeance of an angry God.[1] Imagination, as usual, hastened to assist and expand the nucleus of truth. Cromwell had formed the excellent design, which two years later he carried into effect, of instituting parish registers. A report of his intention had gone abroad, and mingling with the irritating inquiries of the subsidy commissioners into the value of men's properties, gave rise to a rumour that a fine was to be paid to the crown on every wedding, funeral, or christening; that a tax would be levied on every head of cattle, or the cattle should be forfeited; 'that no man should eat in his house white meat, pig, goose, nor capon, but that he should pay certain dues to the King's Grace.'

In the desecration of the abbey chapels and altar-plate a design was imagined against all religion. The clergy were to be despoiled; the parish churches pulled down, one only to be left for every seven or eight miles; the church plate to be confiscated, and 'chalices of tin' supplied for the priest to sing with.[2]

Every element necessary for a great revolt was thus in motion — wounded superstition, real suffering, caused by real injustice, with their attendant train of phantoms. The clergy in the north were disaffected to a man;[3] the people were in the angry humour which looks eagerly for an enemy, and flies at the first which seems to offer. If to a spirit of revolt there had been added a unity of purpose, the results would have been far other than they were. Happily, the discontents of the nobility, the gentlemen, the clergy, the commons, were different, and in many respects, opposite; and although, in the first heat of the commotion, a combination threatened to be possible, jealousy and suspicion rapidly accomplished the work of disintegration. The noble lords were in the interest of Pole, of European Catholicism, the Empire, and the Papacy; the country gentlemen desired only the quiet enjoyment of a right to do as they would with their own, and the quiet maintenance of a Church which was too corrupt to interfere

---

[1] Aske's Deposition: *Rolls House MS.*
[2] Depositions on the Rebellion, *passim.* among the MSS. in the State Paper Office and the Rolls House.
[3] George Lumley, the eldest son of Lord Lumley, said in his evidence that there was not a spiritual man in the whole north of England who had not assisted the rebellion with arms or money.—*Rolls House MS.*

with them. The working people had a just cause, though disguised by folly; but all true sufferers soon learnt, that in rising against the government, they had mistaken their best friends for foes.

It was Michaelmas then, in the year 1536. Towards the fall of the summer, clergy from the southern counties had been flitting northward, and on their return had talked mysteriously to their parishioners of impending insurrections, in which honest men would bear their part.[1] In Yorkshire and Lincolnshire the stories of the intended destruction of parish churches had been vociferously circulated; and Lord Hussey, at his castle at Sleford, had been heard to say to one of the gentlemen of the county, that 'the world would never mend until they fought for it.'[2] September passed away; at the end of the month, the nunnery of Legbourne, near Louth, was suppressed by the visitors, and two servants of Cromwell were left in the house, to complete the dissolution. On Monday, the 2nd of October, Heneage, one of the examiners under the clerical commission, was coming, with the chancellor of the Bishop of Lincoln, into Louth itself, and the clergy of the neighbourhood were to appear and submit themselves to inspection.

The evening before being Sunday, a knot of people gathered on the green in the town. They had the great silver cross belonging to the parish with them; and as a crowd collected about them, a voice cried, 'Masters, let us follow the cross; God knows whether ever we shall follow it hereafter or nay.' They formed in procession, and went round the streets; and after vespers, a party, headed 'by one Nicholas Melton, who, being a shoemaker, was called Captain Cobler,' appeared at the doors of the church, and required the churchwardens to give them the key of the jewel chamber. The chancellor, they said, was coming the next morning, and intended to seize the plate. The churchwardens hesitating, the keys were taken by force. The chests were opened, the crosses, chalices, and candlesticks 'were shewed openly in the sight of every man,' and then, lest they should be stolen in the night,

---

[1] The parish priest of Wyley, in Essex, had been absent for three weeks in the north, in the month of August, and on returning, about the 2nd of September, said to one of his villagers, Thomas Rogers, 'There shall be business shortly in the north, and I trust to help and strengthen my countrymen with ten thousand such as I am myself; and I shall be one of the worst of them all. The king shall not reign long.'—Confession of Thomas Rogers: *MS. State Paper Office*, second series, vol. xxx. p. 112.

[2] Deposition of Thomas Brian: *Rolls House MS.* A 2, 29.

an armed watch kept guard till daybreak in the church aisles.

At nine o'clock on Monday morning Heneage entered the town, with a single servant. The chancellor was ill, and could not attend. As he rode in, the alarm-bell pealed out from Louth Tower. The inhabitants swarmed into the streets with bills and staves; 'the stir and the noise arising hideous.' The commissioner, in panic at the disturbance, hurried into the church for sanctuary; but the protection was not allowed to avail him. He was brought out into the market-place, a sword was held to his breast, and he was sworn at an extemporized tribunal to be true to the commons, upon pain of death. 'Let us swear! let us all swear!' was then the cry. A general oath was drawn. The townsmen swore—all strangers resident swore—they would be faithful to the king, the commonwealth, and to Holy Church.

In the heat of the enthusiasm appeared the registrar of the diocese, who had followed Heneage with his books, in which was enrolled Cromwell's commission. Instantly clutched, he was dragged to the market-cross. A priest was mounted on the stone steps, and commanded to read the commission aloud. He began; but the 'hideous clamour' drowned his voice. The crowd, climbing on his shoulders, to overlook the pages, bore him down. He flung the book among the mob, and it was torn leaf from leaf, and burnt upon the spot. The registrar barely escaped with his life: he was rescued by friends, and hurried beyond the gates.

Meanwhile, a party of the rioters had gone out to Legbourne, and returned, bringing Cromwell's servants, who were first set in the stocks, and thrust afterwards into the town gaol.

So passed Monday. The next morning, early, the common bell was again ringing. Other commissioners were reported to be at Castre, a few miles distant; and Melton the shoemaker, and 'one great James,' a tailor, with a volunteer army of horse and foot, harnessed and unharnessed, set out to seize them. The alarm had spread; the people from the neighbouring villages joined them as they passed, or had already risen and were in marching order. At Castre they found the commissioners fled; but a thousand horse were waiting for them, and the number every moment increasing. Whole parishes marched in, headed by their clergy. A rendezvous was fixed at Rotherwell; and at Rotherwell, on that day, or the next, besides the commons, 'there were priests and monks' (the latter fresh ejected from their monasteries—pensioned, but furious) 'to the number of seven or eight hundred.'[1] Some were 'bidding their bedes,' and praying for the Pope and cardinals; some were in full harness, or armed with such weapons as they could find: all were urging on the people. They had, as yet, no plans. What would the gentlemen do? was the question. 'Kill the gentlemen,' the priests cried; 'if they will not join us, they shall all be hanged.'[2] This difficulty was soon settled. They were swept up from their halls, or wherever they could be found. The oath was offered them, with the alternative of instant death; and they swore against their will, as all afterwards pretended, and as some perhaps sincerely felt; but when the oath was once taken, they joined with a hearty unanimity, and brought in with them their own armed retainers, and the stores from their houses.[3] Sir Edward Madyson came in, Sir Thomas Tyrwhit and Sir William Ascue. Lord Borough, who was in Ascue's company when the insurgents caught him, rode for his life, and escaped. One of his servants was overtaken in the pursuit, was wounded mortally, and shriven on the field.

So matters went at Louth and Castre. On Tuesday, October 3rd, the country rose at Horncastle, in the same manner, only on an even larger scale. On a heath in that neighbourhood there was 'a great muster;' the gentlemen of the county came in, in large numbers, with 'Mr. Dymmock,' the sheriff, at their head. Dr. Mackarel, the Abbot of Barlings, was present, with his canons, in full armour; from the abbey came a waggon-load of victuals; oxen and

[1] We find curious and humorous instances of monastic rage at this time. One monk was seen following a plough, and cursing his day that he should have to work for his bread. Another, a Welshman, 'wished he had the king on Snowdon, that he might souse his head against the stones.'—Depositions on the Rebellion: *Rolls House MS.*

[2] Sir Robert Dighton and Sir Edward Dymmock said they heard many of the priests cry, 'Kill the gentlemen.' The parson of Cowbridge said that the lords of the council were false harlots; and the worst was Cromwell. 'The vicar of Haynton, having a great club in his hand, said that if he had Cromwell there he would beat out his guts.' 'Robert Brownwhite, one of the parsons of Nether Teynton, was with bow and arrows, sword and buckler by his side, and sallet on his head; and when he was demanded how he did, he said, 'None so well;' and said 'it was the best world that ever he did see.' My story, so far, is taken from the Miscellaneous Depositions, *Rolls MS.* A 2, 28; from the Examination of William Moreland, *MS.* A 2, 29; and from the Confession of John Brown, *Rolls House MS.* first series, 892.

[3] Very opposite stories were told of the behaviour of the gentlemen. On one side it was said that they were the great movers of the insurrection; on the other, that they were forced into it in fear of their lives. There were many, doubtless, of both kinds; but it seems to me as if they had all been taken by surprise. Their conduct was that of men who wished well to the rising, but believed it had exploded inopportunely.

sheep were driven in from the neighbourhood; and a retainer of the house carried a banner, on which was worked a plough, a chalice and a host, a horn, and the five wounds of Christ.[1] The sheriff, with his brother, rode up and down the heath, giving money among the crowd; and the insurrection now gaining point, another gentleman 'wrote on the field, upon his saddlebow,' a series of articles, which were to form the ground of the rising.

Six demands should be made upon the crown: 1. The religious houses should be restored. 2. The subsidy should be remitted. 3. The clergy should pay no more tenths and first-fruits to the crown. 4. The Statute of Uses should be repealed. 5. The villein blood should be removed from the privy council. 6. The heretic bishops, Cranmer and Latimer, Hilsey Bishop of Rochester, Brown Archbishop of Dublin, and their own Bishop Longlands the persecuting Erastian, should be deprived and punished.

The deviser and the sheriff sate on their horses side by side, and read these articles, one by one, aloud, to the people. 'Do they please you or not?' they said, when they had done. 'Yea, yea, yea!' the people shouted, waving their staves above their heads; and messengers were chosen instantly, and despatched upon the spot, to carry to Windsor to the king the demands of the people of Lincolnshire. Nothing was required more but that the rebellion should be cemented by a common crime; and this, too, was speedily accomplished.

The rebellion in Ireland had been inaugurated with the murder of Archbishop Allen; the insurgents of Lincolnshire found a lower victim, but they sacrificed him with the same savageness. The chancellor of Lincoln had been the instrument through whom Cromwell had communicated with the diocese, and was a special object of hatred. It does not appear how he fell into the people's hands. We find only that 'he was very sick,' and in this condition he was brought up on horseback into the field at Horncastle. As he appeared he was received by 'the parsons and vicars' with a loud long yell—'Kill him! kill him!' 'Whereupon two of the rebels, by procurement of the said parsons and vicars, pulled him violently off his horse, and, as he knelt upon his knees, with their staves they slew him, the parsons crying continually, 'Kill him! kill him!''

[1] The plough was to encourage the husbandmen; the chalice and host in remembrance of the spoiling of the Church; the five wounds to the couraging of the people to fight in Christ's cause; the horn to signify the taking of Horncastle.—Philip Trotter's Examination: *Rolls House MS.* A 2, 29.

As the body lay on the ground it was stripped bare, and the garments were parted among the murderers. The sheriff distributed the money that was in the chancellor's purse. 'And every parson and every vicar in the field counselled their parishioners, with many comfortable words, to proceed in their journey, saying unto them that they should lack neither gold nor silver.'[1] These, we presume, were Pole's seven thousand children of light who had not bowed the knee to Baal—the noble army of saints who were to flock to Charles's banners.[2]

The same Tuesday there was a rising at Lincoln. Bishop Longlands' palace was attacked and plundered, and the town occupied by armed bodies of insurgents. By the middle of the week the whole country was in movement — beacons blazing, alarm-bells ringing; and, pending the reply of the king, Lincoln became the focus to which the separate bodies from Castre, Horncastle, Louth, and all other towns and villages, flocked in for head quarters.

The duty of repressing riots and disturbances in England lay with the nobility in their several districts. In default of organized military or police, the nobility *ex officio* were the responsible guardians of the peace. They held their estates subject to these obligations, and neglect, unless it could be shown to be involuntary, was treason. The nobleman who had to answer for the peace of Lincolnshire was Lord Hussey of Sleford. Lord Hussey had spoken, as I have stated, in unambiguous language, of the probability and desirableness of a struggle. When the moment came, it seems as if he had desired the fruits of a Catholic victory without the danger of fighting for it, or else had been frightened and doubtful how to act. When the first news of the commotion reached him, he wrote to the mayor of Lincoln, commanding him, in the king's name, to take good care of the city; to buy up or secure the arms; to levy men; and, if he found himself unable to hold his ground, to let him know without delay.[3] His letter fell into the hands of the insurgents; but Lord

---

[1] Examination of Brian Staines: *Rolls House MS.* A 2, 29. In the margin of this document, pointing to the last paragraph, is an ominous finger. ☞, drawn either by the king or Cromwell.

[2] Compare the Report of Lancaster Herald to Cromwell, *MS. State Paper Office*, second series, vol. xix.: 'My especial good lord, so far as I have gone, I have found the most corrupted and malicious spiritualty, inward and partly outward, that any prince of the world hath in his realm; and if the truth be perfectly known, it will be found that they were the greatest corrupters of the temporality, and have given the secret occasion of all this mischief.'

[3] Lord Hussey to the Mayor of Lincoln: *Cotton. MS. Vespasian,* F 13.

Hussey, though he must have known the fate of it, or, at least, could not have been ignorant of the state of the country, sate still at Sleford, waiting to see how events would turn. Yeomen and gentlemen who had not joined in the rising hurried to him for directions, promising to act in whatever way he would command; but he would give no orders—he would remain passive—he would not be false to his prince—he would not be against the defenders of the faith. The volunteers who had offered their services for the crown he called 'busy knaves'—'he bade them go their own way as they would;' and still uncertain, he sent messengers to the rebels to inquire their intentions. But he would not join them, he would not resist them; at length, when they threatened to end the difficulty by bringing him forcibly into their camp, he escaped secretly out of the country; while Lady Hussey, 'who was supposed to know her husband's mind,' sent provisions to a detachment of the Lincoln army.[1] For such conduct the commander of a division would be tried by a court-martial, with no uncertain sentence; but the extent of Hussey's offence is best seen in contrast with the behaviour of Lord Shrewsbury, whose courage and fidelity on this occasion perhaps saved Henry's crown.

The messengers sent from Horncastle were Sir Marmaduke Constable and Sir Edward Madyson. Heneage the commissioner was permitted to accompany them, perhaps to save him from being murdered by the priests. They did not spare the spur, and, riding through the night, they found the king at Windsor the day following. Henry on the instant despatched a courier to Lord Hussey, and another to Lord Shrewsbury, directing them to raise all the men whom they could muster; sending at the same time private letters to the gentlemen who were said to be with the insurgents, to recall them, if possible, to their allegiance. Lord Shrewsbury had not waited for instructions. Although his own county had not so far been disturbed, he had called out his tenantry, and had gone forward to Sherwood with every man that he could collect, on the instant that he heard of the rising. Expecting the form that it might assume, he had sent despatches on the very first day through Derbyshire, Stafford, Shropshire, Worcester, Leicester, and Northampton, to have the powers of the counties raised without a moment's delay.[2]

---

[1] *Rolls House MS.* first series, 416. Cutler's Confession: MS. ibid. 407. Deposition of Robert Sotheby: ibid. A 2, 29.
[2] Lord Shrewsbury to the King: *MS. State Paper Office.* Letter to the king and council, vol. v. Hollinshed tells a foolish story, that Lord

Henry's letter found him at Sherwood on the 6th of October. The king he knew had written also to Lord Hussey; but, understanding the character of this nobleman better than his master understood it, and with a foreboding of his possible disloyalty, he sent on the messenger to Sleford with a further note from himself, entreating him at such a moment not to be found wanting to his duty. 'My lord,' he wrote, 'for the old acquaintance between your lordship and me, as unto him that I heartily love, I will write the plainness of my mind. Ye have always been an honourable and true gentleman, and, I doubt not, will now so prove yourself. I have no commandment from the king but only to suppress the rebellion; and I assure you, my lord, on my truth, that all the king's subjects of six shires will be with me to-morrow at night, to the number of forty thousand able persons; and I trust to have your lordship to keep us company.'[1] His exhortations were in vain; Lord Hussey made no effort; he had not the manliness to join the rising—he had not the loyalty to assist in repressing it. He stole away and left the country to its fate. His conduct, unfortunately, was imitated largely in the counties on which Lord Shrewsbury relied for reinforcements. Instead of the thirty or forty thousand men whom he expected, the royalist leader could scarcely collect three or four thousand. Ten times his number were by this time at Lincoln, and increasing every day; and ominous news at the same time reaching him of the state of Yorkshire, he found it prudent to wait at Nottingham, overawing that immediate neighbourhood till he could hear again from the king.

Meanwhile Madyson and Constable had been detained in London. The immediate danger was lest the rebels should march on London before a sufficient force could be brought into the field to check them. Sir William Fitzwilliam, Sir John Russell, Cromwell's gallant nephew Richard, Sir William Parr, Sir Francis Brian, every loyal friend of the government who could be spared, scattered south and west of the metropolis calling the people on their allegiance to the king's service. The command-in-chief was given to the Duke of Suffolk. The stores in the Tower, a battery of field artillery, bows, arrows, am-

---

Shrewsbury sued out his pardon to the king for moving without orders. As he had done nothing for which to ask pardon, so it is certain, from his correspondence with the king, that he did not ask for any. Let me take this opportunity of saying that neither Hollinshed, nor Stow, nor even Hall, nor any one of the chroniclers, can be trusted in their account of this rebellion.

[1] *MS. State Paper Office*, first series.

munition of all kinds, were sent on in hot haste to
Amptbill; and so little time had been lost, that on Monday, the 9th of October, a week only from the first outbreak at Louth, Sir John Russell with the advanced guard
was at Stamford, and a respectable force was following in
his rear.

Alarming reports came in of the temper of the north-midland and eastern counties. The disposition of the
people between Lincoln and London was said to be as
bad as possible.[1] If there had been delay or trifling, or
if Shrewsbury had been less promptly loyal, in all likelihood the whole of England north of the Ouse would have
been in a flame.

From the south and the west, on the other hand, accounts were more reassuring; Middlesex, Kent, Surrey,
Sussex, Hampshire, Berkshire, Buckinghamshire, all counties
where the bishops had found heaviest work in persecuting
Protestants, had answered loyally to the royal summons.
Volunteers flocked in, man and horse, in larger numbers
than were required; on Tuesday, the 10th, Suffolk was
able to close his muster rolls, and needed only adequate
equipment to be at the head of a body of men as large
as he could conveniently move. But he had no leisure
to wait for stores. Rumours were already flying that
Russell had been attacked, that he had fought and lost a
battle and twenty thousand men.[2] The security against a
spread of the conflagration was to trample it out upon
the spot. Imperfectly furnished as he was, he reached
Stamford only two days after the first division of his
troops. He was obliged to pause for twenty-four hours
to provide means for crossing the rivers, and halt and
refresh his men. The rebels on the Monday had been
reported to be from fifty to sixty thousand strong. A lost
battle would be the loss of the kingdom. It was necessary to take all precautions. But Suffolk within a few
hours of his arrival at Stamford learnt that time was
doing his work swiftly and surely. The insurrection, so

[1] 'My lord: Hugh Ascue, this bearer, hath shewed me that this day
a servant of Sir William Hussey's reported how that in manner, in
every place by the way as his master and he came, he hath heard as
well old people as young pray God to speed the rebellious persons in
Lincolnshire, and wish themselves with them; saying, that if they
came that way, that they shall lack nothing that they can help them
unto. And the said Hugh asked what persons they were which so
reported, and he said *all*; which is a thing as meseemeth greatly to
be noted.—Sir William Fitzwilliam to Lord Cromwell: *MS. State Paper
Office*, second series, vol. vi.

[2] Richard Cromwell to Lord Cromwell: *MS. State Paper Office*, second series, vol. vii.

wide and so rapid, had been an explosion of loose powder, not a judicious economy of it. The burst had been so spontaneous, there was an absence of preparation so complete, that it was embarrassed by its own magnitude. There was no forethought, no efficient leader—sixty thousand men had drifted to Lincoln and had halted there in noisy uncertainty till their way to London was interrupted. They had no commissariat—each man had brought a few days' provisions with him, and when these were gone the multitude dissolved with the same rapidity with which it had assembled. On the Wednesday at noon Richard Cromwell reported that the township of Boston, amounting to twelve thousand men, were gone home. In the evening of the same day five or six thousand others were said to have gone, and not more than twenty thousand at the outside were thought to remain in the camp. The young cavaliers in the royal army began to fear that there would be no battle after all.[1]

Suffolk could now act safely, and preparatory to his advance he sent forward the king's answer to the articles of Horncastle.

'Concerning choosing of councillors,' the king wrote, 'I have never read, heard, nor known that princes' councillors and prelates should be appointed by rude and ignorant common people. How presumptuous, then, are ye, the rude commons of one shire, and that one of the most brute and beastly of the whole realm, and of least experience, to take upon you, contrary to God's law and man's law, to rule your prince whom ye are bound to obey and serve, and for no worldly cause to withstand.

'As to the suppression of religious houses and monasteries, we will that ye and all our subjects should well know that this is granted us by all the nobles, spiritual and temporal, of this our realm, and by all the commons of the same by act of parliament, and not set forth by any councillor or councillors upon their mere will and fantasy as ye falsely would persuade our realm to believe: and where ye allege that the service of God is much thereby diminished, the truth thereof is contrary, for there be none houses suppressed where God was well served, but where most vice, mischief, and abomination of living was used; and that doth well appear by their own con-

[1] 'Nothing we lament so much as that they thus fly; for our trust was that we should have used them like as they have deserved; and I for my part am as sorry as if I had lost five hundred pounds. For my lord admiral (Sir John Russell), he is so earnest in the matter, that I dare say he would eat them with salt.'—Richard Cromwell to Lord Cromwell: *MS. State Paper Office.*

fessions subscribed with their own hands, in the time of our visitation. And yet were suffered a great many of them, more than we by the act needed, to stand; wherein if they amend not their living we fear we have more to answer for than for the suppression of all the rest.'

Dismissing the Act of Uses as beyond their understanding, and coming to the subsidy,—

'Think ye,' the king said, 'that we be so faint-hearted that perforce ye would compel us with your insurrection and such rebellious demeanour to remit the same? Make ye sure by occasion of this your ingratitude, unnaturalness, and unkindness to us now administered, ye give us cause which hath always been as much dedicate to your wealth as ever was king, not so much to set our study for the setting forward of the same, seeing how unkindly and untruly ye deal now with us:

'Wherefore, sirs, remember your follies and traitorous demeanour, and shame not your native country of England. We charge you eftsoons that ye withdraw yourselves to your own houses every man, cause the provokers of you to this mischief to be delivered to our lieutenant's hands or ours, and you yourselves submit yourselves to such condign punishment as we and our nobles shall think you worthy to suffer. For doubt ye not else that we will not suffer this injury at your hands unrevenged; and we pray unto Almighty God to give you grace to do your duties; and rather obediently to consent amongst you to deliver into the hands of our lieutenant a hundred persons, to be ordered according to their demerits, than by your obstinacy and wilfulness to put yourselves, lives, wives, children, lands, goods, and chattels, besides the indignation of God, in the utter adventure of total destruction.'[1]

When the letter was brought in, the insurgent council were sitting in the chapter-house of the cathedral. The cooler-headed among the gentlemen, even those among them who on the whole sympathized in the rising, had seen by this time that success was doubtful, and that if obtained it would be attended with many inconveniences to themselves. The enclosures would go down, the cattle farms would be confiscated. The yeomen's tenures would be everywhere revised. The probability, however, was that, without concert, without discipline, without a leader, they would be destroyed in detail; their best plan would

---

[1] Henry VIII. to the Rebels in Lincolnshire: *State Papers*, vol. i. p. 463, &c.

be to secure their own safety. Their prudence nearly cost them their lives.

'We, the gentlemen,' says one of them, when the letters came, thought 'to read them secretly among ourselves; but as we were reading them the commons present cried that they would hear them read or else pull them from us. And therefore I read the letters openly; and because there was a little clause there which we feared would stir the commons, I did leave that clause unread, which was perceived by a canon there, and he said openly the letter was falsely read, by reason whereof I was like to be slain.'[1]

The assembly broke into confusion. The alarm spread that the gentlemen would betray the cause, as in fact they intended to do. The clergy and the leaders of the commons clamoured to go forward and attack Suffolk, and two hundred of the most violent went out into the cloister to consult by themselves. After a brief conference they resolved that the clergy had been right from the first: that the gentlemen were no true friends of the cause, and they had better kill them. They went back into the chapter-house, and, guarding the doors, prepared to execute their intention, when some one cried that it was wiser to leave them till the next day. They should go with them into action, and if they flinched they would kill them then. There was a debate. The two hundred went out again—again changed their minds and returned; but by this time the intended victims had escaped by a private entrance into the house of the murdered chancellor, and barricaded the door. It was now evening. The cloisters were growing dark, and the mob finally retired to the camp, swearing that they would return at daybreak.

The gentlemen then debated what they should do. Lincoln cathedral is a natural fortress. The main body of the insurgents lay round the bottom of the hill on which the cathedral stands; the gentlemen, with their retinues, seem to have been lodged in the houses round the close, and to have been left in undisputed possession of their quarters for the night. Suffolk was known to be advancing. They determined, if possible, to cut their way to him in the morning, or else to hold out in their present position till they were relieved. Meanwhile the division in the council had extended to the camp. Alarmed by the desertions, surprised by the rapidity with which

[1] Confession of Thos. Mayne: *Rolls House MS first series*, 432.

the king's troops had been collected, and with the fatal distrust of one another which forms the best security of governments from the danger of insurrection, the farmers and villagers were disposed in large numbers to follow the example of their natural leaders. The party of the squires were for peace: the party of the clergy for a battle. The former in the darkness moved off in a body and joined the party in the cathedral. There was now no longer danger. The gentry were surrounded by dependents on whom they could rely; and though still inferior in number, were better armed and disciplined than the brawling crowd of fanatics in the camp. When day broke they descended the hill, and told the people that for the present their enterprise must be relinquished. The king had said that they were misinformed on the character of his measures. It was, perhaps, true, and for the present they must wait and see. If they were deceived they might make a fresh insurrection.[1]

They were heard in sullen silence, but they were obeyed. There was no resistance; they made their way to the king's army, and soon after the Duke of Suffolk, Sir John Russell, and Cromwell rode into Lincoln. The streets, we are told, were crowded, but no cheer saluted them, no bonnet was moved. The royalist commanders came in as conquerors after a bloodless victory, but they read in the menacing faces which frowned upon them that their work was still, perhaps, to be done.

For the present, however, the conflagration was extinguished. The cathedral was turned into an arsenal, fortified and garrisoned;[2] and the suspicion and jealousy which had been raised between the spiritualty and the gentlemen soon doing its work, the latter offered their services to Suffolk, and laboured to earn their pardon by their exertions for the restoration of order. The towns one by one sent in their submission. Louth made its peace by surrendering unconditionally fifteen of the original leaders of the commotion. A hundred or more were taken prisoners elsewhere, Abbot Mackarel and his canons being of the number;[3] and Suffolk was informed that these, who were the worst offenders, being reserved for future punishment, he might declare a free pardon to all the rest 'without doing unto them any hurt or damage in their goods or persons.'[4]

[1] Confession of Thos. Mayne: *Rolls House MS.* first series, 432.
[2] Henry VIII. to the Duke of Suffolk: Ibid. first series, 480.
[3] Wriothesley to Cromwell: *State Papers*, vol. i. p. 471. Examination of the Prisoners: *Rolls House MS.*
[4] Henry VIII. to the Duke of Suffolk: Ibid. first series, 480.

In less than a fortnight a rebellion of sixty thousand persons had subsided as suddenly as it had risen. Contrived by the monks and parish priests, it had been commenced without concert, it had been conducted without practical skill. The clergy had communicated to their instruments alike their fury and their incapacity.

But the insurrection in Lincolnshire was but the first shower which is the herald of the storm.

On the night of the 12th of October there was present at an inn in Lincoln, watching the issue of events, a gentleman of Yorkshire, whose name, a few weeks later, was ringing through every English household in accents of terror or admiration.

Our story must go back to the beginning of the month. The law vacation was drawing to its close, and younger brothers in county families who then, as now, were members of the inns of court, were returning from their holidays to London. The season had been of unusual beauty. The summer had lingered into the autumn, and during the latter half of September young Sir Ralph Ellerkar, of Ellerkar Hall in 'Yorkyswold,' had been entertaining a party of friends for cub-hunting. Among his guests were his three cousins, John, Robert, and Christopher Aske. John, the eldest, the owner of the old family property of Aughton-on-the-Derwent, a quiet, unobtrusive gentleman, with two sons, students at the Temple: Robert, of whom, till he now emerges into light, we discover only that he was a barrister in good practice at Westminster; and Christopher, the possessor of an estate in Marshland in the West Riding. The Askes were highly connected, being cousins of the Earl of Cumberland,[1] whose eldest son, Lord Clifford, had recently married a daughter of the Duke of Suffolk, and niece therefore of the king.[2]

The hunting party broke up on the 3rd of October, and Robert, if his own account of himself was true, left Ellerkar with no other intention than of going direct to London to his business. His route lay across the Humber at Welton, and when in the ferry he heard from the boatmen that the commons were up in Lincolnshire. He wished to return, but the state of the tide would not allow him; he then endeavoured to make his way by by-roads and bridle-paths to the house of a brother-in-law at Sawcliffe; but he was met somewhere near Appleby by a party of the rebels. They demanded who he was, and on

---

[1] 'The captain and the Earl of Cumberland came of two sisters.'— Lord Darcy to Somerset Herald: *Rolls House MS.*
[2] *State Papers*, vol. i. p. 523.

his replying, they offered him the popular oath. It is hard to believe that he was altogether taken by surprise; a man of so remarkable powers as he afterwards exhibited could not have been wholly ignorant of the condition of the country, and if his loyalty had been previously sound he would not have thrown himself into the rising with such deliberate energy. The people by whom he was 'taken,' as he designated what had befallen him,[1] became his body-guard to Sawcliffe. He must have been well known in the district. His brother's property lay but a few miles distant, across the Trent, and as soon as the news spread that he was among the rebels his name was made a rallying cry. The command of the district was assigned to him from the Humber to Kirton, and for the next few days he remained endeavouring to organize the movement into some kind of form; but he was doubtful of the prospects of the rebellion, and doubtful of his own conduct. The commons of the West Riding beginning to stir, he crossed into Marshland; he passed the Ouse into Howdenshire, going from village to village, and giving orders that no bells should be rung, no beacon should be lighted, except on the receipt of a special message from himself.

Leaving his own county, he again hastened back to his command in Lincolnshire; and by this time he heard of Suffolk's advance with the king's answer to the petition. He rode post to Lincoln, and reached the town to find the commons and the gentlemen on the verge of fighting among themselves. He endeavoured to make his way into the cathedral close, but finding himself suspected by the commons, and being told that he would be murdered if he persevered, he remained in concealment till Suffolk had made known the intentions of the government; then, perhaps satisfied that the opportunity was past, perhaps believing that if not made use of on the instant it might never recur, perhaps resigning himself to be guided by events, he went back at full speed to Yorkshire.

And events had decided: whatever his intentions may have been, the choice was no longer open to him.

As he rode down at midnight to the bank of the Humber, the clash of the alarm-bells came pealing far over the water. From hill to hill, from church tower to church tower, the warning lights were shooting. The fishermen on the German Ocean watched them flickering in the darkness from Spurnhead to Scarborough, from

[1] Manner of the taking of Robert Aske: *Rolls House MS.* A 2, 28.

Scarborough to Berwick-upon-Tweed. They streamed westward, over the long marshes across Spalding Moor; up the Ouse and the Wharf, to the watershed where the rivers flow into the Irish Sea. The mountains of Westmoreland sent on the message to Kendal, to Cockermouth, to Penrith, to Carlisle; and for days and nights there was one loud storm of bells and blaze of beacons from the Trent to the Cheviot Hills.

All Yorkshire was in movement. Strangely, too, as Aske assures us, he found himself the object of an unsought distinction. His own name was the watchword which every tongue was crying. In his absence an address had gone out around the towns, had been hung on church doors, and posted on market crosses, which bore his signature, though, as he protested, it was neither written by himself nor with his consent.[1] Ill composed, but with a rugged eloquence, it called upon all good Englishmen to make a stand for the Church of Christ, which wicked men were destroying, for the commonwealth of the realm, and for their own livings, which were stolen from them by impositions. For those who would join it should be well; those who refused to join, or dared to resist, should be under Christ's curse, and be held guilty of all the Christian blood which should be shed.

Whoever wrote the letter, it did its work. One scene out of many will illustrate the effect.

William Stapleton, a friend of Aske, and a brother barrister, also bound to London for the term, was spending a few days at the Grey Friars at Beverley, with his brother Christopher. The latter had been out of health, and had gone thither for change of air with his wife. The young lawyer was to have set out over the Humber on the 4th of October. At three in the morning his servant woke him, with the news that the Lincolnshire beacons were on fire, and the country was impassable. Beverley itself was in the greatest excitement; the sick brother was afraid to be left alone, and William Stapleton agreed for the present to remain and take care of him. On Sunday morning they were startled by the sound of the alarmbell. A servant who was sent out to learn what had happened, brought in word that an address had arrived

[1] 'There was a letter forged in my name to certain towns, which I utterly deny to be my deed or consent.'—Narrative of Robert Aske: *Rolls House MS.* A 2, 28. This is apparently the letter which is printed in the *State Papers*, vol. i. p. 467. It was issued on the 7th or 8th of October (see Stapleton's Confession: *Rolls House MS.* A 2, 28), the days on which, according to Aske's own confession, he seems to have been in the West Riding.

from Robert Aske, and that a proclamation was out, under the town seal, calling on every man to repair to Westwood Green, under the walls of the Grey Friars, and be sworn in to the commons.[1] Christopher Stapleton, a sensible man, made somewhat timid by illness, ordered all doors to be locked and bolted, and gave directions that no one of his household should stir. His wife, a hater of Protestants, an admirer of Queen Catherine, of the Pope, and the old religion, was burning with sympathy for the insurgents. The family confessor appeared on the scene, a certain Father Bonaventure, taking the lady's part, and they two together 'went forth out of the door among the crowd.' 'God's blessing on ye,' William Stapleton heard his sister-in-law cry.—'Speed ye well,' the priest cried; 'speed ye well in your godly purposes.' The people rushed about them. 'Where are your husband and his brother?' they shouted to her. 'In the Freers,' she answered. 'Bring them out!' the cry rose. 'Pull them out by the head; or we will burn the Freers and them within it.' Back flew the lady in haste, and perhaps in scorn, to urge forward her hesitating lord—he wailing, wringing his hands, wishing himself out of the world; she exclaiming it was God's quarrel—let him rise and show himself a man. The dispute lingered; the crowd grew impatient; the doors were dashed in; they rushed into the hall, and thrust the oath down the throat of the reluctant gentleman, and as they surged back they swept the brother out with them upon the green. Five hundred voices were crying, 'Captains! captains!' and presently a shout rose above the rest, 'Master William Stapleton shall be our captain!' And so it was to be: the priest Bonaventure had willed it so; and Stapleton, seeing worse would follow if he refused, consented.

It was like a contagion of madness—instantly he was wild like the rest. 'Forward!' was the cry - whither, who knew or cared? only 'Forward!' and as the multitude rocked to and fro, a splashed rider spurred through the streets, 'like a man distraught,'[2] eyes staring, hair streaming, shouting, as he passed, that they should rise and follow, and flashing away like a meteor.

So went Sunday at Beverley, the 8th of October, 1536; and within a few days the substance of the same scene

---

[1] The oath varied a little in form. In Yorkshire the usual form was, 'Ye shall swear to be true to God, the king, and the commonwealth.'—Aske's Narrative: *Rolls House MS.* The tendency of the English to bind themselves with oaths, explains and partly justifies the various oaths required by the government.

[2] Deposition of William Stapleton: *Rolls House MS.*

repeated itself in all the towns of all the northern counties, the accidents only varying. The same spirit was abroad as in Lincolnshire; but here were strong heads and strong wills, which could turn the wild humour to a purpose—men who had foreseen the catastrophe, and were prepared to use it.

Lord Darcy of Templehurst was among the most distinguished of the conservative nobility. He was an old man. He had won his spurs under Henry VII. He had fought against the Moors by the side of Ferdinand, and he had earned laurels in the wars in France against Louis XII. Strong in his military reputation, in his rank, and in his age, he had spoken in parliament against the separation from the see of Rome; and though sworn like the rest of the peers to obey the law, he had openly avowed the reluctance of his assent — he had secretly maintained a correspondence with the Imperial court.

The king, who respected a frank opposition, and had no suspicion of anything beyond what was open, continued his confidence in a man whom he regarded as a tried friend, and Darcy, from his credit with the crown, his rank and his position, was at this moment the feudal sovereign of the East Riding. To him Henry wrote on the first news of the commotion in Lincolnshire, when he wrote to Lord Hussey and Lord Shrewsbury, but, entering into fuller detail, warning him of the falsehoods which had been circulated to excite the people, and condescending to inform him 'that he had never thought to take one pennyworth of the parish churches' goods from them.' He desired Lord Darcy to let the truth be known, meantime he assured him that there was no cause for alarm, 'one true man was worth twenty thieves and traitors,' and all true men he doubted not would do their duty in suppressing the insurrection.[1]

This letter was written on the same 8th of October on which the scenes which I have described took place at Beverley. Five days later the king had found reason to change his opinion of Lord Darcy.

To him, as to Lord Hussey, the outbreak at this especial crisis appeared inopportune. The Emperor had just suffered a heavy reverse in France, and there was no prospect at that moment of assistance either from Flanders or Spain. . . . . A fair occasion had been lost in the preceding winter—another had not yet arisen. . . . . The conservative English were, however, strong in themselves,

[1] Henry VIII. to Lord Darcy. October 8th: *Rolls House MS.* first series, 282.

and might be equal to the work if they were not crushed prematurely; he resolved to secure them time by his own inaction. .... On the first symptoms of uneasiness he sent his son, Sir Arthur Darcy, to Lord Shrewsbury, who was then at Nottingham. Young Darcy, after reporting as to the state of the country, was to go on to Windsor with a letter to the king. Sharing, however, in none of his father's opinions, he caught fire in the stir of Shrewsbury's camp—he preferred to remain where he was, and, sending the letter by another hand, he wrote to Templehurst for arms and men. Lord Darcy had no intention that his banner should be seen in the field against the insurgents. Unable to dispose of Sir Arthur as he had intended, he replied that he had changed his mind; he must return to him at his best speed; for the present, he said, he had himself raised no men, nor did he intend to raise any—he had put out a proclamation with which he trusted the people might be quieted.[1] The manœuvre answered well. Lord Shrewsbury was held in check by insurrections on either side of him, and could move neither on Yorkshire nor Lincolnshire. The rebels were buying up every bow, pike, and arrow in the country; and Lord Darcy now shut himself up with no more than twelve of his followers in Pomfret Castle, without arms, without fuel, without provisions, and taking no effectual steps to secure either the one or the other. In defence of his conduct he stated afterwards that his convoys had been intercepted. An experienced military commander who could have called a thousand men under arms by a word, could have introduced a few waggon-loads of corn and beer, had such been his wish. He was taking precautions (it is more likely) to enable him to yield gracefully to necessity should necessity arise. The conflagration now spread swiftly. Every one who was disposed to be loyal looked to Darcy for orders. The Earl of Cumberland wrote to him from Skipton Castle, Sir Brian Hastings the sheriff, Sir Richard Tempest, and many others. They would raise their men, they said, and either join him at Pomfret, or at whatever place he chose to direct. But Darcy would do nothing, and would allow nothing to be done. He replied that he had no commission and could give no instructions. The king had twice written to him, but had sent no special directions, and he would not act without them.[2]

[1] Letters to and from Lord Darcy: *Rolls House MS.* first series, 282.
[2] Henry had written him a second letter on the 9th of October, in

Lord Darcy played skilfully into the rebels' hands. The rebels made admirable use of their opportunity. With method in their madness, the townships everywhere organized themselves. Instead of marching in unwieldy tumultuous bodies, they picked their 'tallest and strongest' men; they armed and equipped them; and, raising money by a rate from house to house, they sent them out with a month's wages in their pockets, and a promise of a continuance should their services be prolonged. The day after his return from Lincoln, Aske found himself at the head of an army of horse and foot, furnished admirably at all points. They were grouped in companies by their parishes, and for colours, the crosses of the churches were borne by the priests.

The first great rendezvous in Yorkshire was on Weighton common. Here Stapleton came in with nine thousand men from Beverley and Holderness. The two divisions encamped upon the heath, and Aske became acknowledged as the commander of the entire force. Couriers brought in news from all parts of the country. Sir Ralph Evers and Sir George Conyers were reputed to have taken refuge in Scarborough. Sir Ralph Ellerkar the elder, and Sir John Constable were holding Hull for the king. These places must at once be seized. Stapleton rode down from Weighton to Hull gate, and summoned the town. The mayor was for yielding at once; he had no men, he said, no meat, no money, no horse or harness—resistance was impossible. Ellerkar and Constable, however, would not hear of surrender. Constable replied that he would rather die with honesty than live with shame; and Stapleton carrying back this answer to Aske, it was agreed that the former should lay siege to Hull upon the spot, while the main body of the army moved forward upon York.[1]

Skirting parties meantime scoured the country far and near. They surrounded the castles and houses, and called on every lord, knight, and gentleman to mount his horse, with his servants, and join them, or they would leave neither corn-stack in their yards nor cattle in their sheds, and would burn their roofs over their heads.

Aske himself was present everywhere, or some counterfeit who bore his name. It seemed 'there were six Richmonds in the field.' The Earl of Northumberland lay sick at Wressil Castle. From the day of Anne Boleyn's trial he had sunk, and now was dying. His failing spirit was

which, knowing nothing as yet of the rising in Yorkshire, he had expressed merely a continued confidence in Darcy's discretion.
[1] Stapleton's Confession: *Rolls House MS.* A 2, 28.

disturbed by the news that Aske was at his gates, and that an armed host were shouting 'thousands for a Percy!' If the earl could not come, the rebels said, then his brothers must come—Sir Thomas and Sir Ingram. And then, with side glances, we catch sight of Sir Ingram Percy swearing in the commons, and stirring the country at Alnwick: 'using such malicious words as were abominable to hear; wishing that he might thrust his sword into the Lord Cromwell's belly; wishing the Lord Cromwell were hanged on high, and he standing by to see it.' And again we see the old Countess of Northumberland at her house at Semar, 'sore weeping and lamenting' over her children's disloyalty; Sir Thomas Percy listening, half moved, to her entreaties; for a moment pausing uncertain, then borne away by the contagion, and a few hours later flaunting, with gay plumes and gorgeous armour, in the rebel host.[1]

On Sunday, October the 15th, the main army crossed the Derwent, moving direct for York. On Monday they were before the gates. The citizens were all in the interest of the rebellion; and the mayor was allowed only to take precautions for the security of property and life. The engagements which he exacted from Aske, and which were punctually observed, speak well for the discipline of the insurgents. No pillage was to be permitted, or injury of any kind. The prices which were to be paid for victuals and horse-meat were published in the camp by proclamation. The infantry, as composed of the most dangerous materials, were to remain in the field. On these terms the gates were opened, and Aske, with the horse, rode in and took possession.[2] His first act, on entering the city, was to fix a proclamation on the doors of the cathedral, inviting all monks and nuns dispossessed from their houses to report their names and conditions, with a view to their immediate restoration. Work is done rapidly by willing hands, in the midst of a willing people. In the week which followed, by a common impulse, the king's tenants were universally expelled. The vacant dormitories were again peopled; the refectories were again filled with exulting faces. 'Though it were never so late when they returned, the friars sang matins the same night.'[3]

[1] Examination of Sir Thomas Percy: *Rolls House MS.* Demeanour of Sir Thomas and Sir Ingram Percy: *MS.* ibid. first series, 896.
[2] 'The said Aske suffered no foot man to enter the city, for fear of spoils.'—Manner of the taking of Robert Aske: *Rolls House MS.* A 2, 28.
[3] Earl of Oxford to Cromwell: *MS. State Paper Office*, second series, vol. iii.

Orders were next issued in Aske's name, commanding all lords, knights, and gentlemen in the northern counties to repair to his presence; and now, at last, Lord Darcy believed that the time was come when he might commit himself with safety; or rather, since the secrets of men's minds must not be lightly conjectured, he must be heard first in his own defence, and afterwards his actions must speak for him. On the night of the surrender of York he sent his steward from Pomfret, with a request for a copy of the oath and of the articles of the rising, promising, if they pleased him, to join the confederacy. The Archbishop of York, Dr. Magnus, an old diplomatic servant of the crown, Sir Robert Constable, Lord Neville, and Sir Nicholas Babthorpe, were by this time with him in the castle. His own compliance would involve the compliance of these, and would partially involve their sanction.

On the morning of the 16th or 17th he received a third letter from the king, written now in grave displeasure; the truth had not been told; the king had heard, to his surprise, that Lord Darcy, instead of raising a force and taking the field, had shut himself up, with no more than twelve servants, in Pomfret; 'If this be so,' he said, 'it is negligently passed.'[1] Lord Darcy excused himself by replying that he was not to blame; that he had done his best; but there were sixty thousand men in arms, forty thousand in harness. They took what they pleased — horses, plate, and cattle; the whole population was with them; he could not trust his own retainers; and, preparing the king for what he was next to hear, he informed him that Pomfret itself was defenceless. 'The town,' he said, 'nor any other town, will not victual us for our money; and of such provision as we ourselves have made, the commons do stop the passage so straitly, that no victual can come to us; the castle is in danger to be taken, or we to lose our lives.'[2] The defence may have been partially true. It may have been merely plausible. At all events, it was necessary for him to come to some swift resolution. The occupation of Lincoln by the Duke of Suffolk had set Lord Shrewsbury at liberty; arms had been sent down, and money; and the midland counties, in recovered confidence, had furnished recruits, though in limited numbers. He was now at Newark, in a condition to advance; and on the same 17th of October, on which this despairing letter was written, he sent forward a post to Pomfret, telling Darcy to hold his ground,

---

[1] Henry VIII. to Lord Darcy, October 13: *Rolls House MS.*
[2] Lord Darcy to the King, October 17: MS. ibid.

and that he would join him at the earliest moment possible.[1] Neither the rebels nor Shrewsbury could afford to lose so important a position; and both made haste. Again, on the same Tuesday, the 17th, couriers brought news to Aske, at York, that the commons of Durham were hasting to join him, bringing with them Lord Latimer, Lord Lumley, and the Earl of Westmoreland. Being thus secure in his rear, he rebel leader carried his answer to Lord Darcy in person, at the head of his forces. He reached Pomfret on the afternoon of Thursday, the 19th; finding the town on his side, and knowing or suspecting Darcy's disposition, he sent in a message that the castle must be delivered, or it should be immediately stormed. A conference was demanded and agreed to. Hostages were sent in by Aske. Lord Darcy, the archbishop, and the other noblemen and gentlemen, came out before the gate.

'And there and then the said Aske declared unto the said lords spiritual and temporal the griefs of the commons; and how first the lords spiritual had not done their duty, in that they had not been plain with the King's Highness for the speedy remedy and punishing of heresy, and the preachers thereof; and for the taking the ornaments of the churches and abbeys suppressed, and the violating of relics by the suppressors; the irreverent demeanour of the doers thereof; the abuse of the vestments taken extraordinary; and other their negligences in doing their duty, as well to their sovereign as to the commons.

'And to the lords temporal the said Aske declared that they had misused themselves, in that they had not prudently declared to his Highness the poverty of his realm, whereby all dangers might have been avoided; for insomuch as in the north parts much of the relief of the commons was by favour of abbeys; and that before this last statute made the King's Highness had no money out of that shire in award yearly, for that his Grace's revenues of them went to the finding of Berwick: now the property of abbeys suppressed, tenths, and first-fruits, went out of those parts; by occasion whereof, within short space of years, there should no money nor treasure then be left, neither the tenant have to pay his yearly rent to his lord, nor the lord have money to do the king service. In those

---

[1] Lord Shrewsbury to Lord Darcy: *Rolls House MS.* first series, 282. Darcy certainly received this letter, since a copy of it is in the collection made by himself.

parts were neither the presence of his Grace, execution of his laws, nor yet but little recourse of merchandize; and of necessity the said country should either perish with skaith, or of very poverty make commotion or rebellion: and the lords knew the same to be true, and had not done their duty, for they had not declared the said poverty of the said country to the King's Highness.'[1]

'There were divers reasonings on both parts.' Darcy asked for time; if not relieved, he said he would surrender on Saturday; but Aske, to whom Shrewsbury's position and intentions were well known, and who was informed privately that the few men who were in the castle would perhaps offer no resistance to an attack, 'would not condescend thereto.' He allowed Lord Darcy till eight o'clock the following morning, and no longer. The night passed. At the hour appointed, fresh delay was demanded, but with a certainty that it would not be allowed; and the alternative being an immediate storm, the drawbridge was lowered — Pomfret Castle was in possession of the rebels, and Lord Darcy, the Archbishop of York, and every other man within the walls, high and low, were sworn to the common oath.

The extent of deliberate treachery on the part of Darcy may remain uncertain. The objects of the insurrection were cordially approved by him. It is not impossible that, when the moment came, he could not resign his loyalty without a struggle. But he had taken no precautions to avert the catastrophe, if he had not consciously encouraged its approach; he saw it coming, and he waited in the most unfavourable position to be overwhelmed; and when the step was once taken, beyond any question he welcomed the excuse to his conscience, and passed instantly to the front rank as among the chiefs of the enterprise.[2]

The afternoon of the surrender the insurgent leaders were sitting at dinner at the great table in the hall. A letter was brought in and given to Lord Darcy. He read it, dropped it on the cloth, and 'suddenly gave a great sigh.' Aske, who was sitting opposite to him, stretched his hand for the paper across the board. It was brief,

---

[1] Manner of the taking of Robert Aske: *Rolls House MS.* A 2, 28.

[2] I believe that I am unnecessarily tender to Lord Darcy's reputation. Aske, though he afterwards contradicted himself, stated in his examination that Lord Darcy could have defended the castle had he wished.—*Rolls House MS.* A 2, 29. It was sworn that when he was advised 'to victual and store Pomfret,' he said, 'there was no need; it would do as it was.'—Ibid. And Sir Henry Saville stated that 'when Darcy heard of the first rising, he said, 'Ah! they are up in Lincolnshire. God speed them well. I would they had done this three years ago, for the world should have been the better for it.''—Ibid.

and carried no signature—Lord Shrewsbury, the writer merely said, would be at Pomfret the same night.[1]

The sigh may be easily construed; but if it was a symptom of repentance, Darcy showed no other. A council of war was held when the dinner was over; and bringing his military knowledge into use, he pointed out the dangerous spots, he marked the lines of defence, and told off the commanders to their posts. Before night all the passages of the Don by which Shrewsbury could advance were secured.[2]

Leaving Pomfret, we turn for a moment to Hull, where Stapleton also had accomplished his work expeditiously. On the same day on which he separated from Aske he had taken a position on the north of the town. There was a private feud between Beverley and Hull. His men were unruly, and eager for spoil; and the harbour being full of shipping, it was with difficulty that he prevented them from sending down blazing pitch barrels with the tide into the midst of it, and storming the walls in the smoke and confusion. Stapleton, however, was a resolute man; he was determined that the cause should not be disgraced by outrage, and he enforced discipline by an act of salutary severity. Two of the most unmanageable of his followers were tried by court-martial, and sentenced to be executed. 'A Friar,' Stapleton says, 'was assigned to them, that they might make them clean to God,' and they expected nothing but death. But the object so far was only to terrify. One of them, 'a sanctuary man,' was tied by the waist with a rope, and trailed behind a boat up and down the river, and the waterman did at several times put him down with the oar under the head.' The other seeing him, thought also to be so handled; 'howbeit, at the request of honest men, and being a housekeeper, he was suffered to go unpunished, and both were banished the host; after which there was never spoil more.'[3]

In the town there was mere despondency, and each day made defence more difficult. Reinforcements were thronging into the rebels' camp; the harbour was at their mercy. Constable was for holding out to the last, and then cutting his way through. Ellerkar would agree to surrender if he and his friend might be spared the oath and might leave the county. These terms were accepted, and on Friday Stapleton occupied Hull.

[1] Aske's Deposition: *Rolls House MS.* first series, 414.
[2] Examination of Sir Thomas Percy: *Rolls House MS.*
[3] Stapleton's Confession: *Rolls House MS.* A 2, 28.

So it went over the whole north; scarcely one blow was struck anywhere. The whole population were swept along in the general current, and Skipton Castle alone in Yorkshire now held out for the crown.

With the defence of this place is connected an act of romantic heroism which deserves to be remembered.

Robert Aske, as we have seen, had two brothers, Christopher and John. In the hot struggle the ties of blood were of little moment, and when the West Riding rose, and they had to choose the part which they would take, 'they determined rather to be hewn in gobbets than stain their allegiance.' Being gallant gentlemen, instead of flying the county, they made their way with forty of their retainers to their cousin the Earl of Cumberland, and with him threw themselves into Skipton. The aid came in good time; for the day after their arrival the earl's whole retinue rode off in a body to the rebels, leaving him but a mixed household of some eighty people to garrison the castle. They were soon surrounded; but being well provisioned, and behind strong stone walls, they held the rebels at bay, and but for an unfortunate accident they could have faced the danger with cheerfulness. But unhappily the earl's family were in the heart of the danger.

Lady Eleanor Clifford, Lord Clifford's young wife, with three little children and several other ladies, were staying when the insurrection burst out, at Bolton Abbey. Perhaps they had taken sanctuary there; or possibly they were on a visit, and were cut off by the suddenness of the rising. There, however, ten miles off among the glens and hills, the ladies were, and on the third day of the siege notice was sent to the earl that they should be held as hostages for his submission. The insurgents threatened that the day following Lady Eleanor and her infant son and daughters should be brought up in front of a storming party, and if the attack again failed, they would 'violate all the ladies, and enforce them with knaves' under the walls.[1] After the ferocious murder of the Bishop of Lincoln's chancellor, no villany was impossible; and it is likely that the Catholic rebellion would have been soiled by as deep an infamy as can be found in the English annals but for the adventurous courage of Christopher Aske. In the dead of the night, with the vicar of Skipton, a groom, and a boy, he stole through the camp of the besiegers. He crossed the moors, with led horses, by un-

[1] Examination of Christopher Aske: *Rolls House MS.* first series, 840.

frequented paths, and he 'drew such a draught,' he says, that he conveyed all the said ladies through the commons in safety, 'so close and clean, that the same was never mistrusted nor perceived till they were within the castle;'[1] a noble exploit, shining on the bypaths of history like a rare rich flower. Proudly the little garrison looked down, when day dawned, from the battlements, upon the fierce multitude who were howling below in baffled rage. A few days later, as if in scorn of their impotence, the same gallant gentleman flung open the gates, dropped the drawbridge, and rode down in full armour, with his train, to the market-cross at Skipton, and there, after three long 'Oyez's,' he read aloud the king's proclamation in the midst of the crowd . . . . 'with leisure enough,' he adds, in his disdainful way . . . . 'and that done, he returned to the castle.'

While the north was thus in full commotion the government were straining every nerve to meet the emergency. The king had at first intended to repair in person to Lincolnshire. He had changed his mind when he heard of Suffolk's rapid success.[2] But Yorkshire seemed again to require his presence. The levies which had been sent for from the southern counties had been countermanded, but were recalled within a few hours of the first order. 'The matter hung like a fever, now hot, now cold.' Rumours took the place of intelligence. Each post contradicted the last, and for several days there was no certain news, either of the form or the extent of the danger. Lord Shrewsbury wrote that he had thrown his outposts forwards to the Don; but he doubted his ability to prevent the passage of the river, which he feared the rebels would attempt. He was still underhanded, and entreated assistance. The Earls of Rutland and Huntingdon were preparing to join him; but the reinforcement which they would bring was altogether inadequate, and the Duke of Norfolk and the Marquis of Exeter were sent down to add the weight of their names; their men should follow as they could be raised. Cromwell was collecting money in London. The subsidy had not been paid in; large sums belonging to the crown had fallen into the hands of Aske at York, and the treasury was empty. But 'benevolences' were extorted from the wealthy London clergy: 'they could not help in their persons,' the king said, and 'they must show their good will, if they had any,' in

---
[1] Examination of Christopher Aske: *Rolls House MS.* first series, 840.
[2] Henry VIII. to the Duke of Suffolk: *Rolls House MS.*

another way.[1] Loans could be borrowed, besides, in the City; the royal plate could go to the Mint; the crown jewels, if necessary, could be sold. Henry, more than any of the council, now comprehended the danger. 'His Majesty,' wrote his secretary on the 18th of October, 'appeareth to fear much this matter, specially if he should want money, for in Lord Darcy, his Grace said, he had no great hope.' Ten thousand pounds were raised in two days. It was but a small instalment; but it served to 'stop the gap' for the moment. Three thousand men, with six pieces of field artillery, were sent at once after Norfolk, and overtook him on the 24th of October at Worksop.

Norfolk, it was clear, had gone upon the service most reluctantly. He, too, had deeper sympathy with the movement than he cared to avow; but, even from those very sympathies, he was the fittest person to be chosen to suppress it. The rebels professed to have risen in defence of the nobility and the Catholic faith. They would have to fight their way through an army led by the natural head of the party which they desired to serve.[2] The force under Shrewsbury was now at Doncaster, where, on the 25th, the Duke joined him. The town was in their hands, and the southern end of the bridge had been fortified. The autumn rains had by this time raised the river, securing their flank, and it would have been difficult for an attacking army to force a passage, even with great advantage of numbers. Their situation, at the same time, was most precarious; of the forty thousand men, of whom Shrewsbury had written to Lord Hussey, he had not been able to raise a tenth; and, if rumour was to be believed, the loyalty of the few who were with him would not bear too severe a strain. With Norfolk's reinforcements, the whole army did not, perhaps, exceed eight thousand men, while even these were divided; detachments were scattered up the river to watch and guard the few points at which it might be passed. Under such circumstances the conduct which might be necessary could only be determined on the spot; and the king, in his instructions, left a wide margin of discretion to the generals.[3] He had summoned the whole force of the south and west of England to join him in London, and he intended to

[1] Wriothesley to Cromwell: *State Papers*, vol. i. p. 472.
[2] The Marquis of Exeter, who was joined in commission with the Duke of Norfolk, never passed Newark. He seems to have been recalled, and sent down into Devonshire, to raise the musters in his own county.
[3] *State Papers*, vol. i. p. 493.

appear himself at their head. He directed Norfolk, therefore, to observe the greatest caution; by all means to avoid a battle, unless with a certainty of victory; and 'the chances of war being so uncertain,' he said, 'many times devices meant for the best purpose turning to evil happs and notable misfortunes,' he advised that rather than there should be any risk incurred, the duke should fall back on the line of the Trent, fortify Newark and Nottingham, and wait his own arrival; 'until,' to use the king's own words, 'with our army royal, which we do put in readiness, we shall repair unto you, and so with God's help be able to bear down the traitors before us; yourselves having more regard to the defence of us and of your natural country than to any dishonour that might be spoken of such retirement, which in the end shall prove more honourable than with a little hasty forwardness to jeopard both our honour and your lives.' 'For we assure you,' he said, 'we would neither adventure you our cousin of Norfolk, nor you our cousin of Shrewsbury, or other our good and true subjects, in such sort as there should be a likelihood of wilful casting of any of you away for all the lands and dominion we have on that side Trent.'

The Duke of Norfolk, on his way down, had written from Welbeck, 'all desperately.' By any means fair or foul, he had said that he would crush the rebels; 'he would esteem no promise that he would make to them, nor think his honour touched in the breach of the same.'[1]

To this Henry replied, 'Albeit we certainly know that ye will pretermit none occasion wherein by policy or otherwise ye may damage our enemies, we doubt not, again, but in all your proceedings you will have such a temperance as our honour specially shall remain untouched, and yours rather increased, than by the certain grant of that you cannot certainly promise, appear in the mouths of the worst men anything defaced.' Finally, he concluded, 'Whereas you desire us, in case any mischance should happen unto you, to be good lord unto your children, surely, good cousin, albeit we trust certainly in God that no such thing shall fortune, yet we would you should perfectly know that if God should take you out of this transitory life before us, we should not fail so to remember your children, being your lively images, and in such wise to look on them with our princely favour as others by their example should not be discouraged to follow your steps.'[2]

[1] *State Papers*, vol. i. p. 519.
[2] Ibid. p. 485.

Lord Shrewsbury, as soon as he found himself too late to prevent the capture of Pomfret, sent forward Lancaster Herald with a royal proclamation, and with directions that it should be read at the market cross.[1] The herald started on his perilous adventure 'in his king's coat of arms.' As he approached Pomfret he overtook crowds of the country people upon the road, who in answer to his questions told him that they were in arms to defend Holy Church, which wicked men were destroying. They and their cattle too, their burials and their weddings, were to be taxed, and they would not endure it. He informed them that they were all imposed upon. Neither the king nor the council had ever thought of any such measures; and the people, he said, seemed ready to listen, 'being weary of their lives.' Lies, happily, are canker-worms, and spoil all causes, good or bad, which admit their company, as those who had spread these stories discovered to their cost when the truth became generally known.

Lancaster Herald, however, could do little; he found the town swarming with armed men, eager and furious. He was arrested before he was able to unroll his parchment, and presently a message from the castle summoned him to appear before 'the great captain.'

'As I entered into the first ward,' he said, 'there I found many in harness, very cruel fellows, and a porter with a white staff in his hand; and at the two other ward gates a porter with his staff, accompanied with harnessed men. I was brought into the hall, which I found full of people; and there I was commanded to tarry till the traitorous captain's pleasure was known. In that space I stood up at the high table in the hall, and there shewed to the people the cause of my coming and the effect of the proclamation; and in doing the same the said Aske sent for me into his chamber, there keeping his port and countenance as though he had been a great prince.'

The Archbishop of York, Lord Darcy, Sir Robert Con-

---

[1] This particular proclamation—the same, apparently, which was read by Christopher Aske at Skipton—I have been unable to find. That which is printed in the State Papers from the Rolls House Records, belongs to the following month. The contents of the first, however, may be gathered from a description of it by Robert Aske, and a comparison of the companion proclamation issued in Lincolnshire. It stated briefly that the insurrection was caused by forged stories; that the king had no thought of suppressing parish churches, or taxing food or cattle. The abbeys had been dissolved by act of parliament, in consequence of their notorious vice and profligacy. The people, therefore, were commanded to return to their homes, at their peril. The commotion in Lincolnshire was put down. The king was advancing in person to put them down also, if they continued disobedient.

stable, Mr. Magnus, Sir Christopher Danby, and several other gentlemen were in the room. As the herald entered, Aske rose, and, 'with a cruel and inestimable proud countenance, stretched himself and took the hearing of the tale.' When it was declared to him, he requested to see the proclamation, took it, and read it openly without reverence to any person; he then said he need call no council, he would give an answer of his own wit himself.

'Standing in the highest place in the chamber, taking the high estate upon him, 'Herald,' he replied, 'as a messenger you are welcome to me and all my company, intending as I do. And as for the proclamation sent from the lords from whom you come, it shall not be read at the market cross,[1] nor in no place amongst my people which be under my guiding.''

He spoke of his intentions; the herald enquired what they were. He said 'he would go to London, he and his company, of pilgrimage to the King's Highness, and there to have all the vile blood of his council put from him, and all the noble blood set up again; and also the faith of Christ and his laws to be kept, and full restitution to Christ's Church of all wrongs done unto it; and also the commonalty to be used as they should be.' 'And he bade me trust to this,' the herald said, 'for he would die for it.'

Lancaster begged for that answer in writing. 'With a good will,' Aske replied; 'and he put his hand to his bill, and with a proud voice said, 'This is mine act, whosoever say to the contrary. I mean no harm to the king's person, but to see reformation; I will die in the quarrel, and my people with me.''

Lancaster again entreated on his knees that he might read the proclamation. On his life he should not, Aske answered; he might come and go at his pleasure, and if Shrewsbury desired an interview with the Pomfret council, a safe conduct was at his service; but he would allow nothing to be put in the people's heads which might divert them from their purpose. 'Commend me to the lords,' he said at parting, 'and tell them it were meet they were with me, for that I do is for all their wealths.'[2]

By this time the powers of all the great families, ex-

---

[1] In explanation of his refusal, Aske said afterwards that it was for two causes: first, that if the herald should have declared to the people by proclamation that the commons in Lincolnshire were gone to their homes, they would have killed him; secondly, that there was no mention in the same proclamation neither of pardon nor of the demands which were the causes of their assembly.—Aske's Narrative: *Rolls House MS.* A 2, 2s.

[2] Lancaster Herald's Report: *State Papers*, vol. i. p. 485.

cept the Cliffords, the Dacres, and the Musgraves, had come in to the confederacy. Six peers, or eldest sons of peers, were willingly or unwillingly with Aske at Pomfret. Lord Westmoreland was represented by Lord Neville. Lord Latimer was present in person, and with him Lord Darcy, Lord Lumley, Lord Scrope, Lord Conyers. Besides these, were the Constables of Flamborough, the Tempests from Durham, the Boweses, the Everses, the Fairfaxes, the Strangwayses, young Ellerkar of Ellerkar, the Danbys, St. Johns, Bulmers, Mallorys, Lascelleses, Nortons, Moncktons, Gowers, Ingoldsbys: we scarcely miss a single name famous in Border story. Such a gathering had not been seen in England since the grandfathers of these same men fought on Towton Moor, and the red rose of Lancaster faded before 'the summer sun of York.' Were their descendants, in another bloody battle, to seat a fresh Plantagenet on Edward's throne? No such aim had as yet risen consciously into form; but civil wars have strange issues—a scion of the old house was perhaps dreaming, beyond the sea, of a new and better-omened union; a prince of the pure blood might marry the Princess Mary, restored to her legitimate inheritance. Of all the natural chiefs of the north who were in the power of the insurgents, Lord Northumberland only was absent. On the first summons he was spared for his illness; a second deputation ordered him to commit his powers, as the leader of his clan, to his brothers. But the brave Percy chose to die as he had lived. 'At that time and at all other times, the earl was very earnest against the commons in the king's behalf and the lord privy seal's.' He lay in his bed resolute in loyalty. The crowd yelled before the castle, 'Strike off his head, and make Sir Thomas Percy earl.' 'I can die but once,' he said; 'let them do it; it will rid me of my pain.' 'And therewith the earl fell weeping, ever wishing himself out of the world.'[1]

They left him to nature and to death, which was waiting at his doors. The word went now through the army, 'Every man to Doncaster.' There lay Shrewsbury and the Duke of Norfolk, with a small handful of disaffected men between themselves and London, to which they were going.

They marched from Pomfret in three divisions. Sir Thomas Percy at the head of five thousand men, carried

---

[1] Stapleton's Confession: *Rolls House MS.* A 2, 28. Does this solitary and touching faithfulness, I am obliged to ask, appear as if Northumberland believed that four months before the king and Cromwell had slandered and murdered the woman whom he had once loved?

the banner of St. Cuthbert. In the second division, over ten thousand strong, were the musters of Holderness and the West Riding, with Aske himself and Lord Darcy. The rear was a magnificent body of twelve thousand horse, all in armour: the knights, esquires, and yeomen of Richmondshire and Durham.[1]

In this order they came down to the Don, where their advanced posts were already stationed, and deployed along the banks from Ferrybridge[2] to Doncaster.

A deep river, heavily swollen, divided them from the royal army; but they were assured by spies that the water was the only obstacle which prevented the loyalists from deserting to them.[3]

There were traitors in London who kept them informed of Henry's movements, and even of the resolutions at the council board.[4] They knew that if they could dispose of the one small body in their front, no other force was as yet in the field which could oppose or even delay their march. They had even persuaded themselves that, on the mere display of their strength, the Duke of Norfolk must either retire or would himself come over to their side.

Norfolk, however, who had but reached Doncaster the morning of the same day, lay still, and as yet showed no sign of moving. If they intended to pass, they must force the bridge. Apparently they must fight a battle; and at this extremity they hesitated. Their professed intention was no more than an armed demonstration. They were ready to fight;[5] but in fighting they could no longer maintain the pretence that they were loyal subjects. They desired to free the king from plebeian advisers, and

[1] 'We were 30,000 men, as tall men, well horsed, and well appointed as any men could be.'—Statement of Sir Marmaduke Constable: *MS. State Paper Office*. All the best evidence gives this number.
[2] Not the place now known under this name—but a bridge over the Don three or four miles above Doncaster.
[3] So Aske states.—Examination: *Rolls House MS.*, first series, 838. Lord Darcy went further. 'If he had chosen,' he said, 'he could have fought Lord Shrewsbury with his own men, and brought never a man of the northmen with him.' Somerset Herald, on the other hand, said, that the rumour of disaffection was a feint. 'One thing I am sure of,' he told Lord Darcy, 'there never were men more desirous to fight with men than ours to fight with you.'—*Rolls House MS.*
[4] 'Sir Marmaduke Constable did say, if there had been a battle, the southern men would not have fought. He knew that every third man was theirs. Further, he said the king and his council determined nothing but they had knowledge before my lord of Norfolk gave them knowledge.'—Earl of Oxford to Cromwell: *MS. State Paper Office*.
[5] 'I saw neither gentlemen nor commons willing to depart, but to proceed in the quarrel; yea, and that to the death. If I should say otherwise, I lie.'—Aske's Examination: *Rolls House MS.*

restore the influence of the nobles. It was embarrassing to commence with defeating an army led by four peers of the purest blood in England.[1]

For two days the armies lay watching each other.[2] Parties of clergy were busy up and down the rebel host, urging an advance, protesting that if they hesitated the cause was lost; but their overwhelming strength seems to have persuaded the leaders that their cause, so far from being lost, was won already, and that there was no need of violence.

On the 25th Lancaster Herald came across to desire, in Norfolk's name, that four of them would hold an interview with him, under a safe conduct, in Doncaster, and explain their objects. Aske replied by a counter offer, that eight or twelve principal persons on both sides should hold a conference on Doncaster bridge.

Both proposals were rejected; the duke said that he should remain in his lines, and receive their attack whenever they dared to make it.[3] There was a pause. Aske called a council of war; and 'the lords'—or perhaps Lord Darcy—knowing that in rebellions half measures are suicide, voted for an immediate onset. Aske himself was of a different opinion. Norfolk did not wholly refuse negotiation; one other attempt might at least be made to avoid bloodshed. 'The duke,' he said, in his account of his conduct, 'neither of those days had above six or eight thousand men, while we were nigh thirty thousand at the least; but we considered that if battle had been given, if the duke had obtained the victory, all the knights, esquires, and all others of those parts had been attainted, slain, and undone for the Scots and the enemies of the king; and, on the other part, if the Duke of Norfolk, the Earl of Shrewsbury, the Earl of Rutland, the Earl of Huntingdon, the Lord Talbot, and others, had been slain,

---

[1] Rutland and Huntingdon were in Shrewsbury's camp by this time.

[2] 'They wished,' said Sir Marmaduke Constable, 'the king had sent some younger lords to fight with them than my lord of Norfolk and my lord of Shrewsbury. No lord in England would have stayed them but my lord of Norfolk.'—Earl of Oxford to Cromwell: *MS. State Paper Office*.

[3] The chroniclers tell a story of a miraculous fall of rain, which raised the river the day before the battle was to have been fought, and which was believed by both sides to have been an interference of Providence. Cardinal Pole also mentions the same fact of the rain, and is bitter at the superstitions of his friends; and yet, in the multitude of depositions which exist, made by persons present, and containing the most minute particulars of what took place, there is no hint of anything of the kind. The waters had been high for several days, and the cause of the unbloody termination of the crisis was more creditable to the rebel leaders.

what great captains, councillors, noble blood, persons dread in foreign realms, and Catholic knights had wanted and been lost. What displeasure should this have been to the king's public wealth, and what comfort to the antient enemies of the realm. It was considered also what honour the north parts had attained by the said duke; how he was beloved for his activity and fortune.'[1]

If a battle was to be avoided nevertheless, no time was to be lost, for skirmishing parties were crossing the river backwards and forwards, and accident might at any moment bring on a general engagement. Aske had gained his point at the council; he signified his desire for a further parley, and on Thursday afternoon, after an exchange of hostages, Sir Thomas Hilton, Sir Ralph Ellerkar, Sir Robert Chaloner, and Sir Robert Bowes[2] crossed to the royal camp to attempt, if possible, to induce the duke to agree to the open conference on the bridge.[3] The conditions on which they would consent to admit even this first slight concession were already those of conquerors. A preliminary promise must be made by the duke that all persons who, in heart, word, or deed, had taken part in the insurrection, should have free pardon for life, lands, and goods; that neither in the pardon nor in the public records of the realm should they be described as traitors. The duke must explain further the extent of his powers to treat. If 'the captain' was to be present on the bridge, he must state what hostages he was prepared to offer for the security of so great a person; and as Richard Cromwell was supposed to be with the king's army, neither he nor any of his kin should be admitted among the delegates. If these terms were allowed, the conference should take place, and the objects of the insurrection might be explained in full for the duke to judge of them.[4]

---

[1] Second Examination of Robert Aske: *Rolls House MS.* first series, 638. It is true that this is the story of Aske himself, and was told when, after fresh treason, he was on trial for his life. But his bearing at no time was that of a man who would stoop to a lie. Life comparatively was of small moment to him.

[2] Uncle of Marjory, afterwards wife of John Knox. Marjory's mother, Elizabeth, to whom so many of Knox's letters were addressed, was an Aske, but she was not apparently one of the Aughton family.

[3] Aske's Narrative: *Rolls House MS.* A 2, 28.

[4] Instructions to Sir Thomas Hilton and his Companions: *Rolls House MS.*

There are many groups of 'articles' among the Records. Each focus of the insurrection had its separate form; and coming to light one by one, they have created much confusion. I have thought it well, therefore, to print in full, from Sir Thomas Hilton's instructions, a list, the most explicit, as well as most authentic, which is extant.

Hilton and his companions remained for the night in Doncaster. In the morning they returned with a favourable answer. After dinner the same four gentlemen,

'I. Touching our faith, to have the heresies of Luther, Wickliffe, Huss, Melancthon, Œcolampadius, Bucer's *Confessio Germanica*, *Apologia Melancthonis*, the works of Tyndal, of Barnes, of Marshal, Raskall, St. Germain, and such other heresies of Anabaptists, clearly within this realm to be annulled and destroyed.

'II. To have the supreme head, touching *cura animarum*, to be reserved unto the see of Rome, as before it was accustomed to be, and to have the consecration of the bishops from him, without any first-fruits or pensions to him to be paid out of this realm; or else a pension reasonable for the outward defense of our faith.

'III. We humbly beseech our most dread sovereign lord that the Lady Mary may be made legitimate, and the former statute therein annulled, for the danger if the title might incur to the crown of Scotland. This to be in parliament.

'IV. To have the abbeys suppressed to be restored—houses, lands, and goods.

'V. To have the tenths and first-fruits clearly discharged, unless the clergy will of themselves grant a rent-charge in penalty to the augmentation of the crown.

'VI. To have the friars observants restored unto their houses again.

'VII. To have the heretics, bishops and temporals, and their sect, to have condign punishment by fire, or such other; or else to try the quarrel with us and our partakers in battle.

'VIII. To have the Lord Cromwell, the lord chancellor, and Sir Richard Rich to have condign punishment as subverters of the good laws of this realm, and maintainers of the false sect of these heretics, and first inventors and bringers in of them.

'IX. That the lands in Westmoreland, Cumberland, Kendal, Furness, the abbey lands in Massamshire, Kirkhyshire, and Netherdale, may be by tenant right, and the lord to have at every change two years' rent for gressam [the fine paid on renewal of a lease; the term is, I believe, still in use in Scotland], and no more, according to the grant now made by the lords to the commons there under their seal; and this to be done by act of parliament.

'X. The statute of hand-guns and cross-bows to be repealed, and the penalties thereof, unless it be on the king's forest or park, for the killing of his Grace's deer, red or fallow.

'XI. That Doctor Legh and Doctor Layton may have condign punishment for their extortions in the time of visitation, as bribes of nuns, religious houses, forty pounds, twenty pounds, and so to —— leases under one common seal, bribes by them taken, and other their abominable acts by them committed and done.

'XII. Restoration for the election of knights of shires and burgesses, and for the uses among the lords in the parliament house, after their antient custom.

'XIII. Statutes for enclosures and intakes to be put in execution, and that all intakes and enclosures since the fourth year of King Henry the Seventh be pulled down, except on mountains, forests, or parks.

'XIV. To be discharged of the fifteenth, and taxes now granted by act of parliament.

'XV. To have the parliament in a convenient place at Nottingham or York, and the same shortly summoned.

'XVI. The statute of the declaration of the crown by will, that the same be annulled and repealed.

'XVII. That it be enacted by act of parliament that all recognizances, statutes, penalties under forfeit, during the time of this commotion, may be pardoned and discharged, as well against the king as strangers.

'XVIII. That the privileges and rights of the Church be confirmed by act of parliament; and priests not to suffer by the sword unless

accompanied by Lords Latimer, Lumley, Darcy, Sir Robert Constable, and Sir John Bulmer, went down upon the bridge. They were met by an equal number of knights and noblemen from Norfolk's army; Robert Aske remaining on the bank of the Don, 'the whole host standing with him in perfect array.'[1] The conference lasted till the October day had closed in darkness. What destinies did not hang upon its issue? The insurgents it is likely might have forced the passage of the river; and although the river of time was running with too full a current for them or any man to have stayed its course, yet they might have stained its waters with streams of English blood; the sunrise of the Reformation might have been veiled in storms; and victory, when it came at last, have shone over gory battle-fields and mangled ruins.

Such was not the destiny appointed for England. The insurgents were deceived by their strength. They believed themselves irresistible, and like many others who have played at revolutions, dreamt that they could afford to be moderate.

It was agreed that Sir Robert Bowes and Sir Ralph Ellerkar should carry the articles to the king; that the Duke of Norfolk should escort them in person, and intercede for their favourable hearing. Meanwhile, and till the

---

they be degraded. A man to be saved by his book; sanctuary to save a man for all cases in extreme need; and the Church for forty days, and further, according to the laws as they were used in the beginning of this king's days.

'XIX. The liberties of the Church to have their old customs, in the county palatine of Durham, Beverley, Ripon, St. Peter's at York, and such other, by act of parliament.

'XX. To have the Statute of Uses repealed.

'XXI. That the statutes of treasons for words and such like, made since anno 21 of our sovereign lord that now is, be in like wise repealed.

'XXII. That the common laws may have place, as was used in the beginning of your Grace's reign; and that all injunctions may be clearly decreed, and not to be granted unless the matter be heard and determined in Chancery.

'XXIII. That no man, upon subpœnas from Trent north, appear but at York, or by attorney, unless it be upon pain of allegiance, or for like matters concerning the king.

'XXIV. A remedy against escheators for finding of false offices, and extortionate fees-taking, which be not holden of the king, and against the promoters thereof.'

A careful perusal of these articles will show that they are the work of many hands, and of many spirits. Representatives of each of the heterogeneous elements of the insurrection contributed their grievances; wise and foolish, just and unjust demands were strung together in the haste of the moment.

For the original of this remarkable document, see Instructions to Sir Thomas Hilton, Miscellaneous Depositions on the Rebellion: *Rolls House MS.*

[1] Aske's Narrative: *Rolls House MS.*

king's reply was known, there should be an armistice. The musters on both sides should be disbanded — neither party should 'innovate' upon the *status in quo*.

The loyalists and the rebels alike expected to gain by delay. Letters from all parts of the kingdom were daily pouring in to Aske, full of gratitude, admiration, and promises of help.[1] He had leisure to organize the vast force of which the command had been thrust upon him, to communicate with the Emperor or with the regent's court at Brussels, and to establish a correspondence with the southern counties.

The Duke of Norfolk escaped an immediate danger; agreeing in heart with the general objects of the rising, he trusted that the petition, supported by the formidable report which he would carry up with him, might bring the king to consent to a partial reaction; if not to be reconciled to the Pope, at least to sacrifice Cromwell and the heretical bishops.

The weight of the crisis now rested on Henry himself. Cromwell was powerless where his own person was the subject of contention. He had no friends — or none whose connexion with him did not increase his danger — while by his enemies he was hated as an incarnation of Satan. He left his cause in the king's hands, to be supported or allowed to fall.

But the Tudor princes were invariably most calm when those around them were panic-stricken. From the moment that the real danger was known, the king's own hand was on the helm — his own voice was heard dictating his orders. Lincolnshire had again become menacing, and Suffolk had written despairing letters; the king told him 'not to be frightened at his shadow.'[2] The reactionary members of the council had suggested a call of parliament, and a proclamation that if any of the king's subjects could prove the late measures of the government to be against the laws of God or the interests of the commonwealth, these measures should be undone. They had begged, further, that his Highness would invite all persons who had complaints against Cromwell and the bishops to come forward with their proofs, and would give a promise that if the charges could be substantiated, they should be proceeded against and punished.[3] At such a crisis the king

---

[1] Lord Darcy to Somerset Herald: *Rolls House MS.*
[2] Richard Cromwell to Lord Cromwell: *MS. State Paper Office*, second series, vol. vii.
[3] Devices for the Quieting of the North: *Rolls House MS.* first series, 606.

refused either to call a parliament to embarrass his hands, or to invite his subjects to argue against his policy. 'He dared rather to testify that there never were in any of his predecessors' days so many wholesome, commodious, and beneficial acts made for the commonwealth: for those who were named subverters of God's laws he did take and repute them to be just and true executors of God's laws.' If any one could duly prove to the contrary, they should be duly punished. 'But in case,' he said, 'it be but a false and untrue report (as we verily think it is), then it were as meet, and standeth as well with justice that they should have the self-same punishment which wrongfully hath objected this to them that they should have had if they deserved it.'[1]

On the 29th of October he was on the point of setting off from London; circulars had gone out to the mayors of the towns informing them of his purpose, and directing them to keep watch and ward night and day,[2] when Norfolk reached the court with the two messengers.

Henry received them graciously. Instead of sending them back with an immediate answer, he detained them for a fortnight, and in that interval gained them wholly over to himself. With their advice and assistance he sent private letters among the insurgent leaders. To Lord Latimer and the other nobles he represented the dishonour which they had brought upon themselves by serving under Aske; he implored both them and the many other honourable men who had been led away to return to their allegiance, 'so as we may not,' he said, 'be enforced to extend our princely power against you, but with honour, and without further inconvenience, may perform that clemency on which we have determined.'[3]

By infinite exertion he secured the services, from various parts of England, of fifty thousand reliable men who would join him on immediate notice; while into the insurgent counties he despatched heralds, with instructions to go to the large towns, to observe the disposition of the people, and, if it could be done with safety, to request the assistance of the mayor and bailiffs, 'gently and with good words in his Grace's name.' If the herald 'used himself discreetly,' they would probably make little difficulty; in which case he should repair in his coat of arms, attended by the officers of the corporation, to the market cross, and explain to the people the untruth of

[1] *State Papers*, vol. i. p. 507-8.
[2] Bundle of unassorted MSS. in the State Paper Office.
[3] *Rolls House MS.* second series, 278.

the stories by which they had been stirred to rebellion. The poorest subject, the king said, had at all times access to his presence to declare his suits to him; if any among them had felt themselves aggrieved, why had they not first come to him as petitioners, and heard the truth from his own lips. 'What folly was it then to adventure their bodies and souls, their lands, lives and goods, wives and children, upon a base false lie, set forth by false seditious persons, intending and desiring only a general spoil and a certain destruction of honest people, honest wives, and innocent children. What ruth and pity was it that Christian men, which were not only by God's law bound to obey their prince, but also to provide nutriment and sustentation for their wives and children, should forget altogether, and put them in danger of fire and sword for the accomplishment of a certain mad and furious attempt.' They could not recall the past. Let them amend their faults by submission for the future. The king only desired their good. He had a force in reserve with which he could and would crush them if they drove him to it; he hoped that he might be able only to show them mercy and pardon.[1] As to the suppression of the abbeys, the people should learn to compare their actual condition with the objects for which they were founded. Let them consider the three vows of religion—poverty, chastity, and obedience—and ask themselves how far these vows had been observed.[2]

---

[1] *State Papers*, vol. i. p. 476, and compare p. 500. The instructions varied according to circumstances. There were many forms of them, of which very few are printed in the *State Papers*. I extract from several, in order to give the general effect.

[2] The king's words are too curious to be epitomized. The paper from which I here quote is written by his secretary, evidently from dictation, and in great haste. After speaking of the way in which the vow of chastity had been treated by the monks, he goes on—

'For the point of wilful poverty they have gathered together such possessions, and have so exempted themselves from all laws and good order with the same, that no prince could live in that quiet, in that surety, in that ease, yea, in that liberty, that they lived. The prince must carke and care for the defence of his subjects against foreign enemies, against force and oppression; he must expend his treasures for their safeguard; he must adventure his own blood, abiding all storms in the field, and the lives of his nobles, to deliver his poor subjects from the bondage and thrall of their mortal enemies. The monks and canons meantime lie warm in their demesnes and cloysters. Whosoever wants, they shall be sure of meat and drink, warm clothing, money, and all other things of pleasure. They may not fight for their prince and country; but they have declared at this rebellion that they might fight against their prince and country. Is not this a great and wilful poverty, to be richer than a prince?—to have the same in such certainty as no prince hath that tendereth the weal of his subjects? Is not this a great obedience that may not obey their prince, and against God's commandment, against their duties of allegiance, whereto

The heralds attempted their mission, and partially succeeded; but so hot a fever was not to be cooled on a sudden; and connected with the delay of the messengers, and with information of the measures which the king was procuring, their presence created, perhaps, more irritation and suspicion than their words accomplished good. The siege of Skipton continued; separate local insurrections were continually blazing; the monks everywhere were replaced in the abbeys; and Aske, who, though moderate, was a man of clear, keen decision, determined, since the king was slow in sending up his concessions, to anticipate them by calling a parliament and convocation of the northern notables, to sit at York.[1] 'The king's treasure,' which had fallen into his hands, gave him command of money; the religious houses contributed their plate; circulars were addressed to every parish and township, directing them to have their contingents ready at any moment to march; and, to insure a rapid transmission of orders, regular posts were established from Hull to Templehurst, from Templehurst to York, from York to Durham, from Durham to Newcastle. The roads were patrolled night and day; all unknown persons in town or village were examined and 'ripped.'[2] The harbour at Hull was guarded with cannon, and the town held by a strong garrison under Sir Robert Constable, lest armed ships from Portsmouth might attempt to seize it. Constable himself, with whose name we have already become familiar, was now, after Robert Aske and Lord Darcy, the third great leader of the movement.[3] The weather had changed, an early winter had set in, and the rivers either fell or froze; the low marsh country again became passable, and

they be sworn upon the Holy Evangelists, will labour to destroy their prince and country, and devise all ways to shed Christian blood? The poor husbandman and artificer must labour all weathers for his living and the sustentation of his family. The monk and canon is sure of a good house to cover him, good meat and drink to feed him, and all other things meeter for a prince than for him that would be wilfully poor. If the good subject will ponder and weigh these things, he will neither be grieved that the King's Majesty have that for his defence and the maintenance of his estate, so that he shall not need to molest his subjects with taxes and impositions, which loiterers and idle fellows, under the cloke of holyness, have scraped together, nor that such dissimulers be punished after their demerits, if they will needs live like enemies to the commonwealth.'—*Rolls House MS.* first series, 297.

[1] Sir Brian Hastings to Lord Shrewsbury: *Rolls House MS.* first series, 268.
[2] Ibid.
[3] He was a bad, violent man. In earlier years he had carried off a ward in Chancery, one Anne Grysanis, while still a child, and attempted to marry her by force to one of his retainers.—*Rolls House MS.* second series, 434.

rumours were abroad that Darcy intended to surprise Doncaster, and advance towards Nottingham; and that Aske and Constable would cross the Humber, and, passing through Lincolnshire, would cut off Suffolk, and join him at the same place.[1]

The king, feeling that the only safety was in boldness, replied by ordering Lord Shrewsbury to advance again to his old position. The danger must have been really great, as even Shrewsbury hesitated, and this time preferred to hold the line of the Trent.[2] But Henry would now hear nothing of retreat. His own musters were at last coming up in strength. The fortification of Hull, he said, was a breach of the engagement at Doncaster; and Vernon, one of the lords of the Welsh Marches, Sir Philip Draycote, and Sir Henry Sacheverell, going to Shrewsbury's assistance, the line of the Don was again occupied. The head quarters were at Rotherham, and a depôt of artillery and stores was established at Tickhill.[3]

In Suffolk's camp at Lincoln a suggestion was started whether Aske's attack might not be anticipated—whether, by a swift, silent enterprise, it might not be possible to seize and carry off both him and Sir R. Constable. Two volunteers were found who offered to make the experiment. One of them, Anthony Curtis, a cousin of Aske, 'for private malice, said that if he might have licence, he would find sureties, and would either kill his kinsman or be killed himself.'[4] Another attempt for Aske's destruction was made by the Duke of Norfolk, who had no objection to a coalition of noblemen against Cromwell, but disdained the dictation of an unknown upstart. He supposed that he might tempt Lord Darcy to an act of treachery, and sent a questionable proposal to him by the hands of a servant of Lord Hussey, a certain Percival Cresswell. The attempt failed; but Cresswell's account of his mission is not a little curious.

He arrived at Templehurst on Friday, November the 10th, shortly before dinner. Lord Darcy was walking with Aske himself, who was his guest at the time, and a party of the commons in the castle garden. Cresswell gave him a letter from Norfolk, which was cautiously worded, in case it should fall into wrong hands,' and said he was

[1] Sir Brian Hastings to Lord Shrewsbury: *Rolls House MS.* first series, 626.
[2] Shrewsbury to the King: *MS. State Paper Office*; Letters to the King and Council, vol. v.
[3] *MS. State Paper Office*, second series, vol. xxxvi.
[4] Suffolk to the King: *MS. State Paper Office*; Letters to the King and Council, vol. v.

charged also with a private message. The danger of exciting suspicion was so great that Darcy had a difficulty in arranging a separate conversation. He took Cresswell into the castle, where he left him in an anteroom full of armed men. They gathered about him, and inquired whether Cromwell, 'whom they called most vilipendiously,' was put out of the king's council. He replied that the Duke of Norfolk, Lord Oxford, Lord Sussex, and Sir William Fitzwilliam were with the king. 'God save the king!' they said; 'as long as nohlemen of the true hlood rule ahout the king all will be well. But how of Cromwell? Is he put from the council or no?' Cresswell said that he was still on the council. Then, whatsoever the Lord Darcy say to you, they answered, show the king and the lords that until our petitions are granted we will take no pardon till we have our will.' Darcy had by this time secured a private room and a few private moments. He called Cresswell in. 'Now tell your message,' he said. 'The Duke of Norfolk desires you,' announced the messenger, 'to deliver up Aske, quick or dead, but if possible, alive; and you shall so show yourself a true subject, and the king will so regard you.'[1] Darcy replied like a nobleman. He had given his faith, he said, and he would not stain his coat.[2] He wrote a few lines to Norfolk—'Alas, my Lord!' his letter said, 'that you, being a man of so great honour, should advise or choose me to betray any living man, Frenchman, Scot, yea, or even Turk. To win for me or for mine heirs the hest duke's lands that be in France, I would not do it to no living person.'[3] The next morning, after mass, he again called Cresswell to him, and bade him tell the king that he had never done better service either to him or to his father than he was doing at that moment, and if there was to he peace, he recommended that the answer to the petition should be returned instantly.

The king had written more than one answer; but in each draught which he had made there was a reservation attached to the promise of a general pardon, excluding in one instance ten persons, in another, six, from the benefit of it;[4] and they were withdrawn all of them in

[1] It is to be remembered that Darcy still *professed* that he had been forced into the insurrection by Aske. This is an excuse for Norfolk's request, though it would have been no excuse for Darcy had he consented.
[2] Deposition of Percival Cresswell: *Rolls House MS.* A 2, 29.
[3] *MS. State Paper Office*, first series. Autograph letter of Lord Darcy to the Duke of Norfolk. It is unfortunately much injured.
[4] One of these is printed in the *State Papers*, vol. i. p. 506. The editor of these Papers does not seem to have known that neither this

deference to the protests of the Duke of Norfolk. Ellerkar and Bowes were dismissed on the 14th of November, 'with general instructions of comfort.'[1] Norfolk himself, with other commissioners, would return to the north at the end of the month with a final reply.

The ill-humour of the insurgents was meanwhile increasing; division had begun to show itself; the people suspected the gentlemen, the gentlemen feared the people, and noisy demonstrations showed Aske that a state of inaction was too dangerous to continue. On the return of Bowes and Ellerkar a hasty council was called at York. The question was put whether they should wait or not for the arrival of the commissioners. Especial exasperation had been caused by a letter of Cromwell to Sir Ralph Evers, in which it was said that, 'unless the commons would be soon pacified, there should be such vengeance taken that the whole world should speak thereof.'[2] It was proposed to cut short further parley, and leave the cause to be decided by the sword. Darcy had already selected an agent to the court of Brussels, to beg that arms and ammunition might be sent at once to Hull.[3] Sir Robert Constable declared openly, 'that if his advice might be taken, seeing he had broken one point in the tables with the king, he would yet break another, and have no meeting. He would have all the country made sure from Trent northward; he doubted not they would have joined with them all Lancashire and Cheshire, which would make them strong enough to defend themselves against all men; and then,' he said, 'he would be content to condescend to the meeting.'[4]

Had this advice been taken, the consequences might have been serious; but the fatal moderation of the leader prevailed over the more audacious but safer counsel. The terms offered by the government should be first discussed, but they should be discussed in security. The musters

---

nor any *written* answer was actually sent. Amidst the confusion of the MSS. of this reign, scattered between the State Paper Office, the Rolls House, and the British Museum, some smothered in dirt and mildew, others in so frail a state that they can be scarcely handled or deciphered, far greater errors would be pardonable. The thanks of all students of English history are due to Sir John Romilly for the exertions which he has made and is still making to preserve the remnants of these most curious documents.

[1] Henry VIII. to the Earl of Rutland: *Rolls House MS.* first series, 454.
[2] Aske's Narrative: *Rolls House MS.*
[3] *Rolls House MS.* first series, 1805; and see *State Papers*, vol. i. p. 558.
[4] Deposition of John Selbury: *Rolls House MS.* A 2, 29.

should reassemble in full force.[1] They had summoned a northern parliament and convocation. The two assemblies should sit at Pomfret and not at York, and should meet at the time of the conference.

Thus, on the 26th of November, as the king's commissioners approached the borders of Yorkshire,[2] the news reached them that the beacons were again burning, and the force of the commons was again collecting. The conference, if conference there was to be, must be held with their hands on their sword-hilts. The black squadrons, with St. Cuthbert's banner, would be swarming on the banks of the Don as before.[3] They had brought down extensive powers, but the king had refused absolutely to grant a complete pardon. Five or six of the worst offenders, he insisted, should be surrendered; and if the rebels were obstinate, Norfolk had been directed to protract the discussion, to win time by policy, that he might himself come to them; and in the meantime to consent to nothing, to promise nothing, and yet do and say nothing 'which might give them warning and respite to fortify themselves.'[4]

But the waters had fallen low; the ground was hard; the sharpest winter had set in which had been known for years. The force which Shrewsbury had with him could not now hold its position in the face of the vast numbers which were collecting. When the number of the rebels who had reassembled was known, Sir John Russell was sent back from Nottingham to tell the king that his conditions could not be insisted upon, and to entreat him not only to grant the full pardon, but to promise also to hold a parliament in person at York.

Ignorant what the answer would be, Norfolk, with the other commissioners, went on to Doncaster, having prepared his way by a letter to Lord Darcy, to do away the effect of his late overtures.[5] He arrived at the town on the 28th of November. On Monday the 27th, the northern notables, laity and clergy, had assembled at Pomfret.

---

[1] Sir Anthony Wingfield to the Duke of Norfolk: *Rolls House MS.* first series, 692.

[2] The Duke of Norfolk, Sir William Fitzwilliam, Sir John Russell, and Sir Anthony Brown.

[3] The Duke of Suffolk feared an even larger gathering: where heretofore they took one man, he warned Norfolk, they now take six or seven. *State Paper Office MS.* first series, vol. iii. Lord Darcy assured Somerset Herald that they had a reserve of eighty thousand men in Northumberland and Durham—which, however, the herald did not believe. *Rolls House MS.*

[4] The King to the Duke of Norfolk: *Rolls House MS.* first series, 278.

[5] *MS. State Paper Office.*

Thirty-four peers and knights, besides gentlemen and extemporized leaders of the commons, sate in the castle hall;[1] the Archbishop of York and his convocation in Pomfret church. The discussions of the latter body were opened by the archbishop in a sermon, in which he dared to declare the meeting unlawful and the insurrection traitorous. He was swiftly silenced: a number of soldiers dragged him out of the pulpit, and threw him down upon the pavement. He was rescued and carried off by a party of his friends, or in a few more moments he would have been murdered.[2] The clergy, delivered from his control, drew up a list of articles, pronouncing successively against each step which had been taken in the Reformation;[3] and other articles simultaneously were drawn by the council in the hall. One by one, as the form of each was resolved upon, they were read aloud to the assembly, and were received with shouts of 'Fiat! Fiat!'

Ten knights were then told off, and ten followers for every knight, to ride down to Doncaster and arrange the preliminaries of the meeting. They saw the duke on the day of his arrival; and on Wednesday the 29th, Lord Darcy, Robert Aske, and three hundred of the most eminent of their party, passed the bridge of the Don with a safe conduct into the town. Wearing their pilgrim's badges, the five wounds of Christ crossed on their breasts, 'they made obeisance on their knees before the duke and earls, and did humbly require to have the king's most merciful and free pardon for any their offences committed.' This done, they presented their resolutions, on which they had just determined at Pomfret, and the discussion opened. The duke's hands were tied; he could undertake nothing. The debate continued till Saturday, 'exceeding perplexed,' messengers hurrying to and fro between Doncaster and Pomfret. At length, on Saturday, Sir John Russell came with the king's revised commission.

Against his judgment Henry had yielded to the en-

---

[1] The names of the thirty-four were—Lords Darcy, Neville, Scrope, Conyers, Latimer, and Lumley; Sir Robert Constable, Sir John Danvers, Sir Robert Chaloner, Sir James Strangways, Sir Christopher Danby. Sir Thomas Hilton, Sir William Constable, Sir John Constable, Sir William Vaughan, Sir Ralph Ellerker, Sir Christopher Hellyarde, Sir Robert Neville, Sir Oswald Wolstrop, Sir Edward Gower, Sir George Darcy, Sir William Fairfax, Sir Nicholas Fairfax, Sir William Mallore, Sir Ralph Bulmer, Sir Stephen Hamarton, Sir John Dauncy, Sir George Lawson, Sir Richard Tempest, Sir Thomas Evers, Sir Henry Garrowe, and Sir William Babthorpe.

[2] Examination of John Dakyn: *Rolls House MS.* first series, p. 402.

[3] They have been printed by STRYPE (*Memorials*, vol. ii. p. 266). Strype, however, knew nothing of the circumstances which gave them birth.

treaties of the Privy Council. He foresaw that to allow a commotion of such a kind to pass wholly unpunished, was to acknowledge a virtual defeat, and must encourage conduct which would soon lead to a repetition of the same scenes. He refused to admit that Norfolk was justified in his despondency. Skipton still held out. Lord Clifford and Sir William Musgrave had gained possession of Carlisle, and were raising men there. Lord Derby was ready to move with the musters of Cheshire and Lancashire. Besides Shrewsbury's forces, and the artillery at Tickhill, Suffolk had eight thousand men in high order at Lincoln. He 'marvelled that Norfolk should write to him in such extreme and desperate sort, as though the world were turned upside down.' 'We might think,' he said, 'that either things be not so well looked on as they might be, when you can look but only to the one side; or else that ye be so perplexed with the brutes on the one part, that ye do omit to write the good of the other. We could be as well content to bestow some time in the reading of an honest remedy as of so many extreme and desperate mischiefs.' Nevertheless, he said, if the rebels would be contented with the two concessions which Norfolk had desired—a free pardon and a parliament at York —these, but only these, might be made. No further engagements of any kind should or might be entered into. If more were insisted on, the commissioners should protract the time as skilfully as they could, and send secret expresses to Lord Derby and the Duke of Suffolk, who would advance by forced marches to their support.[1] With this letter he sent a despatch to Suffolk, bidding him hold himself in readiness, and instructing him at the same time to use his influence in the West Riding to induce the people to return to their allegiance, and permitting him to make liberal offers and promises in the name of his government.[2]

The limitation of the new commission was as clear as language could make it. If the Duke of Norfolk com-

---

[1] Henry VIII. to the Duke of Norfolk: *State Papers*, vol. i. p. 511. The council, who had wrung these concessions from the king, wrote by the same courier, advising him to yield as little as possible— 'not to strain too far, but for his Grace's honour and for the better security of the commonwealth, to except from pardon, if by any means he might, a few evil persons, and especially Sir Robert Constable.'— *Hardwicke State Papers*, vol. i. p. 27.

[2] 'You may of your honour promise them not only to obtain their pardons, but also that they shall find us as good and gracious lord unto them as ever we were before this matter was attempted; which promise we shall perform and accomplish without exception.'—Henry VIII. to the Duke of Suffolk: *Rolls House MS.* first series, 476.

mitted himself more deeply, it was against the king's express commands, and in the face of repeated warnings.

On the day of Russell's arrival an agreement was made and signed. The pardon and the parliament were directly promised. It appears, certainly, that further engagements were virtually entered upon, or that words were used, perhaps intentionally vague, which were interpreted by the insurgents through their hopes and wishes. They believed, perhaps they were led to believe, that their entire petition had been granted;[1] they had accomplished the object of their pilgrimage, and they were satisfied.

As the conference closed, Aske again fell upon his knees, 'and most humbly required the Duke of Norfolk and all the earls and lords of his part, to desire the lords of the north part to relinquish and refuse thenceforth to nominate him by the name of captain; and they promised: which done, the said Aske, in the presence of all the lords, pulled off his badge crossed with the five wounds, and in a semblable manner did all the lords there, and all others there present, saying all these words, 'We will wear no badge nor figure but the badge of our sovereign Lord.''[2] A fine scene .... yet, as we sometimes witness with a sudden clearance after rain, leaving hanging vapours in the sky, indicating surely that the elements were still unrelieved.

The king had resolved on concession, but not on such concession as the Pomfret council demanded and Norfolk had seemed to promise. He would yield liberally to the substantial interests of the people, but he would yield little to their imaginative sympathies, and to the clergy and the reactionist lords he would not yield a step. The enclosures he intended should be examined, the fines on renewals of leases should be fixed, and the relations of landlord and tenant so moderated that 'rich and poor men might live together, every one in his degree according to his calling.'[3] The abbey lands would not be restored to the monks, but he saw the inconvenience of attaching them to the domains of the crown. They should be disposed of rapidly on terms favourable to the people and unfavourable to himself. In this direction he was ready to do all that he was desired to do; but undo the Reformation—never.

[1] Aske, in his Narrative, which is in the form of a letter to the king, speaks of 'the articles now concluded at Doncaster, which were drawn, read, argued, and agreed among the lords and esquires' at Pomfret.—*Rolls House MS.*
[2] Aske's Narrative: *Rolls House MS.* A 2, 28.
[3] Instructions to the Earl of Sussex: *Rolls House MS.* first series, 299.

A remarkable state paper, in Cromwell's handwriting, indicates the policy which the king then intended. The northern parliament was to meet the following summer. There is not the smallest doubt that Henry meant to observe his own promises. He would be present in person. The queen would accompany him, and the opportunity would be taken for her coronation. Meanwhile, to clear up all misunderstandings, every nobleman and gentleman who had taken part in the insurrection was to be sent for, and should learn from the king himself the bearing of the measures against which they had clamoured, the motives which had led to the adoption of such measures, and the extent to which they would be further carried. A similar invitation should be sent to the principal persons in all other English counties, to come to London and give their advice on questions of social and local reform; and, further, to receive directions to try various experiments in such matters before the meeting of parliament, 'that his Grace might see what fruit should succeed of them, and so alter and change as he should think meet.' To do away with the suspicion that the government were favouring heresy, copies of the 'Articles of Faith' were to be scattered liberally through England; select preachers were to be sent in sufficient numbers into the north to explain their meaning; and next there follows a passage which, as written by Cromwell, was a foreshadowing of his own fate.

'Forasmuch as the rebels made the maintenance of the faith one of the chief grounds and causes of the rebellion, it shall be necessary that the King's Highness, in the mean season, see his laws, heretofore taken for the establishment of an unity in the points of religion, put in such experience and execution in those parts as it may appear that his Grace earnestly mindeth and desired an agreement specially in those things; which will not be done without his Highness do some notable act in those quarters for that purpose.'

Finally, a lieutenant-general and a council should be permanently established at York as a court of appeal, empowered to hear and decide all local causes and questions. That the government might not again be taken by surprise, garrisons, Cromwell thought, might be established in the great towns, 'in such order as they might be continued without hatred of the people.' The ordnance stores should be kept in better preparation, and should be more regularly examined; and, above all, the treasury must be better furnished to meet unforeseen expenses, 'experience showing that princes be not so easily served save where there is prompt payment for service rendered, and the honest labourer is not kept waiting for his hire.'[1]

These well-considered suggestions were carried at once into effect. By the end of December many of the gentlemen who had been out in the insurrection had been in London; in their interviews with the king they had been won back to an unreserved allegiance, and had returned to do him loyal service. Lord Darcy and Sir Robert Constable had been invited with the rest; they had declined to present themselves: the former pretended to be ill; Constable, when the king's messenger came to him, 'using no reverend behaviour nor making any convenable answer such as might have tended to his Grace's satisfaction,' shut himself up in a remote castle on the Yorkshire

---

[1] Scheme for the Government of the North; *Rolls House MS.* first series, 900. In connexion with the scheme for the establishment of garrisons, a highly curious draft of an act was prepared, to be submitted to the intended parliament.

Presuming that, on the whole, the suppression of the monasteries would be sanctioned, the preamble stated (and the words which follow are underlined in the MS.) that—

'Nevertheless, the experience which we have had by those houses that are already suppressed sheweth plainly unto us that a great hurt and decay is thereby come, and hereafter shall come, to this realm, and great impoverishing of many the poor subjects thereof, for lack of hospitality and good householding that were wont in them to be kept, to the great relief of the poor people of all the counties adjoining the said monasteries, besides the maintaining of many smiths, husbandmen, and labourers that were kept in the said houses.

'It should therefore be enacted:

'1. That all persons taking the lands of suppressed houses must duly reside upon the said lands, and must keep hospitality; and that it be so ordered in the leases.

'2. That all houses, of whatsoever order, habit, or name, lying beyond the river of Trent northward, and not suppressed, should stand still and abide in their old strength and foundation.

'3. That discipline so sadly decayed should be restored among them; that all monks, being accounted dead persons by the law, should not mix themselves in worldly matters, but should be shut up within limited compass, having orchards and gardens to walk in and labour in—each monk having forty shillings for his stipend, each abbot and prior five marks—and in each house a governor, to be nominated by the king, to administer the revenue and keep hospitality.

'4. A thousand marks being the sum estimated as sufficient to maintain an abbey under such management, the surplus revenue was then to be made over to a court, to be called the *Curia Centenariorum*, for the defence of the realm, and the maintenance in peace as well as war of a standing army; the said men of war, being in wages in the time of peace, to remain in and about the towns, castles, and fortresses, within the realm at the appointment of the lord admiral, as he should think most for the surety of the realm.'

A number of provisions follow for the organization of the court, which was to sit at Coventry as a central position, for the auditing the accounts, the employment of the troops, &c. The paper is of great historic value, although, with a people so jealous of their liberties, it was easy to foresee the fate of the project. It is among the *Cotton. MSS. Cleopatra*, E 4, fol. 215.

coast.[1] Of the three leaders who had thrown themselves
into the insurrection with a fixed and peremptory purpose, Aske alone, the truest and the bravest, ventured to
the king's presence. Henry being especially desirous to
see a man who had shaken his throne, paid him the respect of sending his request by the hands of a gentleman
of the bedchamber. He took him now, he said, for his
faithful subject, he wished to talk with him, and to hear
from his own lips the history of the rising.[2]

Aske consulted Lord Darcy. Darcy advised him to go,
but to place relays of horses along the road, to carry six
servants with him, leaving three at Lincoln, Huntingdon,
and Ware, and taking three to London, that in case the
king broke faith, and made him prisoner, a swift message
might be brought down to Templehurst, and Darcy, though
too sick to pay his court to Henry, would be well enough
to rescue Aske from the Tower.[3] They would have acted
more wisely if they had shown greater confidence. Aske
went, however. He saw the king, and wrote out for him
a straightforward and manly statement of his conduct—
extenuating nothing—boasting of nothing—relating merely
the simple and literal truth. Henry repeated his assurance
to him that the parliament should meet at York; and
Aske returned, hoping perhaps against hope; at all events,
exerting himself to make others hope that the promises
which they supposed to have been made to them at Doncaster would eventually be realized. To one person only
he ventured to use other language. Immediately that he
reached Yorkshire, he wrote to the king describing the
agitation which still continued, and his own efforts to appease it. He dwelt upon the expectations which had been
formed; in relating the expressions which were used by
others, he indicated not obscurely his own dissatisfaction.

'I do perceive,' he said, 'a marvellous conjecture in
the hearts of the people, which is, they do think they
shall not have the parliament in convenient time; secondly,
that your Grace hath by your letters written for the most
part of the honourable and worshipful of these shires to
come to you, whereby they fear not only danger to them,
but also to their own selves; thirdly, they be in doubt of
your Grace's pardon by reason of a late book answering
their first articles, now in print,[4] which is a great rumour

---

[1] *Hardwicke State Papers*, vol. i. p. 38.
[2] *State Papers*, vol. i. p. 523.
[3] Confession of George Lascelles: *Rolls House MS.* first series, 774.
[4] And for another reason. They were forced to sue out their pardons individually, and received them only as Aske and Lord Darcy had been obliged to do, by taking the oath of allegiance, and binding

amongst them; fourthly, they fear the danger of fortifying holds, and especially because it is said that the Duke of Suffolk would be at Hull, and to remain there; fifthly, they think your Grace intendeth not to accomplish their reasonable petitions by reason now the tenths is in demand; sixthly, they say the report is my lord privy seal[1] is in as great favour with your Grace as ever he was, against whom they most specially do complain;

'Finally, I could not perceive in all the shires, as I came from your Grace homewards, but your Grace's subjects be wildly minded in their hearts towards commotions or assistance thereof, by whose abetment yet I know not; wherefore, sir, I beseech your Grace to pardon me in this my rude letter and plainness of the same, for I do utter my poor heart to your Grace to the intent your Highness may perceive the danger that may ensue; for on my faith I do greatly fear the end to be only by battle.'[2]

These were the words of a plain, honest man, who was convinced that his conduct had been right, that his demands had been wise, and was ready to return to rebellion when he found his expectations sliding away. Here, as so often in this world, we have to regret that honesty of purpose is no security for soundness of understanding; that high-hearted, sincere men, in these great questions, will bear themselves so perversely in their sincerity, that at last there is no resource but to dismiss them out of a world in which they have lost their way, and will not, or cannot, recover themselves.

But Aske, too, might have found a better fate, if the bad genius of his party had not now, in an evil hour for him and for many more, come forward upon the scene.

themselves to obey the obnoxious statutes so long as they were unrepealed.—*Rolls House MS.* first series, 471.
[1] Cromwell.
[2] Robert Aske to the King: *MS. State Paper Office*, Royal Letters.

CHAPTER XIV.

THE COMMISSION OF CARDINAL POLE.

There were glad hearts at Rome when the news came that the English commons had risen for the Church. The Pope would lose no time in despatching his blessings and his help to his faithful children. His advances had been scorned—his hopes had been blighted—his offers of renewed cordiality had been flung back to him in an insulting act of parliament; the high powers, it seemed, had interfered at last to avenge his quarrel and theirs. Rumour painted the insurgents as in full triumph; but their cause was the cause of the world, and should not be left in their single hands. If France and the Empire were entangled in private quarrels, Scotland was free to act, and to make victory sure.

On Christmas eve, at St. Peter's, at the marvellous mass, when as the clock marked midnight, the church, till then enveloped in darkness, shone out with the brilliance of a thousand tapers, a sword and cap were laid upon the altar,—the sword to smite the enemies of the faith, the cap, embroidered with the figure of a dove, to guard the wearer's life in his sacred enterprise. The enchanted offerings were a present of the Holy Father to James the Fifth; they were to be delivered in Scotland with the same ceremonials with which they had been consecrated;[1] and at Rome prayers were sent up that the prince would use them in defence of Holy Church against those enemies for whom justice and judgment were now prepared; that, in estimating the value of the gifts,

[1] 'Deum deprecantes ut dextram ense firmet caputque tuum hoc pileo vi Spiritûs Sancti per columbam figurati protegat.'—*Paulus III. Regi Scotiæ*: *Epist. Reg. Pol.* vol. ii. p. 269.

he would remember their mystic virtue and spiritual potency.[1]

The Scotch were, indeed, ill-selected as allies to the northern English, their hereditary enemies;[2] but religion had reconciled more inveterate antagonisms, and to the sanguine Paul, and his more sanguine English adviser, minor difficulties seemed as nothing, and vanished in the greatness of their cause.

Reginald Pole was now a cardinal. When hopes of peace with England had finally clouded he was invited to Rome. It was soon after announced that he was to be raised to high dignity in the Roman Church; and although he was warned that the acceptance of such a position would sanction the worst interpretation of his past proceedings, he contented himself with replying with his usual protestations of good meaning, and on the 20th of December he received a cardinal's hat.[3]

His promotion, like the consecration of the cap and sword, was a consequence of the reports from England. He had been selected a representative of the Holy See on the outbreak of the rebellion which he had foretold, and he was armed with a rank adequate to his mission, and with discretionary instructions either to proceed to England or to the nearest point to it, in France or Flanders, to which he could venture.

The condition in which he might find his own country was uncertain. If the first rumours were correct, the king might be in the power of the insurgents, or, at least, be

---

[1] 'Nec tam muneris qualitatem quam mysterium et vim spiritualem perpendes.'—Paulus III. Regi Scotiæ: *Epist. Reg. Pol.* vol. ii. p. 269.

[2] Although the Doncaster petitioners had spoken of 'their antient enemies of Scotland,' an alliance, nevertheless, in the cause of religion, was not, after all, impossible. When James V. was returning from France to Edinburgh, in the spring of 1537, his ship lay off Scarborough for a night to take in provisions—

'Where certain of the commons of the country thereabout, to the number of twelve persons—Englishmen, your Highness's servants' (I am quoting a letter of Sir Thomas Clifford to Henry VIII.)—'did come on board in the king's ship, and, being on their knees before him, thanked God of his healthful and sound repair; showing how that they had long looked for him, and how they were oppressed, slain, and murdered; desiring him for God's sake to come in, and all should be his.'—*State Papers*, vol. v. p. 80.

[3] Among the records in connexion with the entreaties and warnings of the Privy Council are copies of letters to the same effect from his mother and his brother. They are written in a tone of stiff remonstrance; and being found among the government papers, must either have been drafts which the writers were required to transcribe, or copies furnished by themselves as evidence of their own loyalty. Lady Salisbury's implication in the affair of the Nun of Kent may have naturally led the government to require from her some proof of allegiance.

inclined to capitulate. It was possible that the struggle was still in progress—that the friends of the Church might require assistance and direction. It was necessary, therefore, to be provided for either contingency. To the Pope, with whom he had no disguise, and under whose direction he, of course, was acting, he spoke freely of his mission as intended to support the insurrection, that the people of England might have a leader near at hand of the old royal blood, with authority from the Pope to encourage them, yet beyond the reach of the tyrant's hand.[1] With the English government he manœuvred delicately and dexterously. At the end of December he wrote a respectful letter to Henry, making no allusion to any intended commission, but, in his capacity merely of an English subject, going over the points at issue between his country and the Papacy, and giving his reasons for believing the right to be with the See of Rome; but stating at the same time his desire 'to satisfy his Majesty, or else to be himself satisfied,' and offering 'to repair into Flanders, there to discuss and reason with such as his Highness would appoint to entreat that matter with him.'[2]

The proposal seemed so reasonable to Henry, that, if Pole, he said, was coming to Flanders really with no concealed intention, he would consent willingly; and persons were selected who should go over and dispute with him.[3] The mask was carefully sustained. In his general correspondence with his friends, although he did not disguise his commission from the Holy See, or suggest as a possibility that he might himself be convinced in the intended discussion, yet he spoke beforehand of his ex-

[1] Reg. Polus, Paulo Tertio: *Epist. Reg. Pol.* vol. ii. p. 46. The letter to which I refer was written in the succeeding summer, but the language is retrospective, and refers to the object with which the mission had been undertaken.

[2] 'Perceiving by your last letters that there remaineth a little spark of that love and obedience towards his Majesty which your bounden duty doth require, and that by the same as well it appeareth your great suspicion is conveyed to one special point—that is, to the pretended supremacy of the Bishop of Rome—as that you shew yourself desirous either to satisfy his Majesty or to be satisfied in the same, offering yourself for that purpose to repair into Flanders, there to discourse and reason it with such as his Highness shall appoint to entreat that matter with you—for the hearty love and favour we bear to my lady your mother, my lord your brother, and others your friends here, which be right heartily sorry for your unkind proceedings in this behalf, and for that also we all desire your reconciliation to his Highness's grace and favour, we have been all most humble suitors to his Majesty to grant your petition touching your said repair into Flanders, and have obtained our suit in the same, so as you will come thither of yourself, without commission of any other person.'—The Privy Council to Pole. Jan. 18, 1537: *Rolls House MS.*

[3] Ibid.

pedition merely as a peaceful one; and since he intended to commence with argument, he perhaps conceived himself to be keeping within the letter of the truth.

As his legatine credentials, five pastoral epistles were prepared by Paul.

The first was an address to his well-beloved children in England, whose apostacy he knew to have been forced upon them, and who now were giving noble proof of their fidelity in taking arms for the truth. He lauded them for their piety; he exhorted them to receive, obey, and assist his excellent representative in the high work on which he was sent.

The second was to James of Scotland—a companion to another and more explicit letter which accompanied the cap and sword—commending Pole to his care, and again dwelling on the exploits which lay before him to execute in England.

The third and fourth were to Francis and the Regent of the Netherlands. The French and Imperial ambassadors had both been consulted on Pole's intended expedition, and both had signified their approval of it. Paul now implored the King of France to consider the interests which were compromised by the unhappy war in Europe, and to remember his duty as a Christian prince. He urged both Francis and the Regent Mary to receive Pole as they would receive himself, as engaged upon the deepest interests of Holy Church.

A last letter was to the Prince Bishop of Liège, claiming his general assistance, and begging him, should it be necessary, to supply the legate with money.

With these missives, and with purposes of a very plain character, Reginald Pole left Rome in February. France was his first object. The events in England of the few last weeks had prepared a different reception for him from that which he expected.

The king had not lost a moment in correcting the misconceptions which the Duke of Norfolk had permitted at Doncaster. The insurgents supposed that they had done good service to the commonwealth; the king regarded them as pardoned traitors who must reward his forgiveness by loyal obedience for the future. A chasm lay between the two estimates of the same subject, which would not readily be filled. The majority of the gentlemen had returned from their visit to London, converts to Henry's policy—or at any rate determined to support it. The clergy, and such of the people as were under their influence, remained a sullen minority. The intentions of the government were made purposely obvious. Large garrisons, with ammunition and cannon were thrown into Newcastle, Scarborough, and Hull. Royal officers penetrated the country where the power of the knights and nobles was adequate to protect them, compelling suspected persons to sue out their pardons by taking the oath of allegiance in a form constructed for the occasion.[1] The most conspicuous insurgents were obliged to commit themselves to acquiescence in all the measures against which they had risen. They had believed themselves victorious: they were enduring the consequences of defeat.

Loud outcries arose on all sides. The people exclaimed that they were betrayed by the gentlemen. The pardon was a delusion; 'the king,' they said, 'had given them the fawcet and had kept the spigot.'[2] The clergy were described as writhing with fury;[3] they had achieved their magnificent explosion; the smoke which had darkened the sky was clearing off, and the rock was not splintered. The opportunity was not, could not be gone; after all, it was only here and there that the treachery of the gentlemen would be fatal; the king had still but a comparatively inconsiderable force scattered in a few towns; the country generally was in a state of anarchy; the subsidy could not be collected; the monks remained in the abbeys in which they had been reinstated. The agitation began again, at particular points, to gather head.

Sir Francis Bigod, of Mogreve Castle, in Blakemore, was one of those persons who, in great questions, stand aloof from parties, holding some notion of their own, which they consider to be the true solution of the difficulty, and which they will attempt when others have failed; he was a spendthrift; his letters to Cromwell[4] describe him as crippled with debt; he was a pedant; and had written a book on the supremacy, on an original principle;[5] in the first rising, he said, he

[1] 'They shall swear and make sure faith and promise utterly to renounce and refuse all their forced oaths, and that from henceforth they shall use themselves as true and faithful subjects in all things; and that specially they shall allow, approve, support, and maintain to the uttermost of their power all and singular the acts, statutes, and laws which have been made and established in parliament since the beginning of the reign of our most dread Sovereign Lord.'—*Rolls House MS.* first series, 471.

[2] Confession of George Lumley: Ibid.

[3] *MS. State Paper Office*, second series, vol. xix.

[4] Many of them are in the *State Paper Office* in the Cromwell Collection.

[5] John Hallam deposes: 'Sir Francis Bigod did say, at Walton Abbey, that 'the king's office was to have no care of men's souls,

was 'held in great suspect and jealousy because of his learning.'

Mortified, perhaps, that his talents had not been appreciated, he now conceived that he had an occasion for the display of his powers. If the king had selected a leader for the insurgents who would give a deathblow to their cause, he could not have made a better choice.

The council of the north was about to undertake its functions. The Duke of Norfolk was to be the first president, and was to enter upon his duties at the end of January.

Bigod, consulting only a few monks, a certain John Hallam a retainer of Sir Robert Constable, and one or two other insignificant persons, imagined that before his arrival the vantage-ground of Doncaster might be recovered. Had Lord Darcy, or any capable person, been aware of his intentions, he would have been promptly checked; but he kept his secret, except among his own private confederates, till the 12th of January, when he sent out a sudden circular, through Durham and Richmondshire, inviting a muster at Settington. Discontent is an incautious passion. The clergy gave their help, and a considerable number of people collected, though knowing nothing of the object for which they had been called together.[1] Presently Sir Francis Bigod rode up, and mounting a hillock, addressed the crowd.

'He had invited them thither, he said, to warn them that, unless they looked to themselves, they would be all destroyed. Cleveland had risen, and other parts of the bishopric had risen, and all brave men must follow the example. The Duke of Norfolk was coming down with twenty thousand men. The gentlemen were traitors. The people were deceived by a pretended pardon, which was not a pardon, but a proclamation. None were to have the benefit of it, unless they took the king for supreme head of the Church; and that was against the Gospel. If, therefore, he said, you will take my part, I will take yours. You who will follow me, hold up your hands.'[2]

They did not know Bigod; but in their humour they

and did read to this examinate a book made by himself, as he said, wherein was shewed what authority did belong to the Pope, what to a bishop, what to the king; and said that the head of the Church of England must be a spiritual man, as the Archbishop of Canterbury or such; but in no wise the king, for he should with the sword defend all spiritual men in their right.''—*Rolls House MS.* A 2, 29.

[1] Sir Francis Bigod's Confession: *Rolls House MS.* first series. 416. Confession of George Lumley: *Rolls House MS.* The MSS. relating to the later commotions are very imperfect, and much injured.

[2] Lumley's Confession.

would have followed any one who had offered to lead them. Every hand went up. 'Who will not go,' they cried, 'strike off his head!' 'Now is the time to rise, or else never. Forward! forward! forward! forward now! on pain of death. Forward now, or else never; and we shall have captains just and true; and no gentlemen shall stay us.'.... The spent force of the great rising could still issue in noise, if in nothing else.

Among the crowd was the eldest son of Lord Lumley, taken there, if his own word was true, by little else than curiosity. Bigod saw him; and he was pitched upon to head a party to Scarborough, and seize the castle. He went unwillingly, with followers little better than a rabble. The townspeople were languid; the castle had been newly entrenched; the black mouths of cannon gaped between the parapets. The insurgents stood gazing for a few hours on their hopeless enterprise, and at the end Lumley stole away out of the town, and left his men to shift as they could. Hull and Beverley were to be attempted on the same day by Hallam and Bigod. In both cases they hoped to succeed by a surprise. At Hull it happened to be the market day. Hallam went thither in a farmer's dress, with twenty men, the party going in two and two to avoid causing suspicion. He calculated on the assistance of the crowd who would be collected by the market; but he soon discovered that he was mistaken, and that unless he could escape before his disguise was betrayed, he would be taken prisoner. He had gained the open country with two or three of his followers, when, on looking round, he saw the gates closing. 'Fie!' some one cried, 'will you go and leave your men behind you?' He turned his horse, intending a rescue. At that moment his bridle was seized; and though he drew his sword, and, with his servants made a few minutes' defence, he was overpowered, and carried to the town gaol.[1]

Bigod's fortune was scarcely better. He succeeded in getting possession of Beverley; but the late leaders, whose names still possessed the most authority, Aske, Darcy, and Sir Robert Constable, lost not an instant in disclaiming and condemning his proceedings. His men fell away from him; he was obliged to fly, and he, too, soon after found himself a prisoner.

Nothing could have been more fortunate for the government, nothing more vexatious to all intelligent friends of the insurrection, than this preposterous outbreak. If

---

[1] Examination of John Hallam: *Rolls House MS.* A 2, 29.

the king desired to escape from the conditions of Doncaster, a fresh commotion furnished him with a fair excuse. Constable sent out orders,[1] imperiously commanding every one to remain quiet. The Duke of Norfolk, he said, was coming only with his private retinue to listen to the complaints of the people. The king was to follow at Whitsuntide, to hold a parliament in the midst of them. Their present folly was compromising their cause, and would undo their victory. To the king both he and Aske made the most of their exertions to preserve order, and received for them his thanks and acknowledgments.[2] Yet their position was full of danger; and to move either against the rising or in favour of it might equally injure them; they ruined Bigod; but the country people and the clergy, who were half inclined to suspect them before, saw in their circulars only fresh evidence of treachery;[3] their huge party, so lately with the organization of an army, was gaping and splitting everywhere, and they knew not on which side to turn. Bigod's scattered followers appealed to Aske and Darcy for protection, and Aske at least ventured to engage his word for their pardons. Hallam, who was as popular as he was rash and headstrong, had been taken in arms, and was in the hands of the king's soldiers at Hull. They must either rescue

---

[1] 'The King's Highness hath declared by his own mouth unto Robert Aske, that he intendeth we shall have our parliament at York frankly and freely for the ordering and reformation of all causes for the commonwealth of this realm, and also his frank and free convocation for the good stay and ordering of the faith and other spiritual causes, which he supposes shall come down under his great seal by my Lord of Norfolk, who comes down shortly with a mean company after a quiet manner to the great quietness and comfort of all good men. Wherefore, good and loving neighbours, let us stay ourselves and by no means follow the wilfulness of such as are disposed to spoil and to undo themselves and you both, but to resist them in all that ye may, to the best of your power; and so will I do for my part, and so know I well that all good men will do; and if it had not been for my disease which hath taken me so sore that I may neither go nor ride, I would have come and have shewed you this myself for the good stay and quietness of you all, and for the commonwealth of all the country. The parliament and the convocation is appointed to be at York at Whitsuntide, and the coronation of the Queen's Highness about the same time.

'Written in Spaldingmore this 16th day of January.

'ROBERT CONSTABLE, of Flamborough.'

—Letter of Sir R. Constable to the Commons of the North on Bigod's Insurrection: *Rolls House MS.* first series, 276.

[2] For this matter see *Rolls House MS.* first series, 276, 416, 1144, and *State Papers*, vol. i. p. 529.

[3] 'Captain Aske was at London, and had great rewards to betray the commons; and since that he came home they have fortified Hull against the commons, ready to receive ships by the sea to destroy all the north parts.'—Demands of the Rebels who rose with Sir F. Bigod: *Rolls House MS.* first series, 893.

him and commit themselves to fresh treason, or forfeit the influence which they retained. They consulted anxiously. It was still open to them to draw their swords—to fling themselves on the country, and fight out the cause which they saw too clearly was fading away. But they had lost the tide—and they had lost heart, except for half measures, the snare and ruin of revolutionists.

Aske ventured in person to Hull, and interceded, with indirect menaces, to prevent Hallam's execution; a step which compromised himself, and could not benefit the prisoner.[1] The general consequences which he had foreseen all followed as a matter of course. 'Bigod,' he said bitterly, 'had gone about to destroy the effect of the petition.'[2] The Duke of Norfolk came at the end of the month; but, under fair pretext of the continued disorders, he brought with him an army, and an army this time composed of men who would do his bidding and ask few questions.[3]

---

[1] 'Robert Aske, in a letter which he sent to Bigod, shewed that he would do the best he could for the delivery of Hallam. And that he spoke not that feignedly, it should appear that the said Aske, after that Bigod was fled, came to the king's commissioners then sitting at Hull about Hallam's examination, and shewed them how that he had heard of a great commotion that should be in the bishoprick and other places, and therefore advised them not to be hasty in proceeding to the execution of the said Hallam.

'Also divers that had been with Bigod in his commotion came to the said Aske, whom he did not apprehend, but bade them not fear, for he would get their pardon.'—Deposition on the Conduct of Robert Aske, MS. much injured, *Rolls House*, first series, 416.

[2] *Rolls House MS.* A 2, 26.

[3] In the first surprise in October, the Privy Council had been obliged to levy men without looking nicely to their antecedents, and they had recruited largely from the usual depôts in times of difficulties, the sanctuaries. Manslayers, cutpurses, and other doubtful persons might have liberty for a time, and by good conduct might earn their pardon by taking service under the crown. On the present, as on many other occasions, they had proved excellent soldiers; and those who had been with Lord Shrewsbury had been rewarded for their steadiness. Under the circumstances he had perhaps been better able to depend upon them than on the more creditable portion of his force. After the pacification at Doncaster, Norfolk was ashamed of his followers; he proposed to disband them, and supply their place with penitent volunteers from Yorkshire and Lincolnshire. The king, who was already displeased with Norfolk for his other proceedings, approved no better of his present suggestion. 'His Majesty,' wrote the Privy Council, 'marvels that you should be more earnest in the dissuasion of the retainder of them that have been but murderers and thieves (if they so have been), than you were that his Grace should not retain those that have been rebels and traitors. These men have done good rather than hurt in this troublous time, though they did it not with a good mind and intent, but for their own lucre.... What the others did no man can tell better than you. If these men may be made good men with their advancement, his Highness may think his money well employed. If they will continue evil, all the world shall think them the more worthy punishment for that they have so little

On the 3rd of February he was at Pomfret. He was instructed to respect literally the terms of the pardon, but to punish promptly all offences committed since the issue of it. By the gentlemen he was eagerly welcomed, 'being,' he wrote, 'in the greatest fear of the people that ever I saw men.'[1] The East Riding was tolerably quiet; but to the north all was in confusion. The Earl of Westmoreland was in London. The countess was labouring to keep order, 'playing the part rather of a knight than of a lady,' but with imperfect success. The Countess of Northumberland had also exerted herself nobly. But 'there was never so much need of help,' wrote Sir Thomas Tempest to Norfolk, 'as now; Northumberland is wholly out of rule, and without order to be taken in Tyndal and Redesdale, all mischief shall go at large. The barony of Langley and Hexhamshire, taking example by them, be almost as evil as they be.'[2] Similar information came in from Richmond and the Dales, and Westmoreland was in worse condition than either. In place of the disciplined army which had been at Doncaster, an armed mob was spread over the country, pillaging and burning. Happily the latter form of evil was the more easy to deal with. 'The gentlemen be in such terror,' Norfolk said, 'that they be afraid to move for their defence.' 'It shall not be long,' he added, 'ere I will look on these commons;' nor were they slow in giving him an opportunity.

About the 12th of February a rabble from Kendal, Richmond, Hexham, Appleby, and Penrith, collected under one of the Musgraves, about eight thousand in number, and attacked Carlisle. They assaulted the walls, but were beaten back in confusion, and chased for many miles by Sir Thomas Clifford. Clifford's troops, hastily levied, contained a sprinkling of the professional thieves of the Border. The tendencies of these men getting the better of them, they began to pillage; and the rebels rallying, and probably reinforced, attacked them, and gained some advantage. Norfolk hurried to the scene, taking care to bring the southern levies with him;[3] and he trusted that

regarded the clemency of his Highness calling them from their evil doings to honest preferment.'—*Hardwicke State Papers*, p. 33.

[1] Duke of Norfolk to the Earl of Sussex: *State Papers*, vol. i. p. 534.

[2] *MS. State Paper Office*, first series, vol. iv.

[3] 'I did not dare assemble the people of the country, for I knew not how they be established in their hearts, notwithstanding that their words can be no better.'—Norfolk to Cromwell: *MS. State Paper Office*.

he had at last found an opportunity of dealing a blow which would finally restore order, and recover Henry's confidence in him, which had been somewhat shaken. 'I doubt not,' he wrote to Cromwell, 'so to use my company as it shall appear I have seen some wars. This pageant well played, it is likely all this realm shall be in better quiet during our lives. Doubt not, my lord, that I will adventure anything. I know too well what danger it should be to the whole realm if we were overthrown. Now shall appear whether for favour of these countrymen I forbare to fight with them at Doncaster, as ye know the King's Highness showed me it was thought by some I did. Those that so said shall now be proved false liars.'[1]

The result of a battle in Norfolk's humour would have been serious to the rebels.[2] They felt it, and their courage failed them; they broke up in panic and dispersed. On inquiry, the last explosion, like the rest, was traced to the monks; those of Sawley, Hexham, Lanercost, Newminster, and St. Agatha, being the most guilty. The duke had the power in his hands, and was determined, once for all, to close these scenes. The impunity of the first insurrection had borne its natural fruits, and wholesome severity could alone restore quiet. Martial law was proclaimed in Durham, Westmoreland, Cumberland, and the northern angle of Yorkshire; arrests were made on all sides, and a courier was despatched to inform the king of the final flight of the insurgents, and of the steps which had been taken. Henry answered promptly, sending down his thanks to Sir Thomas Clifford and Sir Christopher Dacre, who had defended Carlisle, with his full approbation of Norfolk's conduct. 'The further you wade,' he said, 'in the investigation of the behaviour of those persons that call themselves religious, the more you shall detest the great number of them. Our pleasure is, that before you shall close up our banner again you shall cause such dreadful execution to be done upon a good number of the inhabitants of every town, village, and hamlet that have offended, as they may be a fearful spectacle to all others hereafter that would practise any

---

[1] Norfolk to Cromwell: Ibid.
[2] 'This night I will send two or three hundred horse to them, and have commanded them to set fire in many places of the rebels' dwellings, thinking thereby to make them to steal away, and every man to draw near to his own for the safeguard of his house and goods. I have also commanded them that if the traitors so sparkle they shall not spare shedding of blood; for execution whereof I will send such as I am sure will not spare to fulfil my commandment.'—Norfolk to Cromwell: Ibid.

like matter, remembering that it should be much better that these traitors should perish in their unkind and traitorous follies, than that so slender punishment should be done upon them as the dread thereof should not be a warning to others. Finally, forasmuch as all these troubles have ensued by the solicitation and traitorous conspiracies of the monks and canons of those parts, we desire you at such places as they have conspired or kept their houses with force since the appointment at Doncaster, you shall, without pity or circumstance, cause all the monks and canons that be in any wise faulty, to be tied up without further delay or ceremony.'[1]

The command was obeyed. Before the ordinary course of law was restored, seventy-four persons, laity and clergy, were hanged in various towns in Westmoreland and Cumberland.[2] The severity was not excessive, but it was sufficient to produce the desired result. The rebellion was finished. The flame was trampled out, and a touch of human pathos hangs over the close. I find among the records a brief entry that 'the bodies were cut down and buried by certain women.'[3] Hallam and several of his followers were executed at Hull. Bigod, Lumley, and six others were sent to London, to await their trial with the Lincolnshire prisoners who were still in the Tower.

The turn of events promised ill for Reginald Pole, and the nature of his mission was by this time known in England. The fame had spread of the consecrated sword; and James had given fresh umbrage and caused additional suspicion by having married in the midst of the late events the Princess Magdalen of France, without consulting his uncle. The disturbances had been checked opportunely; but great as the danger was known to have been, a further peril had been on the rise to increase its volume. Pole had professed a desire for a reconciliation. The reconciliation, as Pole understood the word, was to be accomplished by the success of the rebellion which he was hastening to assist by all methods, natural and supernatural; and his affected surprise could scarcely have been genuine when he found himself proclaimed a traitor. Henry, by his success in England, had meantime recovered the judicious respect of foreign sovereigns. The French ambassador had promised the Pope a favourable

---

[1] Henry VIII. to the Duke of Norfolk: *State Papers*, vol. i. p. 537.
[2] Hall says, at Carlisle, but the official reports, as well as the king's directions, imply that the executions were not limited to one place.
[3] *MS. State Paper Office*, first series, vol. ii.

reception for his legate at Paris. The legate, on his arrival at Lyons, met his first disappointment in the reports which reached him from his friends at home: approaching the French capital, he received a second and a worse, in an intimation from Francis that he would not be admitted to his presence; that unless he desired to find himself in the custody of his own government he must leave the kingdom immediately. In the treaties between France and England, a mutual promise to give no protection to political offenders was a prominent article. Henry had required Francis to observe his obligations, and they could only be evaded by Pole's instant disappearance.

In the cruel blight of his hopes the legate had only to comply. He hastened to Cambray, and sending a courier with the Pope's letter to the Regent of the Netherlands, he avenged himself by childish complaints, which he poured out to Cromwell.[1] The King of France had been insulted—the sacred privileges of an ambassador had been violated by the monstrous demand for his surrender. He pretended to be ignorant that treaties are made to be observed, and that foreign courts can confer no sacred privilege on the subjects of other countries, as towards their own governments. He reached Cambray in the beginning of April, but he found in the Netherlands a scarcely more cordial reception than in France. He remained in that town under honourable but uneasy restraint till the end of May, when he was obliged to inform the Pope[2] that the regent was in so great awe and fear of

[1] 'Of the mind of the king towards me I had first knowledge at mine arriving in France; of the which, to shew you the full motive of my mind herein, I was more ashamed to hear, for the compassion I had to the king's honour, than moved by any indignation that I, coming not only as ambassador, but as legate in the highest sort of embassage that is used among Christian princes, a prince of honour should desire another prince of like honour—"Betray the ambassador, betray the legate, and give him into mine ambassador's hands, to be brought unto me." This was the dishonourable request, as I understand, of the king, which to me I promise you was no great displeasure, but rather, if I should say truth, I took pleasure therein, and said forthwith to my company that I never felt myself to be in full possession to be a cardinal as when I heard those tidings, whereby it pleased God to send like fortune to me as it did to those heads of the Church whose persons the cardinals do represent. In this case lived the apostles.'—Pole to Cromwell: STRYPE's *Memorials*, vol. ii. p. 326, &c.

[2] The value of Pole's accusations against Henry depends so much upon his character that I must be pardoned for scrutinizing his conduct rather closely. In his letter to Cromwell, dated the 2nd of May, he insists that his actions had been cruelly misunderstood. Besides making the usual protestations of love and devotion to the king with which all his letters to the English court are filled, he declares, in the most solemn way, that, so far from desiring to encourage the insurgents, he had prevented the Pope from taking the opportunity of

'that adversary,' the King of England, that she no more dared to receive him than Francis; that he lived in daily fear of being taken prisoner and sent to London, and the utmost favour on which she could venture was to send him under an escort to Liège. To Liège, therefore, he was obliged to retire, and there for the present the bishop's hospitality allowed him to remain. If his journey had been attended with no other consequences but his own mortification it would scarcely have required to be noticed. Unhappily it was followed by, and probably it occasioned, the destruction of more than one brave man for whom we could have desired a better fate. While at Liège, and even from his entry into France, it is evident, from his letters to the Pope,[1] that he maintained an active correspondence with England. Whether intercepted despatches found their way into the hands of Cromwell, or whether his presence in the neighbourhood invited suspicion, and suspicion led to discovery, is uncertain; we find only that simultaneously with Pole's arrival at Cambray, Robert Aske, Lord Darcy, and Sir Robert Constable were arrested and taken to the Tower. On mid-Lent Sunday Aske had sent out his letters to 'the captains' of

---

putting out the censures which might have caused more troubles. 'That he had sent at that time his servant purposely to offer his service to procure by all means the king's honour, wealth, and greatness, animating, besides, those that were chief of his nearest kin to be constant in the king's service.'—STRYPE's *Memorials*, vol. ii. p. 321.

I shall lay by the side of these words a passage from his letter to the Pope, written from Cambray on the 18th of the same month.

Both the French and Flemish councils, he says, are urging him to return to Italy:—

'Eo magis quod causa ipsa quæ sola me retinere posset, et quæ huc sola traxit, ne spem quidem ullam ostendere videtur vel minimo periculo dignam, cur in his locis diutius maneam, populi tumultu qui causam ipsam fovebat ita sedato ut multi supplicio sint affecti, duces autem omnes in regis potestatem venerint.'

He goes on to say that the people had been in rebellion in defence of their religion. They had men of noble birth for their leaders; and nothing, it was thought, would more inspirit the whole party than to hear that one of their own nation was coming with authority to assist their cause; nothing which would strike deeper terror into their adversaries, or compel them to more equitable conditions.

For the present the tumult was composed, but only by fair words, and promises which had not been observed. A fresh opportunity would soon again offer. Men's minds were always rather exasperated than conquered by such treatment. The people would never believe the king's word again; and though for the moment held down by fear, would break out again with renewed fury. He thought, therefore, he had better remain in the neighbourhood, since the chief necessity of the party would be an efficient leader; and to know that they had a leader ready to come to them at any moment, yet beyond the king's reach, would be the greatest encouragement which they could receive. —Reginald Pole to the Pope: *Epist. Reg. Pol.* vol. ii. p. 46.

[1] Ibid.

various districts, and meetings had been held in consequence.[1] I am unable to ascertain either the objects or the results of these meetings; but 'to summon the king's lieges' for any object after the restoration of quiet was an act of the highest imprudence. In Easter week there was an obscure insurrection in Cleveland. Sir John and Lady Bulmer (or Margaret Cheyne, as she is termed in her indictment) had been invited to London. Lady Bulmer was proved to have said that she would as soon be torn in pieces as go to London unless the Duke of Norfolk's and Sir Ralph Ellerkar's heads were off, and then she might go where she would at the head of the commons. Her chaplain confessed to a plot between the lady, her husband, and other persons, to seize and carry off Norfolk to Wilton Castle;[2] but in the evidence which I have discovered there is nothing to implicate either Aske or his two friends in this project.

That after the part which the latter had played they should have been jealously watched, that actions of doubtful bearing should be construed to their disfavour, was no more than they had a right to expect. Narrow interpretations of conduct, if severe, are inevitable with men who in perilous times thrust themselves into revolutionary prominence. To estimate their treatment fairly, we must ascertain, if possible, from the fragments of surviving informations against them, whether they really showed symptoms of fresh treasonable intent, or whether they were the victims of the irritation created by Pole's mission, and were less punished for their guilt than because they were dangerous and powerful. The government insisted that they had clear proof of treason;[3] yet the word 'treason' as certainly bore a more general meaning in Cromwell's estimate, than in the estimate of those who continued to regard the first pilgrimage as good service to the state. To the government it was a crime to be expiated by active resistance of all similar attempts, by absolute renunciation of its articles; and if in contrast to

[1] Bishop Hilsey to Cromwell: *MS. State Paper Office*, second series, vol. xxxv.
[2] *Rolls House MS.* first series, 416; much injured.
[3] The Privy Council, writing to the Duke of Norfolk, said: 'You may divulge the cause of their activity to the people of those parts, that they may the rather perceive their miserable fortune, that, being once so graciously pardoned, would eftsoons combine themselves for the attempting of new treasons ... not conceiving that anything is done for their former offences done before the pardon, which his Grace will in nowise remember or speak of; but for those treasons which they have committed again since in such detestable sort as no good subject would not wish their punishment for the same.'—*Hardwicke State Papers*, vol. i. p. 43.

the great body of the northern gentlemen, a few possessed of wide influence continued to maintain that they had done well, if they continued to encourage the people to expect that their petitions would be granted, if they discouraged a renewal of the commotions, avowedly because they would injure the cause; it is certain that by a government surrounded by conspiracy, and emerging with difficulty out of an arduous position, yet determined to persevere in the policy which had created the danger, such men would be regarded with grave suspicion, even if compromised by no further overt acts of disloyalty.

But it can scarcely be said that they were wholly uncompromised. Through the months of February and March a series of evidence shows Aske, Darcy, Sir Robert Constable, a gentleman named Levening, and several others, holding aloof as an isolated group, in close and continued intercourse, yet after Bigod's capture taking no part in the pacification of the country. These men repeatedly, in public and private, assured the people that the Doncaster articles must be conceded. They were in possession of information respecting the risings in Westmoreland and Cleveland, and yet gave no information to the government. In an intercepted letter to Lord Darcy Aske spoke of himself as having accomplished a great enterprise—'as having played his part, and all England should perceive it.'[1] It was proved that Darcy, when commanded in January to furnish Pomfret with stores, had repeated his former neglect—that he and Aske were still in secret possession of cannon belonging to the government, which they had appropriated in the rebellion, and had not restored—that Aske had interfered with the authorities at Hull to prevent the punishment of traitors taken in arms[2]—that Constable, in a letter to Bigod, told him that he had chosen a wrong time of the year, that he ought to have waited till the spring[3]—that Lord Darcy had been heard to say that it was better to rule than be ruled—'and that where before they had had but two sovereign crowns they would now have four.'[4]

[1] *Rolls House MS.* A 2, 28.
[2] Besides his personal interference, Aske, and Constable also, had directed a notorious insurgent named Rudstone, 'in any wise to deliver Hallam from Hull.'—Ibid.
[3] Sir Ralph Ellerkar called on Constable to join him in suppressing Bigod's movement. Constable neither came nor sent men, contenting himself with writing letters.—Ibid.
[4] Part of Pole's mission was to make peace between France and the Empire. The four sovereigns would, therefore, be the Pope, the King of Scotland, Francis, and Charles. I have gathered these accusations out of several groups among the Rolls House MSS., apparently

The lightest of these charges were symptoms of an animus[1] which the crown prosecutors would regard as treasonable. The secretion of the artillery and Aske's conduct at Hull would ensure a condemnation where the judges were so anxious to condemn.

The materials for the prosecution were complete. It remained to proceed with the trials. But I must first mention the fate of the prisoners from Lincolnshire, who had been already disposed of. In their case there was not the complication of a pardon. They had been given up hot-handed by their confederates, as the principal instigators of the rebellion. More than a hundred seem to have been sent originally to the Tower. Upwards of half of these were liberated after a short imprisonment. On the 6th of March Sir William Parr, with a special commission, sat at Lincoln, to try the Abbot of Kirkstead, with thirty of the remainder. The Lincoln jury regarded the prisoners favourably; Thomas Moigne, one of the latter, spoke in his defence for three hours so skilfully, according to Sir William Parr's report, that 'but for the diligence of the king's serjeant,' he and all the rest would have been acquitted. Ultimately the crown secured their verdict: the abbot, Moigne, and another were hanged on the following day at Lincoln, and four others a day or two later at Louth and Horncastle.[2] The commission petitioned for the pardon of the rest. After a delay of a few weeks the king consented, and they were dismissed.[3]

---

heads of information, Privy Council minutes, and drafts of indictments. The particulars which I have mentioned being repeated frequently in these papers, and with much emphasis, I am inclined to think that they formed the whole of the case.

[1] The proofs of 'an animus' were severely construed.
A few clauses from a rough draft of the indictments will show how small a prospect of escape there was for any one who had not resolutely gone over to the government.
Aske wrote to the commons of the north a letter, in which was written, 'Bigod intendeth to destroy the effect of our potition and commonwealth; whereby,' Cromwell concluded, 'it appeareth he continued in his false opinion and traitorous heart.'
In another letter he had said to them, 'Your reasonable petitions shall be ordered by parliament,' 'showing that he thought that their petitions were reasonable, and in writing the same he committed treason.'
Again, both Constable and he had exhorted the commons to wait for the Duke of Norfolk and the parliament, telling them that the duke would come only with his household servants; 'signifying plainly that, if their unreasonable requests were not complied with, they would take the matter in their own hands again.'
There are fifty 'articles' against them, conceived in the same spirit, of more or less importance.

[2] Sir William Parr to Henry VIII: *MS. State Paper Office*, Letters to the King and Council, vol. v. *Rolls House MS.* first series, 76.

[3] Sir William Parr to Cromwell: *MS. State Paper Office*, second series, vol. xxxi.

Twelve more, the Abbot of Barlings, one of his monks, and others who had been concerned in the murder of the chancellor, were then brought to the bar in the Guildhall. They had no claim to mercy; and they found none. They were hung on gibbets, at various towns, in their own county, as signs and warnings. Lord Hussey was tried by the peers. He was guilty obviously of having fled from a post which he was bound to defend. He had obstructed good subjects, who would have done their duty, had he allowed them; and he had held communication with the rebels. His indictment[1] charges him with acts of more direct complicity, the evidence of which I have not discovered. But wherever a comparison has been possible, I have found the articles of accusation in so strict accordance with the depositions of witnesses, that the absent link may be presumed to have existed. The construction may be violent; the fact is always true. He, too, was found guilty, and executed.[2]

With Lord Hussey the Lincolnshire list was closed. Out of fifty or sixty thousand persons who had been in armed rebellion, the government was satisfied with the punishment of twenty. The mercy was perhaps in part dictated by prudence.

The turn of the northern men came next. There were three sections of them—Sir Francis Bigod, George Lumley, and those who had risen in January in the East Riding; Sir Thomas Percy, the Abbot of Fountains, the Abbot of Jervaulx, Sir John and Lady Bulmer, Sir Ralph Bulmer, and Sir Stephen Hamarton, who had been concerned in the separate commotions since suppressed by the Duke of Norfolk; and, finally, Aske, Constable, and

---

[1] *Baga de Secretis.*

[2] Lord Hussey may have the benefit of his own denial. Cromwell promised to intercede for him if he would make a true confession. He replied thus:—

'I never knew of the beginning of the commotion in neither of the places, otherwise than is contained in the bill that I did deliver to Sir Thomas Wentworth, at Windsor. Nor I was never privy to their acts, nor never aided them in will, word, nor deed. But if I might have had 500 men I would have fought with them, or else I forsake my part of heaven; for I was never traitor, nor of none counsel of treason against his Grace; and that I will take my death upon, when it shall please God and his Highness.'

In a postscript he added:

'Now at Midsummer shall be three years, my Lord Darcy, I, and Sir Robert Constable, as we sate at the board, it happened that we spake of Sir Francis Bigod, (how) his priest, in his sermons, likened Our Lady to a pudding when the meat was out, with many words more; and then my Lord Darcy said that he was a naughty priest; let him go; for in good sooth I will be none heretic; and so said I, and likewise Sir Robert Constable; for we will die Christian men.'— *MS. State Paper Office*, second series, vol. xviii.

Lord Darcy, with their adherents. In this instance the proceedings were less simple than in the former, and in some respects unusual. The inferior offenders were first tried at York. The indictments were sent in to the grand jury; and in the important case of Levening, the special confederate of Aske and Darcy, whose guilt was identical with theirs, no bill was found. The king, in high displeasure, required Norfolk to take some severe notice of this obstruction of justice. Norfolk remonstrated; and was requested, in sharper language, to send up a list of the jurors,[1] and unravel, if possible, the cause of the acquittal. The names were forwarded. The panel was composed of fifty gentlemen, relatives, most of them, of one or other of the accused persons, and many among whom had formed part of the insurgent council at Pomfret.[2] Levening's escape was explained; and yet it could not be remedied. The crown was forced to continue its prosecutions, apparently with the same difficulty, and under the same uncertainty of the issue. When the trials of the higher offenders were opened in London, true bills had first to be found against them in their own counties; and the foremen of the two grand juries (for the fifty were divided into two bodies of twenty-five each) were Sir James Strangways and Sir Christopher Danby, noted, both of them, on the list which was forwarded to the crown, as relatives of Lord Darcy, Sir Francis Bigod, and Sir John Bulmer.[3]

On the 9th of May, however, either through intimidation or the force of evidence, the sixteen prisoners who were in the Tower, Lord Darcy, Robert Aske, Sir Robert Constable, and thirteen more, were delivered over for their trials. In the six preceding weeks they had been cross-examined again and again. Of the many strange scenes which must have taken place on these occasions, one

[1] 'And whereas your lordship doth write that, in case the consciences of such persons as did acquit Levening should be examined, the fear thereof might trouble others in like case, the King's Majesty considering his treason to be most manifest, apparent, and confessed, and that all offenders in that case be principals, and none accessories, doth think it very necessary that the means used in that matter may be searched out, as a thing which may reveal many other matters worthy his Highness's knowledge; and doth therefore desire you not only to signify their names, but also to travel all that you can to beat out the mystery.'—Privy Council to the Duke of Norfolk: *Hardwicke State Papers*, vol. i. p. 46.

[2] The list is in the *Rolls MS.* first series, 284. Opposite the name of each juror there is a note in the margin, signifying his connexions among the prisoners.

[3] Compare *Baga de Secretis*, pouch x. bundle 2, and *Rolls House MS.* first series, 284.

picture, but a striking one, is all which I have found. It occurred at the house of the lord chancellor, in the presence of the Privy Council and a crowded audience. Darcy was the subject of examination. Careless of life, and with the prophetic insight of dying men, he turned, when pressed with questions, to the lord privy seal:—

'Cromwell,' he said, 'it is thou that art the very special and chief causer of all this rebellion and mischief, and art likewise causer of the apprehension of us that be——,[1] and dost daily earnestly travel to bring us to our ends, and to strike off our heads. I trust that ere thou die, though thou wouldest procure all the noblemen's heads within the realm to be stricken off, yet shall there one head remain that shall strike off thy head.'[2]

Of Aske, too, we catch glimpses which show that he was something more than a remarkable insurgent leader: a short entry tells us that six or seven days after his arrest, 'his servant, Robert Wall (let his name be remembered), did cast himself upon his bed and cried, 'Oh, my master! Oh, my master! they will draw him, and hang him and quarter him;' and therewith he did die for sorrow.'[3] Aske had lost a friend when friends were needed. In a letter which he wrote to Cromwell, he said that he had been sent up in haste without clothes or money, that no one of his relations would help him, and that unless the king would be his good and gracious lord, he knew not how he would live.[4] His confessions during his imprisonment were free and ample. He asked for his life, yet with a dignity which would stoop to no falsehood, and pretend to no repentance beyond a general regret that he should have offended the king. Then, as throughout, he showed himself a brave, simple, noble-minded man.

But it was in vain; and fate was hungry for its victims. The bills being found, Darcy was arraigned before twenty-two peers, and was condemned, Cromwell undertaking to intercede for his life.[5] The intercession, if made, was not effectual. The fifteen commoners, on the same day, were tried before a special commission in Westminster Hall. Percy, Hamarton, Sir John and Lady Bulmer pleaded guilty. The prosecution against Sir Ralph Bulmer was dropped: a verdict was given without difficulty against Aske, Constable, Bigod, Lumley, and seven more. Sixteen knights, nobles, and gentlemen, who a few months before

[1] Word illegible in the MS.
[2] MS. in Cromwell's own hand: Rolls House, A 2, 29, fol. 160 and 161.
[3] Rolls House MS. first series, 207.   [4] MS. ibid. 1401.
[5] Depositions relating to Lord Delaware: Rolls House MS.

were dictating terms to the Duke of Norfolk, and threatening to turn the tide of the Reformation, were condemned criminals waiting for death.

The executions were delayed from a doubt whether London or York should be the scene of the closing tragedy. There remain some fragments written by Darcy and Aske in the interval after their sentence. Darcy must have been nearly eighty years old; but neither the matter nor the broad, large, powerful handwriting of the following words show signs of agitation:—

'After judgment given, the petition of Thomas Lord Darcy to the King's Grace, by my Lord Privy Seal.

'First to have confession; and at a mass to receive my Maker, that I may depart like a Christian man out of this vale of misery.

'Second, that incontinent after my death my whole body may be buried with my late wife, the Lady Neville, in the Freers at Greenwich.

'Third, that the straitness of my judgment may be mitigated after the king's mercy and pleasure.

'Fourth, that my debts may be paid according to a schedule enclosed.'[1]

Aske, in a few lines addressed also to Cromwell, spoke of his debts, and begged that some provision might be made for his family. 'They,' he said, 'never offended the King's Grace, nor were with me in council in no act during all this time, but fled into woods and houses. Good my Lord, extend your pity herein. And I most humbly ask the King's Highness, and all his council and lords, lowly forgiveness for any mine offences or words attempted or said against his Grace or any of them any time of my life; and that his Grace would save my life, if it be his pleasure, to be his bedesman—or else—to let me be full dead or that I be dismembered, that I may piously give my spirit to God without more pain; and that I desire for the honour of God and for charity.'[2]

The requests relating to the manner of the executions, it is satisfactory to find, were granted; and not only in the case of the two petitioners, but so far as I can learn in that of all the other sufferers. Wherever the scaffold becomes visible, the rope and the axe are the sole discernible implements of death. With respect to the other petition, I find among loose memoranda of Cromwell an entry 'for a book to be made of the wives and poor children of such as have suffered, to the intent his Grace

[1] MS. State Paper Office, Domestic, vol. xii.
[2] Ibid.

may extend his mercy to them for their livings as to his Highness shall be thought convenient, and for payment of their debts.'[1] The 'mercy' seems to have been liberal. The forfeited properties, on the whole, were allowed to descend without diminution, in their natural order.[2]

After some discussion it was settled that Darcy should suffer on Tower Hill; and he was executed on the 20th of June. Sir Thomas Percy, Bigod, the Abbots of Fountains and Jervaulx, Hamarton, Sir John Bulmer, young Lumley, and Nicholas Tempest were hanged at Tyburn; four who had been tried with them and condemned were pardoned. Lady Bulmer died the dreadful death awarded by the English law to female treason.[3] 'On the Friday in Whitsun week,' wrote a town correspondent of Sir Henry Saville, 'the wife of Sir John Bulmer was drawn without Newgate to Smithfield and there burned:' and the world went its light way, thinking no more of Lady Bulmer than if she had been a mere Protestant heretic: the same letter urged Saville to hasten to London for the pleasures of the season, suggesting that he might obtain some share in the confiscated estates, of which the king would be soon disposing.[4] Aske and Sir Robert Constable were to be sent down to Yorkshire. The king had been compelled, by the succession of fresh disorders and the punishments which had followed, to relinquish his intention of holding a summer parliament there. The renewed disturbances had released him from his promise, and the discussion which would inevitably have been opened, would have been alike irritating and useless. He had thought subsequently of going to York on progress,

---

[1] *MS. Cotton. Titus,* B 1, 457.

[2] For instance, Sir Thomas Percy's eldest son inherited the earldom of Northumberland; unfortunately, also his father's politics and his father's fate. He was that Earl of Northumberland who rose for Mary of Scotland against Elizabeth.

[3] Lady Bulmer seems from the depositions to have deserved as serious punishment as any woman for the crime of high treason can be said to have deserved. One desires to know whether in any class of people there was a sense of compunction for the actual measure inflicted by the law. The following is a meagre, but still welcome, fragment upon this subject:—

'Upon Whitsunday, at breakfast, certain company was in the chauntry at Thame, when was had speech and communication of the state of the north country, being that proditors against the King's Highness should suffer to the number of ten; amongst which proditors the Lady Bulmer should suffer. There being Robert Jones, said it is a pity that she should suffer. Then to that answered John Strebilhill, saying it is no pity, if she be a traitor to her prince, but that she should have after her deserving. Then said Robert Jones, let us speak no more of this matter; for men may be blamed for speaking of the truth.'— *Rolls House MS.* first series, 1862.

[4] *MS. State Paper Office:*——to Henry Saville.

and of making his presence the occasion of an amnesty; the condition of the Continent, however, the large armies, French and Imperial, which were in the field in the neighbourhood of Calais, the possibility or the alarm that the Pope might succeed in reconciling and directing them upon England, and still more the pregnancy of the queen and the danger of some anxiety which might cause the loss of the child, combined to make so distant a journey undesirable. These at least were the reasons which he alleged to the world. His chief ground, however, as he stated in private, was the increasing infirmity of his own health and the inhibition of his physician.[1] He resolved, therefore, that Norfolk, and not himself, should 'knit up the tragedy,' by conducting the last executions on the scene of the rebellion, and after they were over, by proclaiming a final and general pardon.

At the beginning of July the two remaining prisoners were placed in the custody of Sir Thomas Wentworth. They were paraded in formal state through the eastern counties, and at each town a few words of warning were addressed on the occasion to the people. Wentworth brought them thus to Lincoln, where they were delivered over to the Duke of Norfolk. Constable suffered first. He was taken to Hull,[2] and there hanged in chains.[3] Before his death he said that, although he had declared on his examination that he had revealed everything of importance which he knew, yet he had concealed some matter connected with Lord Darcy for fear of doing him an injury. 'He was in doubt whether he had offended God in receiving the sacrament in such manner, concealing the truth upon a good purpose.'[4] This secret,

---

[1] A second cause 'is our most dear and most entirely beloved wife the queen, being now quick with child, for the which we give most humble thanks to Almighty God, albeit she is in every condition of that loving inclination and reverend conformity, that she can in all things well content, satisfy, and quiet herself with that thing which we shall think expedient and determine; yet, considering that, being a woman, upon some sudden and displeasant rumours and brutes that might be blown abroad in our absence, she might take impressions which might engender danger to that wherewith she is now pregnant, which God forbid, it hath been thought necessary that we should not extend our progress this year so far from her.'—Henry VIII. to the Duke of Norfolk: *State Papers*, vol. i. p. 552.

[2] *MS. Rolls House*, A 2, 29.

[3] A curious drawing of Hull, which was made about this time, with the plans of the new fortifications erected by Henry, is in the Cotton Library. A gallows stands outside the gate, with a body hanging on it, which was probably meant for Constable's.

[4] 'Immediately tofore Sir Robert Constable should receive his rights, it was asked of him if that his confession put in writing was all that he did know. To which he made answer that it was all. Notwithstanding he knew, besides that, sundry naughty words and high cracks

whatever it was, he carried with him from the world. His own offences he admitted freely, protesting, however, that he had added nothing to them since the pardon.

A fuller account remains of the end of Aske. He, too, like Constable, had some mystery on his conscience which he would not reveal. In a conversation with his confessor he alluded to Darcy's connexion with the Spanish ambassador; he spoke of the intention of sending for help to Flanders, and acknowledged his treason, while he shrunk from the name of traitor. He complained that Cromwell had several times promised him his life if he would make a full confession, and once he said he had a token of pardon from the king; but his bearing was quiet and brave, and if he believed himself hardly dealt with, he said so only in private to a single person.

York was chosen as his place of execution. He was drawn through the streets upon a hurdle, to be hanged afterwards from the top of a tower. On his way he told the people that he had grievously offended God, the king, and the world. God he had offended in breaking his commandments many ways; the King's Majesty he had greatly offended in breaking his laws, to which every subject was bound; and the world he had offended, 'for so much as he was the occasion that many a one had lost their lives, lands, and goods. At the scaffold he begged the people to pray for him, 'and divers times asking the King's Highness' forgiveness, the lord chancellor, the Lord of Norfolk, the lord privy seal, the Lord of Sussex, and all the world, after certain orisons he commended his soul to God.'[1]

---

that my Lord Darcy had blown out, which he thought not best to shew so long as the said lord was on life, partly because they should rather do hurt than good, and partly because he had no proof of them.

'But what these words were he would not declare, but in generality. Howbeit, his open confession was right good.'—*MS. State Paper Office, first series, vol. i.*

[1] A general amnesty was proclaimed immediately after.

'The notable unkindness of the people,' Norfolk said, 'had been able to have moved his Grace to have taken such punishment on the offenders as might have been terrible for all men to have thought on that should hereafter have only heard the names of sedition and rebellion.

'Yet the king's most royal Majesty, of his most tender pity and great desire that he hath rather to preserve you from the stroke of justice imminent upon your deserts, than to put you to the extremity of the same, trusting and supposing that the punishment of a few offenders in respect of the multitude, which have suffered only for an example to others to avoid the like attemptations, will be sufficient for ever to make all you and your posterities to eschew semblable offences, of his inestimable goodness and pity is content by this general proclamation to give and grant to you all, every of you, his general and free pardon.'—*Rolls House MS. A 2, 28; State Papers, vol. i. p. 558.*

So we take leave of Robert Aske, closing his brief greatness with a felon's death—an unhappy ending! Yet, as we look back now, at a distance of three centuries, when the noble and the base, the conquerors and the conquered, have been all long dead together, when nothing remains of any of them but the work, worthy or unworthy, which they achieved, and the few years which weak false hearts could purchase by denying their faith and truckling to the time,[1] appear in the retrospect in their proper insignificance, a man who risked and lost his life for a cause which he believed a just one, though he was mistaken in so believing it, is not among those whose fate deserves the most compassion, or whose career is least to be envied.

The insurrection had sunk down into rest; but it had not been wholly in vain. So far as it was just it had prevailed; and happy were they whose work was sifted for them, who were permitted to accomplish so much only of their intentions as had been wisely formed. If the reins of England had been seized by Aske and Darcy, their signal beacons of insurrection would have become blazing martyr-piles, shining dreadfully through all after ages; and their names would have come down to posterity swathed in such epithets as cling, and will cling, for ever to the Gardiners and the Alvas.

While the noble Catholics were braving danger in England, Reginald Pole sate at safe distance on his Liège watch-tower, scenting the air for the expected battle-field; and at length, hungry and disappointed, turning sullenly away and preparing for flight. He had clung to hope till the last moment with desperate tenacity. He had laboured to inspire his friends in Italy with his own confidence. 'The leaders of the faithful,' he wrote to the Pope, 'had been duped and murdered; but the hate of the people for the government had deepened in intensity. They were subdued for the instant by terror; but their strength was unimpaired. They were furious at the king's treachery.'[2] 'Twice,' he wrote to Contarini, 'the children of Israel went up against Benjamin, and twice they were put to confusion, God having encouraged them to fight, and God permitting their defeat. The third time they

---

[1] Like Cuthbert Tunstall, for instance, who, when upbraided for denying his belief in the Pope, said 'he had never seen the time when he thought to lose one drop of blood therefore, for sure he was that none of those that heretofore had advantage by that authority would have lost one penny to save his life.'—Tunstall to Pole: BURNET's *Collectanea*, p. 481.
[2] *Epist. Reg. Pol.* vol. ii. p. 46.

prevailed. In like manner had the children of the Church been twice conquered, once God so willing it in Ireland, and now again in England. A third time they would take up their cause, and then they would triumph gloriously.'[1] He knew what he meant. Already he was digging fresh graves for other victims; secret messengers were passing between Liège and his mother, and his mother's family, and Lord Montague and Lord Exeter were already contemplating that third effort of which he spoke.[2] 'I do but desire to wait in this place,' he said, 'so long as the farmer waits for his crops. I have sown my seed. It will grow in its allotted time.'[3] Contarini advised his return to Italy; and the Pope believed also that the opportunity was passed. Pole himself, alternately buoyed up with hope and plunged in despondency, seemed at times almost delirious. He spread a wild rumour that the king had sent emissaries to murder him.[4] The Pope believed him, and became more anxious for the safety of so valuable a life. Letters passed and repassed. He could not resign himself to relinquish his enterprise. On the 21st of August he wrote that 'the English government had made itself so detested, and the King of Scotland was so willing to assist, that with the most trifling impulse a revolution would be certain.' Events, however, so far, had not borne out his expectations. He had promised liberally, but there had been no fulfilment; and supposing at length that the chances of success were too slight to justify the risk of his longer stay, Paul put an end to his anxieties by sending him a formal recall.

The disappointment was hard to bear. One only comfort remained to him. Henry had been evidently anxious that his book should not be made known to the world. He might revise, intensify, and then publish it, and taste the pleasure of a safe revenge.

But I have now to mention a minor drama of treachery winding into the interstices of the larger. When Pole first awoke serious suspicion by being raised to the Cardinalate, Michael, younger brother of Sir George Throgmorton, volunteered to Cromwell to go to Rome, make his way into Pole's service, and become a spy upon his

[1] *Epist. Reg. Pol.* vol. ii. p. 64.
[2] Trials of Lord Montague and the Marquis of Exeter: *Baga de Secretis.*
[3] *Epist. Reg. Pol.* vol. ii. p. 73.
[4] Pole to Contarini, *Epist.* vol. ii. p. 64. I call the rumour wild because there is no kind of evidence for it, and because the English resident at Antwerp, John Hutton, who was one of the persons accused by Pole, was himself the person to inform the king of the story. —*State Papers*, vol. vii. p. 703.

actions. His offer was accepted. He went, and became Pole's secretary; but, instead of betraying his master, he betrayed his employers; and to him the 'Liber de Unitate Ecclesiæ' was in all probability indebted for the fresh instalment of scandals which were poured into it before publication,[1] and which have furnished material for the Catholic biographers of Henry the Eighth. Throgmorton's ingenious duplicity enabled him to blind the English government through the spring and summer. He supplied them with reports in a high degree laudatory of the cardinal, affirming entire confidence in the innocency of the legatine mission; and if they were not misled as to Pole's purposes, they believed in the fidelity of the spy. It was not till the day before leaving Liège that he threw off disguise, and wrote to Cromwell in language which was at last transparent.

The excellent intentions of the legate, he said, having been frustrated by events, and his pure and upright objects having been wickedly misconstrued, he was about to return to Rome. The Pope, whose gracious disposition towards England remained unabated, had issued indulgences through all Christendom for a general supplication that the King's Grace and the country might return to the Church. These would be naturally followed by a rehearsal of the king's actions, and accompanied by censures. It was likely, in addition, that, on Pole's return to Rome, his Holiness would request his consent that his book should be set in print, 'as it will be hard for him to deny, for the great confidence they have therein.' 'Hereof,' Throgmorton concluded, 'I have thought it necessary to advertise you, considering the short departure of the legate, upon whose return, as you see, hangs both the divulgating of the censures, the putting forth of his book, and the sending also of new ambassadors to all Christian princes. I suppose you have a great desire for a true knowledge of his mind and acts in this legacy. It makes many men marvel to see the King's Grace so bent to his ruin, rather than to take some way to reconcile him. Your lordship may best think what is best to be done.'[2]

Cromwell's answer to this communication, though long, will not be thought too long by those who desire to comprehend the passions of the time, and with the time the mind of its ruling spirit.

'I thought,' was the abrupt commencement,[3] 'that the

[1] See Appendix to Volume IV.
[2] Michael Throgmorton to Cromwell: MS. *penes me*.
[3] Cromwell to Throgmorton: *Rolls House MS.*

singular goodness of the King's Highness shewed unto you, and the great and singular clemency shewed unto that detestable traitor your master, in promising him not only forgiveness, but also forgetting of his most shameful ingratitude, unnaturalness, conspiracy against his honour, of whom he hath received no more, but even as much, and all that he hath—I thought, I say, that either this princely goodness might have brought that desperate rebel from his so sturdy malice, blindness, and pervicacy, or else have encouraged you to be his Highness's true and faithful subject. But I now remember myself too late. I might better have judged that so dishonest a master could have but even such servants as you are. No, no! loyalty and treason seldom dwell together. There can no faithful servant so long abide the sight of so heinous a traitor to his prince. You could not all this season have been a spy for the king, but at some time your countenance should have declared your heart to be loyal. No! You and your master have both well declared how little fear of God resteth in you, which, led by vain promise of promotion, thus against his laws work treason towards your natural prince and country, to serve an enemy of God, an enemy of all honesty, an enemy of right religion, a defender of iniquity, a merchant and occupier of all deceits.

'You have bleared mine eyes once. Your credit shall never more serve you so far to deceive me the second time. Your part was to do as the king your sovereign lord had commanded you. Your praise was to be sought in obeying his Highness's pleasure, and not in serving your foolish fantasy. But now, to stick unto a rebel, to follow a traitor, to serve a friend of his which mortally hateth your sovereign lord, what folly is it to excuse such mad lewdness? Your good master, who has lately entered into the religion which has been the ruin of all religion, cannot, ye say, but be the king's high friend. He will, as ye write, declare unto the world why the king taketh him for a traitor. In this thing he needeth to travel never a deal. All princes almost know how well he hath deserved this name; yea the King's Highness is much beholden unto some of them from whom his Grace hath learned the godly enterprizes that this silly cardinal went about. Now, if those that have made him thus mad can also persuade him to print his detestable book, where one lie leapeth in every line on another's neck, he shall be then as much bound to them for their good counsel as his family to him for his wise dealing. He will, I trow, have as little joy thereof as his friends and kinsfolk are like to take profit of it. Pity it is that the folly of one brainsick Pole, or, to say better, of one witless fool, should be the ruin of so great a family. Let him follow ambition as fast as he can, these that little have offended (saving that he is of their kin), were it not for the great mercy and benignity of the prince, should and might feel what it is to have such a traitor to their kinsman. Let his goodly book, the fruit of his whole study, come abroad, is there any man but he may well accuse our prince of too much clemency, and must marvel that no way is found to take away the author of such traitory? Surely when answers shall be made to his malice, there shall be very few but they will think as I do, that he hath as he deserveth, if he be brought to a most shameful death. Let him not think but though he can lie largely, there be some with us that can say truth of him. His praise shall be grief when men shall see the King's Highness's benefits towards him, and shall look upon his good heart, his grateful mind, his desire to serve the king's honour.

'Let his lewd work go forth. After that let princes judge whether the king can take the author of so famous a libel to be his true subject. Let the king's high benefits, and, which is far more to be esteemed, his singular benevolence shewed unto him of a child, come and make their plea. - Can he or you think any ground safe for him to stand in? Hath he not just cause to fear lest every honest man should offer himself to revenge this so enormous unkindness? Shall he not think every honest man to be his foe? Shall not his detestable acts, written in his conscience, evermore bring him to continual sorrow? And ye know that, whensoever the king will, his Highness may bring it easily to pass that he shall think himself scarce sure of his life, although he went tied at his master's girdle. There may be found ways enough in Italy to rid a traitorous subject. Surely let him not think but, when justice can take no place by process of law at home, sometimes she may be enforced to take new means abroad.

'Amongst all your pretty news these are very pleasant, that the Bishop of Rome intendeth to make a lamentation to the world and to desire every man to pray that his old gains may return home again. Men will think that he has cause, or at least good time, to lament, not that the King of England hath pulled his realm out of thraldom, but that a great part of the world is like to do the same. Many a man weepeth for less. We blame him not if he lament. Howbeit, doubt ye not he shall find some with us that shall bid him be a better man, though they bid him not be of better cheer. If your good master take upon him to make this lamentation, as indeed I think there is no man that hath better cause to wail than he hath, assure ye him he shall lack no consolation. The Pope will desire the world to pray for the king! The hypocrisy cometh even as it should do, and standeth in place meet for it. The world knoweth right well what other wiles he has practised these three years. They shall laugh to see his Holiness come to prayer because he cannot bring to pass that he most desireth. He that the last day went about to set all princes on his Grace's top, writing letters for the bringing of this to pass, shall he not now be thought holy that thus suddenly casteth away his weapon and falleth to his beads? If sinners be heard at any time, it is when they pray for good things. He shall not pray so fast that we may return to errors, to the defence of tyranny, ungodliness, untruth, as we shall pray that his Grace long may continue our most virtuous prince, and that hypocrites never after these days shall reign over us.

'Michael, if you were either natural towards your country or your family, you would not thus shame all your kin. I pray they bide but the shame of it. This I am sure of, though they bye and hye suffer no loss of goods, yet the least suspicion shall be enough to undo the greatest of them. I can no more, but desire that your master and you may acknowledge your detestable faults and be good witnesses of the king's high mercy. Ye may turn. If ye do so I doubt not but the king will shew the world that he desireth nothing more than the saving of his subjects. If ye continue in your malice and perverse blindness, doubt not but your end shall be as of all traitors. I have done what I may to save you. I must, I think, do what I can to see you condignly punished. God send you both to fare as ye deserve— either shortly to come to your allegiance, or else to a shameful death.'

The scene and the subject change. I must now take my reader below the surface of outward events to the under-current of the war of opinions, where the forces were generated which gave to the time its life and meaning. Without some insight into this region history is but a dumb show of phantoms; yet, when we gaze into it with our best efforts, we catch but uncertain images and fleeting pictures. In palace and cottage, in village church and metropolitan cathedral, at the board of the Privy Council or in the road-side alehouse, the same questions were discussed, the same passions were agitated. A mysterious change was in process in the minds of men. They knew not what it was—they could not control its speed or guide its direction. The articles and the settlement of 1536 were already buried under the froth of the insurrection. New standing-ground was to be sought for, only in its turn to slip away as it seemed to be gained; and the teachers and the taught, the governors and the governed, each separate human being, left to his own direction, was whirled along the rapids which formed the passage into a new era. A few scenes out of this strange time have been preserved for us in the records. They may pass one by one before us like the pictures in a magic slide.

The first figure that appears is a 'friar mendicant, living by the alms of the king's subjects, forming himself to the fashions of the people.' He is 'going about from house to house, and when he comes to aged and simple people he will say to them, 'Father or sister, what a world this is! It was not so in your father's days. It is a perilous world. They will have no pilgrimages. They will not we should pray to saints, or fast, or do any good deeds. Oh Lord, have mercy on us! I will live as my forefathers have done. And I am sure your fathers and friends were good, and ye have followed them hitherto. Continue as ye have done and believe as they believed.'[1]

The friar disappears. A neighbour of the new opinions, who has seen him come and go, takes his place, and then begins an argument. One says 'my father's faith shall be my faith.' And the other, hot and foolish, answers, 'Thy father was a liar and is in hell, and so is my father in hell also. My father never knew Scripture, and now it is come forth.'[2]

The slide again moves. We are in a village church, and there is a window gorgeously painted, representing the various events in the life and death of Thomas à Becket. The king sits on his throne, and speaks fiercely to his four knights. The knights mount their horses and gallop to Canterbury. The archbishop is at vespers in the quire. The knights stride in and smite him dead. Then follows the retribution. In the great central compartment of the window the haughty prince is kneeling

[1] Robert Ward to Cromwell: *MS. State Paper Office*, second series, vol. xlvi.
[2] Depositions relating to the Protestants in Yorkshire: *MS. State Paper Office*, second series, vol. xviii.

naked before the shrine of the martyr, and the monks stand round him and beat him with their rods. All over England in such images of luminous beauty the memory of the great victory[1] of the clergy had been perpetuated.[2] And now the particular church is Woodstock, the court is at the park, and day after day, notwithstanding the dangerous neighbourhood, in the church aisles groups of people assemble to gaze upon the window, and priests and pardoners expatiate with an obvious application on the glories of the martyr, the Church's victory, and the humiliation of the king. Eager ears listen; eager tongues draw comparisons. A groom from the court is lounging among the crowd, and interrupts the speakers somewhat disdainfully; he says that he sees no more reason why Becket was a saint than Robin Hood. No word is mentioned of the profanity to Henry; but a priest carries the story to Gardiner and Sir William Paulet. The groom is told that he might as well reason of the king's title as of St. Thomas's; forthwith he is hurried off under charge of heresy to the Tower; and, appealing to Cromwell, there follows a storm at the council table.[3]

---

[1] The monkish poetry was pressed into the service. The following is from a MS. in Balliol College, Oxford. It is of the date, perhaps, of Henry VII.

> 'Listen, lordlings, both great and small,
> I will tell you a wonder tale,
> How Holy Church was brought in bale,
>   Cum magnâ injuriâ.
>
> The greatest clerke in this land,
> Thomas of Canterbury I understand,
> Slain he was with wicked hand,
>   Malorum potentiâ.
>
> The knights were sent from Henry the king:
> That day they did a wicked thing;
> Wicked men without lesing,
>   Per regis imperia.
>
> They sought the bishop all about,
> Within his palace and without:
> Of Jesu Christ they had no doubt,
>   Pro suâ maliciâ.
>
> They opened their mouths woundily wide,
> They spake to him with much pride:
> 'Traitor! here shalt thou abide,
>   Ferens mortis tædia.'
>
> Before the altar he kneelèd down,
> And there they pared his crown,
> And stirred his braines up and down,
>   Optans cœli gaudia.'

[2] Ward to Cromwell: *MS. State Paper Office*, second series, vol. xlvi.; Miles Coverdale to Cromwell: Ibid. vol. vii.

[3] William Umpton to Cromwell: *MS. State Paper Office*, second series, vol. xlv.

We are next at Worcester, at the Lady Chapel, on the eve of the Assumption. There is a famous image of the Virgin there, and to check the superstition of the people the gorgeous dress has been taken off by Cromwell's order. A citizen of Worcester approaches the figure: 'Ah, Lady,' he cries, 'art thou stripped now? I have seen the day that as clean men had been stripped at a pair of gallows as were they that stripped them.' Then he kisses the image, and turns to the people and says, 'Ye that be disposed to offer, the figure is no worse than it was before,' 'having a remorse unto her.'[1]

The common treads close upon the serious. On a summer evening a group of villagers are sitting at the door of an alehouse on Windermere; a certain master Alexander, a wandering ballad-singer, is 'making merry with them.' A neighbour Isaac Dickson saunters up and joins the party.

'Then the said Isaac commanded the said minstrel to sing a song he had sung at one Fairbank's house in Crossthwaite, in the county of Westmoreland, in the time of the rebellion, which song was called 'Crummock,'[2] which was not convenient, which the said minstrel utterly denied. The said Isaac commanded the said minstrel again in a violent manner to sing the song called 'Cromwell,' and the said minstrel said he would sing none such; and then the said Isaac pulled the minstrel by the arm, and smote him about the head with the pummel of a dagger, and the same song the minstrel would not sing to die for. The third time the said Isaac commanded the minstrel to sing the same song, and the minstrel said it would turn them both to anger, and would not. And then did Isaac call for a cup of ale, and bade the minstrel sing again, which he always denied; then Isaac took the minstrel by the beard and dashed the cup of ale in his face; also, he drew his dagger and hurt master Willan, being the host of the said house, sore and grievously in the thigh, in rescuing of the said minstrel.'[3]

Again, we find accounts of the reception which the English Bible met with in country parishes.

A circle of Protestants at Wincanton, in Somersetshire, wrote to Cromwell complaining of the curate, who

---

[1] *MS. State Paper Office*, second series, vol. xlvi.
[2] Crummock Water is a lake in Cumberland. The point of the song must have some play on the name of Cromwell, pronounced as of old, 'Crummell.'
[3] *Rolls House MS.* first series, 688.

would not teach them or preach to them, but 'gave his time and attention to dicing, carding, bowling, and the cross waster.' In their desire for spiritual food they applied to the rector of the next parish, who had come occasionally and given them a sermon, and had taught them to read the New Testament; when suddenly, on Good Friday, 'the unthrifty curate entered the pulpit, where he had set no foot for years,' and 'admonished his parishioners to give no credence to the new-fangled fellows which read the new books.' 'They be like knaves and Pharisees,' he said; 'they be like a dog that gnaweth a marry-bone, and never cometh to the pith, therefore avoid their company; and if any man will preach the New Testament, if I may hear him, I am ready to fight with him incontinent;' and 'indeed,' the petitioners said, 'he applyeth in such wise his school of fence so sore continually, that he feareth all his parishioners.'[1]

So the parish clerk at Hastings made a speech to the congregation on the faults of the translation: 'It taught heresy,' he said; 'it taught that a priest might have a wife by God's law. He trusted to see the day that the book called the Bible, and all its maintainers and upholders, should be brent.'[2]

Here, again, is a complaint from the parishioners of Langham in Essex, against their village potentate, a person named Vigourous, who with the priest oppressed and ill-used them.

'Upon Ascension day last past did two maidens sit in their pew or school in the church, as all honest and virtuous persons use to do in matins time, saying their matins together upon an English primer. Vigourous this seeing was sore angry, in so much that therefore, and for nothing else, he did bid the maidens to avoid out of the church, (calling them) errant whores, with such other odious and spiteful words. And further, upon a time within this year, one of Vigourous's servants did quarrel and brawl with other children many, whom he called heretics; and as children be light and wanton, they called the said servant again Pharisee. Upon this complained Robert Smyth of our town to Vigourous, saying that it was against reason that the great fellow his servant should quarrel and fight with children. Whereupon Vigourous said to his servant, 'See that thou do cut off their ears, oh errant whoreson, if they so call thee hereafter; and if

---

[1] *MS. State Paper Office*, second series, vol. xlviii.
[2] *Rolls House MS.* A 2, 30.

thou lack a knife, I shall give thee one to do it. And if thou wilt not thus do, thou shalt no longer serve me.'"[1]

On the other hand, the Protestants gave themselves no pains to make their heterodoxy decent, or to spare the feelings of their antagonists. To call 'a spade a spade,' and a rogue a rogue, were Protestant axioms. Their favourite weapons were mystery plays, which they acted up and down the country in barns, in taverns, in chambers, on occasion, before the vicar-general himself;[2] and the language of these, as well as the language of their own daily life, seemed constructed as if to pour scorn on the old belief. Men engaged in a mortal strife usually speak plainly. Blunt words strike home, and the euphuism which, in more ingenious ages, discovers that men mean the same thing when they say opposite things was as yet unknown or unappreciated. We have heard something of the popular impieties, as they were called in the complaints of convocation. I add a few more expressions taken at random from the depositions.—One man said 'he would as soon see an oyster-shell above the priest's head at the sacring time as the wafer. If a knave priest could make God, then would he hire one such God-maker for a year, and give him twenty pounds to make fishes and fowls.'[3] Another said that 'if he had the cross that Christ died on, it should be the first block he would rive to the fire for any virtue that was in it.' Another, 'that a shipload of friars' girdles, nor a dungcart full of friars' cowls and boots, would not help to justification.'

On both sides the same obstinate English nature was stirred into energetic hate.

---

[1] *Rolls House MS.* A 2, 30.

[2] Very few of these are now known to be in existence. Roy's *Satire* is one of the best. It would be excellent if reduced to reasonable length. The fury which the mystery plays excited in the Catholic party is a sufficient proof of the effect which they produced. An interesting letter to Cromwell, from the author of some of them, is among the *State Papers*. I find no further mention of him:—

'The Lord make you the instrument of my help, Lord Cromwell, that I may have liberty to preach the truth. I dedicate and offer to your lordship a 'Reverend receiving of the sacrament,' as a lenten matter declared by six children, representing Christ, the word of God, Paul, Austin, a child, a man called Ignorancy, as a secret thing that shall have an end—once rehearsed afore your eyes. The priests in Suffolk will not receive me into their churches to preach; but have disdained me ever since I made a play against the Pope's councillors, Error, collyclogger of conscience, and Incredulity. I have made a play called *A Rude Commonalty*. I am making of another, called *The Woman on the Rock*, in the fire of faith refining, and a purging in the true purgatory, never to be seen but of your lordship's eye. Aid me, for Christ's sake, that I may preach Christ.'—Thomas Wylley, fatherless and forsaken: *MS. State Paper Office*, second series, vol. 1.

[3] *Rolls House MS.* A 2, 30.

Or, once more to turn to the surviving abbeys, here, too, each house was 'divided against itself, and could not stand.' The monks of Stratford complained to Sir Thomas Cholmondley that their abbot had excommunicated them for breach of oath in revealing convent secrets to the royal visitors. Their allegiance, the brave abbot had said, was to the superior of their order abroad, not to the secular sovereign in England. He cared nothing for acts of parliament or king's commissions. The king could but kill him, and death was a small matter compared to perjury.[1] Death, therefore, he resolutely risked, and in some manner, we know not how, he escaped. Another abbot with the same courage was less fortunate. In the spring and summer of 1537 Woburn Abbey was in high confusion. The brethren were trimming to the times, anxious merely for secular habits, wives, and freedom. In the midst of them, Robert Hobbes the abbot, who in the past year had accepted the oath of supremacy in a moment of weakness, was lying worn down with sorrow, unable to govern his convent, or to endure the burden of his conscience. On Passion Sunday in that spring, dying as it seemed of a broken heart, he called the fraternity to his side, and exhorted them to charity, and prayed them to be obedient to their vows. Hard eyes and mocking lips were all the answer of the monks of Woburn. 'Then, being in a great agony, the abbot rose up in his bed, and cried out, and said, 'I would to God it would please Him to take me out of this wretched world, and I would I had died with the good men that have suffered death for holding with the Pope. My conscience—my conscience doth grudge me for it.'' Abbot Hobbes should have his wish. Strength was left him to take up his cross once more where he had cast it down. Spiteful tongues carried his words to the council, and the law, remorseless as destiny, flung its meshes over him on the instant. He was swept up to London and interrogated in the usual form —'Was he the king's subject or the Pope's?' He stood to his faith like a man, and the scaffold swallowed him.[2]

So went the world in England, rushing forward, rocking and reeling in its course. What hand could guide it! Alone, perhaps, of living men, the king still believed that unity was possible—that these headstrong spirits were as horses broken loose, which could be caught again and harnessed for the road. For a thousand years there had been one faith in Western Christendom. From the Isles

---

[1] *MS. State Paper Office.*
[2] *Rolls House MS.* first series; *MS. Cotton. Cleopatra,* E 4.

of Arran to the Danube thirty generations had followed each other to the grave who had held all to the same convictions, who had prayed all in the same words. What was this that had gone out among men that they were so changed? Why, when he had but sought to cleanse the dirt from off the temple, and restore its original beauty, should the temple itself crumble into ruins?

The sacraments, the Divine mysteries, had existed in the Church for fifteen centuries. For all those ages they had been supposed to be the rivulets which watered the earth with the graces of the Spirit. After so long experience it should have been at least possible to tell what they were, or how many they were; but the question was suddenly asked, and none could answer it. The bishops were applied to. Interrogatories were sent round among them for opinions, and some said there were three sacraments, some seven, some a hundred. The Archbishop of York insisted on the apostolical succession; the Archbishop of Canterbury believed that priests and bishops might be nominated by the crown, and he that was so appointed needed no consecration, for his appointment was sufficient.[1] Transubstantiation remained almost the only doctrine beyond the articles of the three creeds on which a powerful majority was agreed.[2]

Something, however, must be done. Another statement must be made of the doctrine of the Church of England—if the Church of England were to pretend to possess a doctrine—more complete than the last. The slander must be put to silence which confounded independence with heresy; the clergy must be provided with some guide to their teaching which it should be penal to neglect. Under orders, therefore, from the crown, the

---

[1] Answers to Questions on the Sacraments by the Bishops: BURNET's *Collectanea*, p. 114.

[2] In one of the ablest and most liberal papers which was drawn up at this time, a paper so liberal indeed as to argue from the etymology of the word presbyter that 'lay seniors, or antient men, might to some intents be called priests,' I find this passage upon the eucharist: 'As concerning the grace of consecration of the body of our Lord in form of bread and wine, we beseech your Grace that it may be prohibited to all men to persuade any manner of person to think that these words of our Master Christ, when He 'took bread and blest it and brake it, and grave it to his disciples, and said, Take, and eat ye, this is my body that shall be betrayed for you,' ought to be understood figuratively. For since He that spake those words is of power to perform them literally, though no man's reason may know how that may be, yet they must believe it. And surely they that believe that God was of power to make all the world of nought, may lightly believe he was of power to make of bread his very body.'— *Theological MSS. Rolls House.*

bishops agreed at last upon a body of practical divinity, which was published under the title of 'The Bishop's Book,' or 'the Institution of a Christian Man.' It consisted of four commentaries, on the creed, the sacraments, the ten commandments, and the Lord's prayer, and in point of language was beyond question the most beautiful composition which had as yet appeared in English prose. The doctrine was moderate, yet more Catholic, and in the matter of the sacraments, less ambiguous than the articles of 1536. The mystic number seven was restored, and the nature of sacramental grace explained in the old manner. Yet there was a manifest attempt, rather, perhaps, in tendency than in positive statement, to unite the two ideas of symbolic and instrumental efficacy, to indicate that the grace conveyed through the mechanical form was the spiritual instruction indicated in the form of the ceremony. The union among the bishops which appeared in the title of the book was in appearance only, or rather it was assumed by the will of the king, and in obedience to his orders. When the doctrines had been determined by the bench he even thought it necessary to admonish the composers to observe their own lessons.

'Experience,' he wrote to them, 'has taught us that it is much better for no laws to be made, than when many be well made none to be kept; and even so it is much better nothing should be written concerning religion, than when many things be well written nothing of them be taught and observed.... Our commandment is, therefore, that you agree in your preaching, and that vain praise of crafty wits and worldly estimation be laid aside, and true religion sought for. You serve God in your calling, and not your own glory or vile profit. We will no correcting of things, no glosses that take away the text; being much desirous, notwithstanding, that if in any place you have not written so plainly as you might have done, in your sermons to the people you utter all that is in God's Word. We will have no more thwarting—no more contentions whereby the people are much more set against one another than any taketh profit by such undiscreet doctrines. We had much sooner to pray you than command you, and if the first will serve we will leave out the second. Howbeit, we will in any case that all preachers agree; for if any shall dissent, let him that will defend the worser part assure himself that he shall run into our displeasure.'[1]

[1] Henry VIII. to the Bishops: *Rolls House MS.* A 15.

'The wind bloweth where it listeth, and we hear the sound thereof, but we cannot tell whence it cometh nor whither it goeth, so is every one that is born of the Spirit.' Henry would have the bishops agree; as easily could he bind the winds, and bid them blow at his pleasure. Under conditions, and within limits which he did not imagine, some measure of the agreement which he desired would be at last accomplished when the time and season would permit. Meanwhile, though his task was an impossible one, it was better to try and fail, than to sit by and let the dissensions rage. Nor was Henry a man to submit patiently to failure. He would try and try again; when milder methods were unsuccessful he would try with bills of six articles, and pains and penalties. He was wrestling against destiny; yet then, now, and ever, it was, and remains true, that in this great matter of religion, in which to be right is the first condition of being right in anything—not variety of opinion, but unity—not the equal licence of the wise and the foolish to choose their belief, but an ordered harmony, where wisdom prescribes a law to ignorance, is the rule which reasonable men should most desire for themselves and for mankind.

But if Henry erred, his errors might find excuse in the multitude of business which was crowded upon him. Insurrection and controversy, foreign leagues, and Papal censures did not exhaust the number of his difficulties. All evil things in nature seemed to have combined to thwart him.

In the first few years after he became king, he had paid particular attention to the navy. He had himself some skill as a naval engineer, and had conducted experiments in the construction of hulls and rigging, and in ship artillery. Other matters had subsequently called off his attention, and especially since the commencement of the Reformation every moment had brought with it its own urgent claims, and the dockyards had fallen into decay. The finances had been straitened by the Irish wars, and from motives of economy the ships which the government possessed had fallen many of them out of commission, and were rotting in harbour. A few small vessels were kept on the coast of Ireland; but in the year 1536 there was scarcely in all the Channel a single royal cruiser carrying the English flag. Materials to man a fleet existed amply in the fishermen who went year after year in vast numbers to Iceland and to Ireland[1]—hardy sailors, who, taught by necessity, went always armed, and had learnt to fight as well as to work; but, from a neglect not the less injurious, because intelligible, the English authority in their own waters had sunk to a shadow. Pirates swarmed along the coasts—entering fearlessly into the harbours, and lying there in careless security. The war breaking out between Charles and Francis, the French and Flemish ships of war captured prizes or fought battles in the mouths of English rivers, or under the windows of English towns; and through preying upon each other as enemies in the ordinary sense, both occasionally made prey of heretic English as enemies of the Church. While the courts of Brussels and Paris were making professions of goodwill, the cruisers of both governments openly seized English traders and plundered English fishing vessels, and Henry had for many months been compelled by the insurrection to submit to these aggressions, and to trust his subjects along the coasts to such inadequate defences as they could themselves provide. A French galliass and galleon came into Dartmouth harbour and attempted to cut out two merchantmen which were lying there; the mayor attacked them in boats and beat them off:[2] but the harbours in general were poorly defended, and strange scenes occasionally took place in their waters. John Arundel, of Trerice, reports the following story to Cromwell: 'There came into Falmouth haven a fleet of Spaniards, and the day after came four ships of Dieppe, men-of-war, and the Spaniards shot into the Frenchmen, and the Frenchmen shot into the Spaniards, and during three hours great guns shot between them, and the Frenchmen were glad to come higher up the haven; and the morrow after St. Paul's day the Spaniards came up to assault the Frenchmen, and the Frenchmen came up almost to the town of Truro, and went aground there. I went to the admiral of the Spaniards and commanded him to keep the king's peace, and not to follow further; but the Spaniard would

---

[1] The Iceland fleet is constantly mentioned in the *Records*. Before the discovery of Newfoundland, Iceland was the great resort of English fishermen. Those who would not venture so long a voyage, fished the coasts of Cork and Kerry. When Skeffington was besieging Dungarven, in 1535, Devonshire fishing smacks, which were accidentally in the neighbourhood, blockaded the harbour for him. The south of Ireland at the same time was the regular resort of Spaniards with the same object. Sir Anthony St. Leger said that as many as two or three hundred sail might sometimes be seen at once in Valentia harbour.—*State Papers*, vol. v. p. 443, &c.

[2] *MS. State Paper Office*, second series, vol. xxiv.

not, but said 'I will have them, or I will die for it.' And then the Spaniards put their ordnance in their boats, and shot the French admiral forty or sixty shots during a long hour, the gentlemen of the city, Mr. Killigrew and Mr. Trefusis, and others, taking pleasure at it. Then I went to the Spaniards and told them to leave their shooting, or I would raise the country upon them. And so the Spaniards left. My Lord, I and all the country will desire the King's Grace that we may have blockhouses made upon our haven.'[1]

Pirates were enemies to which the people were accustomed, and they could in some measure cope with them; but commissioned vessels of war had now condescended to pirates' practices. Sandwich boatmen were pillaged by a Flemish cruiser in the Downs in the autumn of 1536.[2] A smack belonging to Deal was twice boarded and robbed by a Flemish officer of high rank, the admiral of the Sluys.[3]

The king had for several years been engaged in making a harbour of refuge at Dover. The workmen saw English traders off the coast, and even the very vessels which brought the iron and timber for the harbour-piers, plundered by French and Flemings under their eyes;[4] and the London merchants declared that, although the country was nominally at peace, their ships could not venture out of port unless the government would undertake their convoy.[5] The remonstrances which were made,

---

[1] *MS. State Paper Office*, second series, vol. i. On the other hand the French cut out a Flemish ship from Portsmouth, and another from Southampton.

[2] *Rolls House MS.* A 2, 30.

[3] The inventory of his losses which was sent in by the captain is noticeable, as showing the equipment of a Channel fishing vessel. One last of herring, worth 4l. 13s. Three hagbushes, 15s. In money, 1l. 16s. 8d. Two long bows, 4s. Two bills and a sheaf of arrows, 3s. 8d. A pair of new boots of leather, 3s. 4d. Two barrels of double beer, 3s. 4d. Four mantles of frieze, 12s. A bonnet, 1s. 2d. In bread, candles, and other necessaries, 2s. The second time, one hogshead of double beer, 6s —*MS. State Paper Office*, second series, vol. xxviii.

[4] Sir Thomas Cheyne writes to Cromwell: 'I have received letters from Dover that the Frenchmen on the sea hath taken worth 2000l. of goods since the king being there, and a man-of-war of Dieppe and a pinnace took the king's barge that carries the timber for his Highness's work there, and robbed and spoiled the ship and men of money, victuals, clothes, ropes, and left them not so much as their compass. And another Frenchman took away a pink in Dover roads and carried her away. And on Tuesday last a great fleet of Flemings men-of-war met with my Lord Lisle's ship, laden with wool to Flanders, and one of them took all the victuals and ordnance. Thus the king's subjects be robbed and spoiled every day.'—*MS. State Paper Office*, second series, vol vi.

[5] Sir William Fitzwilliam to Cromwell: *MS. State Paper Office*.

of course in loud terms, at Paris and Brussels, were received with verbal apologies, and the queen regent gave orders that her cruisers should cease their outrages; but either their commanders believed that their conduct would be secretly winked at, or they could not be convinced that heretics were not lawful game; or perhaps the zealous subjects of the Catholic powers desired to precipitate the sluggish action of their governments. At any rate, the same insolences continued, and no redress could be obtained.

Henry could not afford to declare war. The exchequer was ill-furnished. The rebellion had consumed the subsidy, and the abbey lands had as yet returned little profit either by their rentals or by sale. The country, however, had not yet sunk so low as to be unable to defend its own coasts and its own traders. Sufficient money was found for the immediate purpose, and a small but admirably equipped fleet was fitted out silently at Portsmouth. Sir Thomas Seymour, the queen's brother, Sir George Carew, Sir John Dudley, and Christopher Coo, a rough English sailor, were appointed to the command; and, when the ships were ready, they swept out into the Channel. Secrecy had been observed as far as possible, in the hope of taking the offenders by surprise. The greater number of them had, unhappily, been warned, and had escaped to their own harbours; but Coo shortly brought two pirate prizes into Rye. The people of Penzance, one August afternoon, heard the thunder of distant cannon. Carew and Seymour, searching the western coast, had come on the traces of four French ships of war, which had been plundering. They came up with them in Mounts Bay, and, closing against heavy odds, they fought them there till night. At daybreak, one of the four lay on the water, a sinking wreck. The others had crawled away in the darkness, and came no more into English waters.[1] Dudley had been even more fortunate. 'As he was lying between the Needles and the Cowe,' there came a letter to him from the Mayor of Rye, 'that the Flemings had boarded a merchant-ship belonging to that port, and had taken goods out of her valued at three hundred pounds.' 'That hearing,' he said, in his despatch to Henry, 'I, with another of your Grace's ships, made all the diligence that was possible towards the said coast of Rye; and, as it chanced, the wind served us so well

---

[1] Sir William Godolphin to Cromwell: *MS. State Paper Office,* second series, vol. xliii.

that we were next morning before day against the Combe, and there we heard news that the said Flemings were departed the day before. Then we prepared towards the Downs, for the wind served for that place, and there we found lying the admiral of the Sluys, with one ship in his company besides himself, being both as well trimmed for the war as I have lightly seen. And when I had perfect knowledge that it was the admiral of the Sluys, of whom I had heard, both at Rye and at Portsmouth, divers robberies and ill-demeanours by him committed against your Highness's subjects, then I commanded my master to bring my ship to an anchor, as nigh to the said admiral as he could, to the intent to have had some communication with him; who incontinent put himself and all his men to defence, and neither would come to communication nor would send none of his men aboard of me. And when I saw what a great brag they set upon it—for they made their drumsalt to strike alarum, and every man settled them to fight—I caused my master gunner to loose a piece of ordnance, and not touched him by a good space; but he sent one to my ship, and mocked not with me, for he brake down a part of the decks of my ship, and hurt one of my gunners very sore. That done, I trifled no more with him, but caused my master to lay her aboard; and so, within a little fight, she was yielded.' Dudley's second ship had been engaged with the other Fleming; but the latter, as soon as the admiral was taken, slipped her cable and attempted to escape. The Englishman stood after her. Both ships vanished up Channel, scudding before a gale of wind; but whether the Dutchman was brought back a prize, or whether the pursuer followed too far, and found himself, as Dudley feared, caught on a lee shore off the Holland flats, the Records are silent.[1] Pirates, however, and over-zealous privateers, in these and other encounters, were taught their lesson; and it did not, for some time, require to be repeated: 'Your subjects,' Dudley and Seymour told the king in a joint letter, 'shall not only pass and repass without danger of taking, but your Majesty shall be known to be lord of these seas.'[2] They kept their word. In this one summer the Channel was cleared, and the nucleus was formed of the fleet which, eight years after, held in check and baffled the most powerful armament which had left the French shores against England since the Norman William crossed to Hastings.

[1] *MS. State Paper Office*, Letters to the King and Council, vol. i.
[2] Ibid.

But Henry did not rest upon his success The impulse had been given, and the work of national defence went forward. The animus of foreign powers was evidently as bad as possible. Subjects shared the feelings of their rulers. The Pope might succeed, and most likely would succeed at last, in reconciling France and Spain; and experience proved that England lay formidably open to attack. It was no longer safe to trust wholly to the extemporized militia. The introduction of artillery was converting war into a science; and the recent proofs of the unprotected condition of the harbours should not be allowed to pass without leaving their lesson. Commissions were issued for a survey of the whole eastern and southern coasts. The most efficient gentlemen residing in the counties which touched the sea were requested to send up reports of the points where invading armies could be most easily landed, with such plans as occurred to them for the best means of throwing up defences.[1] The plans were submitted to engineers in London; and in two years every exposed spot upon the coast was guarded by an earthwork, or a fort or blockhouse. Batteries were erected to protect the harbours at St. Michael's Mount, Falmouth, Fowey, Plymouth, Dartmouth, Torbay, Portland, Calshot, Cowes, and Portsmouth.[2] Castles (some of them remain to the present day) were built at Dover, Deal, Sandwich, and along both shores of the Thames. The walls and embankments at Guisnes and Calais were repaired and enlarged; and Hull, Scarborough, Newcastle, and Berwick-upon-Tweed were made impregnable against ordinary attack. Each of these places was defended by adequate and trained garrisons;[3] and the musters were kept in training within twenty miles of the coast, and were held in readiness to assemble on any point at any moment.

Money was the chief difficulty. The change in the character of war created unforeseen expenses of many kinds. The cost of regular military and naval establishments, a new feature in the national system, was thrown suddenly on the crown; and the revenue was unequal to so large a demand upon it. A fresh political arrange-

---

[1] Cromwell's Memoranda: *MS. Cotton. Titus*, B 1. Many of the plans are in the Cotton Library, executed, some of them, with great rudeness; some finished with the delicacy of monastic illuminations; some, but very few, are good working drawings. It is a mortifying proof of the backwardness of the English in engineering skill, that the king for his works at Dover sent for engineers to Spain.

[2] 32 Hen. VIII. cap. 50.

[3] Details of the equipments of many of these fortresses lie scattered among the State Papers. The expenses were enormous, but were minutely recorded.

ment was displacing the old; and the finances were necessarily long disordered before the country understood its condition, and had devised methods to meet its necessities.

At this conjuncture the abbey lands were a fortunate resource. They were disposed of rapidly—of course on easy terms to the purchasers. The insurrection as we saw had taught the necessity of filling the place of the monks with resident owners, who would maintain hospitality liberally, and on a scale to contrast favourably with the careless waste of their predecessors. Obligations to this effect were made a condition of the sales, and lowered naturally the market value of the properties. Considerable sums, however, were realized, adequate for immediate objects, though falling short of the ultimate cost of the defences of the country. At the same time the government works found labour for the able-bodied beggars, those sturdy vagrants whose living had been gathered hitherto at the doors of the religious houses, varied only with intervals of the stocks and the cart's-tail.

Thus the spoils of the Church furnished the arms by which the Pope and the Pope's friends could be held at bay; and by degrees in the healthier portion of the nation an English enthusiasm took the place of a superstitious panic. Loyalty towards England went along with the Reformation, when the Reformation was menaced by foreign enemies; and the wide disaffection which in 1536 had threatened a revolution, became concentrated in a vindictive minority, to whom the Papacy was dearer than their country, and whose persevering conspiracies taught England at no distant time to acquiesce with its whole heart in the wisdom which chained them down by penal laws as traitors and enemies to the commonwealth.[1]

Meanwhile, the event to which the king, the whole of England and the Continent, friends and enemies, were looking so anxiously, was approaching near. The king's health was growing visibly weaker; his corpulency was

---

[1] On whatever side we turn in this reign, we find the old and the new in collision. While the harbours, piers, and the fortresses were rising at Dover, an ancient hermit tottered night after night from his cell to a chapel on the cliff, and the tapers on the altar, before which he knelt in his lonely orisons, made a familiar beacon far over the rolling waters. The men of the rising world cared little for the sentiment of the past. The anchorite was told sternly by the workmen that his light was a signal to the king's enemies, and must burn no more; and when it was next seen, three of them waylaid the old man on his road home, threw him down, and beat him cruelly.—*MS. State Paper Office,* second series, vol. xxxiii.

increasing, through disease and weakness of system; an inveterate ulcer had settled in his leg; and the chances of his death in consequence of it were already calculated.[1] The whole fortune of the future seemed to depend on the issue of the queen's pregnancy. Yet, notwithstanding his infirmities, Henry was in high spirits. At the end of the summer he was with a hunting party at Guildford, and was described as being especially affable and good-humoured.[2] In September he was at Hampton Court, where the confinement was expected at the close of the month, or at the beginning of October. Strange inquiries had been made by Pole, or by Pole's secretary,[3] on the probable sex of the child. On the 12th of October the question was decided by the birth of a prince, so long and passionately hoped for. Only a most minute intimacy with the condition of the country can make intelligible the feelings with which the news were received. The crown had an undoubted heir. The succession was sure. The king, who was supposed to be under a curse which refused him male posterity, was relieved from the bane. Providence had borne witness for him, and had rewarded his policy. No revolution need be looked for on his death. The Catholics could not hope for their 'jolly stirring.' The anti-Papal leaders need not dread the stake for their wages. The insurrection was crushed. A prince was born. England was saved. These were the terms which many a heart repeated to itself. The Marchioness of Dorset wrote to Henry that she had received the most joyful news that came to England these many years; for the which she

---

[1] Lord Montague, on the 24th of March, 1537, said, 'I dreamed that the king was dead. He is not dead, but he will die one day suddenly, his leg will kill him, and then we shall have jolly stirring.' —Trial of Lord Montague: *Baga de Secretis*. The king himself, in explaining to the Duke of Norfolk his reason for postponing his journey to Yorkshire in the past summer, said: 'To be frank with you, which we desire you in any wise to keep to yourself, being an humour fallen into our legs, and our physicians therefore advising us in no wise to take so far a journey in the heat of the year, whereby the same might put us to further trouble and displeasure, it hath been thought more expedient that we should, upon that respect only, though the grounds before specified had not concurred with it, now change our determination.'—*State Papers*, vol. i. p. 555.

[2] 'I assure your lordship his Grace is very sorry that ye might not be here to make good cheer as we do. He useth himself more like a good fellow among us that be here, than like a king, and, thanked be God, I never saw him merrier in his life than he is now.' —Sir John Russell to Cromwell: *MS. State Paper Office*, second series, vol. xxxvi.

[3] 'Michael Throgmorton gave great charge to William Vaughan to enquire if there had been any communication upon the opinions of the physicians, whether the Queen's Grace were with child with a man child or not.'—Hutton to Cromwell: *State Papers*, vol. vii. p. 703.

and all his Grace's subjects gave thanks to Almighty God, for that He had remembered his Grace and all his subjects with a prince, to the comfort, universal weal, and quietness of the realm.[1] Latimer, in a letter to Cromwell, was still more emphatic. 'There is no less rejoicing,' he said, 'for the birth of our prince, whom we hungered for so long, than there was, I trow, *inter vicinos*, at the birth of John the Baptist. God give us grace to yield due thanks to our Lord God, the God of England. For verily He hath shewed Himself the God of England; or rather an English God, if we will consider and ponder his proceedings with us. He hath overcome our illness with his exceeding goodness, so that we are now more compelled to serve Him and promote his Word, if the Devil of all devils be not in us. We have now the stop of various trusts and the stay of vain expectations. Let us all pray for his preservation.'[2]

In Latimer's words, the joy and the especial causes of it are alike transparent; but a disaster followed so closely as to show that the mysterious fatality which pursued the king in his domestic relations had not ceased to overshadow him, and to furnish food for fresh superstition and fresh intrigue. The birth took place on the 12th of October. The queen continued to do well up to the 22nd or 23rd,[3] when it seems that, through the carelessness of her attendants, she was allowed to indulge in some improper food, for which she had expressed a wish. She caught a cold at the same time;[4] and although on the evening of the 23rd she appeared still so well that the king intended to leave Hampton Court on the following day, she became in the night alarmingly worse, and was in evident danger. In the morning the symptoms had somewhat improved, and there were hopes that the attack would pass off; but the unfortunate appearances soon returned; in a few more hours she was dead.[5]

A worse calamity could scarcely have befallen the king (unless the loss of the child had been added to that of the mother) than the death of Jane Seymour. Although she makes no figure in history, though she took no part in state questions, and we know little either of her sym-

---

[1] *State Papers*, vol. i. p. 570.
[2] Latimer to Cromwell: *State Paper Office*, vol. i. p. 571.
[3] Hall is made to say she died on the 14th. The mistake was due probably to the printer. He is unlikely himself to have made so large an error.
[4] *State Papers*, vol. viii. p. 1.
[5] Sir John Russell to Cromwell: *MS. State Paper Office*, second series, vol. xxxvi; *State Papers*, vol. i. p. 573.

pathies or opinions, her name is mentioned by both Protestant and Catholic with unreserved respect. She married the king under circumstances peculiarly agitating, without preparation, without attachment, either on her part or on his, but under the pressure of a sudden and tragical necessity. Her uprightness of character and sweetness of disposition had earned her husband's esteem, and with his esteem an affection deeper than he had perhaps anticipated. At her side, at his own death, he desired that his body might be laid.

When he knew that she was gone, he held a single interview with the council, and then retired to the palace at Westminster, where 'he mourned and kept himself close a great while'[1]

In the country the rejoicings were turned to sorrow.[2] Owing to the preternatural excitement of the public imagination, groundless rumours instantly gained currency. It was said that, when the queen was in labour, a lady had told the king that either the child must die or the mother; that the king had answered, Save the child, and therefore 'the child was cut out of his mother's womb.'[3] Catherine's male children had all died in infancy. This child, it was soon believed, was dead also. Some said that the child, some that the king, some that both were dead. The Cæsarian birth passed for an established fact; while a prophecy was discovered, which said that 'He should be killed that never was born, and nature's hand or

---

[1] HALL, p. 825.

[2] Leland wrote an ode on the occasion, which is not without some beauty:—

> Spes erat ampla quidem numerosâ prole Joanna
> Henricum ut faceret regem facunda parentem.
> Sed Superis aliter visum est, cruciatus acerbus
> Distorsit vacuum lethali tormine ventrem.
> Frigora crediderim temere contracta fuisse
> In causâ, superat vis morbi; jamque sainte
> Desperatâ omni, nymphis hæc rettulit almis.
> Non mihi mors curæ est, perituram agnosco creavit
> Omnipotens—Moriar—terram tibi debeo terra:
> At pius Elysiis animus spatiabitur hortis.
> Deprecor hoc unum. Maturos filins annos
> Exigat, et tandem regno det jura paterno.
> Dixit et æternâ clandebat lumina nube.
> Nulla dies pressit graviori clade Britannum.
> *Genethliacon Edwardi Principis.*

[3] *Rolls House MS.* A 2, 30. I trace the report to within a month of Jane Seymour's death. Sanders therefore must be held acquitted of the charge of having invented it. The circumstances of the death itself are so clear as to leave no trace of uncertainty. How many of the interesting personal anecdotes of remarkable people, which have gained and which retain the public confidence, are better founded than this? Prudence, instructed by experience, enters a general caution against all anecdotes particularly striking.

man's had brought it to pass, or soon would bring it to pass.'[1]

These were the mere bubbles of credulity, blown by the general wind; but the interests which now depended upon the infant prince's life, caused to grave persons grave anxiety. He was but one — a single life — between the king's death and chaos, and the king was again a widower. The greater the importance of the child's preservation to one party, the greater the temptation to the other to destroy it; and the precautions with which the royal nursery was surrounded, betray most real alarm that an attempt might be ventured to make away with him.

Instructions to the grand chamberlain were drawn, by some one in high authority, with more than the solemnity of an act of parliament.

'Like as there is nothing in this world so noble, just, and perfect, but that there is something contrary, that evermore envieth it, and procureth the destruction of the same, insomuch as God Himself hath the Devil repugnant to Him, Christ hath his Antichrist and persecutor, and from the highest to the lowest after such proportion, so the Prince's Grace, for all his nobility and innocency (albeit he never offended any one), yet by all likelihood he lacketh not envy nor adversaries against his Grace, who, either for ambition of their own promotion, or otherwise to fulfil their malicious perverse mind, would, perchance, if they saw opportunity, which God forbid, procure to his Grace displeasure. And although his Majesty doubteth not, but like as God for the comfort of this whole realm hath given the said prince, so of his providence He will preserve and defend him; yet, nevertheless, heed and caution ought to be taken, to avoid the evil enterprises which might be devised against his Grace, or danger of his person.'

In pursuance of such caution, it was commanded that no person, of what rank soever, except the regular attendants in the nursery, should approach the cradle, without an order under the king's hand. The food supplied for the child's use was to be largely 'assayed.' His clothes were to be washed by his own servants, and no other hand might touch them. The material was to be submitted to all tests of poison. The chamberlain or vice-chamberlain must be present morning and evening, when the prince was washed and dressed; and nothing, of any kind, bought for the use of the nursery, might be intro-

---

[1] *Rolls House MS.* A 2, 30.

duced till it had been aired and perfumed. No person —not even the domestics of the palace—might have access to the prince's rooms, except those who were specially appointed to them; nor might any member of the household approach London during the unhealthy season, for fear of their catching and conveying infection. Finally, during the infancy, the officers in the establishment were obliged to dispense with the attendance of pages or boys of any kind, for fear of inconvenience from their thoughtlessness.[1]

Regulations so suspicious and minute, betray more than the exaggeration of ordinary anxiety. Fears were evidently entertained of something worse than natural infection; and we can hope only, for the credit of the Catholics, who expected to profit by the prince's death, that they were clear of the intentions which were certainly attributed to them.

Other steps were also taken, in which precaution was mixed with compliment. Should the king die within a few years, the natural protectors of the prince in his minority would be his mother's family. Sir Edward Seymour, her brother, was now created Earl of Hertford, to give him the necessary rank; and for additional security, peerages were bestowed upon three others of the council whose loyalty could be depended upon. Sir William Fitzwilliam, now lord high admiral, was created Earl of Southampton; Sir William Paulet became Lord St. John; and Sir John Russell as Lord Russell, commenced a line of nobles, whose services to England wind like a silver cord through later history.

But inasmuch as, if the danger to the prince was real, the chief cause of it lay in his being an only child, as the temptation to a crime would cease when, by other sons or daughters, of unquestioned legitimacy, the success of the attempt would produce no change, and as all other interests depending now on a single life would be additionally secured, so on the very day of the queen's death, as on the day which followed it, the Privy Council represented to the king the necessity of his undertaking a fresh marriage while the state of his health left a hope that he might be again a father. Henry, suffering deeply from his loss, desired at first to evade a duty in which he had little interest at any time, and which his present sorrow rendered merely distressing. He had consented, under an absolute necessity, on the discovery of the com-

[1] Instructions for the Household of Edward Prince of Wales: *Rolls House MS.*

plicated treasons of Anne. The obligation was now less considerable, and he hoped to be spared.

The council, however, continued to urge what his own judgment united to recommend. He saw that it must be so; and he resigned himself. 'Although his Highness is not disposed to marry again,' wrote Cromwell, in the despatch which communicated to the ambassador in France the death of Queen Jane, 'yet his tender zeal to his subjects hath' already overcome his Grace's said disposition, and framed his mind both to be indifferent to the thing, and to the election of any person, from any part, that with deliberation shall be thought meet for him.'[1]

Persons who are acquainted with the true history of Henry's later marriages, while not surprised at their unfortunate consequences, yet smile at the interpretation which popular tradition has assigned to his conduct. Popular tradition is a less safe guide through difficult passages in history than the word of statesmen who were actors upon the stage, and were concerned personally in the conduct of the events which they describe.

[1] *State Papers*, vol. viii. p. 2.

CHAPTER XV.

THE EXETER CONSPIRACY.

Those who believe that human actions obey the laws of natural causation, might find their philosophy confirmed by the conduct of the great powers of Europe during the early years of the Reformation. With a regularity uniform as that on which we calculate in the application of mechanical forces, the same combinations were attended with identical effects; and given the relations between France and Spain, between Spain and Germany, between England and either of the three, the political situation of all Western Christendom could be estimated with as much certainty as the figure and dimensions of a triangle from the length of one of its sides and the inclination of two of its angles. When England was making advances towards the Lutherans, we are sure that France and Spain were in conjunction under the Papacy, and were menacing the Reformation. When such advances had been pushed forward into prominence, and there was a likelihood of a Protestant league, the Emperor was compelled to neutralize the danger by concessions to the German Diet, or by an affectation of a desire for a reconciliation with Henry, to which Henry was always ready to listen. Then Henry would look coldly on the Protestants, and the Protestants on him. Then Charles could afford again to lay the curb on Francis. Then Francis would again storm and threaten, till passion broke into war. War brought its usual consequences of mutual injury, disaster, and exhaustion; and then the Pope would interfere, and peace would follow, and the same round would repeat itself. Statesmen and kings made, as they imagined, their fine strokes of policy. A wisdom other than theirs condemned them to tread again and again the same ineffectual circle.

But while fact and necessity were thus inexorable, imagination remained uncontrolled; and efforts were made of all kinds, and on all sides, to find openings of escape. The Emperor had boasted, in 1528, that he would rid himself of the English difficulty by a revolution which should dethrone Henry. The experiment had been tried with no success hitherto, and with indifferent prospects for the future. Revolution failing, he believed that he might reconvert England to the Papacy; while both Henry and the Germans on their side had not ceased to hope that they might convert the Emperor to the Reformation. The perspective of Europe varied with the point of view of the various parties. The picture was arranged by prejudice, and coloured by inclination.

The overtures to England which Charles had commenced on the death of Catherine, had been checked by Henry's haughty answer; and Charles had replied by an indirect countenance, through his ambassador, to Pole,[1] and to Lord Darcy. But the motives which had led to these overtures remained to invite their renewal; the insurrection was for the present prostrate, and the Emperor therefore withdrew his first step, and disowned his compromised minister in London. In June, 1537, Diego de Mendoza arrived at the English court, with a commission to express in more emphatic terms the earnest wish of the court of Spain for the renewal of the old alliance.

The king had done enough for the protection of his dignity; prudence now recommended him to believe in Charles's sincerity. A solid understanding with Flanders was the best passport to the hearts of large portions of his subjects, whose interests were connected with the wool trade: he was himself ardently anxious to resume his place in the fraternity of European sovereigns. Mendoza was graciously received. Sir Thomas Wyatt was despatched into Spain with a corresponding mission; and Wyatt's instructions were couched in language which showed that, although the English government were under no delusion as to Charles's late proceedings, they were ready to close their eyes to objects which they did not wish to see. The proposals for a reconciliation which had been made by the late ambassadors had appeared so feeble, Wyatt was to say, as to seem rather a device of policy to prevent the King of England from allying him-

---

[1] Pole to the Bishop of Liège: *Epist.* vol. ii. p. 41.

self with France, than as intended in sincerity; M. de Mendoza, however, had removed all such unpleasant impressions; and although, if the Emperor would consider the past differences between the two courts impartially, he must feel that the fault rested with himself, yet the English government, on their side, were ready to set aside all painful recollections.[1] There were persons, indeed, who affirmed that the Emperor was still trifling, that Mendoza was playing a game, and that, in 'heart, deed, and words,' the Spanish court were 'doing all they could to his Majesty's dishonour.'[2] Nay, even individuals could be found who boasted themselves to have refused some honest offers because they were knit with 'vile and filthy conditions towards his Majesty.'[3] The king, however, set aside these rumours, as either without foundation, or as belonging to the past rather than the present. He required only, as a condition of renewed friendship, that if the Pope found the means of attacking England, Charles should bind himself to be no party to such an enterprise, but should oppose it, 'to the uttermost of his power.'[4] In return, the Emperor might perhaps require that the Lady Mary should 'be restored to her rank as princess.' Some difficulty no doubt continued, and must continue, on this point. But it was a difficulty rather in form than in substance. The king desired that his daughter might be trusted to his honour: she might expect much from his generosity, if he was not pressed to definite promises. Meanwhile, she herself had submitted without reserve; she had entreated pardon for her past disobedience, and accepted her position as illegitimate.[5] It was likely that she would retain her place in the line of succession. Should the king die without legitimate children, she would, in all probability, be his heir.

In confirmation of this language, Mary added a letter to the commission, in which, with her own hand, she assured the Emperor that she was satisfied, entreating him to 'repent,' as she had herself repented; and 'to take of her the tenour.'[6]

---

[1] Nott's Wyatt, p. 312. [2] Ibid. p. 319. [3] Ibid. [4] Ibid. p. 322.
[5] Mary's submission dates from the fall of Anne Boleyn. It was offered by her on the instant, in three successive letters; two of which are printed in the State Papers, a third is in MS. in the State Paper Office.
[6] 'And here Sir Thomas Wyatt shall deliver unto the Emperor the letter written unto him from the said Lady Mary, whereby it shall appear how she doth repent herself, and how she would that he should repent, and take of her the tenour. Whereof it shall like him to consider. It is not to be thought but it will acquit him therein, his Grace, nevertheless, being so good a lord and father to her as he is,

Thus instructed, Wyatt proceeded to Spain; and his reception was, on the whole, auspicious. On both sides, indeed, the hope of agreement, on points of religion disappeared with the first words upon the subject. Mendoza offered in London the Emperor's mediation with the Pope. He received for answer that he might spare his labour. 'The disposition of the King's Highness was immutably against the said Bishop.'[1] The Emperor in his opening interview spoke to Wyatt of the sickness of England, from which he trusted it would soon be recovered. Wyatt replied that England was conscious only of having cast off a chronic sickness which had lasted too long.

On the other hand, Charles, with equal resolution, declined a theological discussion, to which Henry had challenged him. 'If your Majesty,' wrote Wyatt, 'would hearken to the reconciling with the Bishop of Rome, he would be glad to travel in it. But if not, yet he will go through with you, and will continue ever in that mind, the same notwithstanding. And like as he is not lettred, so will he not charge your Majesty with the argument of the Bishop's state, but leave it alone to them that it toucheth.'[2]

On these terms, apparently satisfactory, the *entente cordiale* was restored between England and Spain. It was threatened by a cloud in November, when a truce[3] was concluded between Charles and Francis; but the light suspicion was dispelled by assurances that if the truce was followed by a peace, 'the King of England should be in the same as a principal contrahent;' 'that nothing should be therein concluded which might redound to his dishonour or miscontentment.'[4] The alliance promised stability: by skilful management it might be even more strongly cemented.

The English council were now busily engaged in selecting a successor for Jane Seymour. Mendoza, in the name of the Emperor, proposed the Infanta of Portugal. 'The offer was thankfully taken,'[5] but was for some cause

---

and undoubtedly will be.'—Instructions to Sir Thomas Wyatt: NOTT's *Wyatt*, p. 314.

[1] Cromwell to Wyatt: NOTT, p. 321.
[2] *State Papers*, vol. viii. p. 34.
[3] 'My lord: this shall be to advertise you that the Imperials and Frenchmen have taken a truce for ten months, which, as we think, be great news, and of great weight and moment. Howbeit, my trust is, the King's Highness knows what is the occasion of this sudden turn, or else it will trouble my brain to think of it.'—Sir William Fitzwilliam to Cromwell: *MS. State Paper Office*, second series, vol. xi.
[4] Henry VIII. to Wyatt: NOTT's *Wyatt*.
[5] Cromwell to Wyatt, November 29, 1537: NOTT's *Wyatt*.

unwelcome, and died in its first mention. Cromwell had thrown out feelers in the various European courts. Madame de Longueville was thought of,[1] if she was not already destined for another throne.[2] Hutton, the English agent in Flanders, recommended several ladies as more or less desirable—a daughter of the Lord of Brederode, the Countess of Egmont, Anne of Cleves (of the latter, however, adding, that she was said to be plain), and finally, and with especial emphasis, Christina of Denmark, the young relict of the Duke of Milan, and the niece of the Emperor. The duchess was tall, handsome, and though a widow, not more than sixteen.[3] The alliance would be honourable in itself: it would be a link reconnecting England with the Empire; and, more important still, Charles in his consent would condone before the world the affront of the divorce of Catherine. One obstacle only presented itself, which, with skilful management, might perhaps prove a fresh recommendation. In the eyes of all persons of the Roman communion the marriage with Catherine was of course considered valid, and the lady stood towards her aunt's husband within the degrees of affinity in which marriage was unlawful without a dispensation from the Pope. This certainly was a difficulty; but it was possible that Charles's anxiety for the connexion might induce him to break the knot, and break with the Papacy. On the Duchess of Milan, therefore, the choice of the English government rested; and in January Sir Thomas Wyatt was directed to suggest to the Emperor, as of his own motion, that his niece would be a fit wife for the king.[4] The hint was caught at with gracious eagerness. Mendoza instantly received instructions to make the proposal in form, and, as if this single union was insufficient, to desire at the same time that Henry would bestow the Lady Mary on Don Louis of Portugal. Henry acquiesced, and, seeing Charles so forward, added to his acquiescence the yet further suggestion that the Prince of Wales should be betrothed to the Emperor's daughter, and Elizabeth to one of the many sons of the King of the Romans.[5] Both princes appeared to be overflowing with cordiality. Charles repeated his promises, that when peace was concluded with France, the King of England should be a contracting party. The Queen Regent wrote to Cromwell, thanking him for his

---

[1] Better known as Mary of Guise, mother of Mary Queen of Scots.
[2] Commission of Peter Mewtas to Madame de Longueville: *State Papers*, vol. viii. p. 10.
[3] Hutton to Sir Thomas Wriothesley: Ibid. p. 9.
[4] Henry VIII. to Sir Thomas Wyatt: NOTT's *Wyatt*.
[5] Same to the same: NOTT's *Wyatt*.

zeal in forwarding the Emperor's interests with his master.[1] The Duchess of Milan sate for her picture to Holbein for Henry's cabinet,[2] and professed for herself that she was wholly at her uncle's disposal.[3] Commissioners had only to be appointed to draw the marriage treaty, and all might at once be arranged. The dispensation so far had not been mentioned. Mendoza, indeed, had again pressed Henry to accept the Emperor's good offices at the Vatican; but he had been met with a refusal so absolute as to forbid the further mooting of the question; and the negotiations for these several alliances being continued as amicably as before, the king flattered himself that the difficulty was waived, or else would be privately disposed of.

Either the Emperor's true intentions were better known in Paris than in London, or Francis was alarmed at the

[1] *State Papers*, vol. viii. p. 17.
[2] Hutton to Cromwell: ibid.
[3] A story passes current with popular historians, that the Duchess of Milan, when Henry proposed for her, replied that she had but one head; if she had two, one should be at his Majesty's service. The less active imagination of contemporaries was contented with reporting that she had said that the English ministers need not trouble themselves to make the marriage; 'they would lose their labours, for she minded not to fix her heart that way.' Sir Thomas Wriothesley, who was then resident at Brussels, thought it worth his while to ask her whether these words had really been used by her.

'M. Ambassador,' she replied, 'I thank God He hath given me a better stay of myself than to be of so light sort. I assure you, that neither those words that you have spoken, nor any like to them, have passed at any time from my mouth; and so I pray you report for me.'

Wriothesley took courage upon this answer, and asked what was her real inclination in the matter.

'At this she blushed exceedingly. 'As for mine inclination,' quoth she, 'what should I say? You know I am at the Emperor's commandment.' 'Yea, madam,' quoth Wriothesley; 'but this matter is of such nature, that there must be a concurrence between his commandment and your consent, or else you may percase repent it when it shall be too late. Your answer is such as may serve both for your modesty and for my satisfaction; and yet, if it were a little plainer, I could be the better contented.' With that she smiled, and again said, 'You know I am the Emperor's poor servant, and must follow his pleasure.' 'Marry,' quoth Wriothesley, 'then I may hope to be among the Englishmen that shall be first acquainted with my new mistress, for the Emperor hath instantly desired it. Oh, madam!' quoth he, 'how happy shall you be if it be your chance to be matched with my master. If God send you that hap, you shall be matched with the most gentle gentleman that liveth; his nature so benign and pleasant, that I think till this day no man hath heard many angry words pass his lips. As God shall help me, if he were no king, I think, an you saw him, you would say, that for his virtue, gentleness, wisdom, experience, goodliness of person, and all other qualities meet to be in a prince, he were worthy before all others to be made a king.' . . . . . She smiled, and Wriothesley thought would have laughed out, had not her gravity forbidden it. . . . She said she knew his Majesty was a good and noble prince. Her honest countenance, he added, and the few words that she wisely spake, together with that which he knew by her chamberers and servants, made him to think there could be no doubt of her.'—*State Papers*, vol. viii. p. 146.

rapid friendship, and desired to chill down its temperature. While gracious messages and compliments were passing between England and Spain and Flanders, the Bishop of Tarbes was sent over with an offer on the part of the French to make Henry sole mediator in the peace, and with a promise that, in the matter of the general council, and in all other things, Francis would be 'his good brother and most entire friend.' The Emperor, the bishop asserted on his own knowledge, was playing a part of mere duplicity. Whatever he said, or whatever others said for him, he had determined that England should not be comprehended in the treaty. The king would be left out - dropped out — in some way or other got rid of— when his friendship ceased to be of moment; and so he would find to his cost.

The warning might have been well meant, the offer might have been sincere, but the experience was too recent of the elastic character of French promises. Henry refused to believe that Charles was deceiving him; he replied with a declaration of his full confidence in the Emperor's honour, and declined with cold courtesy the counter-advances of his rival. Yet he was less satisfied than he desired to appear. He sent to Sir T. Wyatt an account of the Bishop of Tarbes's expressions, desiring him to acquaint the Emperor with their nature, and with the answer which he had returned; but hinting at the same time, that although the general language of the Flemish and Spanish courts was as warm as he could desire, yet so far it amounted only to words. The proposal to constitute him sole mediator in the peace was an advance upon the furthest positive step towards him which had been taken by Charles, and he requested a direct engagement in writing, both as to his comprehension in the intended treaty, and on the equally important subject alluded to by the bishop, of the approaching council.[1]

Meanwhile the marriages, if once they were completed, would be a security for good faith in other matters; and on this point no difficulties were interposed till the middle of the spring. The amount of dotes and dowries,

[1] 'Mr. Wyatt, now handle this matter in such earnest sort with the Emperor, as the king, who by your fair words hath conceived as certain to find assured friendship therein, be not deceived. The Frenchmen affirm so constantly and boldly that nothing spoken by the Emperor, either touching the principal contrahents or further alliance, hath any manner of good faith, but such fraud and deceit, that I assure you. on my faith, it would make any man to suspect his proceeding. Lahour, Mr. Wyatt, to cause the Emperor, if it be possible, to write.'—Cromwell to Wyatt: NOTT's *Wyatt*, p. 333.

with the securities for their payment, the conditions under which Mary was to succeed to the crown, and other legal details, were elaborately discussed. At length, when the substance seemed all to be determined, and the form only to remain, the first official conference was opened on the 5th of April, with the Spanish commissioners, who, as was supposed, had come to London for that single and special purpose. The card castle so carefully raised crumbled into instant ruins—the solid ground was unsubstantial air. The commissioners had no commission: they would agree to nothing, arrange nothing, promise nothing. 'I never heard so many gay words, and saw so little effect ensue of the same,' wrote Cromwell in the passion of his disappointment; 'I begin to perceive that there is scarce any good faith in this world.'

Henry's eyes were opening, but opening slowly and reluctantly. Though irritated for the moment, he listened readily to the excuses with which Charles was profusely ready; and if Charles had not been intentionally treacherous, he reaped the full advantage of the most elaborate deception. In the same month it was arranged between the courts of France and Spain that the truce should, if possible, become a peace. The place of mediator, which Henry had rejected at the hands of France, had been offered to and accepted by the Pope, and the consequences foretold by the Bishop of Tarbes were now obviously imminent. Paul had succeeded at last, it seemed, in his great object—the two Catholic powers were about to be united. The effect of this reconciliation, brought about by such means, would be followed in all likelihood by a renewal of the project for an attack on the Reformation, and on all its supporters. Nice was chosen for the scene of the great event of pacification, which was to take place in June. The two sovereigns were to be present in person; the Pope would meet them, and sanctify the reconciliation with his blessing.

The Emperor continued, notwithstanding the change of circumstances, to use the same language of friendship towards Henry, and professed to be as anxious as ever for the maintenance of his connexion with England. Wyatt himself partially, but not entirely, distrusted him, until his conduct no longer admitted any construction but the worst.

The affair at Nice was the central incident of the summer. Wyatt went thither in Charles's train. Paul came accompanied by Pole. Many English were present belonging to both parties: royal emissaries as spies—

passionate Catholic exiles, flushed with hope and triumph. We see them, indistinctly, winding into one another's confidence—'practising' to worm out secrets—treachery undermined by greater treachery; and, at last, expectations but half gratified, a victory left but half gained. The two princes refused to see each other. They communicated only through the Pope. In the end, terms of actual peace could not be agreed upon. The conferences closed with the signature of a general truce, to last for ten years. One marked consolation only the Pope obtained. Notwithstanding the many promises, Henry's name was not so much as mentioned by the Emperor. He was left out, as Wyatt expressed it, 'at the cart's tail.' Against him the Pope remained free to intrigue and the princes free to act, could Pole or his master prevail upon them. The secret history of the proceedings cannot be traced in this place, if indeed the materials exist which allow them to be traced satisfactorily. With infinite comfort, however, in the midst of the diplomatic trickeries, we discover one little island of genuine life on which to rest for a few moments—a group, distinctly visible, of English flesh and blood existences.

Henry, unable, even after the Nice meeting had been agreed upon, to relinquish his hopes of inducing other princes to imitate his policy towards Rome, was determined, notwithstanding avowals of reluctance on the part of Charles, that his arguments should have a hearing; and, as the instrument of persuasion, he had selected the facile and voluble Dr. Bonner. Charles was on his way to the congress when the appointment was resolved upon.

Bonner crossed France to meet him; but the Emperor, either distrustful of his ability to cope with so skilful a polemic, or too busy to be trifled with, declined resolutely to have anything to do with him. Bonner was thus thrown upon Wyatt's hospitality, and was received by him at Villa Franca, where, for convenience and economy, the English embassy had secured apartments remote from the heat and crowd in Nice itself. Sir John Mason, Mr. Blage, and other friends of the ambassadors, were of the party. The future Bishop of London, it seems, though accepted as their guest, was not admitted to their intimacy; and, being set aside in his own special functions, he determined to console himself in a solid and substantial manner for the slight which had been cast upon him. In an evil hour for himself, three years after, he tried to revenge himself on Wyatt's coldness by accusations of loose living, and other calumnies. Wyatt, after briefly disposing of the charges against his own actions, retorted with a sketch of Bonner's.

'Come, now, my Lord of London,' he said, 'what is my abominable and vicious living? Do ye know it, or have ye heard it? I grant I do not profess chastity—but yet I use not abomination. If ye know it, tell with whom and when. If ye heard it, who is your author? Have you seen me have any harlot in my house while you were in my company? Did you ever see a woman so much as dine or sup at my table? None but, for your pleasure, the woman that was in the galley - which, I assure you, may be well seen—for, before you came, neither she nor any other woman came above the mast; but because the gentlemen took pleasure to see you entertain her, therefore they made her dine and sup with you. And they liked well your looks — your carving to Madonna — your drinking to her—and your playing under the table. Ask Mason—ask Blage—ask Wolf that was my steward. They can tell how the gentlemen marked it and talked of it. It was play to them, the keeping your bottles, that no man might drink of them but yourself, and that the little fat priest was a jolly morsel for the signora. This was their talk. It was not my device. Ask others whether I do lie.'[1]

Such was Bonner. The fame, or infamy, which he earned for himself in later years condemns his minor vices to perpetual memory; or perhaps it is a relief to find that he was linked to mankind by participating in their more venial frailties.

Leaving Nice, with its sunny waters, and intrigues, and dissipations, we return to England.

Here the tide, which had been checked for awhile by the rebellion, was again in full flow. The abbeys within the compass of the act had fallen, or were rapidly falling. Among these the demolition was going actively forward. Among the larger houses fresh investigations were bringing secrets into light which would soon compel a larger measure of destruction. The restoration of discipline, which had been hoped for, was found impossible. Monks, who had been saturated with habits of self-indulgence, mutinied and became unmanageable when confined within the convent walls.[2] Abbots in the confidence of the govern-

---

[1] Wyatt's Oration to the Judges: NOTT's *Wyatt*.
[2] 'I have received three houses since I wrote last to your lordship, the which I think would not a little have moved your lordship, if ye had known the order of them: some sticking fast in windows, naked, going to drabs, so that the pillar was fain to be sawed, to have him out; some being plucked from under drabs' beds; some fighting, so

ment were accused as heretics. Catholic abbots were denounced as traitors. Countless letters lie among the State Papers, indicating in a thousand ways that the last hour of monasticism was approaching; that by no care of government, no efforts to put back the clock of time, could their sickly vitality be longer sustained. Everywhere, as if conscious that their days were numbered, the fraternities were preparing for evil days by disposing of their relics,[1] secreting or selling their plate and jewels, cutting down the timber on the estates, using in all directions their last opportunity of racking out their properties. Many, either from a hope of making terms for themselves, or from an honest sense that they were unfit to continue, declared voluntarily that they would burden the earth no longer, and voted their own dissolution. 'We do profoundly consider,' said the warden and friars of St. Francis in Stamford, 'that the perfection of a Christian living doth not consist in douce ceremonies, wearing of a grey coat, disguising ourselves after strange fashions, ducking and becking, girding ourselves with a girdle of knots, wherein we have been misled in times past; but the very true way to please God, and to live like Christian men without hypocrisy or feigned dissimulation, is sincerely declared unto us by our master Christ, his Evangelists and Apostles. Being minded, therefore, to follow the same, conforming ourselves unto the will and pleasure of our Supreme Head under God in earth, and not to follow henceforth superstitious traditions, we do, with mutual assent and consent, surrender and yield up all our said house, with all its lands and tenements, beseeching the king's good grace to dispose of us as shall best stand with his most gracious pleasure.'[2]

'We,' said the prior and convent of St. Andrews, 'called religious persons, taking on us the habit and outward vesture of our rule, only to the intent to lead our lives in idle quietness, and not in virtuous exercise, in a stately estimation, and not in obedient humility, have, under the shadow of the said rule, vainly, detestably, and ungodly devoured the yearly revenues of our possessions in continual ingurgitations and farcings of our bodies, and

---

that the knife hath stuck in the bones; with such other pretty business, of the which I have too much.'—Richard suffragan Bishop of Dover to Cromwell: *Suppression of the Monasteries*, p. 198.

[1] A finger of St. Andrew was pawned at Northampton for 40*l.*; 'which we intend not,' wrote a dry visitor, 'to redeem of the price, except we be commanded so to do.'—*Suppression of the Monasteries*, p. 172.

[2] Printed in FULLER's *Church History*. vol. iii. p. 394.

other supporters of our voluptuous and carnal appetites, to the manifest subversion of devotion and cleanness of living, and to the most notable slander of Christ's holy Evangile, withdrawing from the minds of his Grace's subjects the truth and comfort which they ought to have by the faith of Christ, and also the honour due to the glorious majesty of God Almighty, stirring them with persuasions, engines, and policy to dead images and counterfeit relics for our damnable lucre; which our horrible abominations and long-covered hypocrisy, we revolving daily, and pondering in our sorrowful hearts, constrained by the anguish of our consciences, with hearts most contrite and repentant, do lamentably crave his Highness' most gracious pardon'—they also submitting and surrendering their house.[1]

Six years had passed since four brave Suffolk peasants had burnt the rood at Dovercourt; and for their reward had received a gallows and a rope. The high powers of state were stepping now along the road which these men had pioneered, discovering, after all, that the road was the right road, and that the reward had been altogether an unjust one. The 'materials' of monastic religion were the real or counterfeit relics of real or counterfeit saints, and images of Christ or the Virgin, supposed to work miraculous cures upon pilgrims, and not supposed, but ascertained, to bring in a pleasant and abundant revenue to their happy possessors. A special investigation into the nature of these objects of popular devotion was now ordered, with results which more than any other exposure disenchanted the people with superstition, and converted their faith into an equally passionate iconoclasm. At Hales in Worcestershire was a phial of blood, as famous for its powers and properties as the blood of St. Januarius at Naples. The phial was opened by the visitors in the presence of an awe-struck multitude. No miracle punished the impiety. The mysterious substance was handled by profane fingers, and was found to be a mere innocent gum, and not blood at all, adequate to work no miracle either to assist its worshippers or avenge its violation.[2] Another rare treasure was preserved at Cardigan.

[1] Fuller's *Church History*, vol. iii. p. 398.
[2] 'According to your commission, we have viewed a certain supposed relic, called the blood of Hales, which was enclosed within a round beryll, garnished and bound on every side with silver, which we caused to be opened in the presence of a great multitude of people. And the said supposed relic we caused to be taken out of the said beryll, and have viewed the same, being within a little glass, and also tried the same according to our powers, by all means; and by force of the view and other trials, we judge the substance and matters of

The story of our Lady's taper there has a picturesque wildness, of which later ages may admire the legendary beauty, being relieved by three centuries of incredulity from the necessity of raising harsh alternatives of truth or falsehood. An image of the Virgin had been found, it was said, standing at the mouth of the Tivy river, with an infant Christ in her lap, and the taper in her hand burning. She was carried to Christ Church, in Cardigan, but 'would not tarry there.' She returned again and again to the spot where she was first found; and a chapel was at last built there to receive and shelter her. In this chapel she remained for nine years, the taper burning, yet not consuming, till some rash Welshman swore an oath by her, and broke it; and the taper at once went out, and never could be kindled again. The visitors had no leisure for sentiment. The image was torn from its shrine. The taper was found to be a piece of painted wood, and on experiment was proved submissive to a last conflagration.[1]

Kings are said to find the step a short one from deposition to the scaffold. The undeified images passed by a swift transition to the flames. The Lady of Worcester had been lately despoiled of her apparel. 'I trust,' wrote Latimer to the vicegerent, that 'your lordship will bestow our great sibyll to some good purpose—*ut pereat memoria cum sonitu*—she hath been the devil's instrument to bring many, I fear, to eternal fire. She herself, with her old sister of Walsingham, her younger sister of Ipswich, with their two other sisters of Doncaster and Penrice, would make a jolly muster in Smithfield. They would not be all day in burning.'[2] The hard advice was taken. The objects of the passionate devotion of centuries were rolled

---

the said supposed relic to be an unctuous gum, coloured, which, being in the glass, appeared to be a glistening red, resembling partly the colour of blood. And after, we did take out part of the said substance out of the glass, and then it was apparent yellow colour, like amber or base gold, and doth cleave as gum or bird-lime. The matter and feigned relic, with the glass containing the same, we have enclosed in red wax, and consigned it, with our seals.'—Hugh Bishop of Worcester, with the other Commissioners, to Cromwell: LATIMER's *Remains*, p. 407.

The Abbot of Hales subsequently applied for permission to destroy the case in which the blood had been.

'It doth stand yet in the place where it was, so that I am afraid lest it should minister occasion to any weak person looking thereupon to abuse his conscience therewith; and therefore I beseech for license that I may put it down every stick and stone, so that no manner of token or remembrance of that forged relict shall remain.'—Abbot of Hales to Cromwell: *MS. Tanner*, 105.

[1] Barlow to Cromwell: *Suppression of the Monasteries*, p. 183.
[2] Latimer to Cromwell: *Remains*, p. 395.

in carts to London as huge dishonoured lumber; and the eyes of the citizens were gratified with a more innocent immolation than those with which the church authorities had been in the habit of indulging them.

The fate of the rood of Boxley, again, was a famous incident of the time. At Boxley, in Kent, there stood an image, the eyes of which on fit occasions 'did stir like a lively thing.' The body bowed, the forehead frowned. It dropped its lower lip, as if to speak.[1] The people in this particular rood, beyond all others, saw the living presence of Christ, and offerings in superabundant measure had poured in upon the monks. It happened that a rationalistic commissioner, looking closely, discovered symptoms of motion at the back of the figure. Suspicion caused inquiry, and inquiry exposure. The mystery had a natural explanation in machinery. The abbot and the elder brethren took refuge in surprise, and knew nothing. But the fact was patent; and the unveiled fraud was of a kind which might be useful. 'When I had seen this strange object,' said the discoverer, 'and considering that the inhabitants of the county of Kent had in times past a great devotion to the same image, and did keep continual pilgrimage thither, by the advice of others that were here with me, I did convey the said image unto Maidstone on the market day; and in the chief of the market time did shew it openly unto all the people then being present, to see the false, crafty, and subtle handling thereof, to the dishonour of God and illusion of the said people; who, I dare say, if the late monastery were to be defaced again (the King's Grace not offended), they would either pluck it down to the ground, or else burn it; for they have the said matter in wondrous detestation and hatred.[2]

But the rood was not allowed to be forgotten after a single exhibition; the imposture was gross, and would furnish a wholesome comment on the suppression, if it was shown off in London. From Maidstone, therefore, it was taken to the palace at Whitehall, and performed before the court.[3] From the palace it was carried on to

[1] Geoffrey Chambers to Cromwell: *MS. State Paper Office*, second series.
[2] Ibid.
[3] 'Invisit aulam regis, regem ipsum novus hospes. Conglomerant ipsum risu aulico barones duces marchiones comites. Agit ille, minatur oculis, aversatur ore, distorquet nares; mittit deorsum caput, incurvat dorsum, annuit ant renuit. Rex ipse incertum gavisusne magis ob patefactam imposturam an magis doluerit ex animo tot seculis miseræ plebi fuisse impositum.'—Hooker to Bullinger: *Original Letters on the Reformation*.

its last judgment and execution at Paul's Cross. It was placed upon a stage opposite the pulpit, and passed through its postures, while the Bishop of Rochester lectured upon it in a sermon. When the crowd was worked into adequate indignation, the scaffold was made to give way, the image fell, and in a few moments was torn in pieces.

Thus in all parts of England superstition was attacked in its strongholds, and destroyed there. But the indignation which was the natural recoil from credulity would not be satisfied with the destruction of images. The idol was nothing. The guilt was not with the wood and stone, but in the fraud and folly which had practised with these brute instruments against the souls of men. In Scotland and the Netherlands the work of retribution was accomplished by a rising of the people themselves in armed revolution. In England the readiness of the government spared the need of a popular explosion; the monasteries were not sacked by mobs, or the priests murdered; but the same fierceness, the same hot spirit of anger was abroad, though confined within the restraints of the law. The law itself gave effect, in harsh and sanguinary penalties, to the rage which had been kindled.

The punishments under the Act of Supremacy were not wholly frightful. No governments can permit their subjects to avow an allegiance to an alien and hostile power; and the executions were occasioned, I have observed already, by the same necessity, and must be regarded with the same feelings, as the deaths of brave men in battle, who, in questions of life and death, take their side to kill others or be killed. A blind animosity now betrays itself in an act of needless cruelty, for the details of which no excuse can be pleaded by custom or precedent, which clouds the memory of the greatest of the Reformers, and can be endured only, when regarded at a distance, as an instance of the wide justice of Providence, which punishes wrong by wrong, and visits on single men the offences of thousands.

Forest, the late Prior of the Observants Convent at Greenwich, since the dissolution of his order in consequence of the affair of the Nun of Kent, had halted between a state of concealed disaffection and pretended conformity. In his office of confessor he was found to have instructed his penitents that, for himself, 'he had denied the Bishop of Rome in his outward, but not in his inward man;' and he had encouraged them, notwithstanding their oath, to persevere in their old allegiance.

He had thus laid himself open to prosecution for treason; and whatever penalty was due to an avowal of being the Pope's liegeman had been doubly earned by treachery. If he had been tried and had suffered like Sir Thomas More and the monks of the Charterhouse, his sentence would have ranked with theirs. The same causes which explained the executions of honourable men would have applied with greater force to that of one who had deepened his offences by duplicity. But the crown prosecutors, for some unknown reason, bestowed upon him a distinction in suffering.

When first arrested he was terrified: he acknowledged his offences, submitted, and was pardoned. But his conscience recovered its strength: he returned to his loyalty to the Papacy; he declared his belief that, in matters spiritual, the Pope was his proper sovereign, that the Bishop of Rochester was a martyr, as Thomas à Becket had been a martyr. Becket he held up as the pattern of all churchmen's imitation, courting for himself Becket's fortunes.[1] Like others, he attempted a distinction in the nature of allegiance. 'In matters secular his duty was to his prince.' But, on the threshold of the exception lay the difficulty which no Catholic could evade—what was the duty of a subject when a king was excommunicated, and declared to have forfeited his crown?

Forest, therefore, fell justly under the treason law. But, inasmuch as Catholic churchmen declared the denial of the Pope's supremacy to be heresy, so, for a few unfortunate months, English churchmen determined the denial of the king's supremacy to be heresy; Forest was to be proceeded against for an offence against spiritual truth as well as a crime against the law of the land; and Cranmer is found corresponding with Cromwell on the articles on which he was to be examined.[2] I do not

---

[1] 'He said that blessed man St. Thomas of Canterbury suffered death for the rights of the Church; for there was a great man-meaning thereby King Harry the Second—which, because St. Thomas of Canterbury would not grant him such things as he asked, contrary to the liberties of the Church, first banished him out of this realm; and at his return he was slain at his own church, for the right of Holy Church, as many holy fathers have suffered now of late: as that holy father the Bishop of Rochester: and he doubteth not but their souls be now in heaven.

'He saith and believeth that he ought to have a double obedience: first, to the King's Highness, by the law of God; and the second to the Bishop of Rome, by his rule and profession.

'He confesseth that he used and practised to induce men in confession to hold and stick to the old fashion of belief, that was used in the realm of long time past.'—*Rolls House MS.*

[2] 'The Bishop of Worcester and I will be to-morrow with your lordship, to know your pleasure concerning Friar Forest. For if we

know that the document which I am about to quote was composed for this special occasion. For the first, and happily the last time, the meaning of it was acted upon.

In an official paper of about this date, I find 'heresy' defined to be 'that which is against Scripture.' 'To say, therefore, that Peter and his successors be heads of the universal Church, and stand stubbornly in it, is heresy, because it is against Scripture (Ecclesiastes v.); where it is written, 'Insuper universæ terræ rex imperat servienti' —that is to say, the king commandeth the whole country as his subjects; and therefore it followeth that the Bishop of Rome, which is in Italy where the Emperor is king, is subject to the Emperor, and that the Emperor may command him; and if he should be head of the universal Church, then he should be head over the Emperor, and command the Emperor, and that is directly against the said text, Ecclesiastes v. Wherefore, to stand in it opiniatively is heresy.'[1] In the spirit, if not in the letter of this monstrous reasoning, Forest was indicted for heresy in a court where we would gladly believe that Cranmer did not sit as president. He was found guilty, and was delivered over, in the usual form, to the secular arm.

An accidental coincidence contributed to the dramatic effect of his execution. In a chapel at Llan Dderfel, in North Wales, there had stood a figure of an ancient Welsh saint, called Dderfel Gadern. The figure was a general favourite. The Welsh people 'came daily in pilgrimage to him, some with kyne, some with oxen and horses, and the rest with money, insomuch' (I quote a letter of Ellis Price, the Merionethshire visitor) 'that there were five or six hundred, to a man's estimation, that offered to the said image the fifth day of this month of April. The innocent people hath been sore allured and enticed to worship, insomuch that there is a common saying amongst them that, whosoever will offer anything to the image of Dderfel Gadern, he hath power to fetch him or them that so offer, out of hell.'[2] The visitor desired to know what he should do with Dderfel Gadern, and received orders to despatch the thing at once to London. The parishioners offered to subscribe forty pounds to preserve their pro-

should proceed against him according to the order of the law, there must be articles devised beforehand which must be ministered unto him; and therefore it will be very well done that one draw them against our meeting.'—Cranmer to Cromwell: CRANMER's *Works*, vol. i. p. 239.

[1] *Rolls House MS.* A 1, 7, fol. 213.
[2] Ellis Price to Cromwell: *MS. Cotton. Cleopatra,* E 4.

fitable possession,[1] but in vain—Cromwell was ruthless. The image was sent to the same destination with the rest of his kind; and, arriving opportunely, it was hewn into fuel to form the pile where the victim of the new heresy court was to suffer.

A day at the end of May was fixed for Forest's death. Latimer was selected to preach on the occasion; and a singular letter remains from him from which I try to gather that he accepted reluctantly the ungrateful service. 'Sir,' he addressed Cromwell, 'if it be your pleasure, as it is, that I shall play the fool after my customable manner when Forest shall suffer, I would wish that my stage stood near unto Forest, for I would endeavour myself so to content the people, that therewith I might also convert Forest, God so helping, or, rather, altogether working. Wherefore, I would that he shall hear what I shall say —*si forte.* If he would yet, with his heart, return to his abjuration, I would wish his pardon. Such is my foolishness.'[2] The gleam of pity, though so faint and feeble that it seemed a thing to be ashamed of, is welcome from that hard time. The preparations were made with a horrible completeness. It was the single supremacy case which fell to the conduct of ecclesiastics; and ecclesiastics of all professions, in all ages, have been fertile in ingenious cruelty. A gallows was erected over the stake, from which the wretched victim was to be suspended in a cradle of chains. When the machinery was complete, and the chips of the idol lay ready, he was brought out and placed upon a platform. The Lord Mayor, the Dukes of Norfolk and Suffolk, Lord Southampton, and Cromwell were present with a pardon, if at the last moment his courage should fail, and he would ask for it. The sermon began. It was of the usual kind—the passionate language of passionate conviction. When it was over, Latimer turned to Forest, and asked him whether he would live or die. 'I will die' was the gallant answer. 'Do your worst upon me. Seven years ago you durst not, for your life, have preached such words as these; and now, if an angel from heaven should come down and teach me any other doctrine than that which I learnt as a child, I would not believe him. Take me; cut me to pieces, joint from joint. Burn—hang—do what you will—I will be true henceforth to my faith.'[3]

---

[1] *MS. State Paper Office*, second series, vol. xxxiv.
[2] Latimer to Cromwell: *MS. State Paper Office*, second series, vol. xlix.; LATIMER's *Letters*, p. 391.
[3] STOW's *Chronicle*, p. 575.

It was enough. He was laid upon his iron bed, and slung off into the air, and the flame was kindled. In his mortal agony he clutched at the steps of the ladder, to sway himself out of the blaze; and the pitiless chronicler, who records the scene, could see only in this last weakness an evidence of guilt. 'So impatiently,' says Hall, 'he took his death as never any man that put his trust in God.'[1]

Still the torrent rolled onward. Monasteries and images were gone, and fancied relics, in endless numbers. There remained the peculiar treasures of the great abbeys and cathedrals—the mortal remains of the holy men in whose memories they had been founded, who by martyrs' deaths, or lives of superhuman loftiness, had earned the veneration of later ages. The bodies of the saints had been gathered into costly shrines, which a beautiful piety had decorated with choicest offerings. In an age which believed, without doubt or pretence, that the body of a holy man was incorporated into the body of Christ, that the seeming dust was pure as Christ's body was pure, and would form again the living home of the spirit which had gone away but for awhile, such dust was looked upon with awe and pious fear. Sacred influences were imagined to exhale from it. It was a divine thing, blessed and giving blessing. Alas! that the noblest feelings can pass so swiftly into their opposites, that reverend simplicity should become the parent of a miserable superstition! The natural instinct of veneration had ossified into idolatry, and saints' bones became charms and talismans. The saints themselves became invisible under the swathings of lies. The serpent of healing had become a Nehushtan—an accursed thing, and, with the system to which it belonged, was to pass away and come no more.

The sheriffs and magistrates of the various counties received circulars from the vicegerent, directing that 'whereas prayers were offered at the shrines which were due to God only, that the honour which belonged to the Creator was by a notable superstition given to the creature, and ignorant people, enticed by the clergy, had fallen thereby into great error and idolatry,' they were to repair severally to the cathedrals, churches, or chapels in which any such shrine might be. The relics, reliquaries, gold, silver, or jewels, which they contained, were to be taken out and sent to the king; and they were to see with their own eyes the shrine itself levelled to the ground,

[1] HALL, p. 875, followed by FOXE.

and the pavement cleared of it.[1] The order was fulfilled with or without reluctance. Throughout England, by the opening of the year 1539, there was nothing left to tell of the presence of the saints but the names which clung to the churches which they had built, or the shadowy memories which hung about their desecrated tombs.

Only in one instance was the demolition of a shrine marked by anything peculiar.

The aim from the beginning of the movement, both of the king and the parliament, had been to represent their measures not as new things, but as a reassertion of English independence, a revival of the historical policy of the English kings. From the defeat of Henry II., on the death of Becket, to the accession of the house of Lancaster, the Plantagenet princes had fought inch by inch for the recovery of the ground which had been lost. After sleeping a century and a half, the battle had recommenced; and the crown was determined to inaugurate its victories by the disgrace and destruction of the famous champion whose spirit still seemed to linger in the field. On the 18th of August Cranmer informed the vicegerent that he suspected that the blood of St. Thomas of Canterbury shown in the cathedral was an imposture, like the blood of Hales, 'a feigned thing, made of some red ochre, or such like matter.'[2] He desired that there might be an investigation, and mentioned Dr. Legh and his own chaplain as persons fitted for the conduct of it. The request appears to have been granted, and the suspicion about the blood to have been confirmed.[3] The opportunity was taken to settle accounts in full with the hero of the English Church. On the 30th of September the shrine and the relics were shown, perhaps for the last time, to Madame de Montreuil and a party of French ladies.[4] In

---

[1] *MS. State Paper Office*, unarranged bundle. The command was obeyed so completely, that only a single shrine now remains in England; and the preservation of this was not owing to the forbearance of the government. The shrine of Edward the Confessor, which stands in Westminster Abbey, was destroyed with the rest. But the stones were not taken away. The supposed remains of St. Edward were in some way preserved; and the shrine was reconstructed, and the dust replaced, by Abbot Feckenham, in the first year of Queen Mary.—Oration of Abbot Feckenham in the Parliament House: *MS. Rawlinson*, Bodleian Library.

[2] Cranmer to Cromwell: *State Papers*, vol. i.

[3] 'The abuses of Canterbury' are placed by the side of those of Boxley in one of the official statements of the times.—Sir T. Wriothesley to Henry VIII. Nov. 20, 1538: *State Papers*, vol. viii.

[4] Madame de Montreuil, though a Frenchwoman and a good Catholic, had caught the infection of the prevailing unbelief in saints and saintly relics. 'I showed her St. Thomas's shrine,' writes an attendant, 'and all such other things worthy of sight, of the which she

the following month the bones of the martyr who for centuries had been venerated throughout Europe, which peers and princes had crossed the seas to look upon, which tens of thousands of pilgrims year after year for all those ages had crowded to reverence, were torn from their hallowed resting-place, and burnt to powder, and scattered to the winds. The golden plating of the shrine, the emeralds and rubies, the votive offerings of the whole Christian world, were packed in chests, and despatched to the treasury. The chiselled stone was splintered with hammers. The impressions worn upon the pavement by the millions of knees[1] which had bent in adoration there, alone remained to tell of the glory which had been. Simultaneously with the destruction of his remains, Becket's name was erased out of the service-books, the innumerable church windows in which his history was painted were broken, the day which commemorated his martyrdom was forbidden to be observed; and in explanation of so exceptional a vehemence an official narrative was published by the government of the circumstances of his end, in which he was described as a traitor to the state, who had perished in a scuffle provoked by his own violence.[2]

The executions of More and Fisher had convulsed Europe; but the second shock was felt as much more

was not little marvelled of the great riches thereof, saying it to be innumerable, and that if she had not seen it all the men in the world could never have made her to believe it. Thus overlooking and viewing more than an hour as well the shrine as St. Thomas's head, being at both set cushions to kneel, the prior, opening St. Thomas's head, said to her three times, this is St Thomas's head, and offered her to kiss it, but she neither kneeled nor would kiss it, but (stood), still viewing the riches thereof.'—Penison to Cromwell: *State Papers*, vol. i. p. 583.

[1] These marks are still distinctly visible.

[2] BURNET's *Collectanea*, p. 494. A story was current on the Continent, and so far believed as to be alluded to in the great bull of Paul the Third, that an apparitor was sent to Canterbury to serve a citation at Becket's tomb, summoning 'the late archbishop' to appear and answer to a charge of high treason. Thirty days were allowed him. When these were expired a proctor was charged with his defence. He was tried and condemned—his property, consisting of the offerings at the shrine, was declared forfeited—and he himself was sentenced to be exhumed and burnt. In the fact itself there is nothing absolutely improbable, for the form said to have been observed was one which was usual in the Church, when dead men, as sometimes happened, were prosecuted for heresy; and if I express my belief that the story is without foundation, I do so with diffidence, because negative evidence is generally of no value in the face of respectable positive assertion. All contemporary English authorities, however, are totally silent on a subject which it is hard to believe that they would not at least have mentioned. We hear generally of the destruction of the shrine, but no word of the citation and trial. A long and close correspondence between Cromwell and the Prior of Canterbury covers the period at which the process took place, if it

deeply than the first as the glory of the saint is above the fame of the highest of living men. The impious tyrant, it now seemed, would transfer his warfare even into heaven, and dethrone the gods. The tomb of Becket was the property of Christendom rather than of England. There was scarcely a princely or a noble family on the Continent some member of which had not at one time or other gone thither on pilgrimage, whose wealth had not contributed something to the treasure which was now seized for the royal coffers. A second act had opened in the drama—a crisis fruitful in great events at home and abroad.

The first immediate effect was on the treaty for the king's marriage. Notwithstanding the trifling of the commissioners in April—notwithstanding the pacification of Nice, and the omission of the king's name among the contracting parties — Charles succeeded in persuading Wyatt that he was as anxious as ever for the completion of the entire group of the proposed connexions; and Henry, on his part, was complacently credulous. The country was impatient to see him provided with a wife who might be the mother of a Duke of York. Day after day the council remonstrated with him on the loss of precious time;[1] and however desirable in itself the im-

took place at all, and not a letter contains anything which could be construed into an allusion to it.—Letters of the Prior of Canterbury to Cromwell: *MS. State Paper Office*, second series.

So suspicious a silence justifies a close scrutiny of the authorities on the other side. There exist two documents printed in WILKINS's *Concilia*, vol. iii. p. 835, and taken from POLLINI's *History of the English Reformation*, which profess to be the actual citation and actual sentence issued on the occasion. If these are genuine, they decide the question; but, unfortunately for their authenticity, the dates of the documents are, respectively, April and May, 1538, and in both of them Henry is styled, among his official titles, Rex Hiberniæ. Now Henry did not assume the title of Rex Hiberniæ till two years later. Dominus Hiberniæ, or Lord of Ireland, is his invariable designation in every authentic document of the year to which these are said to belong. This itself is conclusively discrediting. If further evidence is required, it may be found in the word 'Londini,' or London, as the date of both citation and sentence. Official papers were never dated from London, but from Westminster, St. James's, Whitehall; or if in London, then from the particular place in London, as the Tower. Both mistakes would have been avoided by an Englishman, but are exceedingly natural in a foreign inventor.

[1] 'We be daily instructed by our nobles and council to use short expedition in the determination of our marriage, for to get more increase of issue, to the assurance of our succession; and upon their oft admonition of age coming fast on, and (seeing) that the time flyeth and slippeth marvellously away, we be minded no longer to lose time as we have done, which is of all losses the most irrecuperable.'—Henry VIII. to Sir T. Wriothesley: *State Papers*, vol. viii. p. 116.

'Unless his Highness bore a notable affection to the Emperor, and had a special remembrance of their antient amity, his Majesty could

perial alliance appeared, his subjects were more anxious that he should be rapidly married somewhere, than that even for such an object there should be longer delay. But Charles continued to give fair words; and the king, although warned, as he avowed, on all sides, to put no faith in them, refused to believe that Charles would cloud his reputation with so sustained duplicity; and in August he sent Sir Thomas Wriothesley to Flanders, to obtain, if possible, some concluding answer.

The Regent, in receiving Wriothesley, assured him that his master's confidence was well placed—that 'the Emperor was a prince of honour,' and never meant 'to proceed with any practice of dissimulation.' Whatever others might choose to say, both she and her brother remained in one mind and purpose, and desired nothing better than to see the Duchess Christina Queen of England.[1] Her language remained similarly cordial till the beginning of October; and, as the least violent hypothesis is generally the safest, it may be believed that till this time the Emperor had really entertained, or had not as yet relinquished, the intention of bestowing his niece as he professed to wish. But from the end of the autumn the tide turned, and soon flowed visibly the other way. There was no abrupt conclusion—the preliminaries were wearily argued day after day. The English minister was still treated with courtesy; but his receptions had lost their warmth, and with court and people his favour chilled with the changing season. He was taunted with the English apostasy from the Church. 'It is said that religion is extinct among us,' he wrote in November—'that we have no masses—that the saints are burned—and all that was taken for holy clearly subverted.'[2] Each day the prospect became visibly darker: from cordiality there was a change to politeness—from politeness to distance—from distance to something like a menace of hostility. The alteration can without difficulty be interpreted.

The intentions of the Papal court had been made known by Michael Throgmorton, in his letter to Cromwell. The Pope's movements were, perhaps, quickened when the insult to the martyr's bones became known to him. The opportunity was in every way favourable. France and Spain were at peace; the Catholic world was

never have endured to have been kept thus long in balance, his years, and the daily suits of his nobles and council well pondered.'— Wriothesley to Cromwell: Ibid. p. 160.

[1] See the Wriothesley Correspondence: *State Papers*, vol viii.
[2] Wriothesley to Henry VIII. November 20, 1538: Ibid.

exasperated by the outrage at Canterbury. The hour was come—he rose upon his throne, and launched with all his might his long-forged thunderbolt. Clement's censure had been mild sheet lightning, flickering harmlessly in the distance: Paul's was the forked flash, intended to blight and kill. Reginald Pole, his faithful adherent, had by this time re-written his book: he had enriched it with calumnies, either freshly learned, or made credible in his new access of frenzy. It was now printed, and sown broadcast over Christendom. The Pope appended a postscript to his Bull of Deposition, explaining the delay in the issue: not, as he had explained that delay to Henry himself, by pretending that he had executed no more than a form which had never been intended for use; but professing to have withheld a just and necessary punishment at the intercession of the European sovereigns. But his mercy had been despised, his long-suffering had been abused, and the monstrous king had added crime to crime, killing living priests and profaning the sepulchres of the dead. In his contempt for religion he had cited the sainted Thomas of Canterbury to be tried as a traitor; he had passed an impious sentence upon him as contumacious. The blessed bones, through which Almighty God had worked innumerable miracles, he had torn from their shrine of gold, and burnt them sacrilegiously to ashes. He had seized the treasures consecrated to Heaven; he had wasted and robbed the houses of religion; and, as he had transformed himself into a wild beast, so to the beasts of the field he had given honour beyond human beings. He had expelled the monks from their houses, and turned his cattle among the vacant ruins. These things he had done, and his crimes could be endured no longer. As a putrid member he was cut off from the Church.[1]

The book and the excommunication being thus completed and issued, Pole was once more despatched to rouse the Emperor to invasion, having again laid a train to explode, as he hoped successfully, when the Spanish troops should land.

The Pope's intentions must have been made known to Charles before they were put in force, and interpret the change of treatment experienced by Wriothesley. Whether, as a sovereign prince, he would or would not consent to give the active support which was to be demanded of him, the Emperor, perhaps, had not deter-

[1] Bull of Paul III. against Henry VIII: printed in BURNET's *Collectanea*.

mined even in his own mind; but as least he would not choose the opportunity to draw closer his connexion with the object of the Church's censures.

On the 21st of January Wriothesley wrote to Cromwell that he had no more hopes of the Duchess of Milan, and that the king must look elsewhere. 'If this marriage may not be had,' he said, 'I pray his Grace may fix his noble stomach in some such other place as may be to his quiet.' 'And then,' he added, chafed with the slight which had been passed upon his sovereign, 'I fear not to see the day, if God give me life but for a small season, that as his Majesty is father to all Christian kings in time of reign and excellency of wisdom, so his Highness shall have his neighbours in that stay that they shall be glad to do him honour and to yield unto him his own.'[1]

For the present, however, the feeling of the Netherlanders was of mere hostility. The ruin of England was talked of as certain and instant. James of Scotland and Francis were 'to do great things,' and 'the Emperor, it might be, would assist them.' The ambassador tossed aside their presages. 'These men,' said one of his despatches, 'publicly tell me how the Bishop of Rome hath now given a new sentence against the King's Majesty. I discourse to them how much every of the princes of Europe is bound to his Majesty; what every of them hath to do for himself; how little need we have to care for them if they would all break their faith and for kindness show ingratitude: and I show myself, besides, of no less hope than to see his Majesty, as God's minister, correct that tyrant—that usurper of Rome—even within Rome's gates, to the glory of God, and the greatest benefit that ever came to Christendom.'[2]

But, though Wriothesley carried himself proudly, his position was embarrassing. The regent grew daily more distant, her ministers more threatening. The Spaniards resident in England suddenly were observed to be hastening away, carrying their properties with them. At length, on the 21st of February, a proclamation was sent out laying all English ships in Flanders under arrest. Mendoza was recalled from London, and the common conversation on the Bourse at Antwerp was that the united force of France and the Empire would be thrown immediately on the English coasts.[3]

For a closer insight into the Emperor's conduct, I

[1] Wriothesley Correspondence: *State Papers*, vol. viii.
[2] Wriothesley to Cromwell: Ibid.
[3] Stephen Vaughan to Cromwell, Feb. 21, 1539: Ibid.

must again go back over the ground. The history at this point is woven of many fibres.

Pole's book was published in November or December. His expedition into Spain followed immediately after; and, feeling some little misgiving as to the Emperor's approbation of his conduct, he thought it prudent to prepare his appearance by a general defence of his position. A rebellious subject engaged in levying war against his sovereign might interest the Papacy; but the example might easily appear more questionable in the eyes of secular princes. His book, he said in an apology addressed to Charles, had been written originally in obedience to orders from England. He had published it when the Pope instructed him to vindicate the severity of the censures. His present duty was to expose in the European courts the iniquity of the King of England—to show that, as an adversary of the Church, he was infinitely more formidable than the Sultan—and that the arms of the Emperor, if he wished well to the interests of religion, should be specially directed against the chief offender.[1] When the king's crimes were understood in detail the Christian sovereigns would see in their enormity that such a monster must be allowed to vex the earth no longer. He recapitulated the heads of his book, and Henry's history as he there had treated it. In an invective against Cromwell he bathed his name in curses;[2] while the king he compared to Nero, and found the Roman tyrant innocent in the contrast. Finally, he closed his address with a peroration, in which he quoted and applied the prophecy of Daniel on the man of sin. Henry of England was the king of fierce countenance and understanding dark sentences, who was to stand up in the latter time and set himself above all that was called God; whose power should be mighty, but not by his own power; who should destroy wonderfully, and prosper, and practise, and destroy the mighty and the holy people; who should rise

---

[1] 'Of the evils which now menace Christendom those are held most grievous which are threatened by the Sultan. He is thought most powerful to hurt: he must first be met in arms. My words will bear little weight in this matter. I shall be thought to speak in my own quarrel against my personal enemy. But, as God shall judge my heart, I say that, if we look for victory in the East, we must assist first our fellow Christians, whom the adversary afflicts at home. This victory only will ensure the other.'—*Apol. ad Car. Quint.*

[2] He speaks of Cromwell as 'a certain man,' a 'devil's ambassador,' 'the devil in the human form.' He doubts whether he will defile his pages with his name. As great highwaymen, however, murderers, parricides, and others, are named in history for everlasting ignominy, as even the devils are named in Holy Scripture, so he will name Cromwell.—Ibid.

up against the Prince of princes, but in the end be broken without hand.[1]

Pole's business was to supply the eloquent persuasions. A despatch from Paul furnished the more worldly particulars which the Emperor would desire to know before engaging in an enterprise which had been discussed so often, and which did not appear more easy on closer inspection. James the Fifth, the Pope said, would be ready to assist, with his excellent minister, David Beton. If only the war with the Turks were suspended, the other difficulties might be readily overcome. The Turks could be defeated only at a great expense, and a victory over them would do little for religion. The heart of all the mischief in the world lay in England, in the person of the king. Charles must strike there, and minor evils would afterwards heal of themselves.[2]

The English government had agents in Rome whose business was to overhear conversations, though held in the most secret closet in the Vatican; to bribe secretaries to make copies of private despatches; to practice (such was the word) for intelligence by fair means, or else by foul: and they did their work. Pole's movements and Pole's intentions were known in London as soon as they were known at Toledo; and simultaneously another fragment of information was forwarded from Italy, as important in itself, as, doubtless, the manner in which it was procured was questionable. Access was obtained, either by bribery or other form of treachery, to a letter from some person high in Paul's confidence at Rome, to the Cardinal of Seville; opportunity, perhaps, did not permit the completion of a transcript, but an analysis, with considerable extracts, found its way into the hands of Cromwell. The letter stated that an Irish nobleman, evidently the Earl of Desmond, had sent a confidential agent to the Pope to explain at length the weakness of the English authority in Ireland, to describe the impunity with which the earl had resisted and despised it, and to state further how the same illustrious personage, for the discharge of his soul, was now ready to transfer his allegiance to his Holiness. 'England,' so Desmond had declared, was in confusion, utter and hopeless. 'Fathers were against sons, husbands against wives, the commonalty risen one against

---

[1] *Apol. ad Car. Quint.*
[2] Instructions to Reginald Pole: *Epist.* vol. ii. p. 279, &c. Pole's admiring biographer ventures to say that 'he was declared a traitor for causes which do not seem to come within the article of treason.'—PHILIPS's *Life of Reginald Pole*, p. 277.

another;' .... and 'perceiving their divisions, he had been with a great part of Ireland to know their wills and minds, and also with the bishops and the religious houses; and not only the great men of power, but also the people, all with one voice would be ready to give aid against the King of England.' He had added a demand which bore some witness to the energy with which Henry had strengthened the government at Dublin since the Geraldine rebellion. 'Thirty thousand Spaniards,' the earl said, 'with all things necessary for them, with artillery, powder, ships, galleys, and pinnaces, would be required to insure the conquest.' If these could be landed, Desmond would guarantee success. Ireland should be reannexed to the Holy See; and he would himself undertake the government as viceroy, paying a revenue to Paul of one hundred thousand ducats. The expedition would be costly, but the expenses would fall neither on his Holiness nor on the Emperor. Desmond, with armed privateers, would seize and deliver into the hands of the Pope the persons of a sufficient number of the heretical English, whose ransoms would defray the necessary outlay; and an insurrection in behalf of the Holy See might be anticipated with certainty in England itself.

This being the substance of the Irish message, 'His Holiness, perceiving the good mind of these gentlemen in God's behalf, had determined to desire amongst all Christian kings to have aid in this matter for charity, to aid the good Christian people of Ireland.'

'His Holiness says,' concluded the letter, 'that if at the general council amongst the kings he cannot have aid to obtain this holy work, then he will desire them that they will agree and consent that certain pardons may be received in their realms, and that they may give liberty that the bishops may constrain the commonalty to receive the said pardons, and it shall be declared that all such money shall be used for the conquest of Barbary; and that his Holiness will take upon him the said conquest of Barbary with the accord of the Emperor. If the above will not suffice, then his Holiness will give order and desire for the maintenance and defence of the holy faith, to all bishops, archbishops, cardinals, legates, deans, canons, priests, and curates, and also to all sorts of monasteries, to help with certain money which may be needful, to subdue and proceed in this good deed. And he will desire the Most Christian King of France, and also the King of Scots, to have amongst them aid in his behalf, inasmuch as they and their kingdoms is nigh to the said island of Ireland. And immediately that the fleet shall be together to go for Barbary, then shall the most part go for Ireland unto the gentleman that hath written to his Holiness to uphold the Holy See, that his Holiness may sustain Holy Mother Church from that tyrant of England, the which goes to confound the Holy See of St. Peter and the governors and ministers of it. And God give unto all good Christians strength to confound the antichrist of England and the dog Luther his brother.'[1]

Never, perhaps, since the beginning of time had such a provision of 'ways and means' been devised for a military enterprise as was found in the financial suggestions of this Papal Hibernian war scheme. Nevertheless, when so many Spanish ships annually haunted the harbours of Munster, a few thousand men might be thrown on shore there without particular difficulty. The exchequer was in no condition to endure a repetition of the insurrection of Lord Fitzgerald, which had cost forty thousand pounds; and, with the encouragement of an auxiliary force, another similar rising, with its accompanying massacres, might be easily anticipated. Though invasion might be confidently faced in England, it was within the limits of possibility that Ireland might be permanently lost.

With such materials in their hands, more skilful antagonists than Paul III. or Cardinal Pole might have accomplished something considerable; but Paul's practical ability may be measured by his war budget; and the vanity of the English traitor would have ruined the most skilful combinations. Incapable of any higher intellectual effort than declamatory exercises, he had matched himself against the keenest and coolest statesman in Europe. He had run a mine, as he believed, under Henry's throne, to blow it to the moon; and at the expected moment of his triumph his shallow schemes were blasted to atoms, and if not himself, yet his nearest kindred and dearest friends were buried in the ruins.

Lord Darcy had said that fifteen lords and great men had been banded together to put down the Reformation. Two peers had died on the scaffold. Lord Abergavenny, the head of the Nevilles, was dead also; he was, perhaps, a third. The knights and commoners who had suffered after the Pilgrimage of Grace had not covered the whole remaining number. The names revealed by the Nun of

---

[1] News which was sent from Rome unto the Cardinal Bishop of Seville: *Rolls House MS.*

Kent, though unknown to the world, had not been forgotten by the government. Cromwell knew where to watch, and how.

The country was still heaving uneasily from the after-roll of the insurrection, and Pole's expectations of a third commotion, it is likely, were as well known to the Privy Council as they were known to the Pope. Symptoms had appeared in the western counties strikingly resembling those which had preceded the Yorkshire rising, when Cromwell's innocent order was issued for the keeping of parish registers.[1] Rumours were continually flying that the Emperor would come and overthrow all things; and the busy haste with which the coast was being fortified seemed to sanction the expectation. The Pope had made James of Scotland *Defensor fidei*. Fleets were whispered to be on the seas. Men would wake suddenly and find the Spaniards arrived; and 'harness would again be occupied.'[2] Superstition on one side, and iconoclasm on the other, had dethroned reason, and raised imagination to its place; and no sagacity at such times could anticipate for an hour the form of the future.[3]

---

[1] 'There is much secret communication among the king's subjects, and many of them in the shires of Cornwall and Devonshire be in great fear and mistrust what the King's Highness and his council should mean, to give in commandment to the parsons and vicars of every parish, that they should make a book wherein is to be specified the names of as many as be wedded and buried and christened. Their mistrust is, that some charges more than hath been in times past shall grow to them by this occasion of registering.'—Sir Piers Edgecombe to Cromwell: *State Papers*, vol. i. p. 612.

[2] 'George Lascelles shewed me that a priest, which late was one of the friars at Bristol, informed him that harness would yet be occupied, for he did know more than the king's council. For at the last council whereat the Emperor, the French king, and the Bishop of Rome met, they made the King of Scots, by their counsel, *Defensor fidei*, and that the Emperor raised a great army, saying it was to invade the Great Turk, which the said Emperor meaned by our sovereign lord.'—John Babington to Cromwell: *MS. State Paper Office*, second series, vol. iii.

[3] I attach specimens from time to time of the 'informations' of which the Record Office contains so many. They serve to keep the temper of the country before the mind. The king had lately fallen from his horse and broken one of his ribs. A farmer of Walden was accused of having wished that he had broken his neck, and 'had said further that he had a bow and two sheaves of arrows, and he would shoot them all before the king's laws should go forward.' An old woman at Aylesham, leaning over a shop window, was heard muttering a chant, that 'there would be no good world till it fell together by the ears, for with clubs and clouted shoon should the deed be done.' Sir Thomas Arundel wrote from Cornwall, that 'a very aged man' had been brought before him with the reputation of a prophet, who had said that 'the priests should rise against the king, and make a field; and the priests should rule the realm three days and three nights, and then the white falcon should come out of the north-west, and kill almost all the priests, and they that should escape should be fain to hide their crowns with the filth of beasts, because they

Pole's treason had naturally drawn suspicion on his family. The fact of his correspondence with them from Liège could hardly have been a secret from Cromwell's spies, if the contents of his letters were undiscovered; and the same jealousy extended also, and not without cause, to the Marquis of Exeter. Lord Exeter, as the grandson of Edward IV., stood next to the Tudor family in the line of succession. The Courtenays were petty sovereigns in Devonshire and Cornwall; and the marquis, though with no special intellectual powers, was regarded as a possible competitor for the crown by a large and increasing party. Lady Exeter we have already seen as a visitor at the shrine of the oracle of Canterbury; and both she and her husband were on terms of the closest intimacy with the Poles. The Poles and the Nevilles, again, were drawing as closely together as mutual intermarriages would allow. Lady Salisbury, I have said, was regarded as the representative at once of the pure Plantagenet blood and of Warwick the King Maker.[1] Lord Montague had married a daughter of Lord Abergavenny; and as any party in the state in opposition to the government was a formidable danger, so a union between Lord Exeter, Lady Salisbury, and the Nevilles was, on all grounds, religious, political, and historical, the most dangerous which could be formed. It was the knowledge of the influence of his family which gave importance to Reginald Pole. It was this which sharpened the eyes of the government to watch for the first buddings of treason among his connexions.

Exeter's conduct had been for some time unsatisfactory. He had withdrawn for an unknown cause from his share in the command of the royal army on the Pilgrimage of Grace. He had gone down into Devonshire, where his duty would have been to raise the musters of the county; but, instead of it, he had courted popularity by interrupt-

would not be taken for priests.' 'A groom of Sir William Paget's was dressing his master's horse one night: In the stable in the White Horse in Cambridge,' when the ostler came in and began 'to enter into communication with him.' 'The ostler said there is no Pope, but a Bishop of Rome. And the groom said he knew well there was a Pope, and the ostler, moreover, and whosoever held of his part, were strong heretics. Then the ostler answered that the King's Grace held of his part; and the groom said that he was one heretic, and the king was another; and said, moreover, that this business had never been if the king had not married Anne Boleyn. And therewith they multiplied words, and waxed so hot, that the one called the other knave, and so fell together by the ears, and the groom broke the ostler's head with a faggot stick.'—Miscellaneous Depositions: *MSS. State Paper Office*, and *Rolls House*.

[1] Her blood was thought even purer than Lord Exeter's. A cloud of doubtful illegitimacy darkened all the children of Edward IV.

ing the levy of the subsidy.¹ The judges on circuit at the same time complained of the coercion and undue influence which he exercised in the administration of justice, and of the dread with which his power was regarded by juries. No indictment could take effect against the adherents of the Marquis of Exeter; no dependent of the Courtenays was ever cast in a cause.²

From this and other causes altercations had arisen between Exeter and Cromwell at the council-board. High words had passed on Lord Darcy's arraignment. The marquis had been compelled to sit as high steward; and Lord Delaware, in an account of the trial, stated that when the verdict was given of guilty, a promise had been exacted from Cromwell to save Darcy's life, and even to save his property from confiscation.³ Cromwell may have done his best, and Darcy's death have been the act of the king. With Henry guilt was ever in proportion to rank; he was never known to pardon a convicted traitor of noble blood. But the responsibility was cast by the peers on the Privy Seal. Once it was even reported that Exeter drew his dagger on the plebeian adventurer, who owed his life to a steel corslet beneath his dress;⁴ and that Cromwell on that occasion ordered the marquis to the Tower. If the story was true, more prudent counsels prevailed, or possibly there would have been an attempt at rescue in the streets.⁵ The relations between them were evidently approaching a point when one or the other would be crushed. Exeter was boldly confident. When Lord Montague's name was first mentioned with suspicion at the council-board (although, as was discovered afterwards, the marquis knew better than any other person the nature of schemes in which he was himself implicated

¹ 'At my lord marquis being in Exeter at the time of the rebellion, he took direction that all commissions for the second subsidy should stay the levy thereof for a time.'—Sir Piers Edgecombe to Cromwell: *MS. State Paper Office*, second series, vol. x.

² 'The marquis was the man that should help and do them good' (men said). See the experience, how all those do prevail that were towards the marquis. Neither assizes, nisi prius, nor bill of indictment put up against them could take effect; and, of the contrary part, how it prevailed for them.'—Sir Thomas Willoughby to Cromwell: *MS. Cotton. Titus*, B 1, 386.

³ Depositions relating to Lord Delaware: *Rolls House MS.* first series, 426.

⁴ Depositions taken before Sir Henry Capel: *Rolls House MS.* first series, 1286.

⁵ A man named Howett, one of Exeter's dependents, was heard to say, if the lord marquis had been put to the Tower, at the commandment of the lord privy seal, he should have been fetched out again, though the lord privy seal had said nay to it, and the best in the realm besides; and he the said Howett and his company were fully agreed to have had him out before they had come away.'—*MS. ibid.*

so deeply), he stood forward in his friend's defence, and offered to be bound for him, body for body.[1] This was a fresh symptom of his disposition. His conduct, if watched closely, might betray some deeper secrets. About the same time a story reached the government from Cornwall, to which their recent experience in Lincolnshire and the north justified them in attaching the gravest importance.

The parish of St. Kevern had already earned a reputation for turbulence. Here had been born and lived the famous blacksmith Michael Flammock, who forty-five years before had led the Cornish men to Blackheath; and the inhabitants were still true to their character — a wild, bold race, fit instruments for any enterprise of recklessness. A painter from the neighbourhood came one day to Sir William Godolphin, and told him that he had been desired by one of these St. Kevern men to 'make a banner for the said parish, in the which banner they would have, first, the picture of Christ, with his wounds, and a banner in his hand; our Lady on the one side, holding her breasts in her hand, St. John the Baptist on the other; the King's Grace and the queen[2] kneeling, and all the commonalty kneeling, with scrowls above their heads, making petitions to Christ that they might have their holydays.' The painter said he had asked what they intended to do with such a banner. The man gave him an incoherent account of certain people whom he had seen at Southampton, when he had been up selling fish there, and who had asked him why the Cornish men had not risen when the north rose; and now, he said, they had promised to rise, and were sworn upon the book. They wanted the banner to carry round among the neighbouring parishes, and to raise the people in Christ's name.[3] Godolphin would not create an alarm by making sudden arrests; but he despatched a private courier to London, and meanwhile held himself in readiness to crush any mutinous meetings on the instant of their assemblage: 'If there be stirring among them,' he said, 'by the precious body of God I will rid as many as be about the banner, or else I and a great many will die for it.'[4]

Conspiracies against Henry VIII. met usually with ill

---

[1] Deposition of Geoffrey Pole: *Rolls House MS.*

[2] Jane Seymour was dead, and the king was not remarried: I am unable to explain the introduction of the words, unless (as was perhaps the case) the application to the painter was in the summer of 1537, and he delayed his information till the following year.

[3] Sir William Godolphin to Cromwell: *MS. State Paper Office*, second series, vol. xiii.

[4] Ibid.

luck. Lord Exeter had traitors among his domestic servants, who had repeatedly warned the council that all was not right, and that he was meditating some secret movement.[1] At length particular information was given in, which connected itself with the affair at St. Kevern. It was stated distinctly that two Cornish gentlemen named Kendall and Quyntrell had for some time past been secretly employed in engaging men who were to be ready to rise at an hour's warning. When notice should be given they were to assemble in arms, and declare the Marquis of Exeter heir-apparent to the throne. Here was the key to the high promises of Reginald Pole. The government were on the eve of a fresh Pilgrimage of Grace—a fanatical multitude were about to rise again, with a Plantagenet pretender for a leader.

But Henry would not act without clearer proof against a nobleman of so high blood and influence. Cromwell sent orders to Godolphin to secure the man who had ordered the banner.[2] The king despatched two gentlemen of the bedchamber into Cornwall, to make private inquiries, directing them to represent themselves as being merely on a visit to their friends, and to use their opportunities to discover the truth.[3]

The result of the investigation was an entire confirmation of the story. For several years, even before the divorce of Queen Catherine, a project was found to have been on foot for a movement in favour of Exeter. The object had sometimes varied. Originally the enterprise of Blackheath was to have been renewed under more favourable auspices; and the ambition of Cornwall and Devonshire was to avenge their defeat by dethroning Henry, and giving a new dynasty to England. They would be contented now to set aside the Prince of Wales, and to declare Exeter the next in succession. But the enlistment was as certain as it was dangerous. 'Great numbers of the king's subjects' were found to have bound themselves to rise for him.[4] We have here, perhaps, the

---

[1] Wriothesley to Sir Thos. Wyatt: ELLIS, second series, vol. ii.
[2] Godolphin's Correspondence: *MS. State Paper Office*, second series, vol. xiii.
[3] Instructions by the King's Highness to John Becket, Gentleman of his Grace's Chamber, and John Wroth, of the same: printed in the *Archæologia*.
[4] 'Kendall and Quyntrell were as arrant traitors as any within the realm, leaning to and favouring the advancement of that traitor Henry, Marquis of Exeter, nor letting nor sparing to speak to a great number of the king's subjects in those parts that the said Henry was heir-apparent, and should be king, and would be king, if the King's Highness proceeded to marry the Lady Anne Boleyn, or else it should cost a thousand men's lives. And for their mischievous intent to take

explanation of these counties remaining quiet during the great insurrection. Exeter himself might have been willing (if the assistance of the Emperor was contemplated he must have been willing) to acknowledge the higher claims of the Princess Mary. But his adherents had possessed themselves of larger hopes, and a separate purpose would have embarrassed their movements. This difficulty existed no longer. Mary could have no claims in preference to Prince Edward; and the fairest hopes of the revolutionists might now be to close the line of the Tudor sovereigns with the life of the reigning king.

The meshes were thus cast fairly over Exeter. He was caught, and in Cromwell's power. But one disclosure led to another. At or near about the same time, some information led to the arrest of a secret agent of the Poles; and the attitude and objects of the whole party were drawn fully into light. The St. Kevern fisherman had mentioned two men at Southampton who had spoken to him on the subject of the new rebellion. Efforts were made to trace these persons; and although the link is missing, and perhaps never existed, between the inquiry and its apparent consequences, a Southampton 'yeoman' named Holland was arrested on suspicion of carrying letters between Cardinal Pole and his mother and family. There is no proof that papers of consequence were found in Holland's custody; but the government had the right man in their hands. He was to be taken to London; and, according to the usual mode of conveyance, he was placed on horseback, with his feet tied under his horse's belly. On the road it so happened that he was met and recognised by Sir Geoffrey Pole, Reginald's younger brother. The worthlessness of conspirators is generally proportioned to their violence. Sir Geoffrey, the most deeply implicated of the whole family, except the cardinal, made haste to secure his own safety by the betrayal of the rest. A few words which he exchanged with Holland sufficed to show him that Cromwell was on the true scent. He judged Holland's cowardice by his own; and 'he bade him keep on his way, for he would not be long after.'[1]

Lord Exeter's chances of escape were not yet wholly gone. His treasons were known up to a certain point, but forgiveness might generally be earned by confession

---

effect, they retained divers and a great number of the king's subjects in those parts, to be to the lord marquis in readiness within an hour's warning.'—Sir Thomas Willoughby to Cromwell: *MS. Cotton. Titus*, B 1.

[1] Deposition of Alice Paytchet: *MS. State Paper Office*, second series, vol. xxxix.

and submission; and Cromwell sent his nephew Richard to him, with an entreaty that 'he would be frank and plain.'[1] But the accused nobleman would make no revelation which would compromise others. His proud blood perhaps revolted against submission to the detested minister. Perhaps he did not know the extent to which his proceedings had been already discovered, and still less anticipated the treachery by which he was about to be overwhelmed.

Sir Geoffrey Pole made haste to London; and, preventing the accusations which, in a few days, would have overtaken him, he secured the opportunity which had been offered to Exeter of saving himself by confession. He presented himself to the Privy Council, and informed them that he, with Lord Montague, the Marquis and Marchioness of Exeter, Sir Edward Neville, and other persons whom he named, were in treasonable correspondence with his brother Reginald. They had maintained a steady communication with him from the time of his legacy into Flanders. They were watching their opportunities. They had calculated the force which they could raise, the Marquis of Exeter's power in the west forming their especial reliance. The depositions survive only in portions. It does not appear how far the Poles would have supported Exeter's ambition for the crown; they intended, however, this time to avoid Lord Darcy's errors, and not to limit themselves to attacks upon the ministers.[2] The death of Lord Abergavenny had been inopportune;[3] but his brother, Sir Edward Neville, with Lady Salisbury, would supply his place in rallying the Neville powers. The Yorkshire rising had proved how large was the material of an insurrection if adequately managed; and the whole family, doubtless, shared with Reginald, or rather, to them Reginald himself owed the conviction which he urged so repeatedly on the Emperor and the Pope, that, on the first fair opportunity, a power could be raised which the government would be unable to cope with.

If it is remembered that these discoveries occurred when the Bull of Deposition was on the point of publi-

[1] Examination of Lord Montague and the Marquis of Exeter: *Rolls House MS.* first series, 1262.

[2] 'The Lord Darcy played the fool,' Montague said; 'he went about to pluck the council. He should first have begun with the head. But I beshrew him for leaving off so soon.'—*Baga de Secretis*, pouch xi. bundle 2.

[3] 'I am sorry the Lord Abergavenny is dead; for if he were alive, he were able to make ten thousand men.'—Sayings of Lord Montague. Ibid.

cation—when the 'Liber de Unitate' was passing into print—when the pacification of Nice had restored the Continent to the condition most dangerous to England—when the Pope was known to be preparing again a mighty effort to gather against Henry the whole force of Christendom, this was not a time, it will be understood easily, when such plottings would be dealt with leniently by a weaker hand than that which then ruled the destinies of England.

Exeter, Montague, and Neville were sent to the Tower on the 3rd and 4th of November. Lady Exeter followed with her attendant, Constance Beverley, who had been her companion on her secret pilgrimage to the Nun. It is possible that Sir Geoffrey's revelations were made by degrees; for the king was so unwilling to prosecute, that ten days passed before their trial was determined on.[1] Lady Salisbury was not arrested; but Lord Southampton went down to Warblington, her residence in Hampshire, to examine her. She received his questions with a fierce denial of all knowledge of the matters to which they referred, and, for a time, he scarcely knew whether to think her innocent or guilty. 'Surely,' he said, in giving an account of his interview, 'there hath not been seen or heard of a woman so earnest, so manlike in countenance, so fierce as well in gesture as in words; either her sons have not made her privy to the bottom and pit of their stomachs, or she is the most arrant traitress that ever lived.'[2] But her rooms were searched; letters, Papal bulls, and other matters were discovered, which left no doubt of her general tendencies, if they were insufficient to implicate her in actual guilt; and one letter, or copy of a letter, unsigned, but, as Southampton said, undoubtedly hers, and addressed to Lord Montague, was found, the matter of which compromised her more deeply. She was again interrogated, and this time important admissions

[1] 'On Monday, the fourth of this month, the Marquis of Exeter and Lord Montague were committed to the Tower of London, being the King's Majesty so grievously touched by them, that albeit that his Grace hath upon his special favour borne towards them passed over many accusations made against the same of late by their own domestics, thinking with his clemency to conquer their cankeredness, yet his Grace was constrained, for avoiding of such malice as was prepensed, both against his person royal and the surety of my Lord Prince, to use the remedy of committing them to ward. The accusations made against them be of great importance, and duly proved by substantial witnesses. And yet the King's Majesty loveth them so well, and of his great goodness is so loath to proceed against them, that it is doubted what his Highness will do towards them.'—Wriothesley to Sir T. Wyatt: ELLIS, second series, vol. ii.

[2] Southampton to Cromwell: ELLIS, second series, vol. ii. p. 11".

were extracted from her; but she carried herself with undaunted haughtiness. 'We have dealed with such an one,' the earl said, 'as men have not dealed with tofore; we may rather call her a strong and constant man than a woman.'[1] No decisive conclusions could be formed against her; but it was thought well that she should remain under surveillance; and, three days later she was removed to Cowdray, a place belonging to Southampton himself, where she was detained in honourable confinement.

The general case meanwhile continued to enlarge. The surviving materials are too fragmentary to clear the whole circumstances; but allusions to witnesses by name whose depositions have not been preserved, show how considerable those materials were. The world at least were satisfied of the guilt of the chief prisoners. 'They would have made as foul a work,' says a letter written from London on the 21st of November, 'as ever was in England.'[2] Henry made up his mind that they should be proceeded against. Treason at home was too palpably connected with conspiracies against England abroad; and the country could not risk a repetition of the Pilgrimage of Grace.

While preparations were made for the trials, the king took the opportunity of issuing a calming circular to the justices of the peace. The clergy, as before, had been the first to catch the infection of disorder: they had been again eager propagators of sedition, and had spread extravagant stories of the intentions of the government against the Church. Emboldened by the gentleness with which the late insurgents had been handled, 'these miserable and Papistical superstitious wretches,' the king said, 'not caring what danger and mischief our people should incur, have raised the said old rumours, and forged new seditious tales, intending as much as in them lyeth a new commotion. Wherefore, for the universal danger to you and to all our good subjects, and trouble that might ensue unless good and earnest provision to repress them be taken thereupon, we desire and pray you that within the precincts of your charges ye shall endeavour yourselves to enquire and find out all such cankered parsons, vicars, and curates as bid the parishioners do as they did in times past, to live as their fathers, and that the old fashions is best. And also with your most effectual vigilance try out such seditious tale tellers, spreaders of brutes, tidings, and rumours, touching us in honour and surety, or [touching] any mutation of the laws and customs

[1] Southampton to Cromwell: ELLIS, second series, vol. ii. p. 114.
[2] Robert Warren to Lord Fitzwaters: *MS. Cotton. Titus,* B 1, 143.

of the realm, or any other thing which might cause sedition.'[1]

And now once more the peers were assembled in Westminster Hall, to try two fresh members of their order, two of the noblest born among them, for high treason; and again the judges sate with them to despatch the lower offenders. On the 2nd and 3rd of December Lord Montague and Lord Exeter were arraigned successively. On the part of the crown it was set forth generally that 'the king was supreme head on earth of the Church of England, and that his progenitors, from times whereof there was no memory to the contrary, had also been supreme heads of the Church of England; which authority and power of the said king, Paul the Third, Pope of Rome, the public enemy of the king and kingdom, without any right or title, arrogantly and obstinately challenged and claimed; and that one Reginald Pole, late of London, Esq., otherwise Reginald Pole, late Dean of Exeter, with certain others of the king's subjects, had personally repaired to the said Pope of Rome, knowing him to be the king's enemy, and adhered to and became liege man of the said Pope, and falsely and unnaturally renounced the king, his natural liege lord; that Reginald Pole accepted the dignity of a cardinal of the court of Rome without the king's license, in false and treasonable despite and contempt of the king, and had continued to live in parts beyond the seas, and was there vagrant, and denying the king to be upon earth supreme head of the Church of England.'

Caring only to bring the prisoners within the letter of the act, the prosecution made no allusion to Exeter's proceedings in Cornwall. It was enough to identify his guilt with the guilt of the great criminal. Against him, therefore, it was objected—

'That, as a false traitor, machinating the death of the king, and to excite his subjects to rebellion, and seeking to maintain the said Cardinal Pole in his intentions, the Marquis of Exeter did say to Geoffrey Pole the following words in English: 'I like well the proceedings of the Cardinal Pole; but I like not the proceedings of this realm; and I trust to see a change of this world.'

'Furthermore, that the Marquis of Exeter, machinating with Lord Montague the death and destruction of the king, did openly declare to the Lord Montague, 'I trust once to have a fair day upon those knaves which rule about the king; and I trust to see a merry world one day.'

[1] Burnet's *Collectanea*, p. 494, &c.

'And, furthermore persevering in his malicious intention, he did say, 'Knaves rule about the king;' and then stretching his arm, and shaking his clenched fist, spoke the following words: 'I trust to give them a buffet one day.''

Sir Geoffrey Pole was in all cases the witness. The words were proved. It was enough. A verdict of guilty was returned; and the marquis was sentenced to die.

If the proof of language of no darker complexion was sufficient to secure a condemnation, the charges against Lord Montague left him no shadow of a hope. Montague had expressed freely to his miserable brother his approbation of Reginald's proceedings. He had discussed the chances of the impending struggle and the resources of which they could dispose. He had spoken bitterly of the king; he had expressed a fear that when the world 'came to strypes,' as come it would, 'there would be a lack of honest men,' with other such language, plainly indicative of his disposition. However justly, indeed, we may now accuse the equity which placed men on their trial for treason for impatient expressions, there can be no uncertainty that, in the event of an invasion, or of a rebellion with any promise of success in it, both Montague and Exeter would have thrown their weight into the rebel scale. Montague, too, was condemned.

The date of the expressions which were sworn against them is curious. They belong, without exception, to the time when Reginald Pole was in Flanders. That there was nothing later was accounted for by the distrust which Geoffrey said that soon after they had begun to entertain towards him. Evidently they had seen his worthlessness; and as their enterprise had become more critical, they had grown more circumspect. But he remembered enough to destroy them, and to save by his baseness his own miserable life.

He was himself tried, though to receive a pardon after conviction. With Sir Edward Neville and four other persons he was placed at the bar on charges of the same kind as those against Exeter and his brother. Neville had said that he 'would have a day upon the knaves that were about the king;' 'that the king was a beast, and worse than a beast;' 'machinating and conspiring to extinguish the love and affection of the king's subjects.' Sir Geoffrey Pole, beyond comparison the most guilty, had been in command of a company under the Duke of Norfolk at Doncaster; and was proved to have avowed an intention of deserting in the action, if an action was fought

—real, bad, black treason. Of the others, two had spoken against the supremacy; one had carried letters to the cardinal; another had said to Lord Montague, that 'the king would hang in hell for the plucking down of abbeys.'

The last case was the hardest. Sir Nicholas Carew, Master of the Horse, had been on the commission which had taken the indictments against Exeter, and had said 'that he marvelled it was so secretly handled; that the like was never seen.' The expression brought him under suspicion. He was found to have been intimate with Exeter; to have received letters from him of traitorous import, which he had concealed and burnt. With the rest he was brought in guilty, and received sentence as a traitor. On the 9th of December the Marquis of Exeter, Montague, and Sir Edward Neville were beheaded on Towerhill.[1] On the 16th the following proclamation was issued:—

'Be it known unto all men, that whereas Henry Courtenay, late Marquis of Exeter, knight companion of the most noble order of the Garter, hath lately committed and done high treason against the king our dread sovereign lord, sovereign of the said most noble order of the Garter, compassing and imagining the destruction of his most royal person in the most traitorous and rebellious wise, contrary to his oath, duty, and allegiance, intending thereby, if he might have obtained his purpose, to have subverted the whole good order of the commonwealth of England, for the which high and most detestable treason the said Henry hath deserved to be degraded of the said most noble order, and expelled out of the same company, and is not worthy that his arms, ensigns, and hatchments should remain amongst the virtuous and approved knights of the said most noble order, nor to have any benefit thereof.— the right wise king and supreme head of the most noble order, with the whole consent and counsel of the same, wills and commands that his arms, which he nothing deserveth, be taken away and thrown down, and he be clean put from this order, and never from henceforth to be taken of any of the number thereof; so that all others

---

[1] Hall, followed by the chroniclers, says that the executions were on the 9th of January; but he was mistaken. In a MS. in the State Paper Office, dated the 16th of December, 1538, Exeter is described as having suffered on the 9th of the same month. My account of these trials is taken from the records in the *Baga de Secretis*; from the Act of Attainder, 31 Henry VIII. cap. 15, not printed in the Statute Book, but extant on the Roll; and from a number of scattered depositions, questions, and examinations in the Rolls House and in the State Paper Office.

by his example, from henceforth for evermore, may beware how they commit or do the like crime or fault, unto like shame or rebuke.

'God save the King.'

'December, 16, 1538.'

Executions for high treason bear necessarily a character of cruelty, when the peril which the conspiracies create has passed away. In the sense of our own security we lose the power of understanding the magnitude or even the meaning of the danger. But that there had been no unnecessary alarm, that these noblemen were in no sense victims of tyranny, but had been cut off by a compelled severity, may be seen in the consequence of their deaths. Unjust sentences provoke indignation. Indignation in stormy times finds the means, sooner or later, of shaping itself into punishment. But the undercurrent of disaffection, which for ten years had penetrated through English life, was now exhausted, and gradually ceased to flow. The enemy had been held down; it acknowledged its master; and, with the exception of one unimportant commotion in Yorkshire, no symptom of this particular form of peril was again visible, until the king had received notice of departure, in his last illness, and the prospect of his death warmed the hopes of confusion into life again. The prompt extinction of domestic treason, in all likelihood, was the cause which really saved the country from a visit from the Emperor. 'Laud be to God,' said an Englishman, 'we are all now united and knit with a firm love in our hearts towards our prince. Ye never read nor heard that ever England was overcome by outward realms, nor dare any outward prince enterprize to come hither, except they should trust of help within the realm, which I trust in God none such shall ever be found.'[2] The speaker expressed the exact truth; and no one was more keenly aware of it than Charles V.

We must once more go back over our steps. The Emperor being on good terms with France, England, obedient to the necessity of its position, again held out its hand to Germany. No sooner had the pacification of Nice been completed, and Henry had found that he was not, after all, to be admitted as a party contrahent, than,

---

[1] The degrading of Henry Courtenay, late Marquis of Exeter, the 3rd day of December, and the same day convicted; and the 9th day of the said month beheaded at Tower Hill; and the 18th day of the same month degraded at Windsor: *MS. State Paper Office.* Unarranged bundle.

[2] Examination of Christopher Chator: *Rolls House MS.* first series.

without quarrelling with Charles, he turned his position by immediate advances to the Smalcaldic League. In the summer of 1538 Lutheran divines were invited to England to discuss the terms of their confession with the bishops; and though unsuccessful in the immediate object of finding terms of communion, they did not return, without having established, as it seemed, a generally cordial relationship with the English Reformers. Purgatory, episcopal ordination, the marriage of the clergy, were the comparatively unimportant points of difference. On the vital doctrine of the real presence the Lutherans were as jealously sensitive as the vast majority of the English; and on the points on which they continued orthodox the Reformers, German and English, united in a bigotry almost equal to that of Rome. On the departure of the theological embassy, the Landgrave of Hesse took the opportunity of addressing a letter of warning to Henry on the progress of heresy in England, and expressing his anxiety that the king should not forget his duty in repressing and extirpating so dangerous a disorder.[1]

[1] Gibbon professes himself especially scandalized at the persecution of Servetus by men who themselves had stood in so deep need of toleration. The scandal is scarcely reasonable, for neither Calvin nor any other Reformer of the sixteenth century desired a 'liberty of conscience' in its modern sense. The Council of Geneva, the General Assembly at Edinburgh, the Smalcaldic League, the English Parliament, and the Spanish Inquisition held the same opinions on the wickedness of heresy; they differed only in the definition of the crime. The English and Scotch Protestants have been taunted with persecution. When nations can grow to maturity in a single generation, when the child can rise from his first grammar lesson a matured philosopher, individual men may clear themselves by a single effort from mistakes which are embedded in the heart of their age. Let us listen to the Landgrave of Hesse. He will teach us that Henry VIII. was no exceptional persecutor.

The Landgrave has heard that the errors of the Anabaptists are increasing in England. He depicts in warning colours the insurrection at Münster: 'If they grow to any multitude,' he says, 'their acts will surely declare their seditious minds and opinions. Surely this is true, the devil, which is an homicide, carrieth men that are entangled in false opinions to unlawful slaughters and the breach of society. . . . . There are no rulers in Germany,' he continues, 'whether they be Popish or professors of the doctrines of the Gospel, that do suffer these men, if they come into their hands. All men punish them grievously. We use a just moderation, which God requireth of all good rulers. Whereas any of the sect is apprehended, we call together divers learned men and good preachers, and command them, the errors being confuted by the Word of God, to teach them rightlier, to heal them that be sick, to deliver them that were bound; and by this way many that are astray are come home again. These are not punished with any corporal pains, but are driven openly to forsake their errours. If any do stubbornly defend the ungodly and wicked errours of that sect, yielding nothing to such as can and do teach them truly, these are kept a good space in prison, and sometimes sore punished there; yet in such sort are they handled, that death is long deferred for hope of amendment; and, as long as any hope is, favour is shewed to

His advice found Cranmer and Cromwell as anxious as himself. The Catholics at home and abroad persisted more and more loudly in identifying a separation from Rome with heresy. The presence of these very Germans had given opportunity, however absurdly, for scandal; and, taken in connexion with the destruction of the shrines, was made a pretext for charging the king with a leaning towards doctrines with which he was most anxious to disavow a connexion.[1] The political clouds which were gathering abroad, added equally to the anxiety, both of the king and his ministers, to stand clear in this matter; and as Cromwell had recommended, after the Pilgrimage of Grace, that the Articles of Unity should be enforced against some offender or offenders in a signal manner— so, to give force to his principles, which had been faintly acted upon, either he, or the party to which he belonged, now chose out for prosecution a conspicuous member of the Christian brotherhood, John Lambert, who was marked with the dreadful reputation of a sacramentary. Dr. Barnes volunteered as the accuser. Barnes, it will be remembered, had been himself imprisoned for heresy, and had done penance in St. Paul's. He was a noisy, vain man, Lutheran in his views, and notorious for his hatred of more advanced Protestants. Tyndal had warned the brethren against him several years previously; but his German sympathies had recommended him to the vicegerent; he had been employed on foreign missions, and was for the time undergoing the temptation of a brief prosperity. Lambert, the intended victim, had been a friend at Cambridge of Bilney the martyr; a companion at Antwerp of

---

life. If there be no hope left, then the obstinate are put to death.' Warning Henry of the snares of the devil, who labours continually to discredit the truth by grafting upon it heresy, he concludes:—

'Wherefore, if that sect hath done any hurt there in your Grace's realm, we doubt not but your princely wisdom will so temper the matter, that both dangers be avoided, errours be kept down, and yet a difference had between those that are good men, and mislike the abuses of the Bishop of Rome's baggages, and those that be Anabaptists. In many parts of Germany where the Gospel is not preached, cruelty is exercised upon both sorts without discretion. The magistrates which obey the Bishop of Rome (whereas severity is to be used against the Anabaptists) slay good men utterly alien from their opinions. But your Majesty will put a difference great enough between these two sorts, and serve Christ's glory on the one side, and save the innocent blood on the other.'—Landgrave of Hesse to Henry VIII. September 25, 1538: *State Papers*, vol. viii.

[1] 'They have made a wondrous matter and report here of the shrines and of burning of the idol at Canterbury; and, besides that, the King's Highness and council be become sacramentarians by reason of this embassy which the King of Saxony sent late into England.'— Theobald to Cromwell, from Padua, October 22, 1538: ELLIS, third series, vol. iii.

Tyndal and Frith; and had perhaps taken a share in the translation of the Bible. Subsequently, he had been in trouble for suspicion of heresy; he had been under examination before Warham, and afterwards Sir Thomas More; and having been left in prison by the latter, he had been set at liberty by Cranmer. He was now arrested on the charge preferred by Dr. Barnes, of having denied the real presence, contrary to the Articles of Faith. He was tried in the archbishop's court; and, being condemned, he appealed to the king.

Henry decided that he would hear the cause in person. A few years before, a sacramentary was despatched with the same swift indifference as an ordinary felon: a few years later, a sacramentary had ceased to be a criminal. In the interval, the proportions of the crime had so dilated in apparent magnitude, that a trial for it was a national event—an affair of vast public moment.

On the 16th of November, while London was ringing with the arrest of the Marquis of Exeter, the court was opened in Westminster Hall. In the grey twilight of the late dawn, the whole peerage of England, lay and spiritual, took their seats, to the right and left of the throne. The twelve judges placed themselves on raised benches at the back. The prisoner was brought in; and soon after the king entered, 'clothed all in white,' with the yeomen of the guard.

The Bishop of Carlisle rose first to open the case. The king, he said, had put down the usurpations of the Bishop of Rome, but it was not to be thought, therefore, that he intended to give license to heresy. They were not met, at present, to discuss doctrines, but to try a person accused of a crime, by the laws of the Church and of the country.

Lambert was then ordered to stand forward.

'What is your name?' the king asked. 'My name is Nicholson,' he said, 'though I be called Lambert.' 'What!' the king said, 'have you two names? I would not trust you, having two names, though you were my brother.'

The persecutions of the bishops, Lambert answered, had obliged him to disguise himself; but now God had inspired the king's mind, enduing him with wisdom and understanding to stay their cruelty.

'I come not here,' said Henry, 'to hear mine own praises painted out in my presence. Go to the matter without more circumstance. Answer as touching the sacrament of the altar, is it the body of Christ or no?'

'I answer with St. Augustine,' the prisoner said; 'it is the body of Christ after a certain manner.'

'Answer me not out of St. Augustine,' said the king; 'tell me plainly whether it be He.'

'Then I say it is not,' was the answer.

'Mark well,' the king replied, 'you are condemned by Christ's own words—'*Hoc est corpus meum.*'' He turned to Cranmer, and told him to convince the prisoner of his error.

The argument began in the morning. First Cranmer, and after him nine other bishops laboured out their learned reasons—reasons which, for fifteen hundred years, had satisfied the whole Christian world, yet had suddenly ceased to be of cogency. The torches were lighted before the last prelate had ceased to speak. Then once more the king asked Lambert for his opinion. 'After all these labours taken with you, are you yet satisfied?' he said. 'Choose, will you live or will you die!'

'I submit myself to the will of your Majesty,' Lambert said.

'Commit your soul to God,' replied Henry, 'not to me.'

'I commit my soul to God,' he said, 'and my body to your clemency.'

'Then you must die,' the king said. 'I will be no patron of heretics.'

It was over. The appeal was rejected. Cromwell read the sentence. Four days' interval was allowed before the execution. In a country which was governed by law, not by the special will of a despot, the supreme magistrate was neither able, nor desired, so long as a law remained unrepealed by parliament, to suspend the action of it.

The morning on which Lambert suffered he was taken to Cromwell's house, where he breakfasted simply in the hall; and afterwards he died at Smithfield, crying with his last breath, 'None but Christ—none but Christ.'[1] Foxe relates, as a rumour, that Cromwell, before Lambert suffered, begged his forgiveness. A more accurate account of Cromwell's feelings is furnished by himself in a letter written a few days later to Sir Thomas Wyatt:—

'The sixteenth of this present month, the King's Majesty, for the reverence of the holy sacrament of the altar, did sit openly in his hall, and there presided at the disputation, process, and judgment of a miserable heretic sacramentary, who was burnt the twentieth of the same month. It was a wonder to see how princely, with how excellent gravity, and inestimable majesty, his Majesty exercised the very office of a superior head of his Church of England;

---

[1] The history of Lambert's trial is taken from Foxe, vol. v.

how benignly his Grace essayed to convert the miserable man; how strong and manifest reason his Highness alleged against him. I wished the princes of Christendom to have seen it; undoubtedly they should have much marvelled at his Majesty's most high wisdom and judgment, and reputed him none otherwise after the same than in manner the mirror and light of all other kings and princes in Christendom. The same was done openly, with great solemnity.'[1]

The circumstances which accompanied Pole's mission into Spain, and those which occasioned the catastrophe of the marriage treaties, can now be understood. The whole secret of the Emperor's intentions it is not easy, perhaps it is not necessary, to comprehend; but, as it was not till late in the spring that the threatening symptoms finally cleared, so it is impossible to doubt that an enterprise against England was seriously meditated, and was relinquished only when the paralysis of the domestic factions who were to have risen in its support could no longer be mistaken.

The official language of the Spanish court through the winter 'had waxed from colder to coldest.'[2] On Pole's arrival in the Peninsula, Sir Thomas Wyatt, by the king's instructions, protested against his reception. The Emperor, who in 1537 had forbidden his entrance into his dominions when on a similar errand, replied now that, 'if he was his own traitor, he could not refuse him audience, coming as a legate from the Holy Father.' The next step was the arrest of the English ships in Flanders, and the recall of the Spanish ambassador; and meanwhile a mysterious fleet was collected at Antwerp and in other ports, every one asking with what object, and no one being able to answer, unless it were for a descent on Ireland or England.[3] Mendoza's departure from London was followed immediately after by the withdrawal of M. de Chatillon, the ambassador of France. 'It is in every man's mouth,' reported Wriothesley, 'that we shall have war. It has been told me that the commission that was

---

[1] Cromwell to Wyatt: NOTT's *Wyatt*, p. 326.
[2] Cromwell to Wriothesley: *State Papers*, vol. viii. p. 155.
[3] Christopher Mount writes: 'This day (March 5) the Earl William a Furstenburg was at dinner with the Duke of Saxe, which asked of him what news. He answered that there is labour made for truce between the Emperor and the Turk. Then said the duke, to what purpose should be all these preparations the Emperor maketh? The earl answered, that other men should care for. Then said the duke, the bruit is here—it should be against the King of England. Then said the earl, the King of England shall need to take heed to himself.'—*State Papers*, vol. i. p. 606.

sent hither for our matters[1] was dispatched only to keep us in hopes, and to the intent that we might be taken tardy and without provision.'[2]

Wriothesley's duty required him to learn the meaning of the arrests. The ministers at Brussels affected to say that the Emperor required sailors for his fleet, and, until it had sailed on its mysterious errand, no other vessels could leave the harbours. The ambassador refused to accept a reply so insolent and unsatisfactory; he insisted on an interview with the regent herself, and pointing to the clause in the commercial treaty between England and Flanders which stipulated, on behalf of the ships of both nations, for free egress and ingress, he required an explanation of the infringement. 'You give us fair words,' he said to her, 'but your deeds being contrary, the King's Majesty my master shall join words and deeds together, and see that all is but finesse. If you had declared open war, by the law of nations merchant ships should have six weeks allowed them to depart;' while peace remained, they might not be detained a day. The queen regent, like her council, gave an evasive answer. The Emperor must be served, she said; the fleet would soon sail, and the ships would be free. She tried to leave him; his anxiety got the better of his courtesy; he placed himself between her and the door, and entreated some better explanation. But he could obtain nothing. She insisted on passing, and he found himself referred back to the council. Here he was informed that she could not act otherwise; she was obeying absolute orders from the Emperor. Wriothesley warned them that the king would not bear it, that he would make reprisals, and 'then should begin a broiling.' It was no matter; they seemed indifferent.

From their manner Wriothesley did not believe that they would begin a war; yet he could feel no security. 'I have heard,' he wrote to Cromwell, 'that the French king, the Bishop of Rome, and the King of Scots be in league to invade us this summer: and how the Emperor will send to their aid certain Spaniards which shall arrive in Scotland; which Spaniards shall, as it were in fury, upon the arrival in Spain of the ships here prepared, enter the same, half against the Emperor's will, with the oath never to return till they shall revenge the matter of the dowager.' 'This,' he added, 'I take for no gospel, howbeit our master is daily slandered and villanously spoken against. It is possible that all shall be well; but

[1] The negotiations for the marriages.
[2] Wriothesley to Cromwell: *State Papers*, vol. viii. p. 165.

in the mean season, I pray to God to put in the King's Majesty's mind rather to spend twenty thousand pounds in vain, to be in perfect readiness, than to wish it had so been done if any malicious person would attempt anything. Weapons biddeth peace; and good preparation maketh men to look or they leap. The Emperor hath made great provision. It may yet be that he will do somewhat against the Turks; but as many think nay, as otherwise. But he maketh not his preparation in vain. England is made but a morsel among these choppers. They would have the Duke of Orleans a king;[1] and the Duke of Guise, they say, will visit his daughter in Scotland. It is not unlike that somewhat may be attempted; which, nevertheless, may be defeated. God hath taken the King's Majesty into his own tuition.'[2]

Each day the news from Flanders became more alarming. The wharves at Antwerp were covered with ammunition and military stores. Contributions had been levied on the clergy, who had been taught to believe that the money was to be spent in the Pope's quarrel against the King of England. On the 24th of March two hundred and seventy sail were reported as ready for sea; and the general belief was that, if no attack were ventured, the preparations to meet it, which Henry was known to have made, would be the sole cause of the hesitation.[3] Information of a precisely similar kind was furnished from Spain. The agent of a London house wrote to his master: 'You shall understand that, four days past, we had news how the Bishop of Rome had sent a post to the Emperor, which came in seven days from Rome, and brought letters requiring and desiring his Majesty, jointly with the French king and the King of Scots, to give war against the king our sovereign lord; and all his subjects to be heretics and schismatics, and wherever they could win and take any of our nation by land or sea, to take us for Jews

---

[1] *i. e.*, he was to marry the Princess Mary.
[2] Wriothesley to Cromwell: *State Papers*, vol. viii. p. 167.
[3] 'Within these fourteen days, it shall surely break out what they do purpose to do; as of three ways, one—Gueldres, Denmark, or England; notwithstanding, as I think, England is without danger, because they know well that the King's Grace hath prepared to receive them if they come. There be in Holland 270 good ships prepared; but whither they shall go no man can tell. Preparations of all manner of artillery doth daily go through Antwerp.

'All the spiritualty here be set for to pay an innumerable sum of money. Notwithstanding, they will be very well content with giving the aforesaid money, if all things may be so brought to pass as they hope it shall, and as it is promised them—and that is, that the Pope's quarrel may be avenged upon the King's Grace of England.'—March 14, —— to Cromwell: *MS. State Paper Office*, second series, vol. xvi.

or infidels, and to use our persons as slaves. We have hope that in this the Emperor will not grant the request of his Holiness, being so much against charity, notwithstanding that divers our friends in this country give us secret monition to put good order for the safeguard of our goods; and they think, verily, the Emperor will have war with the king our master this March next, and that the army of men and ships in Flanders shall go against England.'[1]

The thing to be feared, if there was cause for fear, was a sudden treacherous surprise. The point of attack would probably be the open coast of Kent. An army would be landed on the beach somewhere between Sandwich and Dover, and would march on London. Leaving Cromwell to see to the defence of the metropolis, Henry went down in person to examine his new fortresses, and to speak a few words of encouragement to the garrisons. The merchant-ships in the Thames were taken up by the government and armed. Lord Southampton took command of the fleet at Portsmouth; Lord Russell was sent into the west; Lord Surrey into Norfolk. The beacons were fresh trimmed; the musters through the country were ordered to be in readiness. Sir Ralph Sadler, the king's private secretary, sent from Dover to desire Cromwell to lose no time in setting London in order: 'Use your diligence,' he wrote, 'for his Grace saith that *diligence passe sense*; willing me to write that French proverb unto your lordship, the rather to quicken you in that behalf. Surely his Majesty mindeth nothing more than, like a courageous prince of valiant heart, to prepare and be in readiness, in all events, to encounter the malice of his enemies; in which part, no doubt, Almighty God will be his helper, and all good subjects will employ themselves to the uttermost, both lives and goods, to serve his Highness truly.... All that will the contrary, God send them ill-hap and short life.'[2]

The inspection proving satisfactory, Sir Thomas Cheyne was left at Dover Castle, with command of the coast from the mouth of the Thames westward. We catch sight through March and April of soldiers gathering and moving. Look-out vessels hung about the Channel, watching the Flanders ports. One morning when the darkness lifted, sixty strange sail were found at anchor in the Downs;[3]

[1] William Ostrich to the worshipful Richard Ebbes, Merchant in London: *MS. State Paper Office*, first series, vol. ii.
[2] Sir Ralph Sadler to Cromwell, from Dover, March 16: Ibid. second series, vol. xxxvii.
[3] Hollinshed, Stow.

and swiftly two thousand men were in arms upon the sandflats towards Deal. Cheyne never took off his clothes for a fortnight. Strong easterly gales were blowing, which would bring the fleet across in a few hours. 'Mr. Fletcher of Rye,' in a boat of his own construction, 'which he said had no fellow in England,' beat up in the wind's eye to Dover, 'of his own mind, to serve the King's Majesty.' At daybreak he would he off Gravelines, on the look-out; at noon he would be in the new harbour, with reports to the English commander. Day after day the huge armada lay motionless. At length sure word was brought that an order had been sent out for every captain, horseman, and footman to be on board on the last of March.[1] In a few days the truth, whatever it was, would be known. The easterly winds were the chief cause of anxiety. If England was their object, they would come so quickly, Cheyne said, that although watch was kept night and day all along the coast, yet, 'if evil were, the best would be a short warning for any number of men to repulse them at their landing.' However, his information led him to think the venture would not be made.

He was right. A few days later the look-out boats brought the welcome news that the fleet had broken up. Part withdrew to the ports of Zealand, where the stores and cannon were relanded, and the vessels dismasted. Part were seen bearing down Channel before the wind, bound for Spain and the Mediterranean; and Cromwell, who had had an ague fit from anxiety, informed the king on the 19th of April that he had received private letters from Antwerp, telling him that the enterprise had been relinquished from the uncertainty which appeared of success.[2]

Such, in fact, was the truth. The Emperor, longing, and yet fearing to invade, and prepared to make the attempt if he could be satisfied of a promising insurrection in his support, saw in the swift and easy extinction of the Marquis of Exeter's conspiracy an evidence of Henry's strength which Pole's eloquence could not gainsay. He had waited, uncertain perhaps, till time had proved the consequences of the execution; and when he found that the country was in arms, but only to oppose the invaders whom the English legate had promised it would welcome as deliverers, he was too wise to risk an overthrow which would have broken his power in Germany, and ensured the enduring enmity of England. The time, he told the

[1] Letters of Sir Thomas Cheyne to Cromwell, March and April, 1539: MS. State Paper Office, second series.
[2] Cromwell to the King: MS. Cotton. Titus, B 1, 271.

Pope, did not serve; and to a second more anxious message he replied that he could not afford to quarrel with Henry till Germany was in better order. The King of France might act as he pleased. He would not interfere with him. For himself, when the German difficulty was once settled, he would then take up arms and avenge the Pope's injuries and his own.[1] Once more Pole had failed. He has been accused of personal ambition; but the foolish expectations of his admirers in Europe have been perhaps mistaken for his own.[2] His worst crime was his vanity; his worst misfortune was his talent—a talent for discovering specious reasons for choosing the wrong side. The deliberate frenzy of his conduct shows the working of a mind not wholly master of itself; or, if we leave him the responsibility of his crimes, he may be allowed the imperfect pity which attaches to failure. The results of his labours to destroy the Reformation had, so far, been to bring his best friends and Lord Montague to the scaffold. His mother, entangled in his guilt, lay open to the same fate. His younger brother was a perjured traitor and a fratricide. In bitter misery he now shrank into the monastery of Carpentras, where, if he might be allowed, he wrote to Contarini, that he would hide his face for ever in mourning and prayer. Often, he said, he had heard the King of England speak of his mother as the most saintly woman in Christendom. First priests, then nobles, and now, as it seemed, women were to follow. Had the faith of Christ, from the beginning, ever known so deadly an enemy?

He went on to bewail the irresolution of Charles:—

'Surely,' he exclaimed, 'if the Emperor had pronounced against the tyrant, this worse antagonist of God than the Turk, he would have found God more favourable to him in the defence of his own empire. I the more dread some judgment upon Cæsar, for that I thought him chosen as a special instrument to do God's work in this matter. God, as we see in the Scriptures, was wont to stir up

---

[1] Phillips's *Life of Pole.* Four letters of Cardinal Alexander Farnese to Paul III.: *Epist. Reg. Pol.* vol. ii. p. 281, &c.

[2] One of these, for instance, writes to him: 'Vale amplissime Pole quem si in meis auguriis aliquid veri est adhuc Regem Angliæ videbimus.' His answer may acquit him of vulgar selfishness: 'I know not where you found your augury. If you can divine the future, divine only what I am to suffer for my country, or for the Church of God, which is in my country.

εἰς οἰωνὸς ἄριστος ἀμύνεσθαι περὶ πάτρης.

For me, the heavier the load of my affliction for God and the Church, the higher do I mount upon the ladder of felicity.'—*Epist. Reg. Pol.* vol. iii. pp. 37-39.

adversaries against those whom he desired to punish; and when I saw that enemy of all good in his decline into impiety commencing with an attack on Cæsar's honour and Cæsar's family, what could I think but that, as Cæsar's piety was known to all men, so God was in this manner influencing him to avenge the Church's wrongs with his own? Now we must fear for Cæsar himself. Other princes are ready in God's cause. He in whom all our hopes were centered is not ready. I have no consolation, save it be my faith in God and in Providence. To Him who alone can save let us offer our prayers, and await his will in patience.'¹

A gleam of pageantry shoots suddenly across the sky. Pole delighted to picture his countrymen to himself cowering in terror before a cruel tyrant, mourning their ruined faith and murdered nobility. The impression was known to have contributed so largely to the hopes of the Catholics abroad, that the opportunity was taken to display publicly the real disposition of the nation. All England had been under arms in expectation of invasion; before the martial humour died away, the delight of the English in splendid shows was indulged with a military spectacle. On the 8th of May a review was held of the musters of the city of London.

'The King's Grace,' says a contemporary record, 'who never ceased to take pains for the advancement of the

---

¹ *Epist. Reg. Pol.* vol. ii. p. 191, &c. The disappointment of the Roman ecclesiastics led them so far as to anticipate a complete apostacy on the part of Charles. The fears of Cardinal Contarini make the hopes so often expressed by Henry appear less unreasonable, that Charles might eventually imitate the English example. On the 8th of July, 1539, Contarini writes to Pole:—

'De rebus Germaniæ audio quod molestissime tuli, indictum videlicet esse conventum Norimburgensem ad Kal. Octobris pro rebus Ecclesiæ componendis, ubi sunt conventuri oratores Cæsaris et Regis Christianissimi; sex autem pro parte Lutheranorum et totidem pro partibus Catholicorum, de rebus Fidei disputaturi; et hoc fieri ex decreto superiorum mensium Conventûs Francford; in quo nulla mentio fit, nec de Pontifice, nec de aliquo qui pro sede Apostolicâ interveniret. Vides credo quo ista tendunt. Utinam ego decipiar; sed hoc prorsus judico; etsi præsentibus omnibus conatibus regis Angliæ maxime sit obstandum, tamen non hunc esse qui maxime sedi Apostolicæ possit nocere; ego illum timeo quem Cato ille in Republicâ Romanâ maxime timebat, qui sobrius accedit ad illam evertendam; vel potius illos timeo (nec enim unus est hoc tempore) et nisi istis privatis conventibus cito obviam eatur, ut non brevi major aciuanra in ecclesiâ cum majori detrimento autoritatis sedis Apostolicæ oriatur, quam multis sæculis fuerit visa, non possum non maxime timere. Scripsit ad me his de rebus primus nuncius ex Hispaniâ; et postea certiora de iisdem ex Reverendissimo et Illustrissimo Farnesio eum huc transiret cognovi cui sententiam meam de toto periculo exposui. Ego certe talem nunc video Ecclesiæ statum, ut si nuquam dixi illâ in causâ cum Isaiâ, mitte me, nunc potius si rogarer dicerem cum Mose, Dominus mitte quem missurus es.'—*Epist. Reg. Pol.* vol. ii. p. 158.

commonwealth, was informed by his trusty friends how that the cankered and venomous serpent Paul, Bishop of Rome, and the archtraitor Reginald Pole, had moved and stirred the potentates of Christendom to invade the realm of England with mortal war, and extermine and destroy the whole nation with fire and sword.'

The king, therefore, in his own person, 'had taken painful and laborious journeys towards the sea coast,' to prevent the invasion of his enemies; he had fortified all the coasts both of England and Wales; he had 'set his navy in readiness at Portsmouth,' 'in all things furnished for the wars.' The people had been called under arms, and the 'harness viewed,' in all counties in the realm; and the Lord Mayor of London was instructed by the Lord Thomas Cromwell that the King's Majesty 'of his most gentle nature' would take the pains to see 'his loving and benevolent subjects muster in order before his Excellent Highness.'

The mayor and his brethren 'determined, after long consultation,' 'that no alien, though he were a denizen, should muster,' but only native-born English; and 'for especial considerations, they thought it not convenient' that all their able-bodied men should be absent from the City at once. They would have but a picked number; 'such as were able persons, and had white harness and white coats, bows, arrows, bills, or poleaxes, and none other except such as bare morris pikes or handguns;' the whole to be 'in white hosen and cleanly shod.'

'And when it was known,' says the record, 'that the king himself would see the muster, to see how gladly every man prepared him, what desire every man had to do his prince service, it was a joyful sight to behold of every Englishman.'

White was the City uniform. The lord mayor and the aldermen rode in white armour, with light coats of black velvet, and the arms of London embroidered on them. Massive gold chains hung on their breasts. Their caps were of velvet with plumes; and steel battle-axes were slung at their side. Every alderman was attended by a body-guard, in white silk, with gilded halberds. The richer citizens were in white silk also, 'with broaches and owches,' and 'breastplates studded with silver.' The remainder had white coats of cotton, worked into a uniform, with the City arms, white shoes, and long woven, closely-fitting hose; 'every man with a sword and dagger,' besides his special arms. The whole number to be reviewed were fifteen thousand men, divided into battles or battalions of five thousand each. The aldermen were at the head each of his ward. The wards were in companies of archers, pikemen, musketeers, and artillery. A preliminary review was held on the evening of the 7th of May. The next morning, before six o'clock, 'all the fields from Whitechapel to Mile-end, from Bethnal-green to Radcliffe and Stepney, were covered with men in bright harness, with glistening weapons.' 'The battle of pikes, when they stood still, seemed a great wood.'

At eight o'clock the advance began to move, each division being attended by a hundred and twenty outriders, to keep stragglers into line. First came thirteen fieldpieces, 'with powder and stones in carts,' followed by the banners of the City, the musketeers, 'five in a rank, every rank five foot from another, and every shoulder even with his fellows;' and next them the archers, five in a rank also, 'and between every man his bow's length.'

After the archers came 'the pikemen,' and then 'the billmen;' the five companies with their officers on horseback, their colours, and their separate bands.

The other divisions were preceded by an equal number of cannon. At the rear of the second, the banner of St. George was carried, and the banner of the Prince of Wales. Behind these, 'at a convenient distance,' the sword-bearer of London, in white damask, 'upon a goodly horse, freshly trapped,' with the sword of the City, 'the scabbard whereof was set full of orient pearl.' Here, too, came the splendid cavalcade of Sir William Foreman, the lord mayor, with himself in person—a blaze of white silk, white satin, gold, crimson, and waving plumes—the choice company of the City; the retinue being composed, for their especial worth and approved valour, of the attorneys, the barristers, their clerks, and the clerks of the courts of law, with white silk over their armour, and chains, and clasps.

The first battalion entered the City at Aldgate, before nine o'clock, and 'so passed through the streets in good order, after a warlike fashion, till they came to Westminster.' Here, in front of the palace, the king was standing on a platform, 'with the nobility.' As the troops passed by, they fired volleys of musketry; the heavy guns were manœuvred, and 'shot off very terribly;' 'and so all three battles, in the order afore rehearsed, one after another, passed through the great Sanctuary at Westminster, and so about the park at St. James's, into a great field before the same place, where the king, standing in his gate-house at Westminster, might both see them that came forward and also them that were passed before. Thence from St. James's fields the whole army passed through Holborn, and so into Cheap, and at Leaden Hall severed and departed: and the last alderman came into Cheap about five of the clock; so that from nine of the clock in the forenoon till five at afternoon this muster was not ended.'

'To see how full of lords, ladies, and gentlemen,' continues the authority, 'the windows in every street were, and how the streets of the City were replenished with people, many men would have thought that they that had mustered had rather been strangers than citizens, considering that the streets everywhere were full of people; which was to strangers a great marvel.

'Whatsoever was done, and whatsoever pains was taken, all was to the citizens a great gladness; as to them also which with heart and mind would serve their sovereign lord King Henry the Eighth, whose High Majesty, with his noble infant Prince Edward, they daily pray unto God Almighty long to preserve in health, honour, and prosperity.'[1]

[1] Account of the Muster of the Citizens of London in the thirty-first Year of the Reign of King Henry VIII., communicated (for the *Archæologia*), from the Records of the Corporation of London, by Thomas Lott, Esq.

CHAPTER XVI.

THE SIX ARTICLES.

The three centuries which have passed over the world since the Reformation have soothed the theological animosities which they have failed wholly to obliterate. An enlarged experience of one another has taught believers of all sects that their differences need not be pressed into mortal hatred; and we have been led forward unconsciously into a recognition of a broader Christianity than as yet we are able to profess, in the respectful acknowledgment of excellence wherever excellence is found. Where we see piety, continence, courage, self-forgetfulness, there, or not far off, we know is the spirit of the Almighty; and, as we look around us among our living contemporaries, or look back with open eyes into the history of the past, we see—we dare not in voluntary blindness say that we do not see—that God is no respecter of 'denominations,' any more than he is a respecter of persons. His highest gifts are shed abroad with an even hand among the sects of Christendom, and petty distinctions of opinion melt away and become invisible in the fulness of a grander truth.

Thus, even among the straitest sects whose theories least allow room for latitude, liberty of conscience has found recognition, and has become the law of modern thought. It is as if the ancient Catholic unity, which was divided in the sixteenth century into separate streams of doctrine, as light is divided by the prism, was again imperceptibly returning; as if the coloured rays were once more blending themselves together in a purer and more rich transparency.

In this happy change of disposition, we have a difficulty in comprehending the intensity with which the different religious parties in England, as well as on the Continent, once detested each other. The fact is manifest; but the understanding refuses to realize its causes. We can perceive, indeed, that there may have been a fiery antagonism between Catholics and Reformers; but the animosities between Protestant and Protestant, the feeling which led Barnes to prosecute Lambert, or the Landgrave of Hesse to urge Henry VIII. to burn the Anabaptists, is obscure and unintelligible. Nevertheless, the more difficult it may be to imagine the nature of such a feeling, the more essential is it to bear in mind the reality of its existence; and a consequent and corollary upon it of no small importance must also be carefully remembered, that in the descending scale of the movement no sect or party recognised any shadow of division among those who were more advanced than themselves. To the Romanist, schism and heresy were an equal crime. All who had separated from the Papal communion were alike outcasts, cut off from grace, children of perdition. The Anglican could extend the terms of salvation only to those who submitted to ordinances, to the apostolical succession, and the system of the sacraments; the Lutherans anathematized those who denied the real presence; the followers of Zuinglius and Calvin, judging others as they were themselves judged, disclaimed such as had difficulties on the nature of the Trinity; the Unitarians gave the same measure to those who rejected the inspiration of Scripture; and with the word 'heretic' went along the full passion of abhorrence which had descended the historical stream of Christianity in connexion with the name.

Desiring the reader, then, to keep these points prominently before him, I must now describe briefly the position of the religious parties in England at the existing crisis.

First, there was the party of insurrection, the avowed or secret Romanists, those who denied the royal supremacy, who regarded the Pope as their spiritual sovereign, and retained or abjured their allegiance to their temporal prince as the Pope permitted or ordered. These were traitors in England, the hope of the Catholic powers abroad. When detected and obstinate they were liable to execution; but they were cowed by defeat and by the death of their leaders, and for the present were subsiding towards insignificance.

Secondly, there were the Anglicans, strictly orthodox in the speculative system of the faith, content to separate from Rome, but only that they might bear Italian fruit more profusely and luxuriantly when rooted in their own soil. Of these the avowed leaders were the majority of the bishops and the peers of the old creation, agreeing for the present to make the experiment of independence, but with a secret dislike to change, and a readiness, should occasion require, to return to the central communion. Weak in their reasoning, and selfish in their objects, the Anglicans were of importance only from the support of the conservative English instinct, which then as ever preferred the authority of precedent to any other guide, and defended established opinions and established institutions because they had received them from their fathers, and because their understandings were slow in entertaining new convictions.

To the third or Lutheran party, belonged Cranmer, Latimer, Barnes, Shaxton, Crome, Hilsey, Jerome, Barlow, all the government Reformers of position and authority, adhering to the real presence, and, in a general sense, to the sacraments, but melting them away in the interpretation. The true creed of these men was spiritual, not mechanical. They abhorred idolatry, images, pilgrimages, ceremonies, with a Puritan fervour. They followed Luther in the belief in justification by faith, they rejected masses, they did not receive the sacerdotal system, they doubted purgatory, they desired that the clergy should be allowed to marry, they differed from the Protestants in the single but vital doctrine of transubstantiation. This party after a few years ceased to exist, developing gradually from the type of Wittenberg to that of Geneva.

Lastly, and still confounded in a common mass of abomination, lay Zuinglians, Anabaptists, sacramentarians, outcasts disowned and cursed by all the rest as a stigma and reproach; those whose hearts were in the matter, who supplied the heat which had melted the crust of habit, and had made the Reformation possible.

For the present the struggle in the state lay between the Anglicans and the Lutherans—the king and Cromwell lying again between them. Cromwell, on the whole orthodox in matters of speculation, cared, nevertheless, little for such matters; his true creed was a hatred of charlatans, and of the system which nursed and gave them power; and his sympathy was gradually bursting the bounds of a tradition which continued to hamper him. The king was constant to his place of mediator; he insisted on the sacraments, yet he abhorred the magical aspect of them. He differed from the Anglican in his zeal for the dissemination of the Bible, in his detestation of the frauds, impostures, profligacies, idlenesses, ignorances, which had disgraced equally the secular and regular clergy, and in his fixed English resolution never more to tolerate the authority of the Pope. He differed from the Lutherans, and thus more and more from Cromwell, in his dislike of theoretic novelties, in an inability to clear himself from attaching a special character to the priesthood, in an adherence generally to the historical faith, and an anxiety to save himself and the country from the reproach of apostacy. A sharp line divided the Privy Council. Cranmer headed the Reformers, supported by the late-created peers, Cromwell, Lord Russell, and for a time Lord Southampton and the lord chancellor; opposed to these were the Dukes of Norfolk and Suffolk, Sir Anthony Brown, Gardiner, Bonner who was now Bishop of London, the Bishops of Durham, Chichester, and Lincoln; and the two parties regarded each other across the board with ever-deepening hatred, with eyes watching for any slip which might betray their antagonists to the powers of the law, and were only prevented by the king's will from flying into open opposition.

In the country, the sympathy of the middle classes was, for the most part, with Henry in preference to either Cranmer or Gardiner, Norfolk or Cromwell. Even in the Pilgrimage of Grace the king had been distinguished from his advisers. A general approbation of the revolt from a foreign usurpation led the body of the nation to support him cordially against the Pope; and therefore, as long as there was danger from Paul or Paul's friends, in England or out of it, Cromwell remained in power as the chief instrument by which the Papal domination had been overthrown. But there was an understanding felt, if not avowed, both by sovereign and subjects, that even loyalty had its limits. If it were true—as the king had ever assured them that it was not true—that Cromwell was not only maintaining English independence and reforming practical abuses, but encouraging the dreaded and hated 'heresy,' then indeed their duties and their conduct might assume another aspect.

And seeing that this 'heresy,' that faith in God and the Bible, as distinguished from faith in Catholicism, was the root and the life of the whole change, that the political and practical revolution was but an *alteration of season*, necessary for the nurture of the divine seed which an invisible hand had sown—seeing that Cromwell himself was opening his eyes to know this important fact, and would follow fearlessly wherever his convictions might lead him, appearances boded ill for the terms on which he might soon be standing with the king, ill for the 'unity and concord' which the king imagined to be possible.

Twice already we have seen Henry pouring oil over the water. The 'Articles of Religion' and the 'Institution of a Christian Man' had contained, perhaps, the highest wisdom on the debated subjects which as yet admitted of being expressed in words. But they had fallen powerless. The decree had gone out, but the war of words had not ceased. The Gospel had brought with it its old credentials. It had divided nation against nation, house against house, child against father. It had brought, 'not peace, but a sword:' the event long ago foretold and long ago experienced. But Henry could not understand the signs of the times; and once again he appealed to his subjects in language of pathetic reproach.

'The King's Highness to all and singular his loving subjects sends his greeting. His Majesty, desiring nothing more than to plant Christ and his doctrine in all his people's hearts, hath thought good to declare how much he is offended with all them that wring and wrest his words, driving them to the maintenance of their fantasies, abuses, and naughty opinions; not regarding how his Highness, as a judge indifferent between two parties, whereof the one is too rash and the other too dull, laboureth for agreement. Seeing the breach of small matters to be cause of great dissension, his Highness had charged his subjects to observe such ceremonies and rites as have been heretofore used in his Church, giving therewith commandment to the bishops and curates to instruct the people what ceremonies are, what good they do when not misused, what hurt when taken to be of more efficacy and strength than they are. His Highness, being careful over all his people, is as loath that the dull party should fancy their ceremonies to be the chief points of Christian religion, as he is miscontent with the rash party which hunt down what they list without the consent of his Grace's authority. His Highness wills that the disobedience of them that seek their lusts and liberties shall be repressed, and they to bear the infirmity and weakness of their neighbours until such time as they, enstrengthened, may be able to go in like pace with them, able to draw in one yoke: for St. Paul would a decent order in the Church; and, because God is a God of peace and not of dissension, it were meet that all they that would be his should agree on all points, and especially in matters of religion.

'God's will, love, and goodness ought. with all reverence, to be kept in memory; and therefore the old forefathers thought it well done that certain occasions might be devised to keep them in remembrance, and so invented signs and tokens which, being seen of the eye, might put the heart in mind of his will and promises. For, as the word is a token that warneth us by the ear, so the sacraments ordained by Christ, and ceremonies invented by men, are sensible tokens to warn us by the eye of that self-same will and pleasure that the word doth; and, as the word is but an idle voice without it be understood, so are all ceremonies but beggarly things, dumb and dead, if the meaning of them be not known. They are but means and paths to religion, made to shew where Christian people must seek their comfort and where they must establish their belief, and not to be taken as savers or workers of any part of salvation. But his Grace seeth priests much readier to deal holy bread, to sprinkle holy water. than to teach the people what dealing or sprinkling sheweth. If the priests would exhort their parishioners, and put them in remembrance of the things that indeed work all our salvation, neither the ceremonies should be dumb nor the people would take that that is the way of their journey, to be the end of their journey. Neither bread nor water nor any indifferent thing can be holy, but it be because it bringeth men to holy thoughts, to godly contemplations, and telleth them where they may and must seek holiness. Ceremonies cannot yet be put down, because the people are evil taught, and would be much offended with the sudden overthrow of them; but, if they be used, their meaning and signification not declared, they are nought else but shadows without a body —shells where there is no kernel—seals of decision without any writing—witnesses without any covenant, text, or promise. And for this cause the King's Highness commanded that ceremonies should be used, and used without superstition; and now, of late, some have blurted in the people's ears that their ceremonies be come home again, taking them as things in themselves necessary—slandering all such as, in their preaching, have reproved the misuse of them.

'The King's Highness, being grounded upon a surer foundation than to waver or revoke any his former injunctions, might worthily punish such wresters of his words and changers of his will and pleasure; but for as much as his Grace is persuaded that clemency often times worketh more than pain can, and seeing many of his loving subjects punished since his last proclamation, not only for evil opinions, but also for words spoken of long time past, his Grace, tendering nothing more than the wealth and comfort of his subjects, doth think it meet rather to heal all diseased, fearful, and hollow hearts, than by dread and fear to keep them still faint friends —faint to God, faint to the truth, faint to his Highness. And, in this consideration, his Highness granteth a general pardon and discharge to all and singular his loving subjects for all and singular causes, matters, suits, preachings, writings, and other things by them or any of them done, had, made, defended, or spoken, touching matters of Christian religion, whereby they might have been brought in danger of the law for suspicion of heresy. And his Highness trusteth that this his gracious pity shall more effectually work the abolishing of detestable heresies and fond opinions than shall the extreme punishment of the law. For, where fear of hurt should be a cause that they should less love his Highness than their duty bound them to do, now shall this be an occasion, his Grace thinketh, not only to make them tender his Highness's will and pleasure, but also to cause them, of honest love, quite to cast away all foolish, fond, evil, and condemned opinions, and joyfully to return to the elect number of Christ's Church.

'All that is past, as touching this matter, his Highness pardoneth and frankly forgetteth it wholly. But, as his Grace desireth the confusion of error, this way so failing of his purpose and expectation, his Highness will use, albeit much against his will, another way—that, when gentleness cannot work, then to provide what the laws and execution of them can do.'[1]

What persuasion could effect this address would have effected; but kindness and menace were alike unavailing. A seed was growing and to grow, which the king knew not of; and it was to grow, as it were, in the disguise of error, with that abrupt violence which so often, among human beings, makes truth a stone of stumbling, and a rock of offence. The young were generally on one side, the old on the other—an inversion of the order of nature when the old are wrong and the young are right.[2] The

---

[1] Royal Proclamation: *Rolls House MS.* A 1, 10.
[2] In 'Lusty Juventus' the Devil is introduced, saying—
'Oh, oh! full well I know the cause
That my estimation doth thus decay:
The old people would believe still in my laws,

learned, again, were on the wrong side, the ignorant were on the right—a false relation, also fertile in evil. Peasant theologians in the public-houses disputed over their ale on the mysteries of justification, and from words passed soon to blows. The Bibles, which lay open in every parish church, became the text-books of self-instructed fanatics. The voluble orator of the village was chosen by his companions, or, by imagined superior intelligence, appointed himself, to read and expound; and, ever in such cases, the most forward was the most passionate and the least wise. Often, for the special annoyance of old-fashioned church-goers, the time of divine service was chosen for a lecture; and opinions were shouted out in 'loud high voices,' which, in the ears of half the congregation, were damnable heresy.[1] The king's proclamations were but as the words of a man speaking in a tempest —blown to atoms as they are uttered. The bishops were bearded in their own palaces with insolent defiance; Protestant mobs would collect to overawe them on their tribunals;[2] and Cromwell was constituted a referee, to whom victims of episcopal persecution rarely appealed without

> But the younger sort lead them a contrary way.
> They will not believe, they plainly say,
> In old traditions made by men;
> But they will live as the Scripture teacheth them.'
>   HAWKINS's *Old Plays*, vol. i. p. 152.

[1] 'The king intended his loving subjects to use the commodity of the reading of the Bible humbly, meekly, reverently, and obediently; and not that any of them should read the said Bible with high and loud voices in time of the celebration of the mass, and other divine services used in the Church; or that any of his lay subjects should take upon them any common disputation, argument, or exposition of the mysteries therein contained.'—Proclamation of the Use of the Bible: BURNET's *Collectanea*, p. 138.
In a speech to the parliament Henry spoke also of the abuse of the Bible: 'I am very sorry to know and hear how unreverendly that most precious jewel, the Word of God, is disputed, rhymed, sung, and jangled in every alehouse and tavern. I am even as much sorry that the readers of the same follow it in doing so faintly and coldly.'— HALL, p. 866.

[2] The Bishop of Norwich wrote to Cromwell, informing him that he had preached a sermon upon grace and freewill in his cathedral;' 'the next day,' he said, 'one Robert Watson very arrogantly and in great fume came to my lodgings for to reason with me in that matter, affirming himself not a little to be offended with mine assertion of free will, saying he would set his foot by mine, affirming to the death that there was no such free will in man. Notwithstanding I had plainly declared it to be of no strength, but only when holpen by the grace of God; by which his ungodly enterprise, perceived and known of many, my estimation and credence concerning the sincere preaching of the truth was like to decay.' The bishop went on to say that he had set Watson a day to answer for 'his temerarious opinions,' and was obliged to call in a number of the neighbouring county magistrates to enable him to hold his court, 'on account of the great number which then assembled as Watson's fautors.'—The Bishop of Norwich to Cromwell: *MS. State Paper Office*, first series, vol. x.

finding protection.[1] Devout communities were scandalized by priests marrying their concubines, or bringing wives whom they had openly chosen to their parsonages. The celibacy of the clergy was generally accepted as a theory; and, though indulgence had been liberally extended to human weakness and frailty, the opinion of the world was less complacent when secret profligacy stepped forward into the open day under the apparent sanction of authority.[2]

The mysteries of the faith were insulted in the celebration of the divine service. At one place, when the priest lifted up the host, a member of the congregation, 'a lawyer' and a gentleman, lifted up a little dog in derision. Another, who desired that the laity should be allowed communion in both kinds, taunted the minister with having drunk all the wine, and with having blessed the people with an empty chalice. The intensity of the indignation which these and similar outrages created in the body of the nation, may be gathered from a scene which took place when an audacious offender was seized by the law, and suffered at Ipswich. When the fire was

---

[1] For instance, in Watson's case he seems to have rebuked the bishop.—*State Paper Office*, first series, vol. x.

[2] Very many complaints of parishioners on this matter remain among the *State Papers*. The difficulty is to determine the proportion of offenders (if they may be called such) to the body of the spirituality. The following petition to Cromwell, as coming from the collective incumbents of a diocese, represents most curiously the perplexity of the clergy in the interval between the alteration of the law and the inhibition of their previous indulgences. The date is probably 1536. The petition was in connexion with the commission of inquiry into the general morality of the religious orders:—

'May it please your mastership, that when of late we, your poor orators the clergy of the diocese of Bangor, were visited by the king's visitors and yours, in the which visitation many of us (to knowledge the truth to your mastership) be detected of incontinency, as it appeareth by the visitors' books, and not unworthy, wherefore we humbly submit ourselves unto your mastership's mercy, heartily desiring of you remission, or at least wise of merciful punishment and correction, and also to invent after your discreet wisdom some lawful and godly way for us your aforesaid orators, that we may maintain and uphold such poor hospitalities as we have done hitherto, most by provision of such women as we have customably kept in our houses. For in case we be compelled to put away such women, according to the injunctions lately given us by the foresaid visitors, then shall we be fain to give up hospitality, to the utter undoing of such servants and families as we daily keep, and to the great loss and harms of the king's subjects, the poor people which were by us relieved to the uttermost of our powers, and we ourselves shall be driven to seek our living at alehouses and taverns, for mansions upon the benefices and vicarages we have none. And as for gentlemen and substantial honest men, for fear of inconvenience, knowing our frailty and accustomed liberty, they will in no wise board us in their houses.'—Petition of the Clergy of Bangor to the Right Hon. Thomas Cromwell: *MS. State Paper Office*, second series, vol. xxxvi.

lighted, a commissary touched the victim with his wand, and urged him to recant. The man spat at him for an answer, and the commissary exclaimed that forty days' indulgence would be granted by the Bishop of Norwich to every one who would cast a stick into the pile. 'Then Baron Curzon, Sir John Audeley, with many others of estimation, being there present, did rise from their seats, and with their swords cut down boughs and threw them into the fire, and so did all the multitude of the people.'[1] It seems most certain that the country only refrained from taking the law into their own hands, and from trying the question with the Protestants, as Aske and Lord Darcy desired, by open battle, from a confidence that the government would do their duties, that in some way the law would interfere, and these excesses would be put down with a high hand.

The meeting of parliament could be delayed no longer; and it must be a parliament composed of other members than those who had sate so long and so effectively.[2] Two years before it had been demanded by the northern counties. The promise had been given, and the expectation of a fresh election had been formed so generally, that the country had widely prepared for it. The counties and towns had been privately canvassed; the intended representation had been arranged. The importance of the crisis, and the resolution of the country gentlemen to make their weight appreciated, was nowhere felt more keenly than in the court.

Letters survive throwing curious light on the history of this election. We see the Cromwell faction straining their own and the crown's influence as far as it would bear to secure a majority—failing in one place, succeeding in another—sending their agents throughout the country, demanding support, or entreating it, as circumstances allowed: or, when they were able, coercing the voters with a high hand. Care was taken to secure the return of efficient speakers to defend the government measures;[3] and Cromwell, by his exertions and by his anxiety, enables

[1] This story rests on the evidence of eye-witnesses.—FOXE, vol. v. p. 251, &c.

[2] The late parliament had become a byword among the Catholics and reactionaries. Pole speaks of the 'Conventus malignantium qui omnia illa decreta contra Ecclesiæ unitatem fecit.'—*Epist. Reg. Pol.* vol. ii. p. 46.

[3] 'For your Grace's parliament I have appointed (for a crown borough) your Grace's servant Mr. Morison, to be one of them. No doubt he shall be able to answer or take up such as should crack on far with litterature of learning.'—Cromwell to Henry VIII.: *State Papers*, vol. i. p. 603.

us to measure the power of the crown, both within parliament and without; to conclude with certainty that danger was feared from opposition, and that the control of the cabinet over the representation of England was very limited.

The returns for the boroughs were determined by the chief owners of property within the limits of the franchise: those for the counties depended on the great landholders. In the late parliament Cromwell wrote to some gentleman, desiring him to come forward as the government candidate for Huntingdonshire. He replied that the votes of the county were already promised, and unless his competitors could he induced to resign be could not offer himself.[1] In Shropshire, on the call of parliament to examine the treasons of Anne Boleyn,[2] there was a division of interest. 'The worshipful of the shire' desired to return a supporter of Cromwell: the sheriff, the under-sheriff, and the town's people, were on the other side. The election was held at Shrewsbury, and the inhabitants assembled riotously, overawed the voters, and carried the opposition member by intimidation. On the present occasion Lord Southampton went in person round Surrey, Sussex, and Hampshire, where his own property was situated. The election for Surrey he reported himself able to carry with certainty. At Guildford he manœuvred to secure both seats, but was only able to obtain one. He was anticipated for the other by a Guildford townsman, whom the mayor and burgesses told him that they all desired. Sir William Goring and Sir John Gage were standing on the court interest for Sussex. Sir John Dawtry, of Petworth, and Lord Maltravers, had promised their support, and Southampton hoped that they might be considered safe. Farnham was 'the Bishop of Winchester's town,' where he 'spared to meddle' without Cromwell's express orders. If the bishop's good intentions could he relied upon, interference might provoke gratuitous ill feeling. He had friends in the town, however, and he could make a party if Cromwell thought it necessary. In Portsmouth and Southampton the government influence was naturally paramount, through the dockyards, and the establishments maintained in them.[3] So far nothing can be detected more irregular than might have been found in the efforts of any prime minister be-

---

[1] Letter to Secretary Cromwell on the Election of the Knights of the Shire for the County of Huntingdon: *Rolls House MS.*
[2] Lady Blount to the King's Secretary: Ibid.
[3] The Earl of Southampton to Cromwell: *MS. Cotton. Cleopatra,* E 4.

fore the Reform Bill to secure a manageable House of Commons. More extensive interference was, however, indisputably practised, wherever interference was possible; at Oxford, we find Cromwell positively dictating the choice of a member, while at Canterbury, at the previous election, a case had occurred too remarkable for its arbitrary character to be passed over without particular mention. Directions had been sent down from London for the election of two government nominees. An answer was returned, stating humbly that the order had come too late—that two members of the corporation of Canterbury were already returned. I have failed to discover Cromwell's rejoinder; but a week later the following letter was addressed to him by the mayor and burgesses:—

'In humble wise we certify you that the 20th day of this present month, at six o'clock in the morning, I, John Alcock, mayor of Canterbury, received your letter directed to me, the said mayor, sheriff, and commonalty of the said city, signifying to us thereby the king's pleasure and commandment, that Robert Sacknell and John Bridges[1] should be burgesses of the parliament for the same city of Canterbury; by virtue whereof, according to our bounden duty, immediately upon the sight of your said letter and contents thereof perceived, we caused the commonalty of the said city to assemble in the court hall, where appeared the number of four score and seventeen persons, citizens and inhabitants of the said city: and according to the king's pleasure and commandment, freely with one voice, and without any contradiction, have elected and chosen the said Robert Sacknell and John Bridges to be burgesses of the parliament for the same city, which shall be duly certified by indenture under the seal of the said citizens and inhabitants, by the grace of the blessed Trinity.'

The first election, therefore, had been set aside by the absolute will of the crown, and the hope that so violent a proceeding might be explained tolerably through some kind of decent resignation is set aside by a further letter, stating that one of the persons originally chosen, having presumed to affirm that he was 'a true and proper burgess of the city,' he had been threatened into submission by a prospect of the loss of a lucrative office which he held under the corporation.[2]

---

[1] The two persons whom Cromwell had previously named.
[2] Letters of the Mayor of Canterbury to Cromwell: *MS. State Paper Office*, second series, vol. v.
In the first edition this affair is referred to the election of 1539.

For the parliament now elected, it is plain that the Privy Seal put out his utmost strength; and that he believed beforehand that his measures had been so well laid as to ensure the results which he desired. 'I and your dedicate councillors,' he wrote to the king, 'be about to bring all things so to pass that your Grace had never more tractable parliament.'[1] The event was to prove that he had deceived himself; a reaction set in too strong for his control, and the spirit which had dictated the Doncaster petition, though subdued and modified, could still outweigh the despotism of the minister or the intrigues of his agents.

The returns were completed; the members assembled in London, and with them as usual the convocation of the clergy. As an evidence of the greatness of the occasion, the two provinces were united into one; the convocation of York held its session with the convocation of Canterbury: a synod of the whole English Church met together, in virtue of its recovered or freshly constituted powers, to determine the articles of its belief.[2]

The opening was conducted by the king in person, on Monday, the 28th of April. The clerk of the House of Lords has recorded (either as if it was exceptional or as if the circumstances of the time gave to a usual proceeding an unusual meaning) the religious service with which the ceremony was accompanied, and the special prayers which were offered for the divine guidance.[3] The first

---

We are left almost invariably to internal evidence to fix the dates of letters, and finding the second of those written by the Mayor of Canterbury, on this subject, addressed to Cromwell as Lord Privy Seal, I supposed that it must refer to the only election conducted by him after he was raised to that dignity. I have since ascertained that the first letter, the cover of which I did not see, is addressed to Sir Thomas Cromwell, chief secretary, &c. It bears the date of the 20th of May, and though the year is not given, the difference of the two styles fixes it to 1536. The election was conducted while Cromwell was a commoner. He was made a peer and Privy Seal immediately on the meeting of parliament on the 2nd of July.

[1] Cromwell to Henry VIII.: *State Papers*, vol. i. p. 693.

[2] 'The King's Highness desiring that such a unity might be established in all things touching the doctrine of Christ's religion, as the same so being established might be to the honour of Almighty God, and consequently redound to the commonwealth of this his Highness's most noble realm, hath therefore caused his most High Court of Parliament to be at this time summoned, and also a synod and convocation of all the archbishops, bishops, and other learned men of the clergy of this his realm to be in like manner assembled.'—31 Henry VIII. cap. 14.

[3] 'Post missarum solemnia, decenter ac devote celebrata, divinoque auxilio humillimi imploranto et invocato.'—*Lords Journals*, 31 Henry VIII.

week passed in unexplained inactivity. On the Monday following the lord chancellor read the speech from the throne, declaring the object for which parliament had been called. The king desired, if possible, to close the religious quarrels by which the kingdom was distracted. With opinions in so furious conflict, the mode of settlement would demand anxious consideration; his Majesty therefore proposed, if the lords saw no objection, that, preparatory to the general debate, a committee of the upper house should compose a report upon the causes and character of the disagreement. The committee should represent both parties. The peers selected were Cromwell, the two archbishops, the Bishops of Bath, Ely, Bangor, Worcester, Durham, and Carlisle.[1] It was foreseen that a body, of which Cranmer and Latimer, Lee and Tunstall were severally members, was unlikely to work in harmony. The committee proceeded, however, to their labours; and up to this time even the Privy Council seem to have been ignorant of the course which events would follow. On some points the king had either formed no intention till he had ascertained the disposition of the House of Commons, or else he had kept his intentions carefully to himself. A paper of suggestions, representing the views of the moderate Reformers, was submitted to him by some one in high authority; and the tone in which they were couched implied a belief in the writer that his advice would be favourably received. It was to the effect that a table of heresies should be drawn out; that the judgment of the bench of bishops and the ecclesiastical lawyers should be taken upon it; that it should then be printed, and copies sent to every justice of the peace, to be read aloud at every assizes, court leet, or sessions, and in the charges delivered to the grand juries. A court might be constituted composed of six masters of chancery, mixed of priests and laymen, to whom all accusations would be referred; and the composite character of the tribunal would be a security against exaggeration or fanaticism. Meanwhile a bill should be prepared to be laid before parliament, relieving the clergy finally from the obligations of celibacy, legalizing the marriages which any among them had hitherto contracted, and for the future permitting them all 'to have wives and work for their living.' 'A little book,' in addition, should be compiled and printed, proving 'that the prayers of men that be here living for the souls of them that be dead

[1] Lords Journals, 31 Henry VIII.

could in no wise be profitable to them that were dead, and could not help them.'¹

It is hard to believe that the king's resolution was fixed, or even that his personal feelings were known to be decided against the marriage of the clergy, when a person evidently high in office could thus openly recommend to him the permission of it, and the reforming preachers at the court had spoken freely to the same effect before him in their sermons.² For the present, however, this matter with the rest waited the determination of the committee of religion, who remained ten days on their labours, and so far had arrived at no conclusions. In the interval the history of the northern rebellion was laid before the houses, with an account of the late conspiracy of the Marquis of Exeter and Lord Montague. Bills of attainder were presented against many of those who had suffered, and in the preambles their offences were stated, though with little detail. The omission in all but two instances is not important, for the act of parliament could have contained only what was proved upon the trials, and the substance of the accusations is tolerably well known. A more explicit statement might have been desired and expected when a parliamentary attainder was the beginning and end of the process. The Marchioness of Exeter and the Countess of Salisbury were not tried, but they were attainted in common with the rest; and it can be gathered only from the language of the act that circumstances were known to the parliament of which the traces are lost.³

¹ A Device for extirpating Heresies among the People: *Rolls House MS.*

² 'Nothing has yet been settled respecting the marriage of the clergy, although some persons have very freely preached before the king upon the subject.'—John Butler to Conrad Pellican, March 8, 1539: *Original Letters on the Reformation*, second series, p. 624.

³ Lady Exeter was afterwards pardoned. Lady Salisbury's offences, whatever they were, seem to have been known to the world, even before Lord Southampton's visit of inspection to Warblington. The magistrates of Stockton in Sussex sent up an account of examinations taken on the 13th of September, 1538, in which a woman is charged with having said, 'If so be that my Lady of Salisbury had been a young woman as she was an old woman, the King's Grace and his council had burnt her.'—*MS. State Paper Office*, second series, vol. xxxix. The act of attainder has not been printed (31 Henry VIII. cap. 15: *Rolls House MS.*); so much of it, therefore, as relates to these ladies is here inserted:

'And where also Gertrude Courtenay, wife of the Lord Marquis of Exeter, hath traitorously, falsely, and maliciously confederated herself to and with the abominable traitor Nicholas Carew, knowing him to be a traitor and a common enemy to his Highness and the realm of England; and hath not only aided and abetted the said Nicholas Carew in his abominable treasons, but also hath herself committed and perpetrated divers and sundry detestable and abominable treasons

Lady Salisbury, after her sentence, was removed from Cowdray to the Tower. A remarkable scene took place in the House of Lords on the last reading of the act. As soon as it was passed, Cromwell rose in his place, and displayed, in profound silence, a tunic of white silk, which had been discovered by Lord Southampton concealed amidst the countess's linen. On the front were embroidered the royal arms of England. Behind was the badge of the five wounds, which had been worn by the northern insurgents.¹ Cromwell knew what he was doing in the exhibition. It was shown, and it was doubtless understood, as conclusive evidence of the disposition of the daughter of the Duke of Clarence and the mother of Reginald Pole. The bill was disposed of rapidly. It was introduced on the 10th of May; it was concluded on the 12th. There was neither dispute nor difficulty; the interest of both houses was fastened on the great question before the committee.

The time passed on. No report was presented, and the peers grew impatient. On the 16th the Duke of Norfolk stated that, so far as he could perceive, no progress was being made in the proper business of the session, and, judging from a conversation which had passed when the committee of opinion was nominated, little progress was likely to be made in a body so composed. He therefore moved that the whole parliament be invited to discuss freely the six ensuing articles. 1. In the eucharist after consecration does there, or does there not, remain any

---

to the fearful peril of his Highness's royal person, and the loss and desolation of this realm of England, if God of his goodness had not in due time brought the same treason to knowledge;

'And where also Margaret Pole, Countess of Salisbury, and Hugh Vaughan, late of Bekener, in the county of Monmouth, yeoman, by instigation of the devil, putting apart the dread of Almighty God, their duty of allegiance, and the excellent benefits received of his Highness, have not only traitorously confederated themselves with the false and abominable traitors Henry Pole, Lord Montague, and Reginald Pole, sons to the said countess, knowing them to be false traitors, but also have maliciously aided, abetted, maintained, and comforted them in their said false and abominable treason, to the most fearful peril of his Highness, the commonwealth of this realm, &c., the said marchioness and the said countess be declared attainted, and shall suffer the pains and penalties of high treason.' I find no account of Vaughan, or of the countess's connexion with him. He was probably one of the persons employed to carry letters to and from the cardinal.

¹ 'Immediate post Billæ lectionem Dominus Cromwell palam ostendit quandam tunicam ex albo serico confectam inventam inter linteamina Comitissæ Sarum, in cujus parte anteriore existebant sola arma Angliæ; in parte vero posteriore insignia illa quibus nuper rebelles in aquilousri parte Angliæ in commotione suâ utebantur.'—*Lords Journals*, 31 Henry VIII.

substance of bread and wine? 2. Is communion in both kinds necessary or permitted to the laity? 3. Are vows of chastity deliberately made of perpetual obligation? 4. Is there or is there not any efficacy in private masses to benefit the souls of the dead? 5. Are priests permitted to have wives? 6. Shall auricular confession be retained or be not retained in the Church? The duke's own opinion on each and every of these points was well known; but the question was not only of the particular opinion of this or that person, but whether difference of opinion was any longer to be permitted; whether after discussion such positive conclusions could be obtained as might be enforced by a penal statute on all English subjects.

On the first no disagreement was anticipated. No member of either house, it is likely, and no member of convocation—not even Latimer—had as yet consciously denied the real presence; but the five remaining articles on which an issue was challenged were the special points on which the Lutheran party were most anxiously interested—the points on which, in the preceding summer, negotiations with the Germans were broken off, and on which Cranmer was now most desirous to claim a liberty for the Church, as the basis of an evangelical league in Christendom. Norfolk, therefore, had opened the battle, and it was waged immediately in full fury in both houses of parliament—in both houses of convocation. There were conferences and counter-conferences. Cromwell, perhaps knowing that direct opposition was useless, was inclined to accept in words resolutions which he had determined to neutralize; Cranmer, more frank, if less sagacious, spoke fearlessly for three days in opposition; and the king himself took part in the debate, and argued with the rest. The settlement was long protracted. There were prorogations for further consideration, and intervals of other business, when acts were passed which at any other moment would have seemed of immeasurable importance. The Romans, in periods of emergency, suspended their liberties and created a dictator. The English parliament, frightened at the confusion of the country, and the peril of interests which they valued even more than liberty, extended the powers of the crown. The preamble of the eighth of the thirty-first of Henry VIII.[1] states that—

[1] In quoting the preambles of acts of parliament I do not attach to them any peculiar or exceptional authority. But they are contemporary statements of facts and intentions carefully drawn, containing an explanation of the conduct of parliament and of the principal events of the time. The explanation may be false, but it is at least possible that it may be true; and my own conclusion is that, on the

'Forasmuch as the King's most Royal Majesty, for divers considerations, by the advice of his council, hath heretofore set forth divers and sundry proclamations, as well concerning sundry articles of Christ's religion, as for an unity and concord among the loving and obedient subjects of his realm, which, nevertheless, divers and many froward and obstinate persons have contemned and broken, not considering what a king by his royal power may do, for lack of a direct statute, to cause offenders to obey the said proclamations, which, being suffered, should not only encourage offenders to disobedience, but also seem too much to the dishonour of the King's Majesty, who may full ill bear it, and also give too great heart to malefactors and offenders; considering also that sudden causes and occasions fortune many times, which do require speedy remedies, and that by abiding for a parliament in the mean time might happen great prejudice to the realm; and weighing also *that his Majesty, which, by the kingly power given him by God, may do many things in such cases, should not be driven to extend the liberty and supremacy of his regal power and dignity by the wilfulness of froward subjects, it is thought in manner more than necessary* that the King's Highness of this realm for the time being, with the advice of his honourable council, should make and set forth proclamations for the good and politic order of this his realm, as cases of necessity shall require, and that an ordinary law should be provided, by the assent of his Majesty and parliament, for the due punishment, correction, and reformation of such offences and disobediences.'[1]

For these reasons the extraordinary privilege was conferred upon the crown of being able, with the consent of the Privy Council, to issue proclamations which should have the authority of acts of parliament; and pains and penalties might be inflicted to enforce submission, provided the specific punishment to follow disobedience was described and defined in each proclamation. A slight

---

whole, the account to be gathered from this source is truer than any other at which we are likely to arrive; that the story of the Reformation as read by the light of the statute book is more intelligible and consistent than any other version of it, doing less violence to known principles of human nature, and bringing the conduct of the principal actors within the compass of reason and probability. I have to say, further, that the more carefully the enormous mass of contemporary evidence of another kind is studied, documents, private and public letters, proclamations, council records, state trials, and other authorities, the more they will be found to yield to these preambles a steady support.

[1] 31 Henry VIII. cap. 8.

limitation was imposed upon this dangerous prerogative. The crown was not permitted to repeal or suspend existing statutes, or set aside the common law or other laudable custom. It might not punish with death, or with unlimited fines or imprisonments. Secondary penalties might be inflicted, on legitimate conviction in the Star Chamber; but they must have been previously defined, both in extent and character. These restrictions interfered with the more arbitrary forms of tyranny; yet the ordinary constitution had received a serious infringement, in order that it might not be infringed further by a compelled usurpation. A measure something larger than the suspension of the Habeas Corpus Act—the most extreme violation of the liberty of the subject to which, in the happier condition of England, we can now be driven, a measure infinitely lighter than the 'declaration of a state of siege,' so familiar to the most modern experience of the rest of Europe, was not considered too heavy a sacrifice of freedom, in comparison with the evils which it might prevent.[1]

While the Six Articles Bill was still under debate, the king at once availed himself of the powers conferred upon him, again to address the people. He spoke of the secret and subtle attempts which certain people were making to restore the hypocrite's religion—the evil and naughty superstitions and dreams which had been abolished and done away; while others, again, he said, were flying in the face of all order and authority, perverting the Scriptures, denying the sacraments, denying the authority of princes and magistrates, and making law and government impossible.[2] He dwelt especially on his disappointment at the bad use which had been made of the Bible: 'His

---

[1] The limitation which ought to have been made was in the time for which these unusual powers should be continued; the bill, however, was repealed duly in connexion with the treason acts and the other irregular measures in this reign, as soon as the crisis had passed away, or when those who were at the head of the state could no longer be trusted with dangerous weapons.—See 1 Edward VI. cap. 7. The temporary character of most of Henry's acts was felt, if it was not avowed. Sir Thomas Wyatt, in an address to the Privy Council, admitted to having said of the Act of Supremacy, 'that it was a goodly act, the King's Majesty being so virtuous, so wise, so learned, and so good a prince; but if it should fall unto an evil prince it were a sore rod:' and he added, 'I suppose I have not mis-said in that; for all powers, namely absolute, are sore rods when they fall into evil men's hands.'—Oration to the Council: NOTT's *Wyatt*, p. 304.

[2] The same expressions had been used of the Lollards a hundred and fifty years before. The description applied absolutely to the Anabaptists; and Oliver Cromwell had the same disposition to contend against among the Independents. The least irregular of the Protestant sects were tainted more or less with anarchical opinions.

Majesty's intent and hope had been, that the Scriptures would be read with meekness, with a will to accomplish the effect of them; not for the purpose of finding arguments to maintain extravagant opinions—not that they should be spouted out and declaimed upon at undue times and places, and after such fashions as were not convenient to be suffered.'[1] So far, it seemed as if the fruit which had been produced by this great and precious gift had been only quarrelling and railing, 'to the confusion of those that used the same, and to the disturbance, and in likelihood to the destruction, of all the rest of the king's subjects.'

Such shameful practices he was determined should be brought to an end. His 'daily study' was to teach his people to live together, not in rioting and disputing, but in unity, in charity, and love. He had therefore called his parliament, prelates, and clergy to his help, with a full resolution to 'extinct diversities of opinion by good and just laws;' and he now gave them his last solemn warning, if they would escape painful consequences, 'to study to live peaceably together, as good and Christian men ought to do.'

The great measure was now in motion; but its advance was still slow, and under the shadow of the absorbing interest which it created, two other statutes passed, without trace of debate or resistance; one of which was itself the closing scene of a mighty destruction; the other (had circumstances permitted the accomplishment of the design) would have constructed a fabric out of the ruins, the incompleteness of which, in these later days, the English Church is now languidly labouring to repair.

The thirteenth of the thirty-first of Henry VIII. confirmed the surrender of all the religious houses which had dissolved themselves since the passing of the previous act, and empowered the king to extend the provisions of that act, at his pleasure, to all such as remained standing. Monastic life in England was at an end, and for ever. A phase of human existence which had flourished in this island for ten centuries had passed out and could not be revived. The effort for the reform of the orders had totally failed; the sentiment of the nation had ceased to be interested in their maintenance, and the determined spirit of treason which the best and the worst conducted of the regular clergy had alike exhibited in the late rebellion, had given the finishing impulse to the resolution of the

---

[1] A considerable part of this address is in Henry's own handwriting.—See STRYPE's *Memorials*, vol. ii. p. 434.

government. The more sincerely 'religion' was professed, the more incurable was the attachment to the Papacy. The monks were its champions while a hope remained of its restoration. In the final severance from Rome the root of their life was divided; and the body of the nation, orthodox and unorthodox alike, desired to see their vast revenues applied to purposes of national utility. They were given over by parliament, therefore, to the king's hands. The sacrifice to the old families, the representatives of the ancient founders, was not only in feeling and associations, but in many instances was substantial and tangible. They had reserved to themselves annual rents. services, and reliefs; they had influence in the choice of superiors; the retainers of the abbeys followed their standard, and swelled their importance and their power.[1] All this was at an end; and although in some instances they repurchased, on easy terms, the estates which their forefathers had granted away, yet in general the confiscated lands fell in smaller proportions to the old-established nobility than we should have been prepared to expect. The new owners of these broad domains were, for the most part, either the rising statesmen—the *nori homines* who had been nursed under Wolsey, and grown to manhood in the storms of the Reformation, Cromwell, Russell, Audeley, Wriothesley, Dudley, Seymour, Fitzwilliam, and the satellites who revolved about them; or else city merchants, successful wood-dealers or manufacturers: in all cases the men of progress—the men of the future—the rivals, if not the active enemies, of the hereditary feudal magnates.

To such persons ultimately fell by far the largest portion of the abbey lands. It was not, however, so intended. Another act, which Henry drew with his own hand,[2] stated that, inasmuch as the slothful and ungodly life of all sorts of persons, bearing the name of religious, was notorious to all the world, ... in order that both they and their estates might be turned to some better account, that the people might be better educated, charity be better exercised, and the spiritual discipline of the country be in all respects better maintained, it was expedient that the king should have powers granted to him to create by letters patent, and endow, fresh bishoprics as he should think fit, and convert religious houses into chapters of deans and prebendaries, to be attached to each of the new sees, and to improve and strengthen those already in existence. The

[1] See FULLER. vol. III. p. 411.
[2] 31 Henry VIII. cap. 9.

scheme, as at first conceived, was on a magnificent scale. Twenty-one new bishoprics were intended, with as many cathedrals and as many chapters; and in each of the latter (unless there had been gross cause to make an exception) the monks of the abbey or priory suppressed would continue on the new foundation, changing little but the name.[1] Henry's intentions, could they have been executed, would have materially softened the dissolution. The twenty-one bishoprics, however, sunk into six;[2] and eight religious houses only were submitted to the process of conversion.[3] The cost of the national defences, followed by three years of ruinous war, crippled at its outset a generous project, and saved the Church from the possession of wealth and power too dangerously great.

On the 23rd of May parliament was prorogued for a week; on the 30th the lord chancellor informed the peers that his Majesty, with the assistance of the bench of bishops, had come to a conclusion on the Six Articles; which, it was assumed—from the course possibly which the many debates had taken—would be acceptable to the two houses. A penal statute would be required to enforce the resolutions; and it was for their lordships to determine the character and the extent of the punishment which would be necessary. To give room for differences of opinion, two committees were this time appointed—the first consisting of Cranmer, the Bishops of Ely and St. David's, and Sir William Petre; the other of the Archbishop of York, the Bishops of Durham and Winchester, and Dr. Tregonwell.[4] The separate reports were drawn and presented; the peers accepted the second. The cruel character of the resolutions was attributed, by sound au-

[1] In some instances, if not in all, this was actually the case.—See the Correspondence between Cromwell and the Prior of Christ Church at Canterbury: *MS. State Paper Office*, second series.
[2] Oxford, Peterborough, Bristol, Gloucester, Chester, and Westminster.
[3] Canterbury, Winchester, Ely, Norwich, Worcester, Rochester, Durham, and Carlisle.
[4] 'Per Dominum cauoellarium declaratum est quod cum non solum proceres spirituales verum etiam regia majestas ad unionem in precedentibus articulis conficiendam multipliciter studuerunt et laboraverunt ita ut nunc unio in eisdem confecta sit regia igitur voluntatis esse ut penale aliquod statutum efficeretur ad coercendum suos subditos, ne contra determinationem in eisdem articulis confectam contradicerent, aut dissentirent, verum ejus majestatem proceribus formam hujusmodi malefactorum hujusmodi committere. Itaque ex eorum communi consensu concordatum est quod Archiepiscopus Cant., Episcopus Elien., Episcopus Menevensis et Doctor Peter, unam formam cujusdam actus, concernentem Punitionem hujusmodi malefactorum dictarent et componerent similiterque quod Archiepisc. Ebor., Episc. Dunelm., Episc. Winton et Doctor Tregonwell alteram ejusmodi effectus dictitarent et componerent formam.'—*Lords Journals*, 31 Henry VIII.

thority, to the especial influence of Gardiner.[1] It was not, in its extreme form, the work of the king, nor did it express his own desires. His opinions on the disputed articles were wholly those contained in the body of the act. He had argued laboriously in their maintenance, and he had himself drawn a sketch for a statute not unlike that which passed into law; but he had added two clauses, from which the bishops contrived to deliver themselves, which, if insisted upon, would have crippled the prosecutions and tied the hands of the Church officials. According to Henry's scheme, the judges would have been bound to deliver in writing to the party accused a copy of the accusation, with the names and depositions of the witnesses; and, if there was but one witness, let his reputation have stood as high as that of any man in the state, it would have been held insufficient for a conviction.[2]

The slight effort of leniency was not approved by the House of Lords. In spite of Cranmer's unwearied and brave opposition, the harshest penalties which were recommended received the greatest favour; and 'the bloody act of the Six Articles,' or 'the whip with six strings,' as it was termed by the Protestants, was the adopted remedy to heal the diseases of England.

After a careful preamble, in which the danger of divisions and false opinions, the peril both to the peace of the commonwealth and the souls of those who were ensnared by heresy, were elaborately dwelt upon, the king, the two houses of parliament, and the convocations of the two provinces declared themselves, after a great and long, deliberate and advised disputation, to have adopted the following conclusions:[3]—

1. That, in the most blessed sacrament of the altar, by the strength and efficacy of Christ's mighty word, it being spoken by the priest, was present really, under the form of bread and wine, the natural body and blood of

---

[1] Foxe's rhetoric might be suspected, but a letter of Melancthon to Henry VIII. is a more trustworthy evidence: 'Oh, cursed bishops!' he exclaims; 'oh, wicked Winchester!'—Melancthon to Henry VIII.: printed in FOXE, vol. v.

[2] 'The judge shall be bounden, if it be demanded of him, to deliver in writing to the party called before him, the copy of the matter objected, and the names and depositions of the witnesses . . . . and in such case, as the party called answereth and denyeth that that is objected, and that no proof can be brought against him but the deposition of one witness only, then and in that case, be that witness never of so great honesty and credit, the same party so called shall be without longer delay absolved and discharged by the judge's sentence freely without further cost or molestation.'—The Six Articles Bill as drawn by the King: WILKINS's *Concilia*, vol. iii. p. 846.

[3] Act for Abolishing Diversity of Opinions: 31 Henry VIII. cap. 14.

Jesus Christ; and that, after consecration, there remained no substance of bread and wine, nor any other but the substance of Christ.

2. That communion in both kinds was not essential to salvation; that, under the form of bread, the blood was present as well as the body; and, under the form of wine, the flesh was present as well as the blood.

3. That it was not permitted to priests, after their ordination, to marry and have wives.

4. That vows of chastity made to God advisedly, by man or woman, ought to be observed, and were of perpetual obligation.

5. That private masses ought to be continued, as meet and necessary for godly consolation and benefit.

6. That auricular confession to a priest must be retained, and continue to be used in the Church.

The lords and commons, in accepting the articles, gave especial thanks to his Majesty for the godly pain, study, and travail with which he had laboured to establish them; and they 'prayed God that he might long reign to bring his godly enterprise to a full end and perfection; and that by these means 'quiet, unity, and concord might be had in the whole body of the realm for ever.'

On their side they enacted against such persons as should refuse to submit to the resolutions:—

That whoever, by word or writing, denied the first article, should be declared a heretic, and suffer death by burning, without opportunity of abjuration, without protection from sanctuary or benefit of clergy. Whoever spoke or otherwise broke the other five articles, or any one of them, should, for the first offence, forfeit his property; if he offended a second time, or refused to abjure when called to answer, he should suffer death as a felon. All marriages hitherto contracted by priests were declared void. A day was fixed before which their wives were to be sent to their friends, and to retain them after that day was felony. To refuse to go to confession was felony. To refuse to receive the sacrament was felony. On every road on which the free mind of man was moving the dark sentinel of orthodoxy was stationed with its flaming sword; and in a little time all cowards, all who had adopted the new opinions with motives less pure than that deep zeal and love which alone entitle human beings to constitute themselves champions of God, flinched into their proper nothingness, and left the battle to the brave and the good.

The feelings with which the bill was received by the

world may be gathered most readily from two letters—one written by an English nobleman, who may be taken to have represented the sentiments of the upper classes in this country; the other written by Philip Melancthon, speaking in the name of Germany and of English Protestantism struggling to be born.

The signature and the address of the first are lost; but the contents indicate the writer's rank.[1]

'For news here, I assure you, never prince showed himself so wise a man, so well learned, and so catholic, as the king hath done in this parliament. With my pen I cannot express his marvellous goodness, which is come to such effect that we shall have an act of parliament so spiritual that I think none shall dare to say that in the blessed sacrament of the altar doth remain either bread or wine after the consecration; nor that a priest may have a wife; nor that it is necessary to receive our Maker *sub utraque specie;* nor that private masses should not be used as they have been; nor that it is not necessary to have auricular confession. And notwithstanding my Lord Canterbury, my Lord of Ely, my Lord of Salisbury, my Lords of Worcester, Rochester, and St. David's defended the contrary long time, yet, finally, his Highness confounded them all with God's learning. York, Durham, Winchester, London, Chichester, Norwich, and Carlisle have shewed themselves honest and well learned men. *We of the temporalty have been all of one opinion;* and my Lord Chancellor and my Lord Privy Seal as good as we can desire. My Lord of Canterbury and all the bishops have given over their opinions and come in to us, save Salisbury, who yet continueth a lewd fool. Finally, all England hath cause to thank God, and most heartily to rejoice, of the king's most godly proceedings.'

There spoke the conservative Englishman, tenacious of old opinions, believing much in established order, and little in the minds and hearts of living human beings—believing that all variation from established creeds could only arise from vanity and licentiousness, from the discontent of an ill-regulated understanding.

We turn to Melancthon, and we hear the protest of humanity, the pleading of intellect against institutions, the voice of freedom as opposed to the voice of order—the two spirits 'between whose endless jar justice resides.'

He reminded the king of the scene described by Thucydides, where the Athenians awoke to their injustice and

[1] Printed in STRYPE's *Cranmer,* vol. II. p. 743.

revoked the decree against Mytilene, and he implored him to reconsider his fatal determination. He was grieved, he said, for those who professed the same doctrines as himself; but he was more grieved for the king, who allowed himself to be the minister of tyranny. For them nothing could happen more glorious than to lose their lives in bearing witness to the truth; but it was dreadful that a prince, who could not plead the excuse of ignorance, should stain his hands with innocent blood. The bishops pretended that they were defending truth; but it was the truth of sophistry, not of God. In England, and through Europe, the defenders of truth were piecing old garments with new cloth, straining to reconcile truth with error, and light with darkness. He was not surprised. It was easy to understand with the reason how such things were; but his feelings recoiled, and pleaded passionately against their hard and cruel hearts. 'If that barbarous decree be not repealed,' he said, 'the bishops will never cease to rage against the Church of Christ without mercy and without pity; for them the devil useth as instruments and ministers of his fury and malice against Christ—he stirreth them up to kill and destroy the members of Christ. And you, O king! all the godly beseech most humbly that you will not prefer such wicked and cruel oppressions and subtle sophistries before their own just and honest prayers. God recompense you to your great reward if you shall grant those prayers. Christ is going about hungry and thirsty, naked and imprisoned, complaining of the rage and malice of the bishops, and the cruelty of kings and princes. He prays, He supplicates, that the members of his body be not rent in pieces, but that truth may be defended, and the Gospel preached among men; a godly king will hear his words, and obey the voice of his entreaty.'[1]

The extremes of opinion were thus visible on either side. Between them the government steered their arduous way, under such guidance as conscience and necessity could furnish. To pass a statute was one thing: to enforce the provisions of it was another. The peers and bishops expected to be indulged forthwith in the pleasures of a hot persecution. The king's first act was to teach them to moderate their ardour. In order to soothe the acrimonies which the debate had kindled, the lords spiritual and temporal were requested to repair to Lambeth to 'animate and comfort the archbishop,' and to bury the

[1] Philip Melancthon to Henry VIII.: Foxe, vol. v.

recollection of all differences by partaking of his hospitality. The history of their visit was, perhaps, diluted through Protestant tradition before it reached the pages of Foxe, and the substance only of the story can be relied upon as true. It is said, however, that on this occasion a conversation arose which displayed broadly the undercurrent of hatred between Cromwell and the peers. One of the party spoke of Wolsey, whom he called 'a stubborn and churlish prelate, and one that never could abide any nobleman;' 'and that,' he added, 'you know well enough, my Lord Cromwell, for he was your master.' Cromwell answered that it was true that he had been Wolsey's servant, nor did he regret his fortune. 'Yet was I never so far in love with him,' he said, 'as to have waited upon him to Rome, which you, my lord, were, I believe, prepared to have done.' It was not true, the first speaker said. Cromwell again insisted that it was true, and even mentioned the number of florins which were to have paid him for his services. The other said 'he lied in his teeth, and great and high words rose between them.'[1]

The king's peace-making prospered little. The impetus of a great victory was not to be arrested by mild persuasions. A commission was appointed by the Catholic leaders to reap the desired fruits. Such of the London citizens as had most distinguished themselves as opponents of reformation in all its forms—those especially who had resisted the introduction of the Bible—formed a court, which held its sittings in the Mercers' Chapel. They 'developed the statute' in what were termed 'branches of inference;' they interpreted 'speaking against masses' to comprehend 'coming seldom to mass.' Those who were slow in holding up their hands 'at sacring time,' or who did not strike their breasts with adequate fervour, were held to have denied the sacrament. In the worst temper of the Inquisition they revived the crippled functions of the spiritual courts: they began to inquire again into private conduct,—who went seldom to church—who refused to receive holy bread or holy water—who were frequent readers of the Bible, 'with a great many other such branches.'[2] 'They so sped with their branches' that in a fortnight they had indicted five hundred persons in

---

[1] Foxe, vol. v. p. 263.
[2] Hall's Chronicle, p. 828. Hall is a good evidence on this point. He was then a middle-aged man, resident in London, with clear eyes and a shrewd, clear head, and was relating not what others told him, but what he actually saw.

London alone. In their imprudent fanaticism they forgot all necessary discretion. There was not a man of note or reputation in the City who had so much as spoken a word against Rome, but was under suspicion, or under actual arrest. Latimer and Shaxton were imprisoned, and driven to resign their bishoprics.[1] Where witnesses were not to be found, Hall tells us significantly, 'that certain of the clergy would procure some, or else they were slandered.' The fury which had been pent up for years, revenge for lost powers and privileges, for humiliations and sufferings, remorse of conscience reproaching them for their perjury in abjuring the Pope, whom they still reverenced, and to whose feet they longed to return, poured out from the reactionary churchmen in a concentrated lava stream of malignity.

The blindness of their rage defeated their object. The king had not desired articles of peace that worthless bigots might blacken the skies of England with the smoke of martyr-fires. The powers given to the crown by the Act of Proclamations recoiled on those who bestowed them, and by a summary declaration of pardon the bishops' dungeon doors were thrown open; the prisoners were dismissed;[2] and though Cromwell had seemed to yield to them in the House of Lords, their victims, they discovered, would not be permitted to be sacrificed so long as Cromwell was in power.

Not contented with granting an indemnity, Henry set the persecutors an example of the spirit in which to enforce the Six Articles. Next to Barnes and Latimer, the most obnoxious of all the reforming clergy, in high orthodox quarters, was Jerome, Vicar of Stepney. While the parliament was in session this person preached in violent denunciation of their proceedings. He denied their authority to make laws to bind the conscience.[3] He had used 'opprobrious words' against the members of the House of Commons, calling them 'butterflies, fools, and knaves;' and when the Act of Opinions was passed, he was seized by the committee at the Mercers'. We need not ask how he would have been dealt with there; but Henry took the cause out of their hands. He sent for

---

[1] In Latimer's case, against Henry's will, or without his knowledge. Cromwell, either himself deceived or desiring to smooth the storm, told Latimer that the king advised his resignation; 'which his Majesty afterwards denied, and pitied his condition.'—*State Papers*, vol. 1. p. 849.

[2] Hall.

[3] Notes of Erroneous Doctrines preached at Paul's Cross by the Vicar of Stepney: *MS. Rolls House.*

the preacher, and, as Jerome reported afterwards, 'so indifferently heard him, so gently used him, so mercifully forgave him, that there was never poor man received like gentleness at any prince's hand.' The preacher consented to revoke his words in the place where he had used them; and appearing again in the same pulpit, he confessed that he had spoken wrongly. The king had shown him that to restrain the power of the government within the limits which he desired, would create confusion in the commonwealth, and that his declamation against the burgesses had been ill and slanderously spoken. He recanted also other parts of his sermon on questions of doctrine; but he added an explanation of his submission characteristic of the man and of the time. 'He was perplexed,' he said, 'but not confounded;' 'he was compelled to deny himself; but to deny himself was no more but when adversity should come, as loss of goods, infamies, and like trouble, than to deny his own will, and call upon the Lord, saying, *Fiat voluntas tua*.'¹ Catholics and Protestants combined to render the king's task of ruling them as arduous as it could be made.

The bill, nevertheless, though it might be softened in the execution, was a hard blow on the Reformation, and was bitterly taken. Good came at last out of the evil. The excesses of the moving party required absolutely to be checked; nor could this necessary result be obtained till the bishops for a time had their way uncontrolled; but the dismissal of Latimer from the bench, the loss of the one man in England whose conduct was, perhaps, absolutely straightforward, upright, and untainted with alloy of baser matter, was altogether irreparable.

We approach another subject of scarcely less importance than this famous statute, and scarcely less stern. Before we enter upon it we may pause for a moment over one of the few scenes of a softer kind which remain among the records of this iron age. It is but a single picture. Richard Cromwell, writing from the court of some unimportant business which the king had transacted, closes his letter with adding: 'This done, his Grace went to the prince, and there hath solaced all the day with much mirth and with dallying with him in his arms a long space, and so holding him in a window to the sight and great comfort of all the people.'² A saying is recorded of Henry: 'Happy those who never saw a king

---

[1] Henry Dowes to Cromwell: ELLIS, third series, vol. III. p. 258.
[2] Richard Cromwell to Lord Cromwell: *MS. State Paper Office*, second series, vol. vii. p. 188.

and whom a king never saw.' It is something, though it be but for once, to be admitted behind the shows of royalty, and to know that he, too, the queller of the Pope, the terror of conspirators, the dread lord who was the pilot of England in the sharpest convulsion which as yet had tried her substance, was nevertheless a man like the rest of us, with a human heart and human tenderness.

But to go on with our story.

The English criminal law was in its letter one of the most severe in Europe; in execution it was the most uncertain and irregular. There were no colonies to draw off the criminals, no galley system, as in France and Spain, to absorb them in penal servitude; the country would have laughed to scorn the proposal that it should tax itself to maintain able-bodied men in unemployed imprisonment; and, in the absence of graduated punishments, there was but one step to the gallows from the lash and the branding-iron. But, as ever happens, the extreme character of the penalties for crime prevented the enforcement of them; and benefit of clergy on the one hand, and privilege of sanctuary on the other, reduced to a fraction the already small number of offenders whom juries could be found to convict. In earlier ages the terrors of the Church supplied the place of secular retribution, and excommunication was scarcely looked upon as preferable even to death. But in the corrupt period which preceded the Reformation the consequences were the worst that can be conceived. Spasmodic intervals of extraordinary severity, when twenty thieves, as Sir Thomas More says, might be seen hanging on a single gibbet,[1] were followed by periods when justice was, perhaps, scarcely executed at all.[2]

[1] More's *Utopia*, Burnet's translation, p. 13.
[2] Respectable authorities, as most of my readers are doubtless aware, inform us that seventy-two thousand criminals were executed in England in the reign of Henry VIII. Historians who are accustomed to examine their materials critically, have usually learnt that no statements must be received with so much caution as those which relate to numbers. Grotius gives, in a parallel instance, the number of heretics executed under Charles V. in the Netherlands as a hundred thousand. The Prince of Orange gives them as fifty thousand. The authorities are admirable, though sufficiently inconsistent, while the judicious Mr. Prescott declares both estimates alike immeasurably beyond the truth. The entire number of victims destroyed by Alva in the same provinces by the stake, by the gallows, and by wholesale massacre, amount, when counted carefully in detail, to twenty thousand only. The persecutions under Charles, in a serious form, were confined to the closing years of his reign. Can we believe that wholesale butcheries were passed by comparatively unnoticed by any one at the time of their perpetration, more than doubling the atrocities which startled subsequently the whole world? Laxity of assertion in matters of number is so habitual as to have lost the character of

The state endeavoured to maintain its authority against the immunities of the Church by increasing the harshness of the code. So long as these immunities subsisted, it had no other resource; but judges and magistrates shrank from inflicting penalties so enormously disproportioned to the offence. They could not easily send a poacher or a vagrant to the gallows while a notorious murderer was lounging in comfort in a neighbouring sanctuary, or having just read a sentence from a book at the bar in arrest of judgment, had been handed over to an apparitor of falsehood. Men not remarkably inaccurate will speak of thousands, and, when cross-questioned, will rapidly reduce them to hundreds, while a single cipher inserted by a printer's mistake becomes at once a tenfold exaggeration. Popular impressions on the character of the reign of Henry VIII. have, however, prevented inquiry into any statement which reflects discredit upon this; the enormity of an accusation has passed for an evidence of its truth. Notwithstanding that until the few last years of the king's life no felon who could read was within the grasp of the law, notwithstanding that sanctuaries ceased finally to protect murderers six years only before his death, and that felons of a lighter cast might use their shelter to the last,—even these considerable facts have created no misgiving, and learned and ignorant historians alike have repeated the story of the 72,000 with equal confidence.

I must be permitted to mention the evidence, the single evidence, on which it rests.

The first English witness is Harrison, the author of the *Description of Britain* prefixed to HOLLINSHED's *Chronicle*. Harrison, speaking of the manner in which thieves had multiplied in England from laxity of discipline, looks back with a sigh to the golden days of King Hal, and adds, 'It appeareth by Cardan, who writeth it upon report of the Bishop of Lexovia, in the geniture of King Edward the Sixth, that his father, executing his laws very severely against great thieves, petty thieves, and rogues, did hang up three score and twelve thousand of them.'

I am unable to discover 'the Bishop of Lexovia'; but, referring to the *Commentaries* of Jerome Cardan, p. 412, I find a calculation of the horoscope of Edward VI., containing, of course, the marvellous legend of his birth, and after it this passage:—

'Having spoken of the son, we will add also the scheme of his father, wherein we chiefly observe three points. He married six wives; he divorced two; he put two to death. Venus being in conjunction with Cauda, Lampas partook of the nature of Mars; Luna in occiduo cardine was among the dependencies of Mars; and Mars himself was in the ill-starred constellation Virgo and in the quadrant of Jupiter Infelix. Moreover, he quarrelled with the Pope, owing to the position of Venus and to influences emanating from her. He was affected also by a constellation with schismatic properties, and by certain eclipses, and hence and from other causes, arose a fact related to me by the Bishop of Lexovia, namely, that two years before his death as many as seventy thousand persons were found to have perished by the hand of the executioner in that one island during his reign.'

The words of some unknown foreign ecclesiastic discovered imbedded in the midst of this abominable nonsense, and transmitted through a brain capable of conceiving and throwing it into form, have been considered authority sufficient to cast a stigma over one of the most remarkable periods in English history, while the contemporary English Records, the actual reports of the judges on assize, which would have disposed effectually of Cardan and his bishop, have been left unstudied in their dust.

the nearest archdeacon's court, and been set at liberty
for a few shillings. I have met with many instances of
convictions for deer stealing in the correspondence of the
reign of Henry VIII.; I have met but one instance where
the letter of the law was enforced against the offender,
unless the minor crime had been accompanied with man-
slaughter or armed resistance—the leaders of a gang who
had for many years infested Windsor Forest were at last
taken and hanged. The vagrancy laws sound terribly
severe; but in the reports of the judges on their assize,
of which many remain in the State Paper Office, I have
not found any one single account of an execution under
them. Felons of the worst kind never, perhaps, had easier
opportunities. The parish constables were necessarily inefficient as a police; many of them were doubtless shaped
after the model of Dogberry; if they bid a man stand
and he would not stand, they would let him go, and thank
God they were rid of a knave. There was a sanctuary
within reach all over England, even under the very walls
of Newgate, where escaped prisoners could secure themselves. The scarcely tolerable licence of ordinary times
had broken its last bonds during the agitations of the
Reformation, and the audacity of the criminal classes had
become so great that organized gangs of them assembled
at the gaol deliveries and quarter sessions to overawe
the authorities. Ambitious or violent knights and noblemen interfered to rescue or protect their own dependents.[1]
They alone were the guardians of the law, and they at
their pleasure could suspend the law; while the habit of
admitting plea of clergy, and of respecting the precincts
of sanctuary, had sunk so deeply into the practice of the
country that, although parliament might declare such privileges curtailed, yet in many districts custom long continued stronger than law. The constables still respected
the boundaries traced by superstition; felons were still
'saved by their book;' the English, like the Romans, were
a people with whom legislation became strong only when
it had stiffened into habit, and had entered slowly and
formally into possession of their hearts and understandings.

So many anomalies have at all times existed among
English institutions, that the nation has been practised
in correcting them; and, even at their worst, the old ar-
rangements may have worked better in reality than under
the naked theory might appear to be possible. In a free

[1] As we saw recently in the complaints of the Marquis of Exeter.
But in this general sketch I am giving the result of a body of correspondence too considerable to quote.

country each definite instinct or tendency represents itself in the general structure of society. When tendencies, as frequently happens, contradict each other, common sense comes in to the rescue, and, on the whole, justice is done, though at the price of consistency.

But at the period at which this history has now arrived, the evils of the system had obtained a conclusive preponderance. Superstition had become powerless to deter from violence, retaining only the means of preventing the punishment of it:[1] I shall proceed to illustrate the actual condition of the criminal administration between the years 1535 and 1540, by specimens, not indeed selected at random, but such as exhibit, in a marked form, a condition of things which may be traced, in greater or less degree, throughout the judicial and magisterial correspondence of the time.

In the spring of 1535, the sessions at Taunton and Bridgewater were forcibly dissolved by an insurrection of 'wilful persons.' Lord Fitzwarren and a number of other gentlemen narrowly escaped being murdered; and the gang, emboldened by success, sent detachments round the country, thirty of whom, the magistrates of Frome reported as having come thither for a similar purpose. The combination was of so serious a kind, that the *posse comitatus* of Somersetshire was called out to put it down. Circulars went round among the principal families, warning them all of what had taken place, and arranging plans for mutual action. Sir John Fitzjames came down from London; and at last, by great exertion, the ringleaders were arrested and brought to trial. The least guilty were allowed to earn their pardon by confession. Twelve who attempted to face out their offence were convicted and executed, four of them at Taunton, four at Bridgewater, and four at the village to which they belonged.[2]

In 1536, 7, 8, or 9,[3] a series of burglaries had been committed in the town and the neighbourhood of Chichester; and there had been a riot also, connected with the robberies, of sufficient importance to be communicated to the government. The parties chiefly implicated were discovered

---

[1] In healthier times the Pope had interfered. A bull of Innocent VIII. permitted felons repeating their crimes, or fraudulent creditors, to be taken forcibly out of sanctuary.—WILKINS's *Concilia*, vol. iii. p. 621.

[2] The Magistrates of Frome to Sir Henry Long: *MS. Cotton, Titus*, B 1, 102. Mr. Justice Fitzjames to Cromwell: *MS. State Paper Office*, second series, vol. xi. p. 43.

[3] The letter which I quote is addressed to Cromwell as 'My Lord Privy Seal,' and dated July 17. Cromwell was created privy seal on the 2nd of July, 1536, and Earl of Essex on the 17th of April, 1540. There is no other guide to the date.

and taken; the evidence against them was conclusive, and no attempt was made to shake it; but three 'froward persons' on the jury, one of whom was the foreman, refused to agree to a verdict. They were themselves, the magistrates were aware, either a part of the gang, or privately in league with them; and the help of the crown was invited for 'the reformation of justice.'[1] I do not find how this matter ended.

Benefit of clergy was taken from felons in 1531-2.[2] At least five years later, when Cromwell was privy seal, three men were arraigned at the gaol delivery at Ipswich, 'upon three several indictments of several felonies.' They were convicted regularly, and their guilt does not seem to have been doubted; but 'every of them prayed their book.' The see of Norwich being vacant at the time, the ecclesiastical jurisdiction was suspended; no 'ordinary' was present in court to 'hear them read;' the magistrates thereupon 'reprieved the said felons, without any judgment upon the said verdict.' The prisoners were remanded to the gaol till the spiritual courts were ready to take charge of them: they were kept carelessly, and escaped.[3]

The following extract from a letter written in 1539 will show, better than any general description, the nature of a sanctuary, and the spirit in which the protection was enjoyed. The number of sanctuaries had been limited by act of parliament previous to their final abolition; certain favoured spots were permitted for a time to absorb the villany of the country; and felons who had taken refuge elsewhere, were to be removed into some one of these. Bewley in Hampshire had been condemned to lose its privilege. Richard Layton, the monastic visitor, describes and pleads for it to the privy seal.

'There be sanctuary men here,' he says, 'for debt, felony, and murder, thirty-two; many of them aged, some very sick. They have all, within four, wives and children, and dwelling-houses, and ground, whereby they live with their families; which, being all assembled before us, and the king's pleasure opened to them, they have very lamentably declared that, if they be now sent to other sanctuaries, not only they, but their wives and children also, shall be utterly undone; and therefore have desired

---

[1] The Magistrates of Chichester to my Lord Privy Seal: *MS. State Paper Office,* second series, vol. x.
[2] 23 Henry VIII. cap. 1.
[3] Humfrey Wingfield to my Lord Privy Seal: *MS. State Paper Office,* second series, vol. li.

us to be mean unto your good lordship that they may remain here for term of their lives, so that none others be received. And because we have certain knowledge that the great number of them, with their wives and children, shall be utterly cast away, their age, impotency, and other things considered, if they be sent to any other place, we have sent this bearer unto you, beseeching your lordship to know the king's pleasure herein.'[1]

The nineteenth century believes, and believes with justice, that in its treatment of criminals it has made advances in humanity on the practice of earlier times; but the warmest of living philanthropists would scarcely consider so tenderly, in a correspondence with the home secretary, the domestic comforts of thirty-two debtors, felons, and murderers.

But the most detailed accounts of the lawlessness which had spread in the wilder districts of the country are to be found in the reports of the remarkable Rowland Lee, Bishop of Lichfield and Coventry, Lord Warden of the Welsh Marches, the last survivor of the old martial prelates, fitter for harness than for bishops' robes, for a court of justice than a court of theology; more at home at the head of his troopers, chasing cattle-stealers in the gorges of Llangollen, than hunting heretics to the stake, or chasing formulas in the arduous defiles of controversy. Three volumes are extant of Rowland Lee's letters.[2] They relate almost wholly to the details of his administration on either side of the frontier line from Chester to the mouth of the Wye. The Welsh counties were but freshly organized under the English system. The Welsh customs had but just been superseded by the English common law. The race whose ancient hardihood the castles of Conway, Carnarvon, and Beaumaris remain to commemorate, whom only those stern towers, with their sterner garrisons, could awe into subjection, maintained a shadow of their independence in a wild lawlessness of character. But the sense of subjection had been soothed by the proud consciousness that they had bestowed a dynasty upon England; that a blood descendant of Cadwallader was seated on the throne of the Edwards. They had ceased to maintain, like the Irish, a feeling of national hostility. They were suffering now from the intermediate disorders which intervene when a smaller race is merging in a stronger and a larger; when traditional customs are falling into

---

[1] Richard Layton to Cromwell: *MS. State Paper Office*, second series, vol. xx.

[2] *MS. State Paper Office*, second series.

desuetude, and the laws designed to take their place have not yet grown actively into operation. Many of the Welsh gentlemen lived peacefully by honest industry; others, especially along the Border, preferred the character of Highland chieftains, and from their mountain fastnesses levied black rent on the English counties. Surrounded with the sentiment of pseudo-heroism, they revelled in the conceit of imaginary freedom; and with their bards and pedigrees, and traditions of Glendower and Prince Llewellyn, they disguised from themselves and others the plain prose truth, that they were but thieves and rogues.

These were the men whom Rowland Lee was sent to tame into civility—these, and their English neighbours, who, from close proximity and from acquired habits of retaliation for their own injuries, had caught the infection of a similar spirit.

From his many letters I must content myself with taking such extracts as bear most immediately on the working of the criminal law, and illustrate the extreme difficulty of punishing even the worst villanies. To strengthen the bishop's hands a Council of the Marches had been established in 1534, with powers similar to those which were given subsequently to the Council of York.

In August, 1537, Lee wrote to Cromwell, 'These shall be to advertise you that where of late I sent unto your lordship a bill of such murders and manslaughters as were done in Cheshire which would not be found until this council set the same forward for condign punishment of the offenders, and although at the late assizes a great number of bills both for murders and riots were put into the great inquest, and good evidence given upon the same—yet, contrary to their duties to our sovereign lord and their oath, neglecting the course and ministration of justice, they have found murders to be manslaughters, and riots to be misbehaviours. The council could do no less but see the same redressed. We have called the said inquest before us, and committed them to ward for their lightness in the premises. And for as much as I think that suit will be made unto your lordship of my straitness and hard dealing herein, if your lordship will have that country in as good order and stay as we have set other parts, there must be punishment done, or else they will continue in their boldness as they have used heretofore. If your lordship will that I shall deal remissively herein, upon the advertisement of your lordship's mind by your letters, I shall gladly follow the same. Or else, if your lordship do mind reformation of the premises, write unto me a sharp letter to see justice ministered, and to punish such as shall be thought offenders according to this council's discretion for their misbehaviours by fines, strait imprisonment, and otherwise. For if we should do nothing but as the common law will, these things so far out of order will never be redressed.'

The bishop's advice was approved. One caution only was impressed upon him by Cromwell—that 'indifferent justice must be ministered to poor and rich according to their demerits;' and gentlemen who were concerned in riots and robberies were not to be spared on account of their position. The bishop obeyed the admonition, which was probably little needed; soon after, at a quarter sessions, in the presence of the Earl of Worcester, Lord Ferrars, and many gentlemen of the shire, 'four of the best blood in the county of Shropshire' were reported to have been hanged.

Carrying his discipline south, the bishop by-and-bye wrote from Hereford—

'By diligent search and pains we have tried out the greatest nest of thieves that was heard of this many years. They have confessed to the robbing of eighteen churches, besides other felonies, already. This nest was rooted in Gloucestershire at a place called Merkyll, and had recourse to a blind inn, to an old man, who, with his two sons, being arrant thieves, were the receitors. Of this affinity were a great number, of whom we have ten or twelve principals and accessories, and do make out daily for more, where we can hear they be. Daily the outlaws submit themselves, or be taken. If he be taken he playeth his pageant. If he come and submit himself, I take him to God's mercy and the king's grace upon his fine.'

Once more, after mentioning the capture of two outlaws, whom he intended to despatch, and of a third, who had been killed in attempting to escape, brought in dead across a horse, and hanged on a market-day at Ludlow, the warden summed up, as a general result of his administration, 'What shall we say further? All the thieves in Wales quake for fear; and at this day we assure you there is but one thief of name, of the sort of outlaws, and we trust to have him shortly; so that now ye may boldly affirm that Wales is redact to that state that one thief taketh another, and one cow keepeth another.'[1]

The bishop's work was rough; but it was good of its kind, and was carried out in the manner which, in the

[1] Correspondence of the Warden and Council of the Welsh Marches with the Lord Privy Seal: *MS. State Paper Office*, second series.

long run, was most merciful—merciful to honest subjects, who were no longer the prey of marauders—merciful to those whom the impunity of these heroes of the Border might have tempted to imitate their example—merciful to the offenders themselves, who were saved by the gallows from adding to the list of their crimes.

But although order could be enforced where an active resolute man had been chosen to supersede the inefficiency of the local authorities, in other parts of England, in Hampshire, Wiltshire, Somersetshire, Devonshire, and Cornwall especially, there was no slight necessity still remaining for discipline of a similar kind; the magistrates had been exhorted again and again in royal proclamations to discharge their duties more efficiently; but the ordinary routine of life was deranged by the religious convulsions; the mainspring of the social system was out of place, and the parts could no longer work in harmony. The expedient would have to be attempted which had succeeded elsewhere; but, before resorting to it, Henry would try once more the effect of an address, and a circular was issued in the ensuing terms:—

'The king to the justices of the peace. Trusty and well-beloved, we greet you well,[1] and cannot a little marvel to hear that, notwithstanding our sundry advertisements lately made unto you for the doing of your duties in such offices as in our commonwealth are committed unto you, many things be nevertheless directed at will and pleasure, than either upon any just contemplation of justice, or with any regard to the good monitions which heretofore we have set forth for the advancement of the same. Minding, therefore, yet once again, before we shall correct the lewdness of the offenders with any extremity of law, to give a more general admonition, to the intent no man shall have colour by excuse of ignorance, we have thought meet to write these our letters unto you, and by the same to desire and pray you, and yet, nevertheless, to charge and command you, upon your duties of allegiance, that for the repairing of all things negligently passed, and for the avoiding of all such damages as may for lack thereof happen unto you, you shall have special care and study to the due and just observation of the points following:—

'First, where we have with our great study, travail, and labour expelled the usurped power of Rome, with all the branches and dependings upon the same, our plea-

[1] *MS. Rolls House,* first series, 494.

sure is that you shall have a principal regard that the privy maintainers of that Papistical faction may be tried out and brought to justice. For by sundry arguments it is manifest unto us that there wanteth not a number that in that matter retain their old fond fantasies and superstitions, muttering in corners, as they dare, to the maintenance and upholding of them, what countenance soever they do shew outwards for avoiding of danger of the law. These kind of men we would have tried out, as the most cankered and venomous worms that be in our commonwealth, both for that they be apparent enemies to God, and manifest traitors to us and to our whole realm, workers of all mischief and sedition within the same.

'Secondly, you shall have special regard that all sturdy vagabonds and valiant beggars may be punished according to the statute made for that purpose. Your default in the execution whereof, proceeding upon an inconsiderate pity to one evil person, without respect to the great multitude that live in honest and lawful sort, hath bred no small inconvenience in our commonwealth. And you shall also have special regard that no man be suffered to use any unlawful games; but that every man may be encouraged to use the longbow, as the law requireth.

'Furthermore, our pleasure and most dread commandment is that, all respects set apart, you shall bend yourselves to the advancement of even justice between party and party, both that our good subjects may have the benefit of our laws sincerely administered unto them, and that evil doers may be punished, as the same doth prescribe and limit. To which points, if you shall upon this monition and advertisement give such diligent regard as you may satisfy your duty in the same, leaving and eschewing from henceforth all disguised corruption, we shall be content the more easily to put in oblivion all your former remissness and negligence. But if, on the other part, we shall perceive that this kind of gentle proceeding can work no kind of good effect in you, or any of you, whom we put in trust under us, assure yourselves that the next advice shall be of so sharp a sort as shall bring with it a just punishment of those that shall be found offenders in this behalf: requiring you, therefore, not only for your own part to wax each a new man, if you shall in your own conscience perceive that you have not done your duty as appertained, but also to exhort others of your sort and condition, whom you shall perceive to digress from the true execution of their offices, rather to reconcile and compose themselves than upon any affection, respect, or displeasure to do any such thing as will hereafter minister unto them further repentance, and will not percase, when it should light on their necks, lightly be redubbed. Wherein you shall shew yourselves men of good instruction, and deserve our right hearty thanks accordingly.'

Menace, as usual, was but partially effectual. At length, in the midst of the general stir and excitement of the spring and summer of 1539, while the loyal portion of the country was still under arms, and the government felt strong enough for the work, we trace the progress of special commissions through the counties where the irregularities had been the greatest, partly to sift to the bottom the history of the Marquis of Exeter's conspiracy, partly to administer discipline to gangs of rogues and vagabonds. Sir Thomas Blunt and Sir Robert Neville went to Worcester and Kidderminster. At the latter place ten felons were hanged.[1] Sir Thomas Willoughby, with Lord Russell and others, was sent into the south and west, where, 'for wilful murders, heinous robberies, and other offences,' Willoughby wrote to Cromwell, that 'divers and many felons suffered.' In Somersetshire four men were hanged for rape and burglary. In Cornwall, Kendall and Quintrell were hanged, with confederates who had acted under them as recruiting agents for Lord Exeter. Other details are wanting; but a general tone of vigour runs through the reports, and the gentlemen had so far taken warning from the last proclamation, that the commissioners were able to conclude: 'I assure you, my lord, in every of these same shires there hath been a great appearance of gentlemen and men of worship who have endeavoured themselves, with much diligence in executing the king's precepts and commandments.'[2] Sir Thomas Wriothesley, who either accompanied the commission, or was in Hampshire independently of it, took advantage of a quarter sessions in that county to stimulate these symptoms of improvement a little further.

The king, he told the magistrates, desired most of all

[1] At the execution Latimer's chaplain, Doctor Tailor, preached a sermon. Among the notes of the proceedings I find a certain Miles Denison called up for disrespectful language.
'The said Miles did say: The bishop sent one yesterday for to preach at the gallows, and there stood upon the vicar's colt and made a foolish sermon of the new learning, looking over the gallows. I would the colt had winced and cast him down.' 'Also during the sermon he did say, I would he were gone, and I were at my dinner.'— *MS. State Paper Office.*
[2] Sir Thomas Willoughby to Cromwell: *MS. Cotton. Titus,* B 1, 386.

things that indifferent justice should be ministered to the poor and the rich, which, he regretted to say, was imperfectly done. Those in authority too much used their powers, 'that men should follow the bent of their bows,' a thing which 'did not need to be followed.' The chief cause of all the evils of the time was 'the dark setting forth of God's Word,' 'the humming and harking of the priests who ought to read it, and the slanders given to those that did plainly and truly set it forth.' At any rate, the fact was as he described it to be; and they would find, he added, significantly, that, if they gave further occasion for complaint, 'God had given them a prince that had force and strength to rule the highest of them.'[1] For the present no further notice was taken of their conduct. There is no evidence that any magistrates were deprived or punished. The work which they had neglected was done for them by others, and they were left again to themselves with a clearer field.[2] One noticeable victim, however, fell in this year. There were three, indeed, with equal claims to interest; but one, through caprice of fame, has been especially remembered. The great abbots, with but few exceptions, had given cause for suspicion during the late disturbances; that is to say they had grown to advanced age as faithful subjects of the Papacy; they were too old to begin life again with a new allegiance. Information had transpired—I do not know the precise nature of it—to persuade Cromwell that the Abbots of Reading, Colchester, and Glastonbury were entangled in some treasonable enterprise or correspondence.[3] The charges against the Abbot of Reading I have been unable to find. The Abbot of Colchester had refused to surrender his house, and concealed or made away with the abbey plate, and had used expressions of most unambiguous anxiety for the success of the rebellions, and of disappointment at their failure.[4] They were both exe-

---

[1] The Sheriff of Hampshire to Cromwell: *MS. State Paper Office*, first series, vol. ix.

[2] The traditions of severity connected with this reign are explained by these exceptional efforts of rigour. The years of licence were forgotten; the seasons recurring at long intervals, when the executions might be counted by hundreds, lived in recollection, and when three or four generations had passed, became the measure of the whole period.

[3] 'These three abbots had joined in a conspiracy to restore the Pope.'—Traherne to Bullinger: *Original Letters on the Reformation*, second series, p. 316.

[4] 'Yesterday I was with the Abbot of Colchester, who asked me how the Abbot of St. Osith did as touching his house; for the bruit was the king would have it. To the which I answered, that he did like an honest man, for he saith, I am the king's subject, and I and

cuted. On the first visitation of the monasteries, Whiting, Abbot of Glastonbury, received a favourable character from the visitors. He had taken the oaths to the king without objection, or none is mentioned. He had acquiesced generally, in his place in the House of Lords, in Cromwell's legislation, he had been present at one reading at least of the concluding statute against the Pope's authority;[1] and there is no evidence that he distinguished himself in any way as a champion of the falling faith. In the last parliament he had been absent on plea of ill health; but he appointed no proxy, nor sought apparently to use on either side his legitimate influence. Cromwell's distrust was awakened by some unknown reason; but both to him and to those who had spoken previously in his favour, it seemed, according to their standard of appreciation, sufficiently grounded. Perhaps some discontented monk had sent up secret informations.[2] An order went out for an inquiry into his conduct, which was to be executed by three of the visitors, Layton, Pollard, and Moyle. On the 16th of September they were at Reading: on the 22nd they had arrived at Glastonbury. The abbot was absent at a country house a mile and a half distant. They followed him, informed him of the

---

my house and all is the king's; wherefore, if it be the king's pleasure, I, as a true subject, shall obey without grudge. To the which the abbot answered, the king shall never have my house but against my will and against my heart; for I know, by my learning, he cannot take it by right and law. Wherefore, in my conscience, I cannot be content; nor he shall never have it with my heart and will. To the which I said beware of such learning; for if ye hold such learning as ye learned in Oxenford when ye were young ye will be hanged; and ye are worthy. But I will advise you to confirm yourself as a good subject, or else you shall hinder your brethren and also yourself.'—Sir John St. Clair to the Lord Privy Seal: *MS. State Paper Office*, second series, vol. xxxviii. The abbot did not take the advice, but ventured more dangerous language.

'The abbot of Colchester did say that the northern men were good men and *mekell* in the mouth, and 'great crackers' and nothing worth in their deeds.' 'Further, the said abbot said, at the time of the insurrection, 'I would to Christ that the rebels in the north had the Bishop of Canterbury, the lord chancellor, and the lord privy seal amongst them, and then I trust we should have a merry world again.''—Deposition of Edmund ——: *Rolls House MS*, second series, No. 27.

But the abbot must have committed himself more deeply, or have refused to retract and make a submission; for I find words of similar purport sworn against other abbots, who suffered no punishment.

[1] *Lords Journals*, 28 Henry VIII.

[2] 'The Abbot of Glastonbury appeareth neither then nor now to have known God nor his prince, nor any part of a good Christian man's religion. They be all false, feigned, flattering hypocrite knaves, as undoubtedly there is none other of that sort.'—Layton to Cromwell: ELLIS, third series, vol. iii. p. 247.

cause of their coming, and asked him a few questions. His answers were 'nothing to the purpose;' that is to say, he confessed nothing to the visitors' purpose. He was taken back to the abbey; his private apartments were searched, and a book of arguments was found there against the king's divorce, pardons, copies of bulls, and a Life of Thomas à Becket—nothing particularly criminal, though all indicating the abbot's tendencies. The visitors considered their discoveries 'a great matter.' The abbot was again questioned; and this time his answers appeared to them 'cankered and traitorous.' He was placed in charge of a guard, and sent to London to the Tower, to be examined by Cromwell himself. The occasion of his absence was taken for the dissolution of the house; and, as the first preliminary, an inventory was made of the plate, the furniture, and the money in the treasury. Glastonbury was one of the wealthiest of the religious houses. A less experienced person than Leyton would have felt some surprise when he found that neither plate, jewels, nor ornaments were forthcoming sufficient for an ordinary parish church. But deceptions of this kind were too familiar to a man who had examined half the religious houses in England. He knew immediately that the abbey treasure was either in concealment or had been secretly made away with. Foreseeing the impending destruction of this establishment, the monks had been everywhere making use of their opportunities of plunder. The altar plate, in some few instances, may have been secreted from a sentiment of piety—from a desire to preserve from sacrilege vessels consecrated to holy uses. But plunder was the rule; piety was the exception. A confession of the Abbot of Barlings contains a frank avowal of the principles on which the fraternities generally acted. This good abbot called his convent into the chapter-house, and by his own acknowledgment, addressed them thus:—

'Brethren, ye hear how other religious men be intreated, and how they have but forty shillings a piece given them and are let go. But they that have played the wise men amongst them have provided aforehand for themselves, and sold away divers things wherewith they may help themselves hereafter. And ye hear also this rumour that goeth abroad that the greater abbeys shall down also. Wherefore, by your advice, this shall be my counsel, that we do take such plate as we have, and certain of the best vestments and copes and set them aside, and sell them if need be, and so divide the money coming thereof when the house is suppressed. And I promise you of my faith and conscience ye shall have your part, and of every penny that I have during my life; and thereupon,' he concluded, 'the brethren agreed thereunto.'[1]

A less severe government than that of Henry VIII. would have refused to tolerate conduct of this kind. Those who decline to recognise the authority of an act of parliament over the property of corporate bodies, cannot pretend that a right of ownership was vested in persons whose tenure, at its best and surest, was limited by their lives. For members of religious houses to make away their plate was justly construed to be felony; and the law, which was necessarily general, could not recognise exceptions on the ground of piety of motive, when such an exception would but have furnished a screen behind which indiscriminate pillage might have been carried on with impunity. The visitors had been warned to be careful,[2] and practice had made them skilful in means of detection. On the first day of the investigation at Glastonbury, 'a fair chalice of gold' came to light, 'with divers other parcels of plate;' all of which the abbot had concealed, committing perjury in doing so, on their previous visitation.[3] The next day brought out more; and the day after more again. Gold and silver in vessels, ornaments, and money were discovered 'mured up in walls, vaults, and other secret places,' some hidden by the abbot, some by the convent. Two monks who were treasurers, with the lay clerks of the vestry, were found to have been 'arrant thieves.' At length as much treasure of various sorts was recovered as would have begun a new abbey.[4] The visitors did not trouble them-

[1] Confession of the Abbot of Barlings: *MS. Cotton. Cleopatra*, E 4.
[2] 'And for as much as experience teacheth that many of the heads of such houses, notwithstanding their oaths, taken upon the holy evangelists, to present to such the King's Majesty's commissioners as have been addressed unto them, true and perfect inventories of all things belonging to their monasteries, many things have been left out, embezzled, stolen, and purloined—many rich jewels, much rich plate, great store of precious ornaments, and sundry other things of great value and estimation, to the damage of the King's Majesty, and the great peril and danger of their own souls, by reason of their wilful and detestable perjury; the said commissioners shall not only at every such house examine the head and convent substantially, of all such things so concealed or unlawfully alienated, but also shall give charge to all the ministers and servants of the same houses, and such of the neighbours dwelling near about them as they shall think meet, to detect and open all such things as they have known or heard to have been that way misused, to the intent the truth of all things may the better appear accordingly.'—Instructions to the Monastic Commissioners: *MS. Tanner*, 105. *Bodleian Library*.
[3] Pollard, Moyle, and Layton to Cromwell: BURNET's *Collectanea*, p. 499.
[4] Same to the same: *State Papers*, vol. i. p. 619.

selves to speculate on the abbot's intentions. There is nothing to show that in collusion with the brethren he was not repeating the behaviour of the Abbot of Barlings; or, like so many of the northern abbots, he might have been hoarding a fund to subsidize insurrection, preserving the treasures of the temple to maintain the temple's defenders; or he might have acted in a simple spirit of piety. His motives were of no moment. The fact of the concealment was patent. The letter communicating these discoveries to the government was written on the 28th of September. Another followed on the 2nd of October, stating that, since the despatch of the last, the visitors 'had come to the knowledge of divers and sundry treasons committed and done by the Abbot of Glastonbury, the certainty whereof would appear in a Book of Depositions,' which they forwarded with the accusers' names attached to their statements, 'very haut and rank treason.'[1] I have not discovered this 'Book of Depositions;' but those who desire to elevate the Abbot of Glastonbury to the rank of the martyr, confess, in doing so, their belief that he was more faithful to the Church than to the State, that he was guilty of regarding the old ways as better than the new, and they need not care to question that he may have acted on his convictions, or at least have uttered them in words. After the recent experience of the Pilgrimage of Grace, an ascertained disposition of disloyalty was enough to ensure a conviction; and the Pope by his latest conduct had embittered the quarrel to the utmost. He had failed to excite a holy war against England, but three English merchants had been burnt by the Inquisition in Spain.[2] Five more had been imprisoned and one had been tortured only for declaring that they considered Henry VIII. to be a Christian. Their properties had been confiscated, they had borne faggots and candles in a procession as sanbenitos,[3] and Paul had issued a promise of indulgence to all pious Catholics who would kill an English heretic.[4]

[1] *State Papers*, vol. i. p. 621.
[2] Butler, Elliot, and Traherne to Conrad Pellican: *Original Letters*, second series, p. 624.
[3] Thomas Perry to Ralph Vane: ELLIS, second series, vol. ii. p. 140.
[4] I should have distrusted the evidence, on such a point, of excited Protestants (see *Original Letters on the Reformation*, p. 626), who could invent and exaggerate as well as their opponents; but the promise of these indulgences was certainly made, and Charles V. prohibited the publication of the brief containing it in Spain or Flanders. 'The Emperor,' wrote Cromwell to Henry, 'hath not consented that the Pope's mandament should be published neither in Spain, neither in any other his dominions, that Englishmen should be destroyed in body,

Six weeks elapsed before the abbot's fate was decided, part or the whole of which time he was in London. At the beginning of November he was sent back into Somersetshire, already condemned at a tribunal where Cromwell sat as prosecutor, jury, and judge. His escape in a more regular court was not contemplated as a possibility; among loose papers of Cromwell still remaining there is a memorandum in his own hand for 'the trial and execution' of the Abbot of Glastonbury.[1] But the appearance of unfair dealing was greater than the reality. Lord Russell, whose stainless character was worthy of his name, was one of the commissioners before whom the trial was conducted; and Russell has left on record his approval of, and acquiescence in the conduct of the case, in plain and unmistakeable language. Whiting was araigned at Wells on Thursday, the 14th of November, with his treasurers, 'before as worshipful a jury as was charged there for many years.'[2] The crime of which he was formally accused was robbing the abbey church; and there was no doubt that he was guilty of having committed that crime, to whatever the guilt may have amounted. But if the government had prosecuted in every instance of abbey-church robbery, a monk would have hung in chains at all the cross-roads in England. The Abbot of Glastonbury was tried and convicted of felony; his real offence was treason, as the word was interpreted by Cromwell. He was unpopular in the county, and among his dependents. 'There were many bills,' Lord Russell said, 'put up against the abbot, by his tenants and others, for wrongs and injuries that he had done them.'[3] He was sentenced to death, and the day following was fixed for the execution. He was taken with the two monks from Wells to Glastonbury; he was drawn through the town in the usual manner, and thence to the top of the conical hill which rises out of the level plain of Somersetshire, called Glastonbury Torre. To the last he was tormented with questions, 'but he would accuse no man but himself;' he only requested the visitors' servants who were present on the Torre to entreat their masters and Lord Russell 'to desire the King's Highness of his merciful goodness and in the way of charity to forgive him his great offences by him committed and done against his Grace.'[4] The modern

in goods, wheresoever they could be found, as the Pope would they should be.'—*State Papers*, vol. i. p. 608.
[1] *MS. Cotton.*
[2] Lord Russell to Cromwell: *MS. Cotton. Cleopatra*, E 4.
[3] Ibid.
[4] Pollard to Cromwell: *Suppression of the Monasteries*, p. 261.

student, to whom the passions and the difficulties of the time are as a long forgotten dream, who sees only the bleak hill-top on the dreary November day, the gallows, and an infirm old man guilty of nothing which he can understand to be a crime, shudders at the needless cruelty. Cromwell, for his share in this policy of death, was soon to receive as he had given; a few more months, and he too on Tower Hill would pass to his account.

CHAPTER XVII.

ANNE OF CLEVES AND THE FALL OF CROMWELL.

The king's marriage could not be longer delayed. Almost three years had been wasted in fruitless negotiations, and the state of his health threatened, more and more clearly, that his life would not be prolonged to any advanced period. The death of the Duke of Richmond[1] was a fresh evidence of the absence of vital stamina in Henry's male children; and the anxious and impatient people saw as yet but a single fragile life between the country and a disputed succession. The disloyal Romanists alone desired to throw obstacles between the king and a fresh connexion—alone calumniated his motives, and looked forward hopefully to the possible and probable confusion.

Among the ladies who had been considered suitable to take the place of Queen Jane, the name had been mentioned, with no especial commendation, of Anne, daughter of the Duke of Cleves, and sister-in-law of the Elector of Saxony. She had been set aside in favour of the Duchess of Milan; but, all hopes in this quarter having been abruptly and ungraciously terminated, Cromwell once more turned his eyes towards a connexion which, more than any other, would make the Emperor repent of his discourtesy—and would further at the same time the great object which the condition of Europe now, more than ever, showed him to be necessary—a league of all nations of the Teutonic race in defence of the Reformation. A marriage between the king and a German Protestant princess would put a final end to Anglo-Imperial trifling; and, committing England to a definite policy abroad, it

---

[1] Henry Fitz Roy, Duke of Richmond, died July 22, 1536.

would neutralize at home the efforts of the framers of the Six Articles, and compel the king, whether he desired it or not, to return to a toleration of Lutheran opinions and Lutheran practices.

The opportunity of urging such an alliance on Henry was more than favourable. He had been deceived, insulted, and menaced by the Emperor; his articles of union had been converted by the bishops into articles of a vindictive persecution; and the Anglicans, in their indiscreet animosity, had betrayed their true tendencies, and had shown how little, in a life-and-death struggle with the Papacy, he could depend upon their lukewarm zeal for independence. Affecting only to persecute heterodoxy, they had extended their vengeance to every advocate for freedom, to every enemy of ecclesiastical exemptions and profitable superstitions; and the king, disappointed and exasperated, was in a humour, while snatching their victims from their grasp, to consent to a step which would undo their victory in parliament. The occasion was not allowed to cool. Parliament was prorogued on the 11th of May, with an intimation from the crown that the religious question was not to be regarded as finally settled.[1] The treaty with Cleves was so far advanced on the 17th of July that Lord Hertford[2] was able to congratulate Cromwell on the consent of Anne's brother and mother.[3] The lady had been previously intended for a son of a Duke of Lorraine; and Henry, whom experience had made anxious, was alarmed at the name of a 'pre-contract.' But Dr. Wotton, who was sent over to arrange the preliminaries, and was instructed to see the difficulty cleared, was informed and believed that the engagement had never advanced to a form which brought with it legal obligations, and that Anne was at liberty to marry wherever

---

[1] 'Animadvertens sua clementia quod maxime hoc convenerat parliamentum pro bono totius Regni publico et concordiâ Christianæ religionis stabiliendâ non tam cito quam propter rei magnitudinem quæ non solum regnum ipsum Angliæ concernit verum etiam alia regna et universi Christianismi Ecclesias quantumvis diversarum sententiarum quæ in eam rem oculos et animum habebant intentos, sua Majestas putavit tam propriâ suâ regiâ diligentiâ et studio quam etiam episcoporum et cleri sui sedulitate rem maturius consultandam, tractandam et deliberandam.'—Speech of the Lord Chancellor at the Prorogation: *Lords Journals*, vol. i. p. 137.

[2] Brother of Jane Seymour; afterwards Protector.

[3] 'I am as glad of the good resolutions of the Duke of Cleves, his mother, and council, as ever I was of anything since the birth of the prince: for I think the King's Highness should not in Christendom marry in no place meet for his Grace's honour that should be less prejudicial to his Majesty's succession.'—Hertford to Cromwell: ELLIS, first series, vol. ii. p. 119.

she pleased.¹ Of her personal attractions Wotton reported vaguely. He said that she had been well brought up; but ladies of rank in Germany were not usually taught accomplishments. She could speak no language except her own, nor could she play on any instrument. He supposed, however, that she would be able to learn English in no long time; and he comforted the king by assuring him that at least she had no taste for 'the heavy-headed revels' of her countrymen.² Wotton could not be accused of having lent himself to a deception as to the lady's recommendations. It would have been well for Cromwell if he too had been equally scrupulous. He had been warned beforehand of an unattractiveness, so great as to have overcome the spontaneous belief in the beauty of royal ladies;³ but, intent upon the success of his policy, he disregarded information which his conduct proves him to have partially believed. Holbein was despatched to take the princess's picture; and Holbein's inimitable skill would not have failed so wholly in conveying a true impression of the original if he had not received an intimation that an agreeable portrait was expected of him; while, as soon as it was brought into England, Cromwell's agents praised to the king 'her features, beauty, and princely proportions,' and assured him that the resemblance was perfect.⁴ The German commission was as expeditious as the Spanish had been dilatory. To allay any uneasiness which might remain with respect to the Six Articles, and to furnish a convincing evidence of the toleration which was practised, Dr. Barnes was sent over as one of the English representatives; and he carried with him the comforting assurance that the persecution had been terminated, and that the Gospel had free way. His assertions were afterwards confirmed by unsuspicious and independent evidence. 'There is no persecution,' wrote a Protestant in London, a few months later, to Bullinger. 'The Word is powerfully preached. Books of every kind may safely be exposed to sale.'⁵ 'Good pastors,' wrote another, 'are freely preaching the truth, nor has any no-

---

¹ 'I find the council willing enough to publish and manifest to the world that by any covenants made by the old Duke of Cleves and the Duke of Lorraine, my Lady Anne is not bounden; but ever hath been and yet is at her free liberty to marry wherever she will.'—Wotton to the King: ELLIS, first series, vol. ii. p. 121.
² Ibid.
³ 'The Duke of Cleves hath a daughter, but I hear no great praise, either of her personage nor beauty.'—Hutton to Cromwell: *State Papers*, vol. viii. p. 5.
⁴ Stow.
⁵ Butler to Bullinger: *Original Letters on the Reformation*, p. 627.

tice been taken of them on account of the articles.'[1] Even the Elector of Saxony, jealous and distrustful as he had ever been of Henry, was so far satisfied as to write to him that he understood 'the sharpness of the decree of the Six Articles to be modified by the wisdom and moderation of his Highness, and the execution of it not put in use.'[2]

All promised well; but it is not to be supposed that Cromwell was allowed without resistance to paralyse a measure which had been carried by an almost unanimous parliament. More than half the Privy Council, the Dukes of Norfolk and Suffolk, the Bishops of Winchester, Durham, and Chichester, were openly and violently opposed to him. The House of Lords and the country gentlemen, baffled, as it seemed to them, by his treachery (for he had professed to go along with their statute while it was under discussion), maintained an attitude of sullen menace or open resistance. If the laws against the heretics might not be put in force, they would lend no help to execute the laws against the Romanists.[3] They despised Cromwell's injunctions, though supported by orders from the crown. They would not acknowledge so much as the receipt of his letters. He was playing a critical and most dangerous game, in which he must triumph or be annihilated. The king warned him repeatedly to be cautious;[4] but the terms on which he had placed himself with the nobility had perhaps passed the point where caution could have been of use. He answered haughtiness by haughtiness; and he left his fate to the chances of fortune, careless what it might be, if only he could accomplish his work while life and power remained to him. One illustration of his relation with the temporal peers shall be given in this place, conveying, as it does, other allusions also, the drift of which is painfully intelligible. The following letter is written in Cromwell's own hand. The address is lost, but the rank of the person or persons to whom it was sent is apparent from the contents:—

'After my right hearty commendations, the King's Highness, being informed that there be two priests in your town, called Sir William Winstanley, which is now

[1] Partridge to Bullinger: *Original Letters on the Reformation*, p. 614.
[2] The Elector of Saxony to Henry VIII.: STRYPE's *Memorials*, vol. ii. p. 437.
[3] See a correspondence between Cranmer and a Justice of the Peace: JENKINS's *Cranmer*, vol. i.
[4] 'I would to Christ I had obeyed your often most gracious grave councils and advertisements. Then it had not been with me as now it is.'—Cromwell to the King: BURNET's *Collectanea*, p. 510.

in ward, the other called Sir William Richardson, otherwise Good Sir William, hath commanded me to signify to you that, upon the receipt hereof, you shall send both the said priests hither as prisoners in assured custody. His Grace cannot a little marvel to hear of the Papistical faction that is maintained in that town, and by you chiefly that are of his Grace's council. Surely his Majesty thinketh that you have little respect either to him, or to his laws, or to the good order of that town, which so little regard him in a matter of so great weight, which, also, his Highness hath so much to heart; and willed me plainly to say to you all and every of you, that in case he shall perceive from henceforth any such abuses suffered or winked at as have been hitherto, in manner in contempt of his most royal estate, his Highness will put others in the best of your rooms that so offend him, by whom he will be better served. It is thought against all reason that the prayers of women, and their fond flickerings, should move any of you to do that thing that should in anywise displease your prince and sovereign lord, or offend his just laws. And, if you shall think any extremity in this writing, you must thank yourselves that have procured it; for neither of yourselves have you regarded these matters, nor answered to many of my letters, written for like purposes and upon like occasions: wherein, though I have not made any accusation, yet, being in the place for these things that I am, I have thought you did me therein too much injury, and such as I am assured his Highness, knowing it, would not have taken it in good part. But this matter needeth no aggravation, ne I have done anything in it more than hath been by his Majesty thought meet, percase not so much; and thus heartily fare you well.

'Your Lordship's assured
'THOMAS CROMWELL.'[1]

Between the minister and the king the points of difference were large and increasing. The conduct which had earned for Cromwell the hatred of the immense majority of the people, could not but at times have been regarded disapprovingly by a person who shared so deeply as Henry in the English conservative spirit; while Cromwell, again, was lavish in his expenditure, and the outlay upon the fleet and the Irish army, the cost of suppression of the insurrection, and of the defences of the coast, at

[1] *MS. Cotton. Cleopatra*, E 4.

once vast and unusual, were not the less irritating because they could not be denied to be necessary. A spirit of economy in the reaction from his youthful extravagance, was growing over Henry with his advancing years; he could not reconcile himself to a profusion to which, even with the addition of the Church lands, his resources were altogether unequal, without trespassing on his subjects' purses; and the conservative faction in the council took advantage of his ill humour to whisper that the fault was in the carelessness, the waste, and the corruption of the privy seal. Cromwell knew it well.[1] Two years previously he had received full warning that they were on the watch to take advantage of any momentary displeasure against him in the king. They were not likely to have been conciliated subsequently by the deaths of the Marquis of Exeter and Lord Montague, for which he personally was held responsible; and he prepared for the fate which he foresaw, in making settlements on his servants, that they

---

[1] He required, probably, no information that his enemies would spare no means, fair or foul, for his destruction. But their plots and proceedings had been related to him two years before by his friend Allen, the Irish Master of the Rolls, in a report of expressions which had been used by George Paulet, brother of the lord treasurer, and one of the English commissioners at Dublin. Cromwell, it seems, had considered that estates in Ireland forfeited for treason, or non-residence, would be disposed of better if granted freely to such families as had remained loyal, than if sold for the benefit of the crown. Speaking of this matter, 'The king,' Paulet said, 'beknaveth Cromwell twice a week, and would sometimes knock him about the pate. He draws every day towards his death, and escaped very hardly at the last insurrection. He is the greatest briber in England, and that is espied well enough. The king has six times as much revenues as ever any of his noble progenitors had, and all is consumed and gone to nought by means of my Lord Privy Seal, who ravens all that he can get. After all the king's charges to recover this land, he is again the only means to cause him to give away his revennes; and it shall be beaten into the king's head how his treasure has been needlessly wasted and consumed, and his profits and revennes given away by sinister means.' 'Cromwell,' Paulet added, 'has been so handled and taunted by the council in these matters, as he is weary of them; but I will so work my matter, as the king shall be informed of every penny that he hath spent here; and when that great expence is once in his head, it shall never be forgotten there is one good point. And then I will inform him how he hath given away to one man seven hundred marks by the year. And then will the king swear by God's body, have I spent so much money and now have given away my land? There was never king so deceived by man. I will hit him by means of my friends.'—*State Papers,* vol. ii. p. 551. It is not clear how much is to be believed of Paulet's story so far as relates to the king's treatment of Cromwell. The words were made a subject of an inquiry before Sir Anthony St. Leger; and Paulet meant, it seemed, that the 'beknaving and knocking about the pate' took place in private before no witnesses; so that, if true, it could only have been known by the acknowledgments of the king or of Cromwell himself. But the character of the intrigues for Cromwell's destruction is made very plain.

might not suffer by his attainder.[1] The noble lords possessed, undoubtedly, one serious advantage against him. His own expenses were as profuse as the expenses of the state under his management. His agents were spread over Europe. He bought his information anywhere, and at any cost; and secret-service money for such purposes he must have provided, like his successor in the same policy, Sir Francis Walsingham, from his own resources. As a self-raised statesman, he had inherited nothing. His position as a nobleman was to be maintained; and it was maintained so liberally, that two hundred poor were every day supplied with food at his gate. The salaries of his offices and the rents of such estates as the king had given to him were inadequate for such irregular necessities. In Cromwell, the questionable practice of most great men of his time—the practice of receiving pensions and presents for general support and patronage—was carried to an extent which even then, perhaps, appeared excessive. It is evident, from his whole correspondence, that he received as profusely as he spent. We trace in him no such ambitious splendour as he had seen in Wolsey. He was contented with the moderate maintenance of a nobleman's establishment. But power was essential to him; and a power like that which Cromwell wielded, required resources which he obtained only by exposing his reputation while alive, and his good name in history, to not unmerited blame.

Weighted as he was with faults, which his high purposes but partially excuse, he fought his battle bravely—alone—against the world. The German marriage did not pass without a struggle at the council board. Cromwell had long recognised his strongest and most dangerous enemy in the person of Stephen Gardiner. So much he dreaded the subtle bishop, that he had made an effort once to entangle him under the Supremacy Act;[2] but

---

[1] FOXE's *History of Cromwell*.

[2] A paper of ten interrogatories is in the Rolls House written in Cromwell's hand, addressed to a Mr. John More. More's opinion was required on the supremacy, and among the questions asked him were these:—

What communication hath been between you and the Bishop of Winchester touching the primacy of the Bishop of Rome?

What answers the said Bishop made unto you upon such questions as ye did put to him?

Whether ye have heard the said Bishop at any time in any evil opinion contrary to the statutes of the realm, concerning the primacy of the Bishop of Rome or any other foreign potentate?—*Rolls House MS.* A 2, 30, fol. 67.

In another collection I found a paper of Mr. More's answers; but it would seem (unless the MS. is imperfect) that he replied only to the

Gardiner had glided under the shadow of the act, and had escaped its grasp. Smooth, treacherous, and plausible, he had held his way along the outer edge of the permitted course, never committing himself, commanding the sympathy of English conservatism, the patron of those suspected of Romanism on one side, as Cromwell was the patron of heretics; but self-possessed and clear-headed, watching the times, knowing that the reaction must have its day at last, and only careful to avoid the precipitancy, in future, into which he had blundered after the Six Articles Bill. His rival's counter-move had checked him, but he waited his opportunity; and when Barnes was sent as commissioner into Germany, Gardiner challenged openly before the council the appointment, for such a purpose, of a man who was 'defamed of heresy.' He was supported, apparently, by the Bishop of Chichester, or the latter ventured to thwart the privy seal in some other manner. Cromwell for the moment was strong enough to bear his opponents down. They were both dismissed from the Privy Council.[1] But this arbitrary act was treated as a breach of the tacit compact by which the opposing parties endured each other's presence. If the Bishop of Durham's chaplain spoke the truth, an attempt was made, in which even Lord Southampton bore a share, to bring Tunstall forward in Gardiner's place.[2] And though this scheme

questions which affected himself. The following passage, however, is curious: 'The cause why I demanded the questions (on the primacy) of my Lord of Winchester was for that I heard it, as I am now well remembered, much spoken of in the parliament house, and taken among many there to be a doubt as ye, Mr. Secretary, well know. And for so much as I esteemed my lord's wisdom and learning to be such, that I thought I would not be better answered, because I heard you, Mr. Secretary, say he was much affectionate to the Papacy.'— *Rolls House MS,* first series, 863.

[1] 'The Bishop of Winchester was put out of the Privy Council, because my Lord Privy Seal took displeasure with him because he should say it was not meet that Dr. Barnes, being a man defamed of heresy, should be sent ambassador. Touching the Bishop of Chichester there was not heard any cause why he was put forth from the Privy Council.' —Depositions of Christopher Chator: *Rolls House MS,* first series.

[2] 'Then said Craye to me, there was murmuring and saying by the progress of time that my Lord Privy Seal should be out of favour with his prince. Marry, said I, I heard of such a thing. I heard at Woodstock of one Sir Launcelot Thornton, a chaplain of the Bishop of Durham, who shewed me that the Earl of Hampton, Sir William Kingston, and Sir Anthony Brown were all joined together, and would have had my Lord of Durham to have had rule and chief saying under the King's Highness. Then said Craye to me, It was evil doing of my lord your master that would not take it upon hand, for he might have amended many things that were amiss; for, if the Bishop of Winchester might have had the saying, he would have taken it upon hand. Well, said I, my lord my master is too good a lawyer, knowing by his book the inconstancy of princes, where there is a text that saith: *Lubricus est primus locus apud Reges.*'— *MS. ibid.*

failed, through the caution of the principal persons interested, the grievances remained, embittered by a forced submission: a fresh debt had been contracted, bearing interest till it was paid.

As great, or a greater, danger embarrassed Cromwell from the folly of his friends. So long as the tide was in their favour, the Protestants indulged in insolent excesses, which provoked, and almost justified the anger with which they were regarded. Hitherto they had held a monopoly of popular preaching. Tradition and authority had been with the Catholics: the rhetoric had been mainly with their adversaries. In the summer the interest of London was suddenly excited on the other side by a Catholic orator of extraordinary powers, a Dr. Watts, unknown before or after this particular crisis, but for the moment a principal figure on the stage. Watts attracted vast audiences; and the Protestants could not endure a rival, and were as little able as their opponents to content themselves with refuting him by argument. He was summoned, on a charge of false doctrine, before the Archbishop of Canterbury; and even moderate persons were scandalized when they saw Barnes sitting by the side of Cranmer as assessor in a cause of heresy.[1] It appeared, and perhaps it was designed, as an insult—as a deliberately calculated outrage. Ten thousand London citizens proposed to walk in procession to Lambeth, to require the restoration of their teacher; and, although the open demonstration was prevented by the City officers, an alderman took charge of their petition, and offered, unless the preacher's offence was high treason, to put in bail for him in the name of the corporation.[2]

There were, perhaps, circumstances in the case beyond those which appear; but, instead of listening to the request of the City, the archbishop spirited away the preacher into Kent, and his friends learned, from the boasts of their adversaries, that he was imprisoned and ill used. He was attached, it seems, to the Victuallers' Company. 'There is no persecution,' wrote a Protestant fanatic, 'except of

[1] 'There was an honest man in London called Dr. Watts, which preacheth much against heresy; and this Dr. Watts was called before my Lord of Canterbury, and Dr. Barnes should be either his judge or his accuser.'—*Rolls House MS.* first series.

[2] 'There was an alderman in Gracechurch-street that came to my Lord of Canterbury, and one with him, and said to my Lord of Canterbury: Please your Grace that we are informed that your Grace hath our master Watts by hold. And if it be for treason we will not speak for him, but if it be for heresy or debt we will be bound for him in a thousand pound; for there was ten thousand of London coming to your lordship to be bound for him, but that we stayed them.'—*MS.* ibid.

the Victuallers; of which sect a certain impostor of the name of Watts, formerly of the order of wry-necked cattle, is now holding forth, oh, shame! in the stocks at Canterbury Bridewell, having been accustomed to mouth elsewhere against the Gospel.'[1]

While England was thus fermenting towards a second crisis, the German marriage was creating no less anxiety on the Continent. As it was Cromwell's chief object to unite England with the Lutherans, so was Charles V. anxious above all things to keep them separate; and no sooner was he aware that the Duke of Cleves had consented to give his sister to Henry than he renewed his offer of the Duchess of Milan. The reply was a cold and peremptory refusal;[2] and the Emperor seeing that the English government would not be again trifled with, determined to repair into Flanders, in order to be at hand, should important movements take place in Germany.[3] To give menace and significance to his journey, he resolved, if possible, to pass through France on his way, and in a manner so unformal and confidential as, perhaps, might contribute towards substantiating his relations with Francis, or, at least, might give the world the impression of their entire cordiality.

The proposal of a visit from the Emperor, when made known at Paris, was met with a warm and instant assent; and many were the speculations to which an affair so unexpected gave occasion in Europe. But the minds of men were not long at a loss, and Henry's intended marriage was soon accepted as an adequate explanation. The danger of a Protestant league compelled the Catholic powers to bury their rivalries; and a legate was despatched from Rome to be present at the meeting at Paris.[4] Reginald

---

[1] Butler to Bullinger: *Original Letters on the Reformation*, p. 627.

[2] 'As to the matter concerning the Duchess of Milan, when his Highness had heard it, he paused a good while, and at the last said, smiling, "Have they remembered themselves now?" To the which I said, "Sir, we that be your servants are much bound to God, they to woo you whom ye have wooed so long." He answered coldly: "They that would not when they might, percase shall not when they would."'—Southampton to Cromwell, Sept. 17, 1539: *State Papers*, vol. i.

[3] 'There should be three causes why the Emperor should come into these parts—the one for the mutiny of certain cities which were dread in time to allure and stir all or the more part of the other cities to the like; the second, for the alliance which the King's Majesty hath made with the house of Cleves, which he greatly stomacheth; the third, for the confederacy, as they here call it, between his Majesty and the Almayns. The fear which the Emperor hath of these three things hath driven him to covet much the French king's amity.'—Stephen Vaughan to Cromwell: *State Papers*, vol. viii. p. 203.

[4] 'There is great suspicion and jealousy to be taken to see these two great princes so familiar together, and to go conjointly in secret

Pole, ever on the watch for an opportunity to strike a blow at his country, caught once more at the opening, and submitted a paper on the condition of England to the Pope, showing how the occasion might be improved. The Emperor was aware, Pole said, that England had been lost to the Holy See in a Spanish quarrel, and for the sake of a Spanish princess; and he knew himself to be bound in honour, however hitherto he had made pretexts for delay, to assist in its recovery. His Imperial oaths, the insults to his family, the ancient alliance between England and the house of Burgundy, with his own promises so often repeated, alike urged the same duty upon him; and now, at last, he was able to act without difficulty. The rivalry between France and Spain had alone encouraged Henry to defy the opinion of Europe. That rivalry was at an end. The two sovereigns had only to unite in a joint remonstrance against his conduct, with a threat that he should be declared a public enemy if he persisted in his course, and his submission would be instant. He would not dare to refuse. He could not trust his subjects: they had risen once of themselves, and he knew too well the broken promises, the treachery and cruelty with which he had restored order, to risk their fury, should they receive effective support from abroad. Without striking a single blow, the Catholic powers might achieve a glorious triumph, and heal the gaping wound in the body of Christ.[1] So wrote, and so thought the English traitor, with all human probabilities in his favour, and only the Eternal Powers on the other side. The same causes which filled Pole with hope struck terror into weak and agitated hearts in the country which he was seeking to betray; the wayfarers on the highroads talked to each other in despair of the impending ruin of the kingdom, left naked without an ally to the attacks of the world.[2]

practices, in which the Bishop of Rome seemeth to be intelligent, who hath lately sent his nephew, Cardinal Farnese, to be present at the parlement of the said princes in France. The contrary part cannot brook the King's Majesty and the Almains to be united together, which is no small fear and terror as well to Imperials as the Papisticals, and no marvel if they fury, fearing thereby some great ruin.'—Harvel to Cromwell from Venice, December 9.

[1] *Epist. Reginaldi Poli*, vol. v. p. 150. In this paper Pole says that the Duke of Norfolk stated to the king in a despatch from Doncaster, when a battle seemed imminent, 'that his troops could not be trusted, their bodies were with the king but their minds with the rebels.' His information was, perhaps, derived from his brother Geoffrey, who avowed an intention of deserting.

[2] 'The said Helyard said to me that the Emperor was come into France, and should marry the king's daughter; and the Duke of Orleans should marry the Duchess of Milan, and all this was by the Bishop of Rome's means; and they were all confederated together, and

Spreading round him such panics and such expectations, the Emperor entered France almost simultaneously with the departure of Anne of Cleves from her mother's side to the shores of England. Pity that, in the game of diplomacy, statesmen are not compelled to use their own persons for their counters! are not forbidden to cast on others the burden of their own failures!

Francis, in order to show Charles the highest courtesy, despatched the constable Montmorency, with the Dauphin and the Duke of Orleans, to Bayonne, and offered, if the Emperor distrusted him, that his sons should be detained as pledges for his good faith. Charles would not be outdone in generosity—when he gave his confidence he gave it without reserve; and, without accepting the security, he crossed the frontier, attended only by his personal train, and made his way to the capital, with the two princes at his side, through a succession of magnificent entertainments. On the 1st of January he entered Paris, where he was to remain for a week; and Henry, at once taking the initiative, made an opportunity to force him, if possible, to a declaration of his intentions. Attached to the Imperial household was a Welshman named Brancetor, uncle of 'young Rice,' who had been executed for a conspiracy against Henry's life in 1531. This man, having been originally obliged to leave England for debt, had contrived, while on the Continent, by assiduity of treason, to assume the more interesting character of a political refugee. He had attached himself to Pole and to Pole's fortunes; he had exerted himself industriously in Spain in persuading English subjects to violate their allegiance; and in the parliament of the previous spring he had been rewarded by the distinction of a place in the list of attainted traitors.

Analogous occupations had brought him to Paris; and, in conformity with treaties, Henry instructed Sir Thomas Wyatt, who was then in England, to repair to the French court, and require his extradition. Wyatt imprudently affected to consider that the affair belonged rather to the police than to the government, and applied to the constable for Brancetor's arrest. Montmorency was unaware of the man's connexion with the Emperor. Wyatt informed him merely that an English subject who had robbed his master, and had afterwards conspired against

---

us for the Scottish king, he was always the French king's man, and we shall all be undone, for we have no help now but the Duke of Cleves, and they are so poor they cannot help us.'—Depositions of Christopher Chator: *Rolls House MS.* first series.

the king, was in Paris, and requested his apprehension. He had been watched to his lodgings by a spy; and the provost-marshal was placed without difficulty at Wyatt's disposal, and was directed to attend him.

The police surrounded the house where Brancetor was to be found. It was night. The English minister entered, and found his man writing at a table. 'I told him,' Wyatt reported in his account of the story, 'that, since he would not come to visit me, I was come to seek him. His colour changed as soon as he heard my voice; and with that came in the provost, and set hand on him. I reached to the letters that he was writing, but he caught them afore me, and flung them backwards into the fire. I overthrew him, and cracked them out; but the provost got them.' Brancetor upon this declared himself the Emperor's servant. He made no attempt to escape, but charged the officer, 'that his writings and himself should be delivered into the Emperor's hands.' He took a number of papers from his pocket, which he placed in the provost's charge; and the latter not daring to act further in such a matter without further instructions, left a guard in the room with Wyatt and the prisoner, and went to make a report to the chancellor. 'In the mean time,' says Wyatt, 'I used all the soberness I could with Brancetor, advising him to submit himself to your Majesty; but he made the Emperor his master, and seemed to regard nothing else. Once he told me he had heard me oft times say that kings have long hands; but God, quoth he, hath longer. I asked him what length he thought that would make when God's and kings' hands were joined together; but he assured himself of the Emperor.' Presently the provost returned, and said that Brancetor was to remain in his charge till the morning, when Wyatt would hear further. Nothing more could be done with the provost; and after breakfast Wyatt had an interview with Cardinal Granvelle and the chancellor. The treaties were plain; a clause stated in the clearest language that neither France, nor Spain, nor England should give shelter to each other's traitors; but such a case as Brancetor's had as clearly not been anticipated when they were drawn; and the matter was referred to the Emperor.

Charles made no difficulty in granting an audience, which he seemed rather to court. He was extremely angry. The man had been in his service, he said, for years; and it was ill done to arrest a member of his household without paying him even the courtesy of a first application on the subject. The English government could scarcely be serious in expecting that he would sacrifice an old attendant in any such manner. Wyatt answered sturdily that Brancetor was his master's subject. There was clear proof, he could vouch for it on his own knowledge, that the man committed treason in Spain; and he again insisted on the treaties. The Emperor cared nothing for treaties. Treaty or no treaty, a servant of his own should pass free; 'and if he was in the Tower of London,' he said, 'he would never consent so to charge his honour and conscience.' Brancetor had come to Paris under his protection; and the French government would never do him the dishonour of permitting the seizure of one of his personal train.

He was so displeased, and there was so much truth in what he said, that Wyatt durst not press him further; but opened ground again with a complaint which he had been instructed also to make, of the ill usage of Englishmen in Spain by the Inquisition. Charles again flashed up with imperious vehemence. In a loud voice, he replied, 'that the authority of the Inquisition depended not upon him. It had been established in his realm and countries for good consideration, and such as he would not break—no, not for his grandame.'

It was unreasonable, Wyatt replied, to punish men merely for their want of allegiance to Rome. They were no heretics, sacramentaries, Anabaptists. They held the Catholic faith as truly as any man.

'The king is of one opinion,' Charles replied, 'and I am of another. If your merchants come with novelties, I can not let the Inquisition. This is a thing that toucheth our faith.'

'What,' Wyatt said, 'the primacy of the Bishop of Rome!'

'Yea, marry,' the Emperor answered, 'shall we now come to dispute of *tibi dabo claves*. I would not alter my Inquisition. No; if I thought they would be negligent in their office, I would put them out, and put others in their rooms.'

All this was uttered with extraordinary passion and violence. Charles had wholly lost his self-command. Wyatt went on to say that the Spanish preached slanders against England, and against the king especially, in their pulpits.

'As to that,' said the Emperor, 'preachers will speak against myself whenever there is cause. That cannot be let. Kings be not kings of tongues; and if men give cause to be spoken of, they will be spoken of.'

He promised at last, with rather more calmness, to inquire into the treatment of the merchants, if proper particulars were supplied to him.[1] If alarm was really felt in the English court at the Emperor's presence in Paris, Wyatt's report of this interview was not reassuring. Still less satisfactory was an intimation, which was not long in reaching England, that Francis, or one of his ministers, had betrayed to Charles a private article in the treaty of Calais, in 1532. Anticipating at that time a war with Spain, Henry had suggested, and Francis had acquiesced in a proposal, should Charles attack them, for a partition of the Flemish provinces. The opportunity of this visit was chosen by the French to give an evidence of unmistakeable goodwill in revealing an exasperating secret.

Keeping these transactions so ominous of evil before our minds, let us now return to the events which were simultaneously taking place in England.

On the 11th of December the Lady Anne of Cleves was conducted, under a German escort, to Calais, where Lord Southampton and four hundred English noblemen and gentlemen were waiting to receive her, and conduct her to her future country. The 'Lion' and the 'Sweepstake' were in the harbour — the ships which two years before had fought the Flemings in the Downs. As she rode into the town the vessels' yards were manned, the rigging was decorated with flags, and a salute of a hundred and fifty guns was fired in her honour. By her expectant subjects she was splendidly welcomed; but the weather was wild; fifteen days elapsed before she could cross with ease and expedition; and meanwhile she was left to the entertainment of the lords. Southampton, in despair at her absence of accomplishments, taught her, as a last resource, to play at cards. Meantime, he wrote to advertise the king of her arrival, and thinking, as he afterwards said, that he must make the best of a matter which it had become too late to remedy, he repeated the praises which had been uttered so loudly by others of the lady's appearance. He trusted that, 'after all the debating, the success would be to the consolation of his Majesty, and the weal of his subjects and realm.'[2]

[1] Sir Thos. Wyatt to Henry VIII.: *State Papers*, vol. viii. p. 219, &c.
[2] Southampton's expressions were unfortunately warm. Mentioning a conversation with the German ambassadors, in which he had spoken of his anxiety for the king's marriage, 'so as if God failed us in my Lord Prince, we might have another sprung of like descent and line to reign over us in peace,' he went on to speak to them of the other ladies whom the king might have had if he had desired; 'but hearing,' he said, 'great report of the notable virtues of my lady now with her excellent beauty, *such as I well perceive to be no less than was reported, in very deed my mind gave me to lean that way*.' These

At length, on Saturday, December the 27th, as the winter twilight was closing into night, the intended Queen of England set her foot upon the shore, under the walls of Deal Castle. The cannon, freshly mounted, flashed their welcome through the darkness; the Duke and Duchess of Suffolk had waited in the fortress for her landing, and the same night conducted her to Dover. Here she rested during Sunday. The next morning she went on, in a storm, to Canterbury; and on Barham Down stood Cranmer, with five other bishops, in the wind and the rain, to welcome, as they fondly hoped, the enchantress who would break the spell of the Six Articles. She was entertained for the evening at Saint Augustine's. Tuesday she was at Sittingbourne. On New-year's Eve she reached Rochester, to which the king was already hastening for the first sight of the lady, the fame of whose charms had been sounded in his ears so loudly. He came down in private, attended only by Sir Anthony Brown, the master of the horse. The interview, agitating under all circumstances, would be made additionally awkward from the fact that neither the king nor his bride could understand each other's language. He had brought with him, therefore, 'a little present,' a graceful gift of some value, to soften the embarrassment and conciliate at first sight the lovely being into whose presence he was to be introduced. The visit was meant for a surprise; the king's appearance at her lodgings was the first intimation of his intention; and the master of the horse was sent in to announce his arrival and request permission for his Highness to present himself.

Sir Anthony, aware of the nature of Henry's expectations, entered the room where Anne was sitting. He described his sensations on the unlooked-for spectacle which awaited him in moderate language, when he said, 'that he was never more dismayed in his life, lamenting in his heart to see the lady so unlike that she was reported.'[1] The graces of Anne of Cleves were moral only, not intellectual, and not personal. She was simple, quiet, modest, sensible, and conscientious; but her beauty existed only in the imagination of the painter. Her presence was ladylike; but her complexion was thick and dark: her features were coarse; her figure large, loose, and corpulent. The

---

words, which might have passed as unmeaning compliment, had they been spoken merely to the lady's countrymen, he repeated in his letters to the king, who of course construed them by his hopes.

[1] Deposition of Sir Anthony Brown: STRYPE'S *Memorials*, vol. ii. p. 252, &c.

required permission was given. The king entered. His heart sank: his presence of mind forsook him; he was 'suddenly quite discouraged and amazed' at the prospect which was opened before him. He forgot his present; he almost forgot his courtesy. He did not stay in the room 'to speak twenty words.' He would not even stay in Rochester. 'Very sad and pensive,' says Brown, he entered his barge and hurried back to Greenwich, anxious only to escape, while escape was possible, from the unwelcome neighbourhood. Unwilling to marry at all, he had yielded only to the pressure of a general desire. He had been deceived by untrue representations, and had permitted a foreign princess to be brought into the realm; and now, as fastidious in his tastes as he was often little scrupulous in his expression of them, he found himself on the edge of a connexion the very thought of which was revolting.' It was a cruel fortune which imposed on Henry VIII., in addition to his other burdens, the labour of finding heirs to strengthen the succession. He 'lamented the fate of princes to be in matters of marriage of far worse sort than the condition of poor men.' 'Princes take,' he said, 'as is brought them by others, and poor men be commonly at their own choice.'²

Cromwell, who knew better than others knew the true nature of the king's adventure, was waiting nervously at Greenwich for the result of the experiment. He presented himself on the king's appearance, and asked him 'how he liked the Lady Anne.' The abrupt answer confirmed his fears. 'Nothing so well as she was spoken of,' the king said. 'If I had known as much before as I know now, she should never have come into the realm.' 'But what remedy?' he added, in despondency.³ The German alliance was already shaking at its base: the court was agitated and alarmed; the king was miserable. Cromwell, to whom the blame was mainly due, endeavoured for a moment to shrink from his responsibility, and accused Southampton of having encouraged false hopes in his letters from Calais. Southampton answered fairly that the fault did not rest with him. He had been sent to bring the queen into

---

[1] Those who insist that Henry was a licentious person, must explain how it was that, neither in the three years which had elapsed since the death of Jane Seymour, nor during the more trying period which followed, do we hear a word of mistresses, intrigues, or questionable or criminal connexions of any kind. The mistresses of princes are usually visible when they exist; the mistresses, for instance, of Francis I., of Charles V., of James of Scotland. There is a difficulty in this which should be admitted, if it cannot be explained.

[2] Deposition of Sir Anthony Denny: STRYPE's *Memorials*, vol. ii.

[3] Cromwell to the King: BURNET's *Collectanea*, p. 109.

England, and it was not his place to 'dispraise her appearance.' 'The matter being so far gone,' he had supposed his duty was to make the best of it.[1]

Among these recriminations passed the night of Friday, while Charles V. was just commencing his triumphal progress through France. The day following, the innocent occasion of the confusion came on to Greenwich. The marriage had been arranged for the Sunday after. The prospects were altogether dark, and closer inspection confirmed the worst apprehensions. The ladies of the court were no less shocked than their husbands. The unfortunate princess was not only unsightly, but she had 'displeasant airs' about her, and Lady Brown imparted to Sir Anthony 'how she saw in the queen such fashions, and manner of bringing up so gross, that she thought the king would never love her.' Henry met her on the stairs when her barge arrived. He conducted her to her apartments, and on the way Cromwell saw her with his own eyes. The sovereign and the minister then retired together, and the just displeasure became visible. 'How say you, my lord?' the king said. 'Is it not as I told you? Say what they will, she is nothing fair. The personage is well and seemly, but nothing else.' Cromwell attempted faintly to soothe him by suggesting that she had 'a queenly manner.' The king agreed to that;[2] but the recommendation was insufficient to overcome the repugnance which he had conceived; and he could resolve on nothing. A frail fibre of hope offered itself in the story of the pre-contract with the Count of Lorraine. Henry caught at it to postpone the marriage for two days; and, on the Sunday morning he sent for the German suite who had attended the princess, and requested to see the papers connected with the Lorraine treaty. Astonished and unprepared, they requested time to consider. The following morning they had an interview with the council, when they stated that, never anticipating any such demand, they could not possibly comply with it on the instant; but the engagement had been nothing. The instrument which they had brought with them declared the princess free from all ties whatever. If the king really required the whole body of the documents, they would send to Cleves for them; but, in the meantime, they trusted he would not refuse to accept their solemn assurances.

[1] Deposition of the Earl of Southampton: STRYPE'S *Memorials*, vol. ii.
[2] Questions to be asked of the Lord Cromwell: *MS. Cotton. Titus*, B 1, 41ᴺ.

Cromwell carried the answer to Henry; and it was miserably unwelcome. 'I have been ill-handled,' he said. 'If it were not that she is come so far into England, and for fear of making a ruffle in the world, and *driving her brother into the Emperor and French king's hands, now being together*, I would never have her. But now it is too far gone; wherefore I am sorry.'[1] As a last pretext for hesitation, he sent to Anne herself to desire a protest from her that she was free from contracts; a proof of backwardness on the side of the king might, perhaps, provoke a corresponding unwillingness. But the impassive constitution of the lady would have been proof against a stronger hint. The protest was drawn and signed with instant readiness. 'Is there no remedy,' Henry exclaimed, 'but that I must needs, against my will, put my neck into this yoke?' There was none. It was inevitable. The conference at Paris lay before him like a thunder-cloud. The divorce of Catherine and the crimes of Anne Boleyn had already created sufficient scandal in Europe. At such a moment he durst not pass an affront upon the Germans, which might drive them also into a compromise with his other enemies. He gathered up his resolution. As the thing was to be done, it might be done at once; delay would not make the bitter dose less unpalatable; and the day remained fixed for the date of its first postponement—Tuesday, the 6th of January. As he was preparing for the sacrifice he called Cromwell to him in the chamber of presence: 'My lord,' he said openly, 'if it were not to satisfy the world and my realm, I would not do that I must do this day for none earthly thing.'

The marriage was solemnized. A last chance remained to the Privy Seal and to the eager prelates who had trembled in the storm on Barham Down, that the affection which could not precede the ceremony might perhaps follow it. But the tide had turned against the Reformers; and their contrivances to stem the current were not of the sort which could be allowed to prosper. Dislike was confirmed into rooted aversion. The instinct with which the king recoiled from Anne settled into a defined resolution. He was personally kind to her. His provocations did not tempt him into discourtesy; but, although she shared his bed, necessity and inclination alike limited the

---

[1] Compare Cromwell's Letter to the King from the Tower, BURNET's *Collectanea*, p. 109, with Questions to be asked of the Lord Cromwell: *MS. Cotton. Titus*, B 1, 418. Wyatt's report of his interview and the Emperor's language could not have arrived till the week after. But the fact of Charles's arrival with Brancetor in his train, was already known and was sufficiently alarming.

companionship to a form; and Henry lamented to Cromwell, who had been the cause of the calamity, that 'surely he would never have any more children for the comfort of the realm.'[1]

The union of France and the Empire, which had obliged the accomplishment of this unlucky connexion, meanwhile prevented, so long as it continued, either an open *fracas* or an alteration in the policy of the kingdom. The relations of the king and queen were known only to a few of the council. Cromwell continued in power, and the Protestants remained in security. The excitement which had been created in London by the persecution of Dr. Watts was kept alive by a controversy[2] between the Bishop of Winchester and three of the Lutheran preachers —Dr. Barnes, for ever unwisely prominent; the Vicar of Stepney, who had shuffled over his recantation; and Garrett, the same who had been in danger of the stake at Oxford for selling Testaments, and had since been a chaplain of Latimer. It is difficult to exaggerate the audacity with which the orators of the moving party trespassed on the patience of the laity. The disputes, which had been slightly turned out of their channel by the Six Articles, were running now on justification — a sufficient subject, however, to give scope for differences, and for the full enunciation of the Lutheran gospel. The magistrates in the country attempted to keep order and enforce the law; but, when they imprisoned a heretic, they found themselves rebuked and menaced by the Privy Seal. Their prison doors were opened, they were exposed to vexatious suits for loss or injury to the property of the discharged offenders, and their authority and persons were treated with disrespect and contumely.[3] The Reformers had out-

---

[1] Cromwell to the King: BURNET's *Collectanea*. The morning after his marriage, and on subsequent occasions, the king made certain depositions to his physicians and to members of the council, which I invite no one to study except under distinct historical obligations. The facts are of great importance. But discomfort made Henry unjust; and when violently irritated he was not careful of his expressions.—See Documents relating to the Marriage with Anne of Cleves: STRYPE's *Memorials*, vol. ii.

[2] Hall.

[3] The discharge of heretics from prison by an undue interference formed one of the most violent accusations against Cromwell. He was, perhaps, held responsible for the general pardon in the summer of 1539. The following letter, however, shows something of his own immediate conduct, and of the confidence with which the Protestants looked to him.

'God save the king.

'Thanks immortal from the Father of Heaven unto your most prudent and honourable lordship, for your mercy, and pity, and great charity that your honourable lordship has had on your poor and true

shot their healthy growth. They required to be toned down by renewed persecution into that good sense and severity of mind without which religion is but as idle and unprofitable a folly as worldly excitement.

In London, on the first Sunday in Lent, the Bishop of Winchester preached on the now prominent topic at Paul's Cross: 'A very Popish sermon,' says Traheron, one of the English correspondents of Bullinger, 'and much to the discontent of the people.'[1] To the discontent it may have been of many, but not to the discontent of the ten thousand citizens who had designed the procession to Lambeth. The Sunday following, the same pulpit was occupied by Barnes, who, calling Gardiner a fighting-cock, and himself another, challenged the bishop to trim his spurs for a battle.[2] He taunted his adversary with concealed Romanism. Like the judges at Fouquier Tinville's tribunal, whose test of loyalty to the republic was the question what the accused had done to be hanged on the restoration of the monarchy, Barnes said that, if he and the Bishop of Winchester were at Rome together, much money would not save his life, but for the bishop there was no fear — a little entreatance would purchase favour enough for him.[3] From these specimens we may con-

---

orator Henry King, that almost was in prison a whole year, rather of pure malice and false suspicion than of any just offence committed by your said orator, to be so long in prison without any mercy, pity, or succour of meat and drink, and all your said orator's goods taken from him. Moreover, whereas your said orator did of late receive a letter from your most honourable lordship by the hands of the Bishop of Worcester, that your said orator should receive again such goods as was wrongfully taken from your said orator of Mr. George Blunt (the committing magistrate apparently); there in your said orator went unto the said George Blunt with your most gentle letter, to ask such poor goods as the said George Blunt did detain from your poor orator; and so with great pain and much entreating your said orator, within the space of three weeks, got some part of his goods, but the other part he cannot get. Therefore, except now your most honourable lordship, for Jesus sake, do tender and consider with the eye of pity and mercy the long imprisonment, the extreme poverty of your said orator, your said orator is clean undone in this world. For where your said orator had money, and was full determined to send for his capacity, all is spent in prison, and more. Therefore, in fond humility your said orator meekly, with all obedience, puts himself wholly into the hands of your honourable lordship, desiring you to help your orator to some succour and living now in his extreme necessity and need; the which is not only put out of his house, but also all his goods almost spent in prison, so that now the weary life of your said orator stands only in your discretion. Therefore, *exaudi preces servi tui*, and Almighty God increase your most honourable lordship in virtue and favour as he did merciful Joseph to his high honour. Amen. Your unfeigned and true orator *ut supra*. Beatus qui intelligit super egenum et pauperem. In die malâ liberabit eum Dominus. — *MS. State Paper Office*, vol. ix. first series.

[1] Traheron to Bullinger; *Original Letters*, p. 316; HALL, p. 837.
[2] FOXE, vol. v. p. 431.   [3] HALL, p. 837.

jecture the character of the sermon; and, from Traheron's delight with it, we may gather equally the imprudent exultation of the Protestants.¹ Gardiner complained to the king. He had a fair cause, and was favourably listened to. Henry sent for Barnes, and examined him in a private audience. The questions of the day were opened.— Merit, works, faith, free-will, grace of congruity, were each discussed—once mystic words of power, able, like the writing on the seal of Solomon, to convulse the world, now mere innocent sounds, which the languid but still eager lips of a dying controversy breathe in vain.

Barnes, too vain of his supposed abilities to understand the disposition with which he was dealing, told the king, in an excess of unwisdom, that he would submit himself to him.

Henry was more than angry: 'Yield not to me,' he said; 'I am a mortal man.' He rose as he spoke, and turning to the sacrament, which stood on a private altar in the room, and taking off his bonnet—'Yonder is the Master of us all,' he said; 'yield in truth to Him; otherwise submit yourself not to me.' Barnes was commanded, with Garrett and Jerome, to make a public acknowledgment of his errors; and to apologize especially for his insolent language to Gardiner. It has been already seen how Jerome could act in such a position. An admirer of these men, in relating their conduct on the present occasion, declared, as if it was something to their credit, 'how gaily they handled the matter, both to satisfy the recantation and also, in the same sermon, to utter out the truth, that it might spread without let of the world.'

Like giddy night-moths, they were flitting round the fire which would soon devour them.

In April, parliament was to meet—the same parliament which had passed the Six Articles Bill with acclamation. It was to be seen in what temper they would bear the suspension of their favourite measure. The bearing of the parliament, was, however, for the moment, of comparative indifference. The king and his ministers were occupied with other matters too seriously to be able to attend it. A dispute had arisen between the Emperor and the Duke of Cleves, on the duchy of Gueldres, to which Charles threatened to assert his right by force; and, galling as Henry found his marriage, the alliance in which it had involved him, its only present recommendation, was too

---

¹ 'The bishop was ably answered by Dr. Barnes on the following Lord's-day, with the most gratifying and all but universal applause.'— Traheron to Bullinger: *Original Letters*, p. 317.

useful to be neglected. The treatment of English residents in Spain, the open patronage of Brancetor, and the haughty and even insolent language which had been used to Wyatt, could not be passed over in silence, whatever might be the consequences; and, with the support of Germany, he believed that he might now, perhaps, repay the Emperor for the alarms and anxieties of years. After staying a few days in Paris, Charles had gone on to Brussels. On the receipt of Wyatt's despatch with the account of his first interview, the king instructed him to require in reply the immediate surrender of the English traitor; to insist that the proceedings of the Inquisition should be redressed and punished; and to signify, at the same time, that the English government desired to mediate between himself and the king's brother-in-law. Nor was the imperiousness of the message to be softened in the manner of delivery. More than once Henry had implied that Charles was under obligations to England for the Empire. Wyatt was instructed to allude pointedly to these and other wounding memories, and particularly, and with marked emphasis, to make use of the word 'ingratitude.' The object was, perhaps, to show that Henry was not afraid of him; perhaps to express a real indignation which there was no longer reason to conceal.

The directions were obeyed; and Wyatt's English haughtiness was likely to have fulfilled them to the letter. The effect was magical. The Emperor started, changed colour, hesitated, and then burst in anger. 'It is too much,' he said, 'to use the term ingrate to me. The inferior may be ingrate to the greater. The term is scant sufferable between like.' Perhaps, he added, as Wyatt was speaking in a foreign language, he might have used a word which he imperfectly comprehended. Wyatt assured him placidly that there was no error: the word was in his instructions, and its meaning perfectly understood. 'The king took it so.' 'Kings' opinions are not always the best,' Charles replied. 'I cannot tell, sir,' the ambassador answered, 'what ye mean by that; but if ye think to note the king my master of anything that should touch him, I assure you he is a prince to give reason to God and the world sufficient in his opinions.' Leaving the word as it stood, he required an answer to the material point.

If Henry was indifferent to a quarrel, the Emperor seemed to be equally willing; Wyatt gathered from his manner, either that he was careless of consequences, or that he desired to provoke the English to strike the first blow. He answered as before, that Brancetor had committed no crime that he knew of. If the King of England would be more explicit in his accusations, he would consider them. His dispute with the Duke of Cleves he intended to settle by himself, and would allow of no interference; and as to the merchants, he had rather they should never visit his countries at all, than visit them to carry thither their heresy.[1] Irritation is a passion which it is seldom politic to excite; and a message like that of Wyatt had been better undelivered, unless no doubt existed of being able to support it by force. A fixed idea in Cromwell's mind, which we trace in all his correspondence, was the impossibility of a genuine coalition between Charles and Francis. Either misled by these impressions, or deceived by rumours, Henry seems to have been acting, not only in a reliance on the Germans, but in a belief that the Emperor's visit to Paris had closed less agreeably than it had opened, that the Milan quarrel had revived, and that the hasty partnership already threatened a dissolution. Some expectations of the kind he had unquestionably formed, for, on the arrival of Wyatt's letter with the Emperor's answer, he despatched the Duke of Norfolk on a mission into France, which, if successful, would have produced a singular revulsion in Europe. Francis was to be asked frankly how the Italian question stood. If the Emperor was dealing in good faith with him, or if he was himself satisfied, nothing more need be desired; if, on the contrary, he felt himself 'hobbled with a vain hope,' there was now an opportunity for him to take fortune prisoner, to place his highest wishes within his grasp, and revenge Pavia, and his own and his children's captivity. The ingratitude story was to be repeated, with Charles's overbearing indignation; redress for the open and iniquitous oppression of English subjects had been absolutely refused; and the Emperor's manner could be interpreted only as bearing out what had long been suspected of him, that he 'aspired to bring Christendom to a monarchy;' that 'he thought himself superior to all kings,' and 'by little and little,' would work his way to universal empire. His insolence might be punished, and all dangers of such a kind for ever terminated, at the present juncture. A league was in process of formation, for mutual defence, between the King of England, the Duke of Cleves, the Elector of Saxony, the Landgrave, and other princes of the Empire. Let Francis join them, and 'they would have the Emperor in such a pitfall, that

---

[1] Wyatt to Henry VIII.: *State Papers*, vol. viii. p. 260, &c.

percase it might be their chance to have him prisoner at their pleasure, his being so environed with them, and having no way to start.'¹

The temptation was so well adjusted to the temperament of Francis that it seemed as if he felt an excuse necessary to explain his declining the combination. The French chancellor told Norfolk that his master was growing old, and that war had lost its charm for him. But, in fact, the proposal was based upon a blunder for which Cromwell's despair was probably responsible. Francis, at the moment, was under the influence of the Cardinal of Ferrara, who had come from Rome on a crusading expedition; and, so far from then desiring to quarrel with Charles, he simply communicated to him Henry's suggestions; while the Queen of Navarre gave a warning to Norfolk that, if the Anglo-German league assumed an organized form, it would be followed by alliance as close and as menacing between France and the Empire.²

Cromwell had again failed; and another and a worse misadventure followed. The German princes, for whose sake the Privy Seal had incurred his present danger, had

---

¹ Henry VIII. to the Duke of Norfolk: *State Papers*, vol. viii. p. 245, &c. Henry held out a further inducement. 'If the duke shall see the French king persevere in his good mind and affection towards the King's Highness, he shall yet further of himself say that his opinion is, and in his mind he thinketh undoubtedly that in such a case as that a new strait amity might now be made between the French king and the king his master, his Majesty would be content to remit unto him the one half of his debt to his Highness, the sum whereof is very great; and also the one half of the pensions for term of the said French king's life, so as it may please him to declare what honourable reciproque he could be content to offer again to his Majesty.'—*State Papers*, vol. viii. p. 251.

² Ibid. p. 318. The Queen of Navarre, who was constant to the English interests, communicated to the secretary of Sir John Wallop (the resident minister at Paris), an account of a conversation between herself and the Papal nuntio.

Ferrara had prayed her 'to help and put her good hand and word that the French king might join the Emperor and his master for the wars against the Almayns and the King of England, which king was but a man lost and cast away.'

'Why, M. l'Ambassadeur,' the queen answered, 'what mean you by that? how and after what sort do you take the King of England?' 'Marry,' quoth he, 'for a heretic and a Lutheryan. Moreover, he doth make himself head of the Church.' 'Do you say so?' quoth she. 'Now I would to God that your master, the Emperor, and we here, did live after so good and godly a sort as he and his doth.' The nuntio answered, 'the king had pulled down the abbeys,' 'trusting by the help of God it should be reformed or it were long.' She told him that were easier to say than to do. England had had time to prepare, and to transport an army across the Channel was a difficult affair. Ferrara said, 'It could be landed in Scotland.' 'The King of Scotland,' she replied, 'would not stir without permission from France;' and then (if her account was true) she poured out a panegyric upon the Reformation in England, and spoke out plainly on the necessity of the same thing in the Church of Rome.—*State Papers*, vol. viii. p. 289, &c.

their own sense of prudence, and were reluctant to quarrel with the Emperor, so long as it was possible to escape. Experience had taught Charles the art of trifling with their credulity, and he flattered them with a hope that from them he would accept a mediation in behalf of the Duke of Cleves, which he had rejected so scornfully when offered by England.

Thus was Henry left alone, having been betrayed into an attitude which he was unable to support, and deserted by the allies for whom he had entangled himself in a marriage which he detested. Well might his confidence have been shaken in the minister whose fortune and whose sagacity had failed together. Driven forward by the necessity of success or destruction, Cromwell was, at the same time, precipitating the crisis in England. Gardiner, Tunstall, and Sampson the Bishop of Chichester, were his three chief antagonists. In April Sampson was sent to the Tower, on a charge of having relieved 'certain traitorous persons' who had denied the king's supremacy.[1] The two others, it is likely, would soon have followed: the Bishop of Chichester accused them of having been the cause of his own misconduct, to such extent as he admitted himself to have erred;[2] and although Tunstall equivocated, he at least would not have escaped imprisonment, had the Privy Seal remained in power, if imprisonment had been the limit of his sufferings.[3] To the eyes of the

---

[1] HALL, p. 839. The case broke down, and Sampson was afterwards restored to favour; but his escape was narrow. Sir Ralph Sadler, writing to Cromwell, said, 'I declared to the King's Majesty how the Bishop of Chichester was committed to ward to the Tower, and what answer he made to such things as were laid to his charge, which in effect was a plain denial of the chief points that touched him. His Majesty said little thereto, but that he liked him and the matter much the worse because he denied it, seeing his Majesty perceived by the examinations there were witnesses enough to condemn him in that point.'—*State Papers*, vol. i. p. 627.

[2] The Bishop of Chichester to Cromwell: STRYPE's *Memor.*, vol. li. p. 381.

[3] Another instance of Tunstall's underhand dealing had come to light. When he accepted the oath of supremacy, and agreed to the divorce of Queen Catherine, he entered a private protest in the Register Book of Durham, which was afterwards cut out by his chancellor. Christopher Chator, whose curious depositions I have more than once quoted, mentions this piece of evasion, and adds a further feature of some interest. Relating a conversation which he had held with a man called Craye, Chator says, 'We had in communication the Bishop of Rochester and Sir Thomas More attainted of treason. Craye said to me he marvelled that they were put to death for such small trespasses; to whom I answered that their foolish conscience was so to die. Then I shewed him of one Burton, my Lord of Durham's servant, that told me he came to London when the Bishop of Rochester and Thomas More were endangered, and the said More asked Burton, "Will not thy master come to us and be as we are?" and he said he could not tell. Then said More, "If he do, no force, for if he live he may do more good than to die with us."—*Rolls House MS.* first series.

world, the destroyer of the monasteries, the 'hammer of the monks,' remained absolute as ever. No cloud, as yet, was visible in the clear sky of his prosperity; when the moment came, he fell suddenly, as if struck by lightning, on the very height and pinnacle of his power. If events had been long working towards the catastrophe, it was none the less abrupt, surprising, unlooked for.

On the 12th of April, amidst failure abroad and increased discontent at home, parliament assembled. After the ordinary address from the chancellor, Cromwell rose to speak a few words on the state of the kingdom.

'The King's Majesty,' he said, 'knowing that concord is the only sure and true bond of security in the commonwealth, knowing that if the head and all the members of the body corporate agree in one, there will be wanting nothing to the perfect health of the state, has therefore sought, prized, and desired concord beyond all other things. With no little distress, therefore, he learns that there are certain persons who make it their business to create strife and controversy; that in the midst of the good seed tares also are growing up to choke the harvest. The rashness and carnal license of some, the inveterate corruption and obstinate superstition of others, have caused disputes which have done hurt to the souls of pious Christians. The names of Papist and heretic are bandied to and fro. The Holy Word of God, which his Highness, of his great clemency, has permitted to be read in the vulgar tongue, for the comfort and edification of his people—this treasure of all sacred things—is abused, and made a servant of errour or idolatry; and such is the tumult of opinion, that his Highness ill knows how to bear it. His purpose is to shew no favour to extremes on either side. He professes the sincere faith of the Gospel, as becomes a Christian prince, declining neither to the right hand nor to the left, but setting before his eyes the pure Word of God as his only mark and guide. On this Word his princely mind is fixed; on this Word he depends for his sole support; and with all his might his Majesty will labour that errour shall be taken away, and true doctrines be taught to his people, modelled by the rule of the Gospel. Of forms, ceremonies, and traditions he will have the reasonable use distinguished from the foolish and idolatrous use. He will have all impiety, all superstition, abolished and put away. And, finally, he will have his subjects cease from their irreverent handling of God's book. Those who have offended against the faith and the laws shall suffer the punishment by the laws appointed; and his first and last prayer is for the prevailing of Christ – the prevailing of the Word of Christ—the prevailing of the truth.'[1]

A general intimation of intentions, which being so stated every one would approve, passed quietly, and the subject dropped. It is the peculiarity of discourses on theological subjects, that they are delivered and they are heard under an impression, both on the part of the speaker and of his audience, that each is in possession of the only reasonable and moderate truth; and so long as particulars are avoided, moderation is praised, and all men consent to praise it—excess is condemned, and all agree in the condemnation. Five days after, a public mark of the king's approbation was bestowed on Cromwell, who was created Earl of Essex; and the ordinary legislation commenced quietly. The complaints against the Statute of Uses were met by a measure which silently divided the leading root of the feudal system. Persons holding lands by military tenure were allowed to dispose of two-thirds in their wills, as they pleased. Lands held under any other conditions might be bequeathed absolutely, without condition or restriction.[2] To prevent disputes on titles, and to clear such confusion of claims as had been left remaining by the Uses Act, sixty years' possession of property was declared sufficient to constitute a valid right; and no claim might be pressed which rested on pretensions of an older date.[3] The Privy Seal's hand is legible in several acts abridging ecclesiastical privileges, and restoring monks, who had been dead in law, to some part of their right as human beings. The suppression of the religious houses had covered England with vagrant priests, who, though pensioned, were tempted by idleness and immunity from punishment, into crimes. If convicted of felony, and admitted 'to their clergy,' such persons were in future to be burnt in the hand.[4] A bill in the preceding year had relieved them from their vows of poverty; they were permitted to buy, inherit, or other-

[1] *Lords Journals*, 32 Henry VIII.
[2] 32 Henry VIII. cap. 1. [3] 32 Henry VIII. cap. 2.
[4] 32 Henry VIII. cap. 3. 'Many goes oft begging.' 'and it causeth much robbing.'—Deposition of Christopher Chator. Here is a special picture of one of these vagabonds. Gregory Cromwell, writing to his father from Lewes, says, 'The day of making hereof came before us a fellow called John Dancy, being apparelled in a friese coat, a pair of black hose, with fustian slops, having also a sword, a buckler, and a dagger; being a man of such port, fashion, and behaviour that we at first took him only for a vagabond, until such time as he, being examined, confessed himself to have been heretofore a priest, and sometime a monk of this monastery.'—*MS. State Paper Office*, second series, vol. vii.

wise occupy property. They were freed by dissolution from obedience to their superiors, and the reflection naturally followed, that the justice which had dispensed with two vows would dispense with the third, and that a permission to marry, in spite of the Six Articles, would soon necessarily follow. Further inroads were made also upon the sanctuaries. Institutions which had worn so deep a groove in the habits of men could not be at once put away; nor, while the letter of the law continued so sanguinary, was it tolerable to remove wholly the correctives which had checked its action, and provide no substitute. The last objection was not perhaps considered a serious one; but prejudice and instinct survived, as a safeguard of humanity. The protection of sanctuary was withdrawn for the more flagrant felonies, for murder, rape, robbery, arson, and sacrilege. Churches and churchyards continued to protect inferior offenders; and seven towns — Wells, Westminster, Manchester, Northampton, York, Derby, and Launceston — retained the same privileges, until, finding that their exemption only converted them into nests of crime, they petitioned of themselves for desecration. Some other regulations were also introduced into the system. Persons taking refuge in a church were allowed to remain not longer than forty days; at the end of which they were to abjure before the coroner and leave the country, or were to be consigned for life to one of the specified towns, where they were to be daily inspected by the governor, and if absent three days consecutively — no very barbarous condition — were to forfeit their security.[1] An act was passed for the better maintenance of the navy; and next, bringing inevitable ill-will with it to the unpopular minister, appeared the standard English grievance, a Money Bill. In the preceding session the Duke of Norfolk had laid before the Lords a statement of the extraordinary expenses which had been cast upon the Crown, and of the inadequacy of the revenue.[2] Twelve months' notice had been given, that the Houses might consider at their leisure the demand which was likely to be made upon them. It appeared in a bill introduced on the 3rd of May, requiring a subsidy of four fifteenths and four tenths, the payments to be spread over a period of four years.[3]

[1] 32 Henry VIII. cap. 12.
[2] *Lords Journals*, 31 Henry VIII.
[3] It was so difficult to calculate at the time the amount likely to be raised by this method of taxation, or the degree in which it would press, that it is impossible at present even to guess reasonably on either of these points. In 1545, two fifteenths and tenths which were

The occasion of a demand of money was always carefully stated: the preamble set forth that the country had prospered, had lived in wealth, comfort, and peace under the king, for thirty-one years. His Highness, in the wisdom which God had given him, had brought his subjects out of blindness and ignorance to the knowledge of God and his holy Word. He had shaken off the usurpations of the Bishop of Rome, by whose subtle devices large sums had been annually drained out of the realm. But in doing this he had been forced to contend against insurrections at home and the peril of invasion from the powers of the Continent. He had built a navy and furnished it. He had raised fortresses, laid out harbours, established permanent garrisons in dangerous places, with arsenals for arms and all kinds of military stores. Ireland after an arduous struggle was at length reduced to obedience; but the conquest was maintained at a great and continuing cost. To meet this necessary outlay, no regular provision existed; and the king threw himself confidently upon his subjects, with an assurance that they would not refuse to bear their share in the burden.

The journals throw no light upon the debate, if debate there was. The required sum was voted: we know no more.[1] The sand in Cromwell's hour-glass was almost run. Once more, and conspicuously, his spirit can be seen in a bill of attainder against four priests, three of whom, Abel, Fetherston, and Powell, had been attached to the household of Queen Catherine, and had lingered in the Tower, in resolute denial of the supremacy; the fourth, Robert Cook, of Doncaster, 'had adhered to the late arrogant traitor Robert Aske.' In companionship with them was a woman, Margaret Tyrrell, who had refused to acknowledge Prince Edward to be heir to the crown. These five were declared by act of parliament guilty of high treason; their trial was dispensed with; they were sentenced to death, and the bill was passed without a dissentient voice.[2] This was on the 1st of June.[3] It was

---

granted by parliament are described as extending to 'a right small sum of money,' and a five per cent. income tax was in consequence added.—37 Henry VIII. cap. 25. Aliens and clergy generally paid double, and on the present occasion the latter granted four shillings in the pound on their incomes, to be paid in two years, or a direct annual tax of ten per cent.—32 Henry VIII. cap. 23. But all estimates based on conjecture ought to be avoided.

[1] 32 Henry VIII. cap. 50.
[2] 32 Henry VIII. cap. 57. Unprinted *Rolls House, MS.*
[3] 'Hodie lecta est Billa attincturæ Ricardi Fetherstone, etc.; et communi omnium Procerum assensu nemine discrepante expedita.'— *Lords Journals*, 32 Henry VIII.

the same week in which the Tower seemed likely to be the destiny of Tunstall and Gardiner; the struggling parties had reached the crisis when one or the other must fall. Nine days more were allowed to pass; on the tenth the blow descended.

But I must again go back for a few steps, to make all movements clear.

From the day of the king's marriage 'he was in a manner weary of his life.'[1] The public policy of the connexion threatened to be a failure. It was useless abroad, it was eminently unpopular at home; while the purpose for which the country had burdened him with a wife was entirely hopeless.[2] To the queen herself he was kindly distant; but, like most men who have not been taught in early life to endure inconvenience, he brooded in secret over his misfortune, and chafed the wound by being unable to forget it. The documents relating to the precontract were not sent; his vexation converted a shadow into a reality. He grew superstitious about his repugnance, which he regarded as an instinct forbidding him to do an unlawful thing. 'I have done as much to move the consent of my heart and mind as ever man did,' he said to Cromwell, 'but without success.'[3] 'I think before God,' he declared another time, 'she has never been my lawful wife.'[4] The wretched relations continued without improvement till the 9th of May. On that day a royal circular was addressed to every member of the Privy Council, requiring them to attend the king's presence, 'for the treaty of such great and weighty matters as whereupon doth consist the surety of his Highness's person, the preservation of his honour, and the tranquillity and quietness of themselves and all other his loving and faithful subjects.'[5] It may be conjectured that the king

---

[1] Stow.
[2] The Ladies Rutland, Rochford, and Edgecombe, all being together with the queen, 'they wished her Grace with child, and she answered and said she knew well she was not with child. My Lady Edgecombe said, "How is it possible for your Grace to know that?" "I know it well I am not," said she. Then said my Lady Edgecombe, "I think your Grace is a maid still." With that she laughed; "How can I be a maid," said she, "and sleep every night with the king? When he comes to bed he kisses me, and takes me by the hand, and bids me 'Good night, sweetheart;' and in the morning kisses me, and bids me 'Farewell, darling.' Is not this enough?" Then said my Lady Rutland, "Madame, there must be more than this, or it will be long or we have a Duke of York, which all this realm most desireth." "Nay," said the queen, "I am contented I know no more."'—Deposition on the Marriage of the Lady Anne of Cleves: STRYPE's *Memorials*, vol. ii. p. 462.
[3] STRYPE's *Memorials*, vol. i. p. 556.
[4] Cromwell to the King: BURNET's *Collectanea*, p. 109.
[5] The Letter sent to Cromwell is printed in *State Papers*, vol. i. p. 628.

had at this time resolved to open his situation for discussion. No other matter can be ascertained to have existed at the time worthy of language so serious. Yet he must have changed his purpose. For three weeks longer the secret was preserved, and his course was still undecided. On the evening of the 6th or 7th of June Sir Thomas Wriothesley repaired to Cromwell's house with the ordinary reports of public business. He found the minister alone in a gallery, leaning against a window. 'Were there any news abroad?' Cromwell asked. Wriothesley said he knew of none. 'There is something,' the minister said, 'which troubles me. The king loves not the queen, nor ever has from the beginning; insomuch as I think assuredly she is yet as good a maid for him as she was when she came to England.' 'Marry, sir,' Wriothesley answered, 'I am right sorry that his Majesty should be so troubled. For God's sake, devise how his Grace may be relieved by one way or the other.' 'Yes,' Cromwell said, 'but what and how?' Wriothesley said he could not tell on the moment; but standing the case as it did, he thought some way might be found. 'Well, well,' answered the minister, 'it is a great matter.' The conversation ended; and Wriothesley left him for the night.

'The next day following,' Wriothesley deposed, 'having occasion eftsoons for business to repair unto him, I chanced to say, 'Sir, I have thought somewhat of the matter you told me, and I find it a great matter. But, sir, it can be made better than it is. For God's sake, devise for the relief of the king; for if he remain in this grief and trouble, we shall all one day smart for it. If his Grace be quiet we shall all have our parts with him.' 'It is true,' quoth he; 'but I tell you it is a great matter.' 'Marry,' quoth I, 'I grant; but let the remedy be searched for.' 'Well,' quoth he; and thus brake off from me.'[1]

Wriothesley's remedy was of course a divorce. It could be nothing else. Yet, was it not a remedy worse than any possible disorder? Cromwell, indeed, knew himself responsible. He it was who, with open eyes, had led the king into his embarrassment. Yet, was a second divorce to give mortal affront to the Lutherans, as the first had done to the Catholics? Was another marriage scandal to taint a movement which had already furnished too much of such material to insolence? What a triumph to the Pope! What a triumph to the Emperor! How would his own elaborate policy crumble to ruins! It was a great matter indeed to Cromwell.

[1] STRYPE's *Memorials*, vol. ii. p. 459.

But how would the whisper of the word sound in the ears of the English reactionaries? What would the clergy think of it in whose, only not unanimous, convictions the German alliance had been from the first a pollution? What would the parliament think of it, who had seen the fruit of their theological labours so cunningly snatched from them? What would the Anglican bishops think of it, who had found themselves insulted from the pulpit, from behind the shield of the hateful connexion—with one of their body already in the Tower, and the same danger hanging before them all? Or the laity generally —the woolgrowers of the counties, the merchants of the cities, the taxpayers charged with the new subsidy, who, in the connexion with the house of Cleves, saw a fresh cause of quarrel with the Emperor and the ruin of the trade with Flanders; what, to all these, in the heat and rage of party, must have seemed the natural remedy for the king's difficulty? Let Queen Catherine and her friends be avenged by a retribution in kind. Their opinions on the matter were shortly expressed.

Meanwhile, the minister who, in the conduct of the mighty cause which he was guiding, had stooped to dabble in these muddy waters of intrigue, was reaping, within and without, the harvest of his errors. The consciousness of wrong brought with it the consciousness of weakness and moody alternations of temper. The triumph of his enemies stared him in the face, and rash words dropped from him, which were not allowed to fall upon the ground, declaring what he would do if the king were turned from the course of the Reformation. Carefully his antagonists at the council-board had watched him for years. They had noted down his public errors; spies had reported his most confidential language. Slowly, but surely, the pile of accusations had gathered in height and weight, till the time should come to make them public. Three years before, when the northern insurgents had demanded Cromwell's punishment, the king had answered that the laws were open, and were equal to high and low. Let an accuser come forward openly, and prove that the Privy Seal had broken the laws, and he should be punished as surely and as truly as the meanest criminal. The case against him was clear at last; if brought forward in the midst of the king's displeasure, the charges could not fail of attentive hearing, and the release from the detested matrimony might be identified with the punishment of the author of it.

For struck down Cromwell should be, as his master

Wolsey had been, to rise no more. Not only was he hated on public grounds, as the leader of a revolution, but, in his multiplied offices, he had usurped the functions of the ecclesiastical courts; he had mixed himself in the private concerns of families; he had interfered between wives and husbands, fathers and sons, brothers and sisters. In his enormous correspondence[1] he appears as the universal referee—the resource of all weak or injured persons. The mad Duchess of Norfolk chose him for her patron against the duke. Lady Burgh, Lady Parr, Lady Hungerford,[2] alike made him the champion of their domestic wrongs. Justly and unjustly, he had dragged down upon himself the animosity of peers, bishops, clergy, and gentlemen, and their day of revenge was come.

On the 10th of June he attended as usual at the

[1] *MSS. State Paper Office*, second series, 52 volumes.

[2] Lady Elizabeth Burgh's letter to him will show the character of interference which he was called upon to exercise: 'My very good lord, most humbly I beseech your goodness to me your poor bounden bedewoman, considering the great trouble I am put onto by my Lord Burgh, who always hath lien in wait to put me to shame and trouble, which he shall never do, God willing, you being my good and gracious lord, as I have found you merciful to me ever hitherto; and so I most humbly beseech you of your good continuance, desiring now your good lordship to remember me, for I am comfortless, and as yet not out of the danger of death through the great travail that I had. For I am as yet as a prisoner comfortless, only trusting to your lordship's goodness and to the King's Grace's most honourable council. For I hear say my Lord Burgh hath complained on me to your lordship and to all the noble council; and has enformed your lordship and them all that the child that I have borne and so dearly bought is none of his son's my husband. As for me, my very good lord, I do protest afore God, and also shall receive him to my eternal damnation, if ever I designed for him with any creature living, but only with my husband; therefore now I most lamentably and humbly desire your lordship of your goodness to stay my Lord Burgh that he do not fulfil his diabolical mind to disinherit my husband's child.

'And thus am I ordered by my Lord Burgh and my husband (who dare do nothing but as his father will have him do), so that I have nothing left to help me now in my great sickness, but am fain to lay all that I have to gage, so that I have nothing left to help myself withal, and might have perished ere this time for lack of succour, but through the goodness of the gentleman and his wife which I am in house withal. Therefore I most humbly desire your lordship to have pity on me, and that through your only goodness ye will cause my husband to use me like his wife, and no otherwise than I have deserved; and to send me money, and to pay such debts as I do owe by reason of my long being sick, and I shall pray for your lordship daily to increase in honour to your noble heart's desire. Scribbled with the hand of your bounden bedewoman, Elizabeth Burgh.'—*MS. State Paper Office*, first series, vol. xiii.

I should have been glad to have added a more remarkable letter from Lady Hungerford, who was locked up by her husband in a country house for four years, and 'would have died for lack of sustenance,' 'had not,' she wrote, 'the poor women of the country brought me, to my great window in the night, such poor meat and drink as they had, and gave me for the love of God.' But the letter contains other details not desirable to publish.—*MS. Cotton. Titus*, B 1, 397.

morning sitting of the House of Lords. The Privy Council sat in the afternoon, and, at three o'clock the Duke of Norfolk rose suddenly at the table: 'My Lord of Essex,' he said, 'I arrest you of high treason.' There were witnesses in readiness, who came forward and swore to have heard him say 'that, if the king and all his realm would turn and vary from his opinions, he would fight in the field in his own person, with his sword in his hand, against the king and all others; adding that, if he lived a year or two, he trusted to bring things to that frame that it should not lie in the king's power to resist or let it.'[1] The words 'were justified to his face.' It was enough. Letters were instantly written to the ambassadors at foreign courts, desiring them to make known the blow which had been struck and the causes which had led to it.[2] The twilight of the summer evening found Thomas Cromwell within the walls of that grim prison which had few outlets except the scaffold; and far off, perhaps, he heard the pealing of the church bells and the songs of revelry in the streets, with which the citizens, short of sight, and bestowing on him the usual guerdon of transcendent merit, exulted in his fall. 'The Lord Cromwell,' says Hall, 'being in the council chamber, was suddenly apprehended and committed to the Tower of London; the which many lamented, but more rejoiced, and specially such as either had been religious men or favoured religious persons; for they banqueted and triumphed together that night, many wishing that that day had been seven years before, and some, fearing lest he should escape, although he were imprisoned, could not be merry; others,

[1] *State Papers*, vol. viii. p. 349.
[2] 'His Majesty remembering how men wanting the knowledge of the truth would else speak diversely of it, considering the credit he hath had about his Highness, which might also cause the wisest sort to judge amiss thereof if that his ingratitude and treason should not be fully opened unto them.'—Ibid. The opening sentences of the letter (it was evidently a circular) also deserve notice: 'These shall be to advertise you that when the King's Majesty hath of long season travelled, and yet most godly travaileth to establish such an order in matters of religion as neither declining on the right or on the left hand, God's glory might be advanced, the temerity of such as would either obscure or refuse the truth of his Word refrained, stayed, and in cases of obstinacy duly corrected and punished; so it is that the Lord Privy Seal, to whom the King's Majesty hath been so special good and gracious a lord, hath, only out of his sensual appetite, wrought clean contrary to his Grace's intent, secretly and indirectly advancing the one of the extremes, and leaving the mean, indifferent, true, and virtuous way which his Majesty so entirely desired, but also hath shewed himself so fervently bent to the maintenance of that his outrage, that he hath not spared most privily, most traitorously to devise how to continue the same, and in plain terms to say,' &c. Then follow the words in the text.—Ibid.

who knew nothing but truth by him, both lamented him and heartily prayed for him. But this is true, that, of certain of the clergy, he was detestably hated; and specially of such as had borne swing, and by his means were put from it; for indeed he was a man that, in all his doings, seemed not to favour any kind of Popery, nor could not abide the snuffing pride of some prelates.'[1]

The first intention was to bring him to trial,[2] but a parliamentary attainder was a swifter process, better suited to the temper of the victorious reactionists. Five Romanists but a few days previously had been thus sentenced under Cromwell's direction. The retribution was only the more complete which rendered back to him the same measure which he had dealt to others. The bill was brought in a week after his arrest. His offences, when reduced into ordinary prose out of the passionate rhetoric with which they were there described, were generally these:—

1. He was accused of having taken upon himself, without the king's permission, to set at liberty divers persons convicted and attainted of misprision of high treason, and divers others being apprehended and in prison for suspicion of high treason. No circumstances and no names were mentioned; but the fact seemed to be ascertained.

2. He was said to have granted licences for money; to have issued commissions in his own name and by his own authority; and to have interfered impertinently and unjustly with the rights and liberties of the king's subjects.

3. Being a detestable heretic and disposed to set and sow common sedition and variance amongst the people, he had dispersed into all shires in the realm great numbers of false, erroneous books, disturbing the faith of the king's subjects on the nature of the Eucharist and other articles of the Christian faith. He had openly maintained that the priesthood was a form—that every Christian might equally administer the sacraments. Being vicegerent of the king in matters ecclesiastical, and appointed to correct heresy, he had granted licences to persons detected or openly defamed of heresy to teach and preach.

4. He had addressed letters to the sheriffs in various shires, causing many false heretics to be set at liberty, some of whom had been actually indicted, and others

[1] HALL, p. 838.
[2] 'He is committed to the Tower of London, there to remain till it shall please his Majesty to have him tried according to the order of his laws.'—*State Papers*, vol. viii. p. 350.

who had been for good reason apprehended and were in prison.

5. On complaint being made to him of particular heretics and heresies, he had protected the same heretics from punishment; 'he had terribly rebuked their accusers,' and some of them he had persecuted and imprisoned, 'so that the king's good subjects had been in fear to detect the said heretics and heresies.'

6. In fuller explanation of the expressions sworn against him on his arrest, he had made a confederation of heretics, it was said, through the country; and supposing himself to be fully able, by force and strength, to maintain and defend his said abominable treasons and heresies, on declaration made to him of certain preachers, Dr. Barnes and others, preaching against the king's proclamation, 'the same Thomas Cromwell affirming the same preaching to be good, did not let to declare and say, 'If the king would turn from it, yet I would not turn; and if the king did turn, and all his people, I would fight in the field, with my sword in my hand, against him and all others; and if that I live a year or two, it shall not lie in the king's power to let it if he would.''

7. By bribery and extortion he had obtained vast sums of money; and being thus enriched, he had held the nobles in disdain.

8. Finally, being reminded of his position with respect to the lords, and of the consequences which he might bring upon himself, he had said, 'If the Lords would handle him so, he would give them such a breakfast as never was made in England, and that the proudest of them should know.'[1]

The amount and character of the evidence on which these charges were brought we have no means of judging; but the majority of them carry probability on their front; and we need not doubt that the required testimony was both abundant and sound. The case, of course, had been submitted in all its details to the king before the first step had been taken; and he was called upon to fulfil the promise which he had made of permitting justice to have its way. How was the king to refuse? Many a Catholic had gone to the scaffold for words lighter than those which had been sworn against Cromwell, by Cromwell's own order. Did he or did he not utter those words? If it be these to which he alluded in a letter which he

---

[1] Act of Attainder of Thomas Lord Cromwell, 32 Henry VIII. The act is not printed in the Statute Book, but it is in very good condition on the parliament roll. Burnet has placed it among his *Collectanea*.

wrote from the Tower to the king,[1] Sir George Throgmorton and Sir Richard Rich were the witnesses against him; and though he tried to shake their testimony, his denial was faint, indirect — not like the broad, absolute repudiation of a man who was consciously clear of offence.[2] Could he have cleared himself on this one point, it would have availed him little if he had suspended the action of the law by his own authority, if he had permitted books to circulate secretly which were forbidden by act of parliament, if he had allowed prisoners for high treason or heresy to escape from confinement. Although to later generations acts such as these appear as virtues, not as crimes, the king could not anticipate the larger wisdom of posterity. An English sovereign could know no guidance but the existing law, which had been manifestly and repeatedly broken. Even if he had himself desired to shield his minister, it is not easy to see that he could have prevented his being brought to trial, or, if tried, could have prevented his conviction, in the face of an exasperated parliament, a furious clergy, and a clamorous people. That he permitted the council to proceed by attainder, in preference to the ordinary forms, must be attributed to the share which he, too, experienced in the general anger.

Only one person had the courage or the wish to speak for Cromwell. Cranmer, the first to come forward on behalf of Anne Boleyn, ventured, first and alone, to throw a doubt on the treason of the Privy Seal. 'I heard yesterday, in your Grace's council,' he wrote to the king, 'that the Earl of Essex is a traitor; yet who cannot be sorrowful and amazed that he should be a traitor against your Majesty—he whose surety was only by your Majesty—he who loved your Majesty, as I ever thought, no less than God—he who studied always to set forwards whatsoever was your Majesty's will and pleasure—he that cared for no man's displeasure to serve your Majesty—he that was such a servant, in my judgment, in wisdom, diligence, faithfulness, and experience as no prince in this realm ever had—he that was so vigilant to preserve your Majesty from all treasons, that few could be so secretly conceived but he detected the same in the beginning!—I loved him as my friend, for so I took him to be; but I chiefly loved

---

[1] BURNET'S *Collectanea*, p. 500.
[2] 'Most Gracious Lord, I never spoke with the chancellor of the augmentation and Throgmorton together at one time. But if I did, I am sure I never spake of any such matter, and your Grace knows what manner of man Throgmorton has ever been towards your Grace's proceedings.'—BURNET'S *Collectanea*, p. 500.

him for the love which I thought I saw him bear ever towards your Grace, singularly above all others. But now, if he be a traitor, I am sorry that ever I loved or trusted him; and I am very glad that his treason is discovered in time; but yet, again, I am very sorrowful; for who shall your Grace trust hereafter, if you may not trust him? Alas! I lament your Grace's chance herein. I wot not whom your Grace may trust.'[1]

The intercession was bravely ventured; but it was fruitless. The illegal acts of a minister who had been trusted with extraordinary powers were too patent for denial; and Cranmer himself was forced into a passive acquiescence, while the enemies of the Reformation worked their revenge. Heresy and truth, treason and patriotism! these are words which in a war of parties change their meaning with the alternations of success, till time and fate have pronounced the last interpretation, and human opinions and sympathies bend to the deciding judgment. But while the struggle is still in progress—while the partisans on either side exclaim that truth is with them, and error with their antagonists, and the minds of this man and of that man are so far the only arbiters—those, at such a time, are not the least to be commended who obey for their guide the law as it in fact exists. Men there are who need no such direction, who follow their own course—it may be to a glorious success, it may be to as glorious a death. To such proud natures the issue to themselves is of trifling moment. They live for their work or die for it, as their Almighty Father wills. But the law in a free country cannot keep pace with genius. It reflects the plain sentiments of the better order of average men; and if it so happen as in a perplexed world of change it will happen and must, that a statesman, or a prophet, is beyond his age, and in collision with a law which his conscience forbids him to obey, he bravely breaks it, bravely defies it, and either wins the victory in his living person, or, more often, wins it in his death. In fairness, Cromwell should have been tried; but it would have added nothing to his chances of escape. He could not disprove the accusations. He could but have said that he had done right, not wrong—a plea which would have been but a fresh crime. But, in the deafening storm of denunciation which burst out, the hastiest vengeance was held the greatest justice. Any charge, however wild, gained hearing: Chatillon, the French ambassador, informed his court

---

[1] Cranmer to the King: a fragment printed by Lord Herbert.

that the Privy Seal had intended privately to marry the Lady Mary, as the Duke of Suffolk had married the king's sister, and on Henry's death proposed to seize the crown.[1] When a story so extravagant could gain credence, the circular of the council to the ambassadors rather furnishes matter of suspicion by its moderation.

The attainder passed instantly, with acclamation. Francis wrote a letter of congratulation to the king on the discovery of the 'treason.'[2] Charles V., whose keener eyes saw deeper into the nature of the catastrophe, when the news were communicated to him, 'nothing moved outwardly in countenance or word,' said merely, 'What, is he in the Tower of London, and by the king's commandment?'[3] He sent no message, no expression of regret or of pleasure, no word of any kind; but from that moment no menacing demonstrations or violent words or actions ruffled his relations with England, till a new change had passed upon the stage. His own friends were now in power. He knew it, and acknowledged them.[4]

The barrier which had stemmed the reactionary tide had now fallen. Omnipotent in parliament and convocation, the king inclining in their favour, carrying with them the sympathy of the wealth, the worldliness, and the harder intellect of the country, freed from the dreaded minister, freed from the necessity of conciliating the German Protestants, the Anglican leaders made haste to redeem their lost time, and develope their policy more wisely than before.

---

[1] 'The said Privy Seal's intent was to have married my Lady Mary, and the French king and the Cardinal du Bellay had much debated the same matter, reckoning at length by the great favour your Majesty did bear to him he should be made some earl or duke, and therefore presumed your Majesty would give to him in marriage the said Lady Mary your daughter, as beforetime you had done the French queen unto my Lord of Suffolk. These things they gathered of such hints as they had heard of the Privy Seal, before knowing him to be fine witted, in so much as at all times when any marriage was treated of for my said Lady Mary, he did always his best to break the same.'—*State Papers*, vol. viii. p. 379, and see p. 362.

[2] Ibid. p. 362.

[3] Pate to the Duke of Norfolk: Ibid. p. 355.

[4] Richard Pate, a priest of high Anglican views, and now minister at the Imperial court, supplied the Emperor's silence by his own enthusiasm. He wrote to Henry an ecstatic letter on the 'fall of that wicked man who, by his false doctrines and like disciples, so disturbed his Grace's subjects, that the age was in manner brought to desperation, perceiving a new tradition taught.' 'What blindness,' he exclaimed, 'what ingratitude is this of this traitor's, far passing Lucifer's, that, endeavouring to pluck the sword out of his sovereign's hand, hath deserved to feel the power of the same. But lauded be our Lord God that hath delivered your Grace out of the bear's claws, as not long before of a semblable danger of the lioness!'—Pate to Henry VIII.: Ibid. p. 364.

Their handiwork is to be traced in the various measures which occupied the remainder of the session. The first step was to despatch the Bishop of Bath to the Duke of Cleves, to gain his consent, if possible, to his sister's separation from the king; Anne, herself, meanwhile, being recommended, for the benefit of her health, to retire for a few days to Richmond. The bill of attainder was disposed of on the 19th of June; on the 22nd the bishops brought in a bill for the better payment of tithes, which in the few years last past certain persons had contemptuously presumed to withhold.[1] On the 1st of July a bill was read enacting that, whereas in the parliament of the year preceding 'a godly act was made for the abolishment of diversity of opinion concerning the Christian religion,' the provisions of which, for various reasons, had not been enforced, for the better execution of the said act the number of commissioners appointed for that purpose should be further increased; and the bishops and the bishops' chancellors should be assisted by the archdeacons and the officials of their courts.[2] This measure, like the attainder, was passed unanimously.[3] On the 5th a general pardon was introduced, from which heretics were exempted by a special proviso.[4] The new spirit was rapid in its manifestation. The day after (for it was not thought necessary to wait for a letter from Germany) the Cleves' marriage was brought forward for discussion; and the care with which the pleadings were parodied which had justified the divorce of Catherine, resembled rather a deliberate intention to discredit the first scandal than a serious effort to defend the second; but we must not judge the conduct of a party blinded

---

[1] 32 Henry VIII. cap. 7; *Lords Journals*, 32 Henry VIII. Session June 22.
[2] 32 Henry VIII. cap. 15; *Lords Journals*, 32 Henry VIII. July 1.
[3] Communi omnium procerum consensu nemine discrepante.
[4] 'Excepted alway all and all manner of heresies and erroneous opinions touching or concerning, plainly, directly, and only the most holy and blessed sacrament of the altar; and these heresies and erroneous opinions hereafter ensuing: that infants ought not to be baptized, and if they be baptized, they ought to be rebaptized when they come to lawful age; that it is not lawful for a Christian man to bear office or rule in the commonwealth; that no man's laws ought to be obeyed; that it is not lawful for a Christian man to take an oath before any judge; that Christ took no bodily substance of our blessed Lady; that sinners, after baptism, cannot be restored by repentance; that every manner of death, with the time and honr thereof, is so certainly prescribed, appointed, and determined to every man of God, that neither any prince by his sword can alter it, nor any man by his own wilfulness prevent or change it; that all things be common and nothing several.'—32 Henry VIII. cap. 49.

with passion by the appearance which such conduct seems to wear in a calmer retrospect.

The chancellor, once more reminding the lords of the wars of the Roses, and the danger of a disputed succession, informed them that certain doubts had arisen affecting the legality of the king's present marriage. The absence of a prospect of issue was the single palliative of the present proceedings. The chancellor injured the case so far as it admitted of injury, by dwelling on the possibility of an issue of doubtful legitimacy. The questions raised, however, belonged, he said, to the canon law, and he proposed that they should be submitted to the clergy then sitting in convocation.

When the chancellor had ceased, the peers desired to communicate with the other House. Six delegates were sent down to repeat the substance of what they had heard, and returned presently, followed by twenty members of the House of Commons, who signified a wish to speak with the king in person. The lords assented, and repaired in a body with the twenty members to Whitehall. The formality of state interviews may not be too closely scrutinized. They requested to be allowed to open to his Majesty a great and important matter, which his Majesty, they were well aware, had alone permitted them to discuss. His Majesty, being confident that they would make no improper demands, they laid before him the proposition which they had heard from the woolsack, and added their own entreaties that he would be pleased to consent.[1] The king was gracious, but the canon law required also the consent of the queen; for which, therefore, the Duke of Suffolk, the Bishop of Winchester, and other noblemen were despatched to Richmond, and with which they soon returned.[2] Six years were spent over the affair with Queen Catherine: almost as many days sufficed to dispose of Anne of Cleves.

On the Wednesday morning the clergy assembled, and

---

[1] *Lords Journals*, 32 Henry VIII. July 6.

[2] 'Upon Tuesday, the sixth of this month, our nobles and commons made suit and request unto us to commit the examination of the justness of our matrimony to the clergy; upon which request made we sent incontinently our councillors the Lord Chancellor, the Duke of Suffolk, the Bishop of Winchester, &c., advertising the queen what request was made, and in what sort, and thereupon to know what answer she would make unto the same. Whereunto, after divers conferences at good length, and the matter by her thoroughly perceived and considered, she answered plainly and frankly that she was contented that the discussion of the matter should be committed to the clergy as unto judges competent in that behalf.'—*State Papers*, vol. viii. p. 404; and see Anne of Cleves to the King; ibid. vol. i. p. 637.

Gardiner, in 'luminous oration,'[1] invited them to the task which they were to undertake. Evidence was sent in by different members of the Privy Council whom the king had admitted to his confidence; by the ladies of the court who could speak for the condition of the queen; and, finally, by Henry himself, in a paper which he wrote with his own hand, accompanying it with a request that, after reviewing all the circumstances under which the marriage had been contracted, they would inform him if it was still binding; and adding at the same time, an earnest adjuration, which it is not easy to believe to have been wholly a form, that, having God only before their eyes, they would point out to him the course which justly, honourably, and religiously he was at liberty to pursue.[2]

His personal declaration was as follows:—[3]

'I depose and declare that this hereafter written is merely the verity, intended upon no sinister affection, nor yet upon none hatred or displeasure, and herein I take God to witness. To the matter I say and affirm that, when the first communication was had with me for the marriage of the Lady Anne of Cleves, I was glad to hearken to it, trusting to have some assured friend by it, I much doubting at that time both the Emperor, and France, and the Bishop of Rome, and also because I heard so much both of her excellent beauty and virtuous behaviour. But when I saw her at Rochester, which was the first time that ever I saw her, it rejoiced my heart that I had kept me free from making any pact or bond before with her till I saw her myself; for I assure you that I liked her so ill and [found her to be] so far contrary to that she was praised, that I was woe that ever she came into England, and deliberated with myself that if it were possible to find means to break off, I would never enter yoke with her; of which misliking both the Great Master (Lord Russell), the Admiral that now is, and the Master of the Horse (Sir Anthony Brown) can and will bear record. Then after my repair to Greenwich, the next day after, I think, I doubt not but the Lord of Essex will and can declare what I then said to him in

---

[1] Luculentâ Oratione: STRYPE's *Memorials*, vol. i. p. 553.
[2] 'Inspectâ hujus negotii veritate ac solum Deum præ oculis habentes, quod verum, quod honestum, quod sanctum est, id nobis, de communi consilio scripto authentico renunoietis et de communi consensu licere diffiniatis. Nempe hoc unum a vobis nostro jure postulamus ut tanquam fida et proba ecclesiæ membra causæ huic ecclesiasticæ quæ maxima est in justitiâ et veritate adesse velitis.'—*State Papers*, vol. i. p. 630.
[3] MS. Cotton. Otho, x. p. 240.

that case, not doubting but, since he is a person which knoweth himself condemned to die by act of parliament, he will not damn his soul, but truly declare the truth not only at that time spoken by me, but also continually until the day of the marriage, and also many times after; wherein my lack of consent I doubt not doth or shall well appear, and also lack enough of the will and power to consummate the same, wherein both he and my physicians can testify according to the truth.'

Nearly two hundred clergy were assembled, and the ecclesiastical lawyers were called in to their assistance. The deliberation lasted Wednesday, Thursday, and Friday.¹ On Saturday they had agreed upon their judgment, which was produced and read in the House of Lords.

The contract between the Lady Anne of Cleves and the Marquis of Lorraine was sufficient, they would not say to invalidate, but to perplex and complicate any second marriage into which she might have entered.

Before the ceremony the king had required the production of the papers relating to that engagement with so much earnestness, that the demand might be taken as a condition on which the marriage was completed. But the papers had not been produced, the uncertainties had not been cleared ... and thus there had not only been a breach of condition, but, if no condition had been made, the previous objection was further increased.

Consent had been wanting on the part of the king. False representations had been held out to bring the lady into the realm and force her upon his Majesty's acceptance.

The solemnization of the marriage was extorted from his Majesty against his will under urgent pressure and compulsion by external causes.

Consummation had not followed, nor ought to follow, and the convocation had been informed—as indeed it was matter of common notoriety—that if his Majesty could, without the breach of any divine law, be married to another person, great benefits might thereby accrue to the realm, the present welfare and safety whereof depended on the preservation of his royal person, to the honour of God, the accomplishment of His will, and the avoiding of sinister opinions and scandals.

Considering all these circumstances, therefore, and weighing what the Church might and could lawfully do in such cases, and had often before done,² the convo-

¹ *State Papers*, vol. viii. p. 404.
² 'Tum vero quid ecclesia in ejusmodi casibus et possit facere et

cation, by the tenor of those their present letters, declared his Majesty not to be any longer bound by the matrimony in question, which matrimony was null and invalid; and both his Majesty and the Lady Anne were free to contract and consummate other marriages without objection or delay.

To this judgment two archbishops, seventeen bishops, and a hundred and thirty-nine clergy set their hands.[1] Their sentence was undoubtedly legal, according to a stricter interpretation of the canon law than had been usual in the ecclesiastical courts. The case was of a kind in which the queen, on her separate suit, could, with clear right, have obtained a divorce *a vinculo* had she desired; and the country had been accustomed to see separations infinitely more questionable obtained in the court of the Rota or at home, with easy and scandalous levity.[2] Nor could the most scrupulous person, looking at the marriage between Henry and Anne of Cleves on its own merits, pretend that any law, human or divine, would have been better fulfilled, or that any feeling entitled to respect would have been less outraged, by the longer maintenance of so unhappy a connexion. Yet it is much to be regretted that the clergy should have been compelled to meddle with it; under however plausible an aspect the

---

sæpenumero antebac fecerit perpendentes.'—Judgment of the Convocation: *State Papers*, vol. i. p. 632.

[1] Ibid. p. 633.

[2] 'Heretofore divers and many persons, after long continuance together in matrimony, and fruit of children having ensued of the same, have nevertheless, by an unjust law of the Bishop of Rome (which is upon pretence of a former contract made and not consummate by carnal copulation, for proof whereof two witnesses by that law were only required), been divorced and separate contrary to God's law, and so the true matrimonies solemnized in the face of the Church and confirmed by fruit of children, have been clearly frustrate and dissolved. Further, also, by reason of other prohibitions than God's law admitteth, for their lucre by that court invented, the dispensation whereof they always reserved to themselves, as in kindred or affinity between cousin germains, and so to the fourth and fifth degree, and all because they would get money by it, and keep a reputation to their usurped jurisdiction, not only much discord between lawful married persons hath, contrary to God's ordinances, arisen, much debate and suit at the law, with the wrongful vexation and great danger of the innocent party bath been procured, and many just marriages brought in doubt and danger of undoing, and also many times undone; marriages have been brought into such uncertainty, that no marriage could be so surely knit and bounden but it should lie in either of the parties' power and arbitre, casting away the fear of God, by means and compasses to prove a precontract, a kindred, an alliance, or a carnal knowledge, to defeat the same, and so, under the pretence of these allegations afore rehearsed, to live all the days of their lives in detestable adultery, to the utter destruction of their own souls and the provocation of the terrible wrath of God upon the places where such abominations were suffered and used.'—32 Henry VIII. cap. 38.

divorce might be presented, it gave a colour to the interpretation which represented the separation from Catherine as arising out of caprice, and enabled the enemies of the Church of England to represent her synods as the instruments of the king's licentiousness.[1]

For good or for evil, however, the judgment was given. The Bishop of Winchester spoke a few words in explanation to the two houses of parliament when it was presented;[2] and the next day the Duke of Suffolk and Wriothesley waited on the queen, and communicated the fortune which was impending over her. Anne herself— who, after the slight agitation which the first mooting of the matter naturally produced, had acquiesced in everything which was proposed to her—received the intimation with placidity. She wrote at their request to the king, giving her consent in writing. She wrote also to her brother, declaring herself satisfied, and expressing her hope that he would be satisfied as well. So much facility increased the consideration which her treatment entitled her to claim. The Bishop of Bath had taken with him to the Duke of Cleves an offer, which ought to have been an insult, of a pecuniary compensation for his sister's injury. It was withdrawn or qualified, before it was known to have been refused, to increase the settlement on the ex-queen. For many reasons the king desired that she should remain in England; but she had rank and precedence assigned to her as if she had been a princess of the blood. Estates were granted for her maintenance producing nearly three thousand a year. Palaces, dresses, jewels, costly establishments were added in lavish profusion, to be her dowry, as she was significantly told, should she desire to make a fresh experiment in matrimony. And she not only (it is likely) preferred a splendid independence to the poverty of a petty court in Germany, but perhaps, also, to the doubtful magnificence which she had enjoyed as Henry's bride.[2]

Parliament made haste with the concluding stroke. On Monday the 12th the bill for the divorce was introduced: it was disposed of with the greatest haste which

---

[1] The Protestant refugees became at once as passionate, as clamorous, and as careless in their statements as the Catholics.—See especially a letter of Richard Hilles to Bullinger (*Original Letters*, 195): to which Burnet has given a kind of sanction by a quotation. This letter contains about as trustworthy an account of the state of London as a letter of a French or Austrian exile in England or America would contain at present of the Courts of Paris or Vienna.

[2] *Lords Journals*, 32 Henry VIII.
See *State Papers*, vol. i. p. 637, and vol. viii. p. 403, &c.

the forms of the Houses would allow; and the conclusion
of the matter was announced to the queen's own family
and the foreign powers almost as soon as it was known
to be contemplated. The Duke of Cleves, on the first
audience of the Bishop of Bath, had shown himself 'heavy
and hard to pacify and please.' When all was over, the
Bishops of Winchester and Durham, with other noble
lords, wrote to him themselves, persuading him to acquiesce in a misfortune which could no longer be remedied; his sister had already declared her own satisfaction; and Henry, through his commissioners, informed him
in detail of the proceedings in parliament and convocation,
and trusted that the friendship between the courts would
not be interrupted in consequence. It would have been
well had he added nothing to a bare narrative of facts;
but questionable actions are rarely improved in the manner
of their execution. The king was irritated at the humiliation to which the conduct of the German powers had
exposed him in the spring; and the Duke of Cleves had
afterwards increased his displeasure by a secret intrigue
with the court of Paris. Satisfied with his settlements
upon Anne, he avowed an anxiety to be extricated from
his offer of money to the duke, 'who might percase, to
his miscontentment, employ it by the advice of others,
or at least without commodity to the giver.'[1] In fact, he
said, as he had done nothing but what was right, 'if the
lady's contentation would not content her friends, it should
not be honourable for him, with detriment and waste of
his treasure, to labour to satisfy those who without cause
misliked his doings, which were just, and without injury
to be passed over.'[2] Finally, he concluded: 'In case the
duke sheweth himself untractable and high-couraged, in
such sort as devising interests and respects, he shall
further set forth the matter, and increase it with words
more largely than reason would be should, alledging, percase, that though the lady is contented, yet he is not contented, her mother is not contented, requiring why and
wherefore, and such other behaviour as men in high
stomach, forgetting reason, shew and utter, in that case
you, the Bishop of Bath, declaring unto the duke how
we sent you not thither to render an account of our just
proceedings, but friendly to communicate them, you shall
desire the duke to license you to depart.'[3]

The high style of Henry contrasts unfavourably with
the more dignified moderation of the answer. The duke

[1] *State Papers*, vol. viii. p. 407.
[2] Ibid. p. 408.   [3] Ibid. p. 410.

wrote himself briefly to the king: he replied through his minister to the ambassador, that 'he was sorry for the chance, and would well have wished it had been otherwise; yet, seeing it was thus, he would not depart from his amity for his Majesty for any such matter. He could have wished that his sister should return to Germany; but, if she was satisfied to remain, he had confidence that the king would act uprightly towards her, and he would not press it.' Of the offer of money he took little notice or none.[1] The bishop laboured to persuade him to pay respect to the judgment of the Church; this, however, the duke resolutely refused, altogether ignoring it as of no manner of moment; neither would he allow that the Lady Anne had been treated honourably, although the bishop much pressed for the admission. A cold acquiescence in an affront which he was too weak to resent, and a promise that his private injuries should not cause the dissolution of an alliance which had been useful to the interests of religion, was the most which could be extorted from the Duke of Cleves; and, in calmer moments, Henry could neither have desired nor looked for more. But no one at that crisis was calm in England. The passions roused in the strife of convictions which divided rank from rank, which divided families, which divided every earnest man against himself, extended over all subjects which touched the central question. The impulse of the moment assumed the character of right, and everything was wrong which refused to go along with it.

Sir Edward Karne made the communication to Francis, prefacing his story with the usual prelude of the succession, and the anxiety of the country that the king should have more children. 'Even at that point' Francis started, expecting that something serious was to follow. When Sir Edward went on to say that 'the examination of the king's marriage was submitted to the clergy,' 'What,' he

---

[1] The bishop, nevertheless, was not satisfied that it would be refused, if it could be had. He thought, evidently, that Henry would act prudently by being liberal in the matter. Speaking of the miscontentment which had been shown, he added: 'For any overture that yet hath been opened you may do your pleasure. How be it, in case of their suit unto your Majesty, if the duke shall be content by his express consent to approve your proceeding, specially the said decree of your clergy, whereby all things may be here ended and brought to silence, and the lady there remaining still, this duke, without kindling any further fire, made your Majesty's assured friend with a demonstration thereof to the world, and that with so small a sum of money to be given unto him (sub colore restitutionis pecuniæ pro oneribus et dote licet vere nulla interesset), or under some other good colour. . . . . God forbid your Majesty should much stick thereat.'—Bishop of Bath to Henry VIII.: *State Papers*, vol. viii. p. 425.

said, 'the matrimony made with the queen that now is?' Karne assented. 'Then he fetched a great sigh, and spake no more' till the conclusion, when he answered, 'he could nor would take any other opinion of his Highness but as his loving brother and friend should do;' for the particular matter, 'his Highness's conscience must be judge therein.'[1]

'The Emperor,' wrote the resident Pate, 'when I declared my commission, gave me good air, with one gesture and countenance throughout, saving that suddenly, as I touched the pith of the matter, thereupon he steadfastly cast his eye upon me a pretty while, and then interrupting me, demanded what the causes were of the doubts concerning the marriage with the daughter of Cleves.' Pate was not commissioned to enter into details; and Charles, at the end, contented himself with sending his hearty recommendations, and expressing his confidence that, as the king was wise, so he was sure he would do nothing 'which should not be to the discharge of his conscience and the tranquillity of his realm.'[2] In confidence, a few days later, he avowed a hope that all would now go well in England; the enormities of the past had been due to the pernicious influence of Cromwell; or were 'beside the king's pleasure or knowledge, being a prince,' the Emperor said, 'no less godly brought up than endued and imbued with so many virtuous qualities as whom all blasts and storms could never alter nor move, but as vice might alter true virtue.'[3] On the whole, the impression left by the affair on the Continent was that Henry 'had lost the hearts of the German princes, but had gained the Emperor instead.'[4] But the loss and the gain were alike welcome to the English conservatives. The latter, happy in their victory, and now freed from all impediments, had only to follow up their advantage.

On the 12th of July the persecuting bill was passed, and the Tithe Bill also, after having been recast by the Commons.[5] On the 16th the Six Articles Bill was moderated, in favour not of heresy, but of the more venial offence of incontinency. Married clergy and incontinent

---

[1] *State Papers*, vol. viii. p. 392.   [2] Ibid. p. 386.   [3] Ibid. p. 397.
[4] Pate to the Duke of Suffolk: ibid. p. 412.
[5] No draft of the bill exists in its original form. As it passed it conferred on lay impropriators the same power of recovering tithes as was given to the clergy. The members of the lower house had been, many of them, purchasers of abbey lands, and impropriated tithes formed a valuable item of the property. It is likely that the bishops overlooked, and that the commons remembered this important condition.—*Lords Journals*, 32 Henry VIII. Session of July 12.

priests by the Six Articles Bill were, on the first offence, to forfeit their benefices; if they persisted they were to be treated as felons. The King's Highness, graciously considering 'that the punishment of death was very sore, and too much extreme,' was contented to relax the penalty into three gradations. For the first offence the punishment was to be forfeiture of all benefices but one; for the second, forfeiture of the one remaining; for the third, imprisonment for life.[1] A few days later the extension given to the prerogative, by the Act of Proclamations, was again shortened by communicating to the clergy a share of the powers which had been granted absolutely to the crown; and the parliament at the same time restored into the hands of the spiritualty the control of religious opinion. The Protestants had shifted their ground from purgatory and masses to free-will and justification; and had thus defied the bishops, and left the law behind them. The king's proclamations had failed through general neglect. A committee of religion was now constituted, composed of the archbishops, bishops, and other learned doctors of divinity; and an act, which passed three readings in the House of Lords in a single day, conferred on this body a power to declare absolutely, under the king's sanction, the judgment of the English Church on all questions of theology which might be raised, either at home or on the Continent, and to compel submission to their decrees, under such pains and penalties as they might think proper to impose, limited only by the common law and by the restrictions attached to the Act of Proclamations.[2]

One important matter remained. This statute conferred no powers of life and death; and there were certain chosen champions of Protestantism who had resisted authority, had scoffed at recantation, and had insulted the Bishop of Winchester. Although a penal measure could not be extended to comprehend their doctrine by special definition, an omnipotent parliament might, by a stretch of authority, vindicate the bishop's dignity, and make a conspicuous example of the offenders. A case of high treason was before the Houses. At the time when the invasion was impending, a party of conspirators, Sir Gregory Botolph, Clement Philpot, and three others, had contrived a project to betray Calais either to the French or the Spaniards. The plot had been betrayed by a con-

[1] 32 Henry VIII. cap. 10.
[2] 32 Henry VIII. cap. 26.

federate;[1] and the Anglo-Catholics did not intend to repeat the blunder of showing a leaning towards the Romanists, which had wrecked their fortunes in the preceding summer: they sentenced the offenders to death by an attainder; and after so satisfactory a display of loyalty, the friends of the bishops added three more names to the list in the following words:[2] 'And whereas Robert Barnes, late of London, clerk, Thomas Garret, late of London, clerk, and William Jerome, late of Stepney, in the county of Middlesex, clerk, being detestable and abominable heretics, and amongst themselves agreed and confederated to set and sow common sedition and variance amongst the king's true and loving subjects within this his realm, not fearing their most bounden duty to God nor yet their allegiance towards his Majesty, have openly preached, taught, set forth, and delivered in divers and sundry places of this realm, a great number of heresies, false, erroneous opinions, doctrines, and sayings; and thinking themselves to be men of learning, have taken upon them most seditiously and heretically to open and declare divers and many texts of Scripture, expounding and applying the same to many perverse and heretical senses, understandings, and purposes, to the intent to induce and lead his Majesty's said subjects to diffidence and refusal of the

---

[1] Philpot's confession is preserved. He describes how Sir Gregory Botolph, returning to Calais from a journey to Rome, took him one night upon the walls, and after swearing him to secrecy, showed himself a worthy pupil of Reginald Pole.

'If England have not a scourge in time,' Botolph said, 'they will be all infidels, and no doubt God to friend, there shall be a redress; and know ye for a truth what my enterprise is, with the aid of God and such ways as I shall devise. I shall get the town of Calais into the hands of the Pope and Cardinal Pole, who is as good a Catholic man as ever I reasoned with; and when I had declared everything of my mind unto them, no more but we three together in the Pope's chamber, I had not a little cheer of the Pope and Cardinal Pole; and after this at all times I might enter the Pope's chamber at my pleasure.'

Philpot asked him how he intended to proceed, Calais being so strong a place. 'It shall be easy to be done,' Botolph said. 'In the herring time they do use to watch in the lantern gate, whereat there be in the watch about a dozen persons, and against the time which shall be appointed in the night, you, with a dozen persons well appointed for the purpose, shall enter the watch and destroy them. That done, ye shall recoil back with your company and keep the stairs, and at the same time I with my company shall be ready to scale the walls over the gate. I will have five or six hundred men that shall enter with me on the first burst. We shall have aid both by sea and land, within short space.'—Confession of Clement Philpot: *Rolls House MS.* Viscount Lisle, the old commandant of Calais, an illegitimate son of Edward IV., was suspected of having been privy to the conspiracy, and was sent for to England. His innocence was satisfactorily proved, but he died in the Tower on the day when he would have been liberated.

[2] 32 Henry VIII. cap. 58: unprinted, *Rolls House MS.*

true, sincere faith and belief which Christian men ought to have in Christian religion, the number whereof were too long here to be rehearsed. . . . Be it, therefore, enacted that the said persons Robert Barnes, Thomas Garret, and William Jerome, shall be convicted and attainted of heresy, and that they and every of them shall be deemed and adjudged abominable and detestable heretics, and shall have and suffer pains of death by burning or otherwise, as shall please the King's Majesty.'

This was the last measure of consequence in the session. Three days after it closed. On the 24th the king came down to Westminster in person, to thank the parliament for the subsidy. The Speaker of the House of Commons congratulated the country on their sovereign. The chancellor replied, in his Majesty's name, that his only study was for the welfare of his subjects; his only ambition was to govern them by the rule of the Divine law, and the Divine love, to the salvation of their souls and bodies. The bills which had been passed were then presented for the royal assent; and the chancellor, after briefly exhorting the members of both houses to show the same diligence in securing the due execution of these measures as they had displayed in enacting them, declared the parliament dissolved.[1]

The curtain now rises on the closing act of the Cromwell tragedy. In the condemned cells in the Tower, the three Catholics for whose sentence he was himself answerable—the three Protestants whom his fall had left exposed to their enemies—were the companions of the broken minister; and there for six weeks he himself, the central figure, whose will had made many women childless, had sat waiting his own unpitied doom. Twice the king had sent to him 'honourable persons,' to receive such explanations as he could offer. He had been patiently and elaborately heard.[2] Twice he had himself written—

[1] *Lords Journals*, 32 Henry VIII. The clerk of the parliament has attached a note to the summary of the session declaring that throughout its progress the peers had voted unanimously. From which it has been concluded, among other things, that Cranmer voted for Cromwell's execution. The archbishop was present in the house on the day on which the bill for the attainder was read the last time. There is no evidence, however, that he remained till the question was put; and as he dared to speak for him on his arrest, he is entitled to the benefit of any uncertainty which may exist. It is easy to understand how he, and the few other peers who were Cromwell's friends, may have abstained from a useless opposition in the face of an overwhelming majority. We need not exaggerate their timidity or reproach them with an active consent, of which no hint is to be found in any contemporary letter, narrative, or document.

[2] ELLIS, second series, vol. ii. p. 160.

once, by Henry's desire, an account of the Anne of Cleves marriage—once a letter, which his faithful friend Sir Ralph Sadler carried to Henry for him; and this last the king caused the bearer three times to read over, and 'seemed to be moved therewith.'[1] Yet what had Cromwell to say? That he had done his best in the interest of the commonwealth? But his best was better than the laws of the commonwealth. He had endeavoured faithfully to serve the king; but he had endeavoured also to serve One higher than the king. He had thrown himself in the breach against king and people where they were wrong. He had used the authority with which he had been so largely trusted to thwart the parliament and suspend statutes of the realm. He might plead his services; but what would his services avail him! An offence in the king's eyes was ever proportioned to the rank, the intellect, the character of the offender. The *via media Anglicana*, on which Henry had planted his foot, prescribed an even justice; and as Cromwell, in this name of the *via media*, had struck down without mercy the adherents of the Church of Rome, there was no alternative but to surrender him to the same equitable rule, or to declare to the world and to himself that he no longer held that middle place which he so vehemently claimed. To sustain the Six Articles and to pardon the vicegerent was impossible. If the consent to the attainder cost the king any pang, we do not know; only this we know, that a passionate appeal for mercy, such as was rarely heard in those days of haughty endurance, found no response; and on the 28th of July the most despotic minister who had ever governed England passed from the Tower to the scaffold.

A speech was printed by authority, and circulated through Europe, which it was thought desirable that he should have been supposed to have uttered before his death. It was accepted as authentic by Hall, and from Hall's pages has been transferred into English history; and 'the Lord Cromwell' is represented to have confessed that he had been seduced into heresy, that he repented, and died in the faith of the holy Catholic Church. Reginald Pole, who, like others, at first accepted the official report as genuine, warned a correspondent, on the authority of persons whose account might be relied upon, that the words which were really spoken were very different, and to Catholic minds were far less satisfac-

[1] ELLIS, second series, vol. ii. p. 160; this is apparently the letter printed by BURNET, *Collectanea*, p. 500.

tory.[1] The last effort of Cromwell's enemies was to send him out of the world with a lie upon his lips, to call in his dying witness in favour of falsehoods which he gave up his life to overthrow. Clear he was not, as what living man was clear? of all taint of superstition; but a fairer version of his parting faith will be found in words which those who loved him, and who preserved no record of his address to the people, handed down as his last prayer to the Saviour:—

'O Lord Jesu, which art the only health of all men living, and the everlasting life of them which die in Thee, I, wretched sinner, do submit myself wholly to thy most blessed will; and, being sure that the thing cannot perish which is submitted to thy mercy, willingly now I leave this frail and wicked flesh, in sure hope that Thou wilt in better wise restore it to me again at the last day in the resurrection of the just. I beseech Thee, most merciful Lord Jesu Christ, that Thou wilt by thy grace make strong my soul against all temptation, and defend me with the buckler of thy mercy against all the assaults of the devil. I see and acknowledge that there is in myself no hope of salvation; but all my confidence, hope, and trust is in thy most merciful goodness. I have no merits nor good works which I may allege before Thee: of sin and evil works, alas! I see a great heap. But yet, through thy mercy, I trust to be in the number of them to whom Thou wilt not impute their sins, but wilt take and accept me for righteous and just, and to be the inheritor of everlasting life. Thou, merciful Lord, wast born for my sake; Thou didst suffer both hunger and thirst for my sake; all thy holy actions and works Thou wroughtest for my sake; Thou sufferedst both grievous pains and torments for my sake; finally, Thou gavest thy most precious body and blood to be shed on the cross for my sake. Now, most merciful Saviour, let all these things profit me that Thou hast freely done for me, which hast given Thyself also for me. Let thy blood cleanse and wash away the spots and foulness of my sins. Let thy righteousness hide and cover my unrighteousness. Let the merits of thy passion and bloodshedding be satisfaction for my sins. Give me, Lord, thy grace, that the faith in my salvation in thy blood waver not, but

[1] Vereor ne frustra cum Reverendissimâ Dominatione vestrâ per litteras de Cromwelli resipiscentiâ sim gratulatus, nec enim quæ typis sunt excusa quœ ad me missa sunt, in quibus novissima ejus verba recitantur, talem animum mihi exprimunt qualem eorum narratio qui de ejus exitu et de extremis verbis mecum sunt locuti.'—Pole to Beccatelli: *Epist.* vol. iii.

may ever be firm and constant; that the hope of thy mercy and life everlasting never decay in me; that love wax not cold in me; finally, that the weakness of my flesh be not overcome with fear of death. Grant me, merciful Saviour, that when death hath shut up the eyes of my body, yet the eyes of my soul may still behold and look upon Thee; and when death hath taken away the use of my tongue, yet my heart may cry and say unto Thee, Lord, into thy hands I commend my soul. Lord Jesu, receive my spirit. Amen.'[1]

With these words upon his lips perished a statesman whose character will for ever remain a problem.[2] For eight years his influence had been supreme with the king —supreme in parliament—supreme in convocation; the nation, in the ferment of revolution, was absolutely controlled by him; and he has left the print of his individual genius stamped indelibly, while the metal was at white heat, into the constitution of the country. Wave after wave has rolled over his work. Romanism flowed back over it under Mary. Puritanism, under another even grander Cromwell, overwhelmed it. But Romanism ebbed again, and Puritanism is dead, and the polity of the Church of England remains as it was left by its creator.

And not in the Church only, but in all departments of the public service, Cromwell was the sovereign guide. In the Foreign Office and the Home Office, in Star Chamber and at council table, in dockyard and law court, Cromwell's intellect presided — Cromwell's hand executed. His gigantic correspondence remains to witness for his varied energy. Whether it was an ambassador or a commissioner of sewers, a warden of a company or a tradesman who was injured by the guild, a bishop or a heretic, a justice of the peace, or a serf crying for emancipation, Cromwell was the universal authority to whom all officials looked for instruction, and all sufferers looked for redress. Hated by all those who had grown old in an earlier system—by the wealthy, whose interests were touched by his reforms— by the superstitious, whose prejudices he wounded—he was the defender of the weak, the defender of the poor, defender of the 'fatherless and forsaken;' and for his work, the long maintenance of it has borne witness that it was good — that he did the thing which England's true interests required to be done.

[1] Prayer of the Lord Cromwell on the Scaffold: FOXE, vol. v.
[2] His death seems to have been needlessly painful through the awkwardness of the executioner, 'a ragged and butcherly miser, who very ungoodly performed the office.'—HALL.

Of the manner in which that work was done it is less easy to speak. Fierce laws fiercely executed—an unflinching resolution which neither danger could daunt nor saintly virtue move to mercy—a long list of solemn tragedies—weigh upon his memory. He had taken upon himself a task beyond the ordinary strength of man. His difficulties could be overcome only by inflexible persistence in the course which he had marked out for himself and for the state; and he supported his weakness by a determination which imitated the unbending fixity of a law of nature. He pursued an object, the excellence of which, as his mind saw it, transcended all other considerations—the freedom of England and the destruction of idolatry: and those who from any motive, noble or base, pious or impious, crossed his path, he crushed, and passed on over their bodies.

Whether the same end could have been attained by gentler methods is a question which many persons suppose they can answer easily in the affirmative. Some diffidence of judgment, however, ought to be taught by the recollection that the same end was purchased in every other country which had the happiness to attain to it at all, only by years of bloodshed, a single day or week of which caused larger human misery than the whole period of the administration of Cromwell. Be this as it will, his aim was noble. For his actions he paid with his life; and he followed his victims by the same road which they had trodden before him, to the high tribunal, where it may be that great natures who on earth have lived in mortal enmity may learn at last to understand each other.

Two days after, Barnes, Garret, and Jerome died bravely at the stake, their weakness and want of wisdom all atoned for, and serving their Great Master in their deaths better than they had served Him in their lives. With them perished, not as heretics, but as traitors, the three Romanizing priests. The united executions were designed as an evidence of the even hand of the council. The execution of traitors was not to imply an indulgence of heresy; the punishment of heretics should give no hope to those who were disloyal to their king and country. But scenes of such a kind were not repeated. The effect was to shock, not to edify.[1] The narrow theory could be carried out to both its cruel extremes only where a special purpose was working upon passions specially excited.

[1] 'Men know not what part to follow or to take.'—FOXE, vol. v.

END OF VOL. III.

Printed by F. A. Brockhaus, Leipzig.

CONTENTS OF VOLUME III.

	PAGE.
CHAPTER XII. FOREIGN AND DOMESTIC ASPECTS OF THE REFORMATION IN ENGLAND	1
CHAPTER XIII. THE PILGRIMAGE OF GRACE	53
CHAPTER XIV. THE COMMISSION OF CARDINAL POLE	113
CHAPTER XV. THE EXETER CONSPIRACY	164
CHAPTER XVI. THE SIX ARTICLES	221
CHAPTER XVII. ANNE OF CLEVES AND THE FALL OF CROMWELL	267

www.ingramcontent.com/pod-product-compliance
Lightning Source LLC
Chambersburg PA
CBHW030013240426
43672CB00007B/937